Teacher's Edition Level 6

BASIC GOALS IN SPELLING

fifth edition   **William Kottmeyer & Audrey Claus**

About the Levels: To avoid the problems associated with grade-labeled materials in a multilevel setting, level numerals have been omitted from the covers of all books in the fifth edition. Levels may be determined by referring to the title pages of the teachers' editions or by checking the second-to-last digit in the code number on the back covers of the pupils' books.

About the Covers: The fifth edition emphasizes the concept of symbolization by presenting linguistic sound symbols in all levels and international visual symbols in the first four levels. The covers of the books in the series reflect this feature. The cover symbols are reproduced here, along with level designations, symbol identifications, and code numbers.

Level 1
Airport
Terminal
0-07-034321-7

Level 2
Parking
Garage
0-07-034302-0

Level 3
Picnic
Area
0-07-034303-9

Level 4
Elevator
0-07-034304-7

Level 5
Film-
making
0-07-034305-5

Level 6
Elevated
Train
0-07-034306-3

Level 7
Sailing
0-07-034307-1

Level 8
Hockey
0-07-034308-X

Webster Division, McGraw-Hill Book Company

New York   St. Louis   San Francisco   Dallas   Atlanta

William Kottmeyer has served in the St. Louis Public Schools as teacher, principal, reading specialist, and superintendent. A nationally recognized educational innovator, Dr. Kottmeyer has created a wide variety of basic language-skills materials. Currently author-in-residence in the Webster Division, his publications include *Basic Goals in Spelling*, the *+4 Reading Booster*, *Decoding and Meaning*, the *+10 Vocabulary Booster*, the *Classroom Reading Clinic*, *Dr. Spello*, and the *Everyreader Series.*

Audrey Claus has served in the St. Louis Public Schools as teacher, consultant, elementary principal, and curriculum coordinator. Presently author-in-residence in the Webster Division, Miss Claus is co-author of *Basic Goals in Spelling* and the *+10 Vocabulary Booster.*

Sponsoring Editor: Richard Paul
Editing Supervisor: Carol Boyer
Designer: George Ibera
Production Supervisor: Gail Paubel

ISBN 0-07-034316-0

TABLE OF CONTENTS

The BASIC GOALS IN SPELLING

    Program   T-4

Overview of Levels 4, 5, and 6   T-6

Level 6 Skills Outline   T-12

Level 6 Diagnostic Charts of

    Test Words   T-18

Spelling Alphabet   T-36

Sound-Spelling Alphabet   1

Unit Teaching Suggestions

1   Short-Vowel Words   2

2   Long-Vowel Words   6

3   Two-Letter Vowels   10

4   Vowel-*r* Words   14

5   Long and Short Vowels in

      Compounds   18

6   Two-Letter Vowels in

      Compounds   22

7   Vowel-*r* Compound Words   26

8   Snurks   30

9   Homonyms   34

10   Soft-Syllable Endings   38

11   VCCV and VCCCV Patterns   42

12   VCV Patterns   46

13   Longer Snurks   50

14   Prefix-Root Words   54

15   Root-Suffix Words   58

16   Three-Syllable Words   62

17   Combinations with /a/   66

18   Combinations with /e/   71

19   Combinations with /i/   76

20   Combinations with /o/

      and /ô/   81

21   Combinations with /u/   86

22   Combinations with /ā/   91

23   Combinations with /ē/   96

24   Combinations with /ī/   101

25   Combinations with /ō/   106

26   Combinations with /ū/

      and /ü/   111

27   *oo* Spelling Combinations   116

28   Combinations with /ou/   121

29   Combinations with /oi/   126

30   Combinations with /ô/   131

31   Combinations with /är/   136

32   Combinations with /ãr/   141

33   Combinations with /ôr/   146

34   Combinations with /ėr/   151

35   Prefix-Root-Suffix Words   156

36   Four-Syllable Words   160

Guide to the Dictionary   164

Spelling Dictionary   165

THE BASIC GOALS IN SPELLING PROGRAM

The Fifth Edition of BASIC GOALS IN SPELLING is a flexible elementary spelling program designed both for conventional classes and for classes using small-group individualization. Like its widely used predecessors, this completely new edition takes a pioneering direction in the teaching of spelling and provides a unique and thoroughly researched learning progression through all the spelling patterns of the language. Beginning with Level 2, each study unit is organized around either a major, high-frequency speech sound or a syllabic pattern and presents one or more spellings of that sound or syllabic pattern. In addition, most units in Levels 2 through 6 feature a Read and Spell word list that coordinates the encoding and decoding skills of spelling and reading and extends the learning objectives of the basic unit list. Each basic text for Levels 1 through 6 is supplemented by Webstermasters that provide correlated enrichment activities for Levels 1 through 3 and end-of-unit mastery tests for Levels 4 through 6.

The cumulative learning goal of the series is a thorough mastery of every basic spelling pattern and a competence in handling inflectional endings, prefixes and suffixes, multisyllabic words, and all the other related language processes which enable pupils to expand the basic word list into a virtually unlimited personal spelling vocabulary. To enable pupils to achieve this goal, the series is structured according to precise linguistic principles and incorporates the following learning strategies.

1   Presentation of words in the order of their frequency of use, grouped by their most important linguistic characteristics, to emphasize the basic relationship between the sounds and the written symbols of American-English words.

2   Introduction of a simple, easily mastered system of linguistic symbols for the forty-odd speech sounds of the language to enable pupils to identify these sounds rapidly and precisely and to analyze them more accurately within the context of words.

3   Sequential development of all the regular, or expected, spelling options for each of the speech sounds in American-English words.

4   Systematic attention in each appropriate study unit to the relatively small number of high-frequency irregular words that violate the expected spelling options.

5 Continuous comparison of similar and dissimilar vowel sounds through activities focused upon the interrelationship of short, long, and other vowel sounds and the shifting spelling patterns by which these sounds are represented in words.

6 Expansion of the spelling vocabulary introduced at each level to demonstrate a natural skills correlation with the much broader reading vocabularies of current basal readers.

7 Synchronization of the complementary skills of encoding and decoding by first introducing sound-symbol and structural generalizations as an encoding concept and then immediately reversing the application of these generalizations in corresponding decoding activities.

8 Integration of a comprehensive program of instruction in dictionary skills with proofreading, the study of word meanings, the mechanics of writing, and other related language arts skills.

9 Implementation of an innovative, individualized testing program that incorporates a continually reinforcing and precisely paced review as well as a criterion-referenced diagnosis of spelling errors.

10 Emphasis of the concept of symbolization by correlating linguistic symbols with a broad variety of internationally standardized symbols and by developing an appreciation of how visual symbols can transmit ideas, as well as speech sounds, instantaneously.

OVERVIEW OF LEVELS 4, 5, AND 6

The principal objective of the texts for Levels 4, 5, and 6 of the Fifth Edition of BASIC GOALS IN SPELLING is to teach pupils the spelling options for the various vowel and consonant sounds. Pupils are taught to look at words discriminatingly and to note agreement with or deviation from an expected phonetic or structural spelling pattern. Since the coding system of sound-symbol relationships is common to the processes of both spelling and reading, the texts at these levels follow the precedent of earlier levels and synchronize encoding instruction with decoding instruction.

To enable pupils to apply their knowledge of sound-symbol relationships to the multisyllabic words that appear with increasing frequency in the vocabulary at these levels, a comprehensive program of instruction in the analysis of syllables and in the deciphering of a sound-spelling alphabet has been designed as a basic focus of the learning activities throughout each text. These activities dealing with syllables and pronunciations are intended to provide pupils with a set of skills that will allow them to analyze and master multisyllabic words in the same way that they analyze and master monosyllabic words.

Related language skills are also presented, practiced, reviewed, and evaluated in every unit of the texts. Included are activities in capitalization, punctuation, and other basic conventions of written communication. Opportunities for the application and evaluation of these skills are regularly provided, both in the proofreading exercises and in the end-of-unit Mastery Tests. Pupils are given intensive instruction in the use of the dictionary, not only as a resource tool for correct spellings and word meanings, but also as a useful reference for identifying parts of speech, synonyms and antonyms, irregular plurals, and inflectiona endings. In all units there are carefully struc tured activities that require pupils to use th Spelling Dictionary at the back of each book. A additional feature of the language skills stran is the inclusion of Handwriting Models in eac unit as a guide to good legibility for pupils t follow in their written work.

Sound-Symbol Relationships

In these three levels pupils review the conso nant spellings that were introduced in the ear lier levels of the series. A few problems ma occasionally be encountered with consonants For example, some consonant letters are use to represent more than one sound (c spells /s and /k/, g spells /g/ and /j/), some consonan letters are doubled to spell one sound (ll in bel gg in egg), and some consonant pairs spe completely unexpected sounds (ph spells /f gh spells /f/). But, by and large, consonant cause far fewer spelling problems than d vowels. Consequently, the attention of pupil at these levels is directed primarily to study o the vowels.

The spelling patterns for the vowel sound are logically grouped into four categories short-vowel spellings, long-vowel spellings, di graphic-vowel spellings, and vowel-r spellings The various spelling options for these four cate gories of vowels are introduced in monosyllabi vocabulary and then carefully reiterated and ap plied to the stressed syllables of multisyllabi vocabulary. Pupils are also assisted in learning vowel spellings in unstressed syllables—sylla bles in which the vowel sounds are usually in distinguishable. This assistance takes the for of training pupils to look at and to say the ind vidual syllables of multisyllabic words as if the were regular monosyllabic words. By artificially placing stress on all syllables (and thereby creating distinguishable vowel sounds which provide spelling cues), pupils are taught to apply the standard vowel spellings that they have learned for monosyllabic words. Pupils are regularly reminded, of course, that the practice of placing equal stress on all syllables is a device to be used only for learning to spell a multisyllabic word and that we always say these words as whole words with the normal stresses of standard pronunciation.

Eye-Syllables and Ear-Syllables

In order to help pupils utilize the sound-symbol relationships in multisyllabic words, we have developed two singularly important devices for dealing with the basic concepts of written and spoken language. The learning device that relates to the written concept of our multisyllabic vocabulary we call the *eye-syllable.* The device relating to the pronunciation concept of multisyllables we call the *ear-syllable.*

Eye-syllables are visual groupings of letters into those word parts that make multisyllabic words easiest to spell. We signal eye-syllables in the word lists within the texts by using brackets in this fashion: ˏreˏmemˏber. As pupils analyze the parts called out by brackets, they learn to break long letter sequences into smaller visual segments to which they can readily apply sound-symbol generalizations.

All multisyllabic words in Levels 4, 5, and 6 are shown with the eye-syllables clearly bracketed. The eye-syllable breaks are, of course, somewhat arbitrary. They represent our judgment concerning the most logical visual segments for each multisyllabic word. The eye-syllable brackets are especially useful with the vocabulary at these levels because of the frequency of compound words and of words with inflectional endings, prefixes, or suffixes.

Ear-syllables are the word parts we hear when a multisyllabic word is spoken. The pronunciations that lexicographers show for entry words are their attempts to represent the ear-syllables of spoken words. In this series, ear-syllables are shown by sound symbols between slant marks in this fashion: /rē mem′ bər/.

The sound symbols between slant marks represent our effort to identify the most common pronunciations of the spelling vocabulary. There may be variations between the symbols we use and those used in some dictionaries. And there will undoubtedly be regional differences in pronunciations. Some of these regional differences are noted in the unit activities as well as in the Spelling Dictionary at the back of each text. Pupils should be encouraged to note other differences between the pronunciations in these texts and the pronunciations of their own dialect. Such linguistic comparisons are a valuable learning experience, and they will further increase the usefulness of the system of pronunciation symbols used in these texts.

In a continuing effort to help pupils master the various spelling options for the sounds they hear, the texts for Levels 4, 5, and 6 rely heavily on the use of ear-syllable representation. We refer to this representation as *sound-spelling* in the pupil texts. In order to assist pupils in interpreting sound-spelling, a Sound-Spelling Alphabet immediately precedes Unit 1 in both the pupils' text and the Teacher's Edition. Throughout the course of study, this chart will serve as a useful reference for translating sound-spellings and for understanding the sounds for which the various symbols stand.

Irregular Spellings

There are a number of words that are not spelled according to a regular, or expected, spelling pattern. The Fifth Edition of BASIC GOALS IN SPELLING offers pupils a systematic and concentrated study of these irregular spellings.

We have identified 115 violators of the sound-symbol generalizations among the one thousand most frequently used words of English. In Levels 1, 2, and 3 of this series, we have introduced these words as total configurations to be memorized and practiced.

In Levels 4, 5, and 6, we continue to alert pupils to the problems of irregular spellings. Violators from the earlier levels are reviewed in many units by being placed in juxtaposition with words that illustrate regular spelling patterns. They are used repeatedly in the end-of-unit tests. In addition, new monosyllabic and multisyllabic violators are introduced and systematically reviewed. These violators also appear in the end-of-unit tests.

In order to highlight our concern for and our treatment of the study of spelling violators, we consistently refer to them as *snurks.* We define a snurk as follows:

> **snurk** /snėrk/ *n.* A violator of an expected spelling pattern. (A coined word made up of parts of *sneak* and *lurk.*) — *adj.* **snurky.**

Correlation of Spelling and Reading

A close harmony exists between the encoding skills of spelling and the decoding skills of reading. Since the sound-symbol relationships are identical for both sets of skills, it seems natural and sensible that the learning and application of those relationships should be taught in both contexts. This new edition of BASIC GOALS IN SPELLING has been designed to do so.

In Levels 4, 5, and 6, the presentation of spelling material has been organized in such a manner that the application of spelling generalizations to the process of decoding is made apparent. The principal device for achieving this correlation is a Read and Spell list included in each unit of study. The Read and Spell list illustrates the same phonetic or structural generalizations as those presented in the spelling list at the beginning of the unit.

Several research studies, one of which analyzes the vocabulary of commonly used basal reading texts, have been used to verify the vocabulary of both the unit lists and the Read and Spell lists.* When pupils decode the Read

*Harris, Albert J., and Jacobson, Milton D. *Basic Elementary Reading Vocabularies.* New York: The Macmillan Co., 1972.

Rinsland, Henry D. *A Basic Vocabulary of Elementary School Children.* New York: The Macmillan Co., 1945.

Thorndike, Edward L. *The Teacher's Word Book of 30,000 Words.* New York: Teachers College Press, Columbia University, 1944.

and Spell words, they will get practice in dealing with a vocabulary that appears again and again in their reading books.

Each Read and Spell list is recommended for use as a diagnostic decoding test. It may also be used as practice material in the development of word perception skills. It can be of considerable use as a convenient source for the study of word meanings. And, of course, the list may serve as a supplementary spelling list. Words from the Read and Spell lists have been incorporated into the activities of all units.

Dictionary Instruction

At these levels the vocabulary of content area textbooks proliferates, and competence in using the dictionary becomes essential. To develop this competence, the Fifth Edition of BASIC GOALS IN SPELLING includes a uniquely comprehensive program of systematic instruction in dictionary skills. Every unit of Levels 4, 5, and 6 includes a formal dictionary activity that requires pupils to apply a variety of dictionary skills. Moreover, other activities in each unit provide pupils with additional practice by causing them to use the Spelling Dictionary at the back of the texts for Levels 4, 5, and 6. Extensive practice in reading dictionary sound-spelling is provided in conjunction with spelling activities and is utilized in the testing program. The Guide to the Dictionary serves as a convenient reference for dictionary usage by demonstrating standard dictionary format. The comprehensive scope of dictionary instruction is detailed in the Dictionary Skills section of the Skills Outline.

Proofreading Practice

Many errors in written work occur because of failure to proofread. Regular practice in this important skill is provided in every unit of Levels 4, 5, and 6. Practice in locating and correcting common errors in capitalization, punctuation, and spelling is carefully sequenced and is based on instruction provided in the texts. The writing conventions are systematically reviewed, and pupils are continually alerted to the value and need of proofreading all their written work. Thus, they develop the habit of looking for errors, not only in spelling but also in the basic conventions of written communication.

Enrichment Activities

Each of the Level 4, 5, and 6 texts has at least one activity in every unit designed to stimulate pupils' interest in symbols, words, or word sources. An exercise requiring a written response is provided to structure and guide pupils' use of this material. Pupils are thus given additional opportunities for applying and extending the language skills presented in these texts.

Handwriting

The Spelling Alphabet, which immediately precedes Unit 1 of the text, offers pupils a complete set of cursive models in both capital and lower-case forms for each of the twenty-six letters of the alphabet. For the benefit of those teachers who wish to correlate handwriting instruction with the spelling activities, a display of the unit words in cursive, prominently labeled *Handwriting Models,* is included in each unit.

Organization of the Units

All of the foregoing features are logically and visibly organized in each of the thirty-six units at each level. Unit titles clearly indicate the generalizations to be studied. The unit spelling list and the block of study material presented at the beginning of each unit serve as vehicles for discussion and a reference for the written work.

The various writing activities in each unit are separated into four precisely focused sections. Following are the symbols which identify the *sequence* of these four sections in each unit:

 = Section One

 = Section Two

 = Section Three

 = Section Four

Paired with each sequence symbol or placed beside an individual exercise are the *content* symbols, which signal the purpose of each activity:

 = Spelling Activity

 = Dictionary Activity

 = Read and Spell Activity

 = Proofreading Activity

It should be noted that the traditional periodic review units have been deleted from this edition of BASIC GOALS IN SPELLING in favor of an expanded developmental program. A significant feature of this expanded developmental approach is a continuous spiral review built into the activities of all units, as well as into the innovative testing program that is discussed in the following section.

Testing for Mastery and Diagnosis

The end-of-unit tests, which immediately follow the Teaching Suggestions in each unit of the Teacher's Edition, are an integral part of the instructional strategy of the Fifth Edition of BASIC GOALS IN SPELLING. These tests have been meticulously designed to test pupils' mastery of the words and generalizations taught in the units, to serve as a diagnosis of spelling progress, and to provide systematic review of the words and generalizations taught previously. The total vocabulary of the tests is purposefully controlled. Included in each test are the words of the unit, review words from previous units and earlier levels, snurks, and homonyms.

As discussed earlier, when the spelling patterns for the various vowel and consonant sounds are introduced in the basic text, the linguistic symbols for the sounds are also presented. These dictionary sound-spelling symbols, which represent the pronunciations of the spelling vocabulary, have been utilized to develop the innovative silent tests provided as part of the testing program in Levels 4, 5, and 6.

Two versions of each Mastery Test are offered in this Teacher's Edition. The format of the recommended version is a transcription test. The same test content is also provided in dictation form. The two forms of the test may be used in a variety of ways. An example of Part A of a typical two-part Mastery Test as it appears at the end of the Teaching Suggestions for each unit at these levels follows:

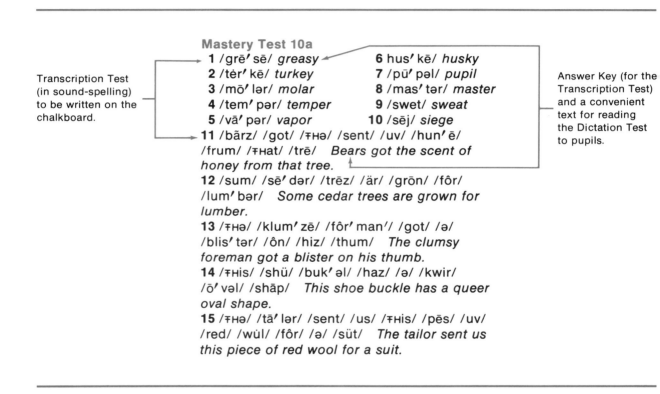

Transcription Test (in sound-spelling) to be written on the chalkboard.

Mastery Test 10a

1 /grē′sē/ *greasy*   **6** hus′kē/ *husky*
2 /tėr′kē/ *turkey*   **7** /pū′pəl/ *pupil*
3 /mō′lər/ *molar*   **8** /mas′tər/ *master*
4 /tem′pər/ *temper*   **9** /swet/ *sweat*
5 /vā′pər/ *vapor*   **10** /sēj/ *siege*
11 /bārz/ /got/ /ɸHə/ /sent/ /uv/ /hun′ē/ /frum/ /ɸHat/ /trē/ *Bears got the scent of honey from that tree.*
12 /sum/ /sē′dər/ /trēz/ /är/ /grōn/ /fôr/ /lum′bər/ *Some cedar trees are grown for lumber.*
13 /ɸHə/ /klum′zē/ /fôr′man′/ /got/ /ə/ /blis′tər/ /ôn/ /hiz/ /thum/ *The clumsy foreman got a blister on his thumb.*
14 /ɸHis/ /shü/ /buk′əl/ /haz/ /ə/ /kwir/ /ō′vəl/ /shāp/ *This shoe buckle has a queer oval shape.*
15 /ɸHə/ /tā′lər/ /sent/ /us/ /ɸHis/ /pēs/ /uv/ /red/ /wül/ /fôr/ /ə/ /süt/ *The tailor sent us this piece of red wool for a suit.*

Answer Key (for the Transcription Test) and a convenient text for reading the Dictation Test to pupils.

The transcription test is preferred over the dictation version for several reasons. First, since pupils at these levels receive a concentrated program of instruction in the use and interpretation of sound symbols, it is appropriate to use a sound-symbol test. In addition, the transcription format provides an effective silent testing program of spelling skills. The transcription test may be copied on the chalkboard for all pupils to see and to transcribe into traditional orthography.

The dictation version of the test in each unit is given for several reasons. First, it is offered as a convenient answer key for the transcription test. Second, the dictation test is an alternate form which some teachers may prefer over the transcription version.

It is hoped, however, that teachers will be able to make good use of both forms of the tests. For example, some teachers may prefer to use the transcription tests as additional practice material and to give the end-of-unit tests in the form of dictation. Or this procedure may be reversed by giving the dictation test as additional practice and concluding the unit with the transcription version as a final test.

Each end-of-unit test is separated into two equivalent parts, which together make up the complete test. The two parts may, depending upon the needs of individual pupils, be administered in one or two sittings.

Beginning on page T-18 of this Teacher's Edition, there appears a Diagnostic Chart of Test Words for each of the thirty-six Mastery Tests. The charts show at a glance the words that are used in the tests. Use of the charts will enable the teacher to determine the kinds of spelling errors pupils make and to give individual pupils special attention as required. It will be useful to maintain folders of the completed tests and to refer to the diagnostic charts for the purpose of systematically reviewing and analyzing pupils' spelling progress.

The thirty-six tests are also available in the form of duplicating masters.* They can be used to make the testing less cumbersome. Use of the Webstermasters eliminates the need to write the test on the board and enables the pupils to complete the tests as individual assignments.

Individualizing the Spelling Program

Teachers are naturally concerned about the wide range of spelling performance among pupils. In some cases the range is so wide that the use of a single spelling textbook for all pupils in a graded class is not feasible. Some pupils can make accelerated progress through a spelling program, while others may require more time, according to their abilities and experiences. Tailoring the use of spelling materials to individual differences within a classroom should be undertaken as soon as possible.

It is reasonable to expect, for example, that some kindergarten pupils may be able to make profitable use of the Level 1 text. There is a strong probability that those pupils would be able to complete the first three textbook levels in two school years. Since these accelerated beginners will probably continue their rapid progress, they need not be restricted to the use of one spelling text each school year.

Proceeding at an accelerated rate, some pupils may be capable of completing seven or eight levels of BASIC GOALS IN SPELLING in six years of study. Such accelerated progress has the dual advantage of challenging the able pupils, while not depriving them of the essential related language-arts content built into the series.

To facilitate a more flexible use of the texts and the correlated supplementary materials in this series, grade-level designations are not shown on the pupil material. Teachers, therefore, will find it easier to use materials from various levels within the same class.

The Webster Spelling Placement Test

The Webster Spelling Placement Test is available as an aid to individualizing the spelling program. The test is designed to be administered to pupils who will be using the Fifth Edition of BASIC GOALS IN SPELLING for the first time. The Webster Spelling Placement Test is not a standardized test, but it does provide information about pupils' readiness to use the text that most pupils of a given grade level would be expected to use. Recommendations for placement accompany the test. However, the test data should be weighed carefully and supplemented with other available information about the pupils being tested.

The Webster Spelling Placement Test is constructed so that information may be gathered about pupils' specific spelling deficiencies in any of the basic categories of sound-symbol and structural generalizations. Suggestions for remediation of these deficiencies are included with the test.

* Level 4 *Basic Goals in Spelling Webstermasters,* Fifth Edition ISBN 0-07-034344-6
Level 5 *Basic Goals in Spelling Webstermasters,* Fifth Edition ISBN 0-07-034345-4
Level 6 *Basic Goals in Spelling Webstermasters,* Fifth Edition ISBN 0-07-034346-2

LEVEL 6 SKILLS OUTLINE

ENCODING SKILLS

REGULAR MONOSYLLABIC SPELLINGS		UNIT*
Consonants	• /b/ *b*, /d/ *d*, /g/ *g*, /h/ *h*, /l/ *l*, /m/ *m*, /n/ *n*, /p/ *p*, /r/ *r*, /t/ *t*, /v/ *v*, /w/ *w*, /y/ *y*, /hw/ *wh*, /ks/ *x*, /kw/ *qu*, /sh/ *sh*, /th/ *th*, /ŦH/ *th*, /zh/ *s*	1–36
	• /ch/ *ch*, *tch*; /f/ *f*, *ph*; /j/ *j*, *g*, *dge*; /k/ *k*, *c*, *ck*, *ch*; /m/ *m*, *mb*; /n/ *n*, *kn*; /ng/ *ng*, *n(k)*; /s/ *s*, *c*, *sc*; /z/ *z*, *s*; /l/ *ll*, /s/ *ss*, /g/ *gg*, etc.	1–4
Short Vowels	• /a/ *a*	1, 17
	• /e/ *e*	1, 18
	• /i/ *i*	1, 19
	• /o/ or /ô/ *o*	1, 20
	• /u/ *u*	1, 21
Long-Vowel Options	• /ā/ *ai, ay, a*-consonant-*e*	2, 22
	• /ē/ *ee, ea, e*-consonant-*e*	2, 23
	• /ī/ *y, igh, ie, i*-consonant-*e*	2, 24
	• /ō/ *oa, ow, o*-consonant-*e*	2, 25
	• /ū/ or /ü/ *ue, ui, ew, u*-consonant-*e*	2, 26
Digraphic-Vowel Options	• /u̇/ and /ü/ *oo*	3, 27
	• /ou/ *ou, ow*	3, 28
	• /oi/ *oi, oy*	3, 29
	• /ô/ *au, aw, a(l)*	3, 30
Vowel-*r* Options	• /är/ *ar*	4, 31
	• /ãr/ *are, air*	4, 32
	• /ôr/ *or, ore, oar*	4, 33
	• /ėr/ *er, ir, ur*	4, 34
	• /ir/ *ear, eer*	4

*Numerals indicate the unit or units in which each skill is presented or given concentrated attention. Following its introduction, each skill is regularly reviewed and reinforced.

IRREGULAR MONOSYLLABIC SPELLINGS	UNIT
Snurks • *chief, field, brief, yield, niece, siege, shriek; eight, freight; thread, dread, sweat; weird; post, though, dough, host, toll, stroll; thought, trough; wash, squash, squad; glove, shove, dove; mild, pint, ninth*	8
• *pear, piece, vein, isle, aisle, prey, yolk, bass*	9
• *wealth, spread*	18
• *build, sieve*	19
• *ton, sponge*	21
• *steak*	22
• *piece, grief, shield*	23
• *guide, height*	24
• *poll, roll*	25
• *truth, youth*	26
• *blood, flood*	27
• *tough, cough*	28
• *their, heir*	32

REGULAR COMPOUND SPELLINGS

Short Vowels • /a/ *a*	5, 17
• /e/ *e*	5, 18
• /i/ *i*	5, 19
• /o/ or /ô/ *o*	5, 20
• /u/ *u*	5, 21
Long-Vowel Options • /ā/ *ai, ay, a*-consonant-*e*	5, 22
• /ē/ *ee, ea*	5, 23
• /ī/ *y, i*-consonant-*e*	5, 24
• /ō/ *oa, ow, o*-consonant-*e*	5, 25
• /ū/ or /ü/ *ew, u*-consonant-*e*	5, 26
Digraphic-Vowel Options • /ù/ and /ü/ *oo*	6, 27
• /ou/ *ou, ow*	6, 28
• /oi/ *oi, oy*	6, 29
• /ô/ *au, aw, a(l)*	6, 30
Vowel-*r* Options • /är/ *ar*	7, 31
• /ār/ *are, air*	7, 32
• /ôr/ *or, ore, oar*	7, 33
• /èr/ *er, ir, ur;* /ir/ *ear*	7

REGULAR MULTISYLLABIC SPELLINGS

Words with Soft-Syllable Endings • /ē/ *y, ey*	10, 16, 17–34
• /ər/ *er, or, ar*	10, 16, 17–34
• /əl/ *le, el, al*	10, 16, 17–34

		UNIT
VCCV Words	● VC/CV, VCC/V, V/CCV	11, 17–36
VCCCV Words	● VC/CCV, VCC/CV	11, 17–36
VCV Words	● V/CV, VC/V	12, 17–36
Words with Prefixes	● *re, ex, com, con, en, in, im, pre, pro, de, dis, un*	14, 17–35
Words with Suffixes	● *ness, ment, tion, sion, ance, ence, ful, less, ant, ent, ous, able, ible*	15, 17–35
Words with Prefixes and Suffixes	● *contraction, delightful, impossible,* etc.	20, 26, 29, 30, 32, 33, 34, 35
Four-Syllable Words	● *ceremony, patriotic, caterpillar,* etc.	36

IRREGULAR MULTISYLLABIC SPELLINGS

Snurks	● *carol, honey*	10
	● *postpone*	11
	● *bushel, bullet, butcher; only, poster, hostess; smother, wonder, shovel; remove, approve; machine, sardine, gasoline; barrel, carrot, narrow, parrot, caravan; heaven, sweater, steady, weapon, meadow; believe, relieve, belief, relief, achieve, movie*	13
	● *bulletin*	16
	● *improve*	20
	● *berry, bury*	34
	● *unpleasant*	35

HOMONYMS

Consonant and Vowel Spelling Options	● *cent-scent-sent, pair-pare-pear, loan-lone, peace-piece, vain-vane-vein, cell-sell, isle-aisle-I'll, birth-berth, pray-prey, yoke-yolk, bough-bow, base-bass, cord-chord*	9
	● *some-sum, rung-wrung, waste-waist, steak-stake, piece-peace, die-dye, idol-idle, roll-role, poll-pole, fare-fair, hair-hare, fur-fir, berry-bury*	21–25, 32, 34

STRUCTURAL CONVENTIONS

Plural Forms	● *mercy-mercies, donkey-donkeys, foreman-foremen, piano-pianos, banjo-banjos* and *banjoes, suffix-suffixes,* etc.	7, 10, 11, 12, 13, 16, 19, 20, 33, 36

		UNIT
Verb Forms	● *brand-branding, dodge-dodging,* etc.	1–4, 9, 10, 14, 17, 22, 24, 25, 31–34, 36
	● *prefer-preferred-preferring,* etc.	12, 14, 20
	● *rival-rivaled-rivaling,* etc.	10
	● *send-sent-sending, build-built-building,* etc.	9, 21, 34
	● *panic-panicked-panicking,* etc.	12
Adjective Forms	● *coarse-coarser-coarsest,* etc.	4, 26
	● *weary-wearier-weariest,* etc.	10, 17, 19, 20, 25, 27, 28, 34
Suffix Forms	● *uneasy-uneasiness, response-responsible,* etc.	15, 24, 35

DICTIONARY SKILLS

PRONUNCIATIONS

Consonant Sound Symbols	● /b/, /d/, /f/, /g/, /h/, /j/, /k/, /l/, /m/, /n/, /p/, /r/, /s/, /t/, /v/, /w/, /y/, /z/, /ch/, /sh/, /th/, /ᵮн/, /hw/, /ng/, /zh/	1–36
Vowel Sound Symbols	● /a/ *damp,* /ā/ *grace*	1–2, 5, 17, 22
	● /e/ *flesh,* /ē/ *feast*	1–2, 5, 18, 23
	● /i/ *swift,* /ī/ *chime*	1–2, 5, 19, 24
	● /o/ *bomb,* /ō/ *pose*	1–2, 5, 20, 25
	● /u/ *punch,* /ū/ *huge*	1–2, 5, 21, 26
	● /ù/ *nook,* /ü/ *booth*	3, 6, 27
	● /ou/ *bough*	3, 6, 28
	● /oi/ *broil*	3, 6, 29
	● /ô/ *sprawl*	3, 6, 30
	● /ä/ *arch*	4, 7, 31
	● /ã/ *fair*	4, 7, 32
	● /ô/ *port*	4, 7, 33
	● /èr/ *verb*	4, 7, 34
	● /ə/ *taken, about, pencil, lemon, circus*	10, 12–36
Ear-Syllables in Multisyllabic Words	● compounds	5–7, 17–34
	● soft-syllable endings	10, 17–34
	● VCCV, VCCCV, and VCV patterns	11, 12, 17–36
	● prefixes and suffixes	14, 15, 17–35
	● four-syllable words	36
Stress in Multisyllabic Words	● primary and secondary accent	5–7, 36
	● unaccented syllables	10–36

MEANINGS AND USES OF ENTRY WORDS

		UNIT
Definitions	• sample entries	1–36
	• numbered definitions	2
	• sentences or phrases to show meaning	1–4
	• additional information in entry	17
	• synonyms and antonyms	23, 24
	• pictures with labels	7, 17, 36
	• special meanings	11, 33
Parts of Speech	• n., v., adj., adv., etc.	1–36
	• multiple parts of speech	3, 14, 18

STRUCTURAL CHANGES IN ENTRY WORDS

Plural Forms	• firefly-fireflies, foundry-foundries, etc.	6, 13
	• donkey-donkeys, turkey-turkeys, etc.	13
	• tobacco-tobaccos and tobaccoes, etc.	16
Verb Forms	• bathe-bathed-bathing, etc.	2
	• sell-sold-selling, etc.	9, 34
	• tremble-trembled-trembling, etc.	10
	• admit-admitted-admitting, etc.	12, 14
Adjective Forms	• coarse-coarser-coarsest, etc.	4, 26
	• crafty-craftier-craftiest, etc.	19, 25

CONVENTIONS OF FORMAT

Form and Arrangement of Entries	• alphabetical order	1, 6
	• numbered definitions	2
	• multiple spellings	27
	• multiple pronunciations	18, 31
	• prefixes as entries	29, 30
	• suffixes as entries	32
	• numbered entries	8, 22, 28
	• singular and plural	6, 16, 31
	• inflectional endings	19, 24, 26

CORRELATED LANGUAGE SKILLS

DECODING

Sound-Symbol Generalizations	• Read and Spell lists	1–36
	• Read and Spell exercises	1–36
Structural Generalizations	• Read and Spell lists	5–7, 10–36
	• Read and Spell exercises	5–7, 10–36

PROOFREADING

		UNIT
Spelling Errors	• new words and review words	1–36
	• plural forms	6, 16, 17, 22, 23, 33
	• verb forms	6, 13, 16, 23, 25
	• possessives and contractions	4, 5, 7, 8, 15, 20, 27, 29, 36
Punctuation and Capitalization	• periods and question marks	3, 4, 7, 13, 23
	• commas	1, 2, 22, 25
	• capitalization	1, 2, 5, 10, 13, 17, 22, 34
	• run-on sentences	3, 7, 12, 29, 34
Word Meaning	• synonyms and antonyms	9, 14, 28, 32, 35
	• parts of speech	21, 26, 31, 35
	• words in context	11, 18, 19, 24, 27, 33
Errors in Fact	• expository paragraphs	6, 7, 20, 29

ENGLISH ACTIVITIES

Identification of Parts of Speech	• nouns, verbs, adjectives, adverbs	15–36
	• suffixes to change parts of speech	15, 20, 24, 26, 27, 29, 31, 35
Word Meanings	• synonyms and antonyms	1–4, 8–10, 12–17, 19–21, 23–35
	• homonyms	3, 4, 9, 21–25, 32, 34
	• word origins	1–36
	• prefixed words and suffixed words	14, 15, 17–35
	• definitions	3, 12, 16, 18, 22, 24, 29, 30, 36
	• words in context	4, 7, 9, 11–36
Writing Conventions in Compositions and Lists	• original dictionary entries	1–36
	• proofreading activities	1–36
	• word origin activities	1–36

LEVEL 6 DIAGNOSTIC CHARTS OF TEST WORDS

UNIT 1   Diagnostic Chart of Test Words*

Regular Spellings	back 2, badge 5, best 3, Black 2, boss 5, box 1, can 2, chest 3, crutch 5, desks 2, dish 2, fence 3, hand 2, hedge 5, help 2, his 2, hot 2, if 2, is 1, just 3, kept 3, left 2, lids 2, lift 3, lock 2, long 2, loss 4, Miss 2, on 2, patch 5, pink 2, plums 5, scrub 3, shrug 5, soft 2, strength 5, that 2, this 2, thumb 3, twins 3, us 1, whiz 3, with 2, yelled 2
Homonyms	in 1, it's 4, some 2, to 2, two 2
Snurks	are 2, from 2, have 2, most 3, of 2, said 2, want 2, you 2, your 2

* The Mastery Test for Unit 1 also includes the new basic unit words, which are not shown on this chart. The numeral following a word indicates the level at which that word is introduced. Underscored words are those that appear in the unit Study Chart as review words.

UNIT 2   Diagnostic Chart of Test Words*

Regular Spellings	bathe 4, bay 5, beef 5, broth 6, cheese 5, chest 3, clock 3, cups 2, Dad 2, damp 6, dodge 6, faint 5, fox 1, girls 2, goal 5, had 2, hat 2, he 2, him 1, huge 4, is 1, lock 2, lunch 2, my 2, numb 6, old 2, on 2, patch 5, phone 5, pink 2, row 5, runs 2, sand 4, slice 5, sly 5, smell 6, squeal 5, strong 3, swift 6, that 2, think 3, those 2, tongs 6, when 2, whisk 6, with 2
Homonyms	be 3, for 2, knew 2, new 2, not 2, road 2, through 4, to 2, too 2, two 2
Snurks	bought 3, child 3, have 2, of 2, said 2, should 2, want 2, you 2, young 2

* The Mastery Test for Unit 2 also includes the new basic unit words, which are not shown on this chart. The numeral following a word indicates the level at which that word is introduced. Underscored words are those that appear in the unit Study Chart as review words.

UNIT 3   Diagnostic Chart of Test Words*

Regular Spellings

bake 2, bit 2, broth 6, <u>caught</u> 2, chest 3, chime 6, <u>claws</u> 4, cloth 2, <u>crook</u> 4, dent 6, down 2, gave 2, grace 6, has 1, hat 2, hew 6, huge 4, <u>joy</u> 2, junk 6, just 3, known 6, <u>moist</u> 5, must 2, my 2, needs 3, <u>noun</u> 4, on 2, pan 2, phone 5, pink 2, plate 4, plume 6, <u>poor</u> 5, quail 6, rang 2, roast 6, <u>salt</u> 3, <u>scowl</u> 5, seeds 4, she 1, shed 2, small 3, <u>smooth</u> 4, squeal 5, steep 6, strength 5, this 2, those 2, thrill 6, when 2, whisk 6, with 2

Homonyms

in 1, its 4, knew 2, new 2, not 2, or 2, to 2, two 2, would 2

Snurks

from 2, have 2, of 2, put 2, who 2, you 2, your 2

> * The Mastery Test for Unit 3 also includes the new basic unit words, which are not shown on this chart. The numeral following a word indicates the level at which that word is introduced. Underscored words are those that appear in the unit Study Chart as review words.

UNIT 4   Diagnostic Chart of Test Words*

Regular Spellings

<u>arch</u> 5, art 3, at 1, <u>barge</u> 5, birds 2, boy 2, came 2, <u>chore</u> 4, <u>clear</u> 2, don't 3, drag 3, drawings 2, drawl 6, drought 6, <u>fair</u> 5, <u>firm</u> 4, fly 2, house 2, is 1, it 2, known 6, load 3, long 2, much 2, must 2, my 2, needs 3, nook 6, nouns 4, ounce 6, paint 2, part 2, poor 5, <u>porch</u> 4, quails 6, quite 6, <u>roar</u> 4, row 5, sand 4, show 2, sides 2, sprawl 6, sprouts 6, <u>spur</u> 5, <u>square</u> 5, stuck 6, that 2, thumb 3, toil 6, trash 6, troop 6, <u>verbs</u> 4, wall 3, warm 3, when 2, with 2

Homonyms

<u>deer</u> 2, for 2, four 2, in 1, its 4, it's 4, some 2, sun 1, there's 4, to 2, too 2

Snurks

are 2, from 2, have 2, of 2, was 2, words 2, your 2

> * The Mastery Test for Unit 4 also includes the new basic unit words, which are not shown on this chart. The numeral following a word indicates the level at which that word is introduced. Underscored words are those that appear in the unit Study Chart as review words.

UNIT 5 Diagnostic Chart of Test Words*

Regular Spellings

at 1, bad 2, barge 5, called 2, calves 5, clerks 6, cook 3, cows 2, crossroad 4 daydream 5, flagpole 5, grew 2, grownups 5, jukebox 5, leaped 3, like 2, long 2, lot 3 near 2, on 2, paint 2, pancake 5, patch 5, pink 2, porch 4, port 6, queer 6, railway 5 roast 6, sailors 4, ship 2, skyline 4, smear 6, sometimes 3, spent 3, spite 5, squall 6 squirt 6, starve 6, that 2, thorn 6, those 2, tunes 4, weekend 5, we'll 3, withdrew 5

Homonyms

base 4, fair 2, for 2, hear 2, in 1, sale 3, some 2, to 2

Snurks

are 2, brought 3, don't 3, from 2, have 2, of 2, puts 2, they 2

* The Mastery Test for Unit 5 also includes the new basic unit words, which are not shown on this chart. The numeral following a word indicates the level at which that word is introduced. Underscored words are those that appear in the unit Study Chart as review words.

UNIT 6 Diagnostic Chart of Test Words*

Regular Spellings

all 2, cars 2, catch 2, causeway 5, cleaned 2, clockwise 6, day 2, downtown 4, drive 3, driveway 6, each 3, fireplace 6, foe 5, grapevine 6, hallway 5, let's 4, mainland 6, marched 3, near 2, need 3, offspring 6, oilskin 4, on 2, out 2, outfit 5, past 4, peanut 6, picnic 3, play 2, pledged 6, row 5, run 2, sawmill 5, snow 2, snowplow 5, soybean 4, spoiled 2, stagecoach 6, swift 6, teaspoon 4, textbook 5, told 2, trains 2, troops 6, twice 3, use 2, wide 2

Homonyms

do 2, in 1, meet 3, not 2, our 2, their 2, there 2, to 2, two 2

Snurks

are 2, child 3, from 2, you 2

* The Mastery Test for Unit 6 also includes the new basic unit words, which are not shown on this chart. The numeral following a word indicates the level at which that word is introduced. Underscored words are those that appear in the unit Study Chart as review words.

UNIT 7   Diagnostic Chart of Test Words*

Regular Spellings

as 2, at 1, barnyard 5, best 3, birthday 4, can't 3, cardboard 4, cheese 5, coat 2, cowboys 4, downstream 6, eardrum 4, fish 2, forenoon 4, get 2, go 2, haircut 5, hang 2, harm 3, iceberg 4, if 2, is 1, let's 4, my 2, near 2, nickname 6, oilskin 4, on 2, past 4, pay 3, pointblank 6, popcorn 4, ride 2, roundup 6, row 5, sawmill 5, scarecrow 4, she's 1, small 3, softball 6, strawstack 6, take 3, team 3, this 2, trimmed 5, turnpike 5, well 2, when 2, yuletide 6

Homonyms

fair 2, fare 5, hear 2, here 2, I'll 3, in 1, our 2, sell 2, there's 4, through 3, to 2

Snurks

have 2, you 2, your 2

> * The Mastery Test for Unit 7 also includes the new basic unit words, which are not shown on this chart. The numeral following a word indicates the level at which that word is introduced. Underscored words are those that appear in the unit Study Chart as review words.

UNIT 8   Diagnostic Chart of Test Words*

Regular Spellings

beehive 6, boys 2, carefree 6, causeways 5, chores 4, cream 4, cupcake 6, did 2, down 2, drive 3, each 3, falsehood 6, farmhouse 6, good 2, grease 6, had 2, has 1, he 2, his 2, hit 2, horseback 6, huge 3, need 3, old 2, on 2, patch 5, pay 3, quail 6, she 1, shirt 3, soap 3, soybeans 4, stoop 6, that 2, these 3, this 2, tree 2, turnpikes 5, use 2, we 1, when 2, whirlpool 6, will 2, with 2

Homonyms

blue 2, bough 6, eight 2, for 2, hear 2, new 2, or 2, some 2, sun 1, to 2, two 2

Snurks

bought 3, chief 4, field 4, from 2, gloves 4, head 2, mild 5, of 2, post 5, shields 6, though 3, thought 3, thread 4, was 2, wash 2, you 2, your 2

> * The Mastery Test for Unit 8 also includes the new basic unit words, which are not shown on this chart. The numeral following a word indicates the level at which that word is introduced. Underscored words are those that appear in the unit Study Chart as review words.

UNIT 9   Diagnostic Chart of Test Words*

Regular Spellings

all 2, barnyard 5, birds 2, church 3, cupcakes 6, deep 4, did 2, down 2, eat 2, farmhouse 6, find 2, flew 2, game 2, grownups 5, hawks 6, into 3, let's 4, like 2, men 2, on 2, pancakes 5, quails 6, this 2, tree 2, tried 2, we 1, went 2

Homonyms

ate 3, by 2, <u>cent</u> 3, eight 2, fair 2, fare 5, for 2, fore 6, four 2, hear 2, here 2, in 1, <u>loan</u> 5, <u>lone</u> 5, made 3, <u>pair</u> 4, <u>pared</u> 4, <u>peace</u> 4, <u>pear</u> 4, piece 2, <u>scent</u> 5, sea 3, see 2, <u>sent</u> 3, their 2, there 2, through 3, to 2, two 2, woods 2, would 2

Snurks

could 2, doves 6, field 4, from 2, host 6, of 2, shove 6, shriek 6, stroll 6, they 2, trough 6, you 2, you've 4, weird 6

> * The Mastery Test for Unit 9 also includes the new basic unit words, which are not shown on this chart. The numeral following a word indicates the level at which that word is introduced. Underscored words are those that appear in the unit Study Chart as review words.

UNIT 10   Diagnostic Chart of Test Words*

Regular Spellings

all 2, at 1, <u>beggar</u> 5, <u>clumsy</u> 4, cupcake 6, egg 3, foreman 6, gave 2, got 1, <u>grumble</u> 5, has 1, his 2, known 6, lumber 4, mainland 6, mom 3, <u>nickels</u> 4, on 2, pledged 6, <u>plural</u> 5, poor 5, <u>pupil</u> 4, queer 6, repair 4, rowed 5, sailors 4, schoolboy 5, shape 4, sing 2, streets 3, suit 4, <u>symbol</u> 5, <u>tailor</u> 5, <u>temper</u> 5, that 2, these 3, this 2, thumb 3, town 3, trees 2, <u>turkey</u> 5, us 1, we 1, well 2, with 2, wool 3, yuletide 6

Homonyms

bears 2, eight 2, for 2, grown 4, in 1, it's 3, oars 4, piece 2, red 2, scent 5, sent 3, some 2, their 2, to 2, two 2, yolks 6

Snurks

are 2, dough 6, from 2, of 2, put 2, shoe 2, siege 6, squash 6, sweat 6, toll 6

> * The Mastery Test for Unit 10 also includes the new basic unit words, which are not shown on this chart. The numeral following a word indicates the level at which that word is introduced. Underscored words are those that appear in the unit Study Chart as review words.

UNIT 11   Diagnostic Chart of Test Words*

Regular Spellings

at 1, beads 2, buckle 6, cedar 6, <u>chicken</u> 4, churches 3, <u>costume</u> 5, cross 2, dine 3, <u>elbow</u> 5, food 2, game 2, gave 2, grade 3, is 1, <u>lobster</u> 5, much 2, my 2, <u>necklace</u> 5, ninth 6, on 2, panel 6, <u>pantry</u> 5, part 2, past 4, <u>program</u> 4, <u>pumpkin</u> 3, pupil 4, seaport 6, <u>secret</u> 4, ships 2, softball 6, symbol 5, this 2, <u>tickets</u> 4, town 3, vessel 6, we 1, weary 6, when 2

Homonyms

for 2, hauled 3, here 2, hour 3, in 1, it's 3, made 3, our 2, sailed 3, sale 3, some 2, their 2, there 2, to 2, two 2

Snurks

are 2, built 4, could 2, freight 6, have 2, niece 6, of 2, pint 6, thought 6, was 2, you 2, young 2

> * The Mastery Test for Unit 11 also includes the new basic unit words, which are not shown on this chart. The numeral following a word indicates the level at which that word is introduced. Underscored words are those that appear in the unit Study Chart as review words.

UNIT 12   Diagnostic Chart of Test Words*

Regular Spellings

athletes 6, brand 6, canned 2, cash 2, caused 2, <u>climate</u> 5, council 6, custom 6, <u>event</u> 5, farmhouses 6, <u>fever</u> 5, fish 2, foil 6, <u>frozen</u> 5, game 2, grow 2, help 2, her 2, is 1, it 2, lunch 2, makes 3, <u>menu</u> 5, met 2, <u>mimic</u> 5, <u>modest</u> 5, nephew 6, <u>olives</u> 5, on 2, path 3, plans 3, plastic 6, postpone 6, rival 6, sky 3, slice 4, <u>spider</u> 5, that 2, <u>timid</u> 5, tiny 3, took 2, town 3, trademark 6, warm 3, we 1, will 2

Homonyms

by 2, for 2, heard 3, hour 3, in 1, knew 2, new 2, one 2, our 2, sell 2, tail 3, tale 3, to 2, two 2, won 2

Snurks

build 2, could 2, have 2, of 2, thief 4, was 2, weird 6, who 2, you 2

> * The Mastery Test for Unit 12 also includes the new basic unit words, which are not shown on this chart. The numeral following a word indicates the level at which that word is introduced. Underscored words are those that appear in the unit Study Chart as review words.

UNIT 13   Diagnostic Chart of Test Words*

Regular Spellings

athletes 6, comet 6, cut 2, day 2, fat 2, few 2, good 2, he 2, his 2, honor 4, if 2, into 3, lasted 2, let's 4, like 2, melon 6, my 2, off 2, on 2, own 2, pistol 6, poor 5, roast 6, safe 2, showed 2, take 3, that 2, this 2, town 3, trash 6, visitors 5, vivid 6, weekend 5, will 2

Homonyms

be 2, cords 6, in 1, it's 3, one 2, sell 2, their 2, to 2, too 2, two 2, weak 3, weeks 3, wood 2, would 2

Snurks

<u>barrel</u> 5, <u>believe</u> 4, brought 3, <u>bushel</u> 4, child 3, from 2, great 3, <u>heaven</u> 5, honey 6, host 6, journey 5, <u>machine</u> 4, ninth 6, of 2, <u>only</u> 4, <u>remove</u> 4, <u>smother</u> 5, tastes 3, was 2, wealth 5, yield 6, you 2, your 2

---

* The Mastery Test for Unit 13 also includes the new basic unit words, which are not shown on this chart. The numeral following a word indicates the level at which that word is introduced. Underscored words are those that appear in the unit Study Chart as review words.

UNIT 14   Diagnostic Chart of Test Words*

Regular Spellings

about 3, at 1, blister 6, care 2, <u>complain</u> 5, <u>convince</u> 5, <u>destroy</u> 5, did 2, <u>displease</u> 5, donate 6, <u>enjoy</u> 3, <u>exchange</u> 5, goods 2, he 2, him 1, his 2, <u>impress</u> 5, <u>includes</u> 5, lands 4, melon 6, menu 5, noon 3, on 2, <u>predict</u> 5, <u>produce</u> 5, <u>return</u> 5, she 1, store 2, take 3, that 2, these 3, <u>unkind</u> 5, verses 6, virus 6, we 1, western 6, will 2, with 2

Homonyms

be 2, hear 2, heel 3, here 2, in 1, not 2, our 2, to 2

Snurks

achieve 6, bought 3, country 4, does 2, don't 3, gasoline 6, honey 6, many 2, movies 6, of 2, other 2, shovel 6, was 2, weapon 6, who 2, wonder 6, you 2

---

* The Mastery Test for Unit 14 also includes the new basic unit words, which are not shown on this chart. The numeral following a word indicates the level at which that word is introduced. Underscored words are those that appear in the unit Study Chart as review words.

UNIT 15 Diagnostic Chart of Test Words*

Regular Spellings

<u>ambulance</u> 5, at 1, <u>audience</u> 5, brave 4, carving 5, cause 2, <u>collection</u> 5, decay 6, dismiss 6, downtown 4, drivers 3, <u>elegant</u> 5, events 5, failed 4, <u>faithful</u> 5, falsehoods 6, feel 2, <u>frequent</u> 5, <u>generous</u> 5, <u>honorable</u> 5, import 6, is 1, it 2, king 2, last 2, man 2, mimic 5, old 2, outlaw 4, perform 5, poor 3, prefer 6, price 4, proceed 6, ranch 2, <u>reckless</u> 5, roundups 6, <u>settlement</u> 5, showed 2, takes 3, tell 2, that 2, <u>visible</u> 5, went 2, when 2, <u>witness</u> 5

Homonyms

knight 5, night 2, not 2, one 2, our 2, see 2, some 2, to 2, wood 2, would 2

Snurks

are 2, bought 3, carrot 6, gloves 4, great 3, movie 6, of 2, preview 6, they 2, was 2, you 2

> * The Mastery Test for Unit 15 also includes the new basic unit words, which are not shown on this chart. The numeral following a word indicates the level at which that word is introduced. Underscored words are those that appear in the unit Study Chart as review words.

UNIT 16 Diagnostic Chart of Test Words*

Regular Spellings

at 1, blast 4, <u>carnivals</u> 5, climate 5, <u>continue</u> 4, cross 2, <u>desperate</u> 5, <u>factory</u> 4, farms 2, fashion 6, few 2, frightful 6, has 1, <u>hesitate</u> 5, house 2, is 1, it 2, judgment 6, least 3, makes 3, <u>moccasins</u> 5, notes 4, on 2, opponent 6, patience 6, <u>pioneers</u> 5, raised 3, reasonable 6, refuse 6, <u>regular</u> 4, <u>satisfy</u> 4, takes 3, that 2, this 2, those 2, three 1, times 2, vessels 6, visits 3, <u>volcano</u> 5, warm 3, we 1, weakness 6

Homonyms

chord 6, in 1, made 3, main 5, read 2, their 2, there 2, to 2

Snurks

are 2, children 3, comfort 4, have 2, journeys 5, leather 4, many 2, month 4, only 4, pleasure 4

> * The Mastery Test for Unit 16 also includes the new basic unit words, which are not shown on this chart. The numeral following a word indicates the level at which that word is introduced. Underscored words are those that appear in the unit Study Chart as review words.

UNIT 17   Diagnostic Chart of Test Words*

Regular Spellings	action 4, agent 6, ailment 6, all 2, alley 5, anchor 5, atmosphere 6, attendant 6, attracts 5, audiences 5, bananas 4, bulletin 6, celery 6, climates 5, command 5, constant 5, days 2, dynamite 6, elegant 5, enjoy 3, equator 6, fancy 4, find 2, found 2, gave 2, grammar 5, grandstand 3, grasp 5, house 2, is 1, lands 4, large 3, mansion 5, much 2, near 2, occupy 6, olives 5, on 2, plain 4, platters 5, prefer 6, quiet 4, rent 3, sandal 5, scramble 5, set 2, table 3, tenant 6, that 2, this 2, travel 3, use 2, we 1, without 3
Homonyms	do 2, for 2, in 1, ones 2, or 2, see 2, there 2, to 2
Snurks	are 2, could 2, from 2, mild 5, of 2, water 2, were 2, you 2, your 2

* The Mastery Test for Unit 17 also includes the new basic unit words, which are not shown on this chart. The numeral following a word indicates the level at which that word is introduced. Underscored words are those that appear in the unit Study Chart as review words.

UNIT 18   Diagnostic Chart of Test Words*

Regular Spellings	around 3, at 1, avenue 6, bold 4, camel 6, can 2, can't 3, cellar 3, comet 6, cucumber 6, driveway 6, eat 2, energy 6, flower 2, foreman 5, gentlemen 3, helmet 5, helpful 6, his 2, house 2, lend 5, level 4, melons 6, messenger 5, opponents 6, pajamas 6, pancakes 5, pebble 5, penny 3, petals 5, plowed 4, protect 4, pupils 4, settlement 5, sky 3, slender 5, swift 6, textbooks 5, those 2, tobacco 6, tractor 4, we 1, will 2, with 2, wore 2, wren 4
Homonyms	ate 3, eight 2, for 2, in 1, knight 5, new 2, night 2, not 2, see 2, steel 4, their 2, there 2, to 2, whole 2
Snurks	are 2, brought 3, field 4, fought 3, heavy 4, honey 6, months 4, of 2, wealth 5, were 2, who 2, you 2

* The Mastery Test for Unit 18 also includes the new basic unit words, which are not shown on this chart. The numeral following a word indicates the level at which that word is introduced. Underscored words are those that appear in the unit Study Chart as review words.

UNIT 19   Diagnostic Chart of Test Words*

Regular Spellings

action 4, actor 6, at 1, audience 5, <u>chisel</u> 5, dismissed 6, <u>dizzy</u> 5, driveway 6, farm 2, <u>finishing</u> 4, first 2, gave 2, halted 4, is 1, <u>jingle</u> 5, jug 3, known 6, <u>limp</u> 5, <u>lipstick</u> 4, <u>metal</u> 3, near 2, neglect 6, noise 2, o'clock 3, on 2, <u>pilgrims</u> 5, plenty 6, pupils 4, <u>recess</u> 4, rust 5, <u>sentence</u> 4, settlement 5, she 1, shows 2, <u>similar</u> 5, spoke 3, squad 6, stroll 6, these 3, this 2, <u>twist</u> 5, <u>visitors</u> 5, verb 4, when 2, <u>whisker</u> 5

Homonyms

for 2, in 1, made 3, not 2, sea 3, see 2, their 2, there 2, to 2, weight 3

Snurks

are 2, barrels 5, <u>build</u> 2, could 2, of 2, one 2, rough 3, spread 6, wealth 5, were 2, what 2

* The Mastery Test for Unit 19 also includes the new basic unit words, which are not shown on this chart. The numeral following a word indicates the level at which that word is introduced. Underscored words are those that appear in the unit Study Chart as review words.

UNIT 20   Diagnostic Chart of Test Words*

Regular Spellings

at 1, <u>boss</u> 5, <u>bottles</u> 3, <u>bottom</u> 3, can't 3, commerce 6, <u>copy</u> 4, cucumbers 6, cut 2, difference 6, <u>doctor</u> 3, <u>dollars</u> 3, down 2, dress 2, eating 2, fifty 6, finished 6, foundry 6, games 2, gave 2, has 1, huge 4, <u>impossible</u> 5, is 1, I've 3, <u>jockey</u> 5, mattress 6, may 2, me 2, metal 3, <u>moccasin</u> 5, <u>model</u> 4, much 2, my 2, on 2, pebbles 5, play 2, <u>plot</u> 5, price 4, racket 6, recess 4, salt 3, scissors 6, <u>softness</u> 4, that 2, this 2, throwing 3, <u>topnotch</u> 5, vinegar 6, vitamins 6, we 1, with 2, without 3

Homonyms

berth 6, dear 2, for 2, hear 2, here 2, it's 3, made 3, piece 2, to 2, too 2, two 2

Snurks

<u>bother</u> 4, build 2, children 3, could 2, earn 3, from 2, health 4, <u>income</u> 5, leather 4, of 2, sieve 6, wealth 5, you 2, your 2

* The Mastery Test for Unit 20 also includes the new basic unit words, which are not shown on this chart. The numeral following a word indicates the level at which that word is introduced. Underscored words are those that appear in the unit Study Chart as review words.

UNIT 21   Diagnostic Chart of Test Words*

Regular Spellings

arms 2, audience 5, <u>bathtub</u> 5, bells 2, <u>bunch</u> 5, <u>butter</u> 3, clay 4, <u>clumsy</u> 4, cotton 6 <u>customer</u> 4, dentists 6, doctors 3, dry 3, enjoyed 3, farmhouse 6, flowers 3, grew 2 hands 2, has 1, her 2, his 2, hobby 6, hockey 6, <u>honored</u> 4, king's 2, molding 4 near 2, project 6, <u>pumpkins</u> 3, rag 3, salesman 6, she 1, show 2, signal 6, single 6 sold 3, strength 5, <u>study</u> 3, ten 3, times 2, <u>trustful</u> 5, <u>tumble</u> 5, <u>tunnel</u> 5, <u>unlucky</u> 4 volunteer 6, wet 3, with 2, years 2

Homonyms

bare 2, birth 6, blue 2, cents 3, for 2, I 1, in 1, <u>some</u> 2, son 3, <u>sum</u> 5, their 2, there's 4 to 2, too 2, two 2

Snurks

bought 3, field 4, many 2, of 2, <u>ton</u> 5, was 2, were 2

* The Mastery Test for Unit 21 also includes the new basic unit words, which are not shown on this chart The numeral following a word indicates the level at which that word is introduced. Underscored word are those that appear in the unit Study Chart as review words.

UNIT 22   Diagnostic Chart of Test Words*

Regular Spellings

as 2, actors 6, <u>bacon</u> 4, breezes 5, carols 6, <u>celebrate</u> 5, city 3, cook 3, <u>disgrace</u> 5 game 2, ground 3, had 2, <u>haystack</u> 3, his 2, hopscotch 6, impossible 5, <u>lady</u> 4, let 2 let's 4, lights 2, <u>maker</u> 3, <u>naval</u> 5, on 2, <u>painless</u> 4, <u>place</u> 3, platter 5, please 3 <u>raised</u> 3, rise 4, sculptor 6, set 2, singing 2, skirt 4, soft 2, sponsor 6, stage 5, <u>stray</u> 5 <u>table</u> 3, <u>tailor</u> 5, this 2, those 2, thumbtack 6, trees 2, umbrella 6, we 1, when 2, with 2 wrench 6, yuletide 6

Homonyms

blew 3, blue 2, boughs 6, bowed 6, by 2, for 2, hour 3, it's 3, not 2, one 2, our 2 piece 2, sewed 3, their 2, there 2, to 2, two 2, <u>waist</u> 4, <u>waste</u> 3

Snurks

bread 3, dough 6, from 2, have 2, of 2, said 2, sponge 6, they 2, thread 4, were 2

* The Mastery Test for Unit 22 also includes the new basic unit words, which are not shown on this chart. The numeral following a word indicates the level at which that word is introduced. Underscored words are those that appear in the unit Study Chart as review words.

UNIT 23   Diagnostic Chart of Test Words*

Regular Spellings	appealing 5, at 1, bald 5, basin 6, candidate 6, cloth 2, cotton 6, daily 6, <u>daydream</u> 5, drifted 6, driveway 6, <u>eagle</u> 4, earning 3, <u>explain</u> 3, fatal 6, <u>fever</u> 5, flew 5, good 2, <u>greet</u> 5, honorable 5, huge 4, involved 6, king 2, ladies 4, mayor 6, men 2, much 2, <u>needles</u> 3, <u>needy</u> 3, on 2, parked 3, <u>peach</u> 5, politics 6, <u>readable</u> 5, <u>season</u> 4, <u>seaweed</u> 5, shore 2, sign 4, storms 3, tailors 5, tests 3, <u>these</u> 3, this 2, those 2, top 1, use 2, we 1
Homonyms	be 3, for 2, four 2, hour 3, in 1, it's 3, not 2, our 2, <u>peace</u> 4, <u>piece</u> 2, sew 3, so 3, to 2, two 2
Snurks	belief 6, have 2, money 3, of 2, should 2, sweater 6, toward 4, was 2, were 2, women 4, your 2

* The Mastery Test for Unit 23 also includes the new basic unit words, which are not shown on this chart. The numeral following a word indicates the level at which that word is introduced. Underscored words are those that appear in the unit Study Chart as review words.

UNIT 24   Diagnostic Chart of Test Words*

Regular Spellings	all 2, caused 2, causes 2, chest 3, darkness 6, dauntless 6, daydreaming 5, dress 2, exceeds 6, extreme 6, feet 2, <u>final</u> 5, <u>firefly's</u> 5, <u>flight</u> 5, <u>glide</u> 5, gold 2, her 2, hid 2, his 2, <u>hydrant</u> 5, is 1, lazy 3, legs 2, <u>likeness</u> 5, praises 6, <u>recite</u> 5, rifle 4, scheme 6, serious 4, she 1, <u>shy</u> 5, silver 3, <u>siren</u> 5, six 2, <u>spider</u> 5, splendor 6, steeple 6, such 2, time 2, <u>tiny</u> 3, trees 2, verse 6
Homonyms	<u>die</u> 2, <u>dyed</u> 5, eight 2, in 1, lead 3, led 3, made 3, or 2, our 2, passed 3, red 2, tail 3, through 3, to 2, way 3
Snurks	child 3, does 2, grief 6, <u>guide</u> 5, have 2, of 2, shield 6, wealth 5, what's 4, you'll 3

* The Mastery Test for Unit 24 also includes the new basic unit words, which are not shown on this chart. The numeral following a word indicates the level at which that word is introduced. Underscored words are those that appear in the unit Study Chart as review words.

UNIT 25   Diagnostic Chart of Test Words*

Regular Spellings

actor 6, age 3, all 2, at 1, athletes 6, can 2, <u>clover</u> 5, cost 3, cotton 6, <u>cyclone</u> 5, dollars 3, down 2, eat 2, fifty 6, <u>flow</u> 5, <u>globe</u> 5, hibernate 6, is 1, like 2, liquid 6, <u>locate</u> 4, <u>lonely</u> 4, <u>motion</u> 5, <u>motor</u> 4, my 2, ninety 6, novels 6, nylon 6, play 2, <u>polar</u> 5, prefer 6, <u>promote</u> 5, public 6, <u>railroad</u> 4, retire 6, she 1, showed 2, shy 5, skill 4, sky 3, suitcase 4, sweet 4, that 2, thick 2, this 2, <u>throat</u> 5, title 6, <u>total</u> 4, vehicle 6, vitamin 6, western 6, with 2, yard 2

Homonyms

blew 3, blue 2, eight 2, for 2, I 1, in 1, made 3, new 2, read 2, <u>role</u> 5, <u>roll</u> 2, see 2, some 2, their 2, there's 4, to 2, too 2, would 2

Snurks

are 2, does 2, from 2, front 3, height 6, most 3, movie 6, of 2, people 3, what 2, you 2, your 2

---

* The Mastery Test for Unit 25 also includes the new basic unit words, which are not shown on this chart. The numeral following a word indicates the level at which that word is introduced. Underscored words are those that appear in the unit Study Chart as review words.

UNIT 26   Diagnostic Chart of Test Words*

Regular Spellings

all 2, avenue 6, <u>bruise</u> 4, can't 3, celebrate 5, choose 2, <u>confuse</u> 5, <u>confusion</u> 5, crown 3, cyclone 5, <u>drew</u> 4, <u>duty</u> 4, equator 6, fifth 3, <u>fuel</u> 4, <u>glue</u> 4, he 2, his 2, <u>humor</u> 4, humorous 6, is 1, like 2, located 4, miser's 6, motion 5, motor 4, <u>museum</u> 4, <u>music</u> 3, must 2, near 2, <u>newsreel</u> 5, newsstand 6, on 2, parts 2, ports 6, quite 6, recites 5, resist 6, <u>rude</u> 4, <u>ruler's</u> 5, she 1, <u>suitable</u> 5, tells 2, this 2, tools 4, verses 6, we 1, when 2, witness 5, wrenches 6

Homonyms

for 2, heard 3, here 2, I 1, idol 6, in 1, it's 3, no 2, sailed 3, sale 3, there's 4, to 2

Snurks

are 2, have 2, many 2, of 2, stroll 6, taste 3, <u>truth</u> 3, wealth 5, were 2, world 3, you 2

---

* The Mastery Test for Unit 26 also includes the new basic unit words, which are not shown on this chart. The numeral following a word indicates the level at which that word is introduced. Underscored words are those that appear in the unit Study Chart as review words.

UNIT 27 Diagnostic Chart of Test Words*

Regular Spellings

after 2, balloon 3, bloom 5, bring 2, caught 2, chisel 5, claws 4, conclusion 6, confusion 5, consume 6, cooker 3, cooky 4, days 4, deep 4, destroyed 5, did 2, down 2, eagle 4, eat 2, foolish 5, good 2, goodness 5, his 2, homes 2, hood 5, humid 6, into 3, is 1, it 2, jewel 6, latitude 6, left 2, may 2, museum 4, my 2, on 2, poodle 5, proofread 5, recess 4, rooster 4, schoolroom 5, scoop 5, small 3, snow 2, tent 2, toolbox 4, trail 5, unhook 5, we 1, with 2, wrench 6

Homonyms

for 2, hear 2, hole 3, I 1, in 1, not 2, some 2, stake 6, steak 6, to 2, too 2, whole 2

Snurks

are 2, blood 5, could 2, great 3, of 2, put 2, was 2, were 2, work 2, you 2, your 2

> * The Mastery Test for Unit 27 also includes the new basic unit words, which are not shown on this chart. The numeral following a word indicates the level at which that word is introduced. Underscored words are those that appear in the unit Study Chart as review words.

UNIT 28 Diagnostic Chart of Test Words*

Regular Spellings

about 3, around 3, at 1, balance 4, bloom 5, boys 2, conclusion 6, cookies 4, counter 5, county 4, cruise 6, dogs 2, dismount 4, drowsy 5, exert 6, feet 2, fables 6, famous 4, flowers 3, helpful 6, hockey 6, hundred 3, is 1, lesson 3, lonely 4, needed 3, night 2, now 2, on 2, places 3, proof 6, prowl 5, raccoon 6, rulers 5, scout 5, snowplows 5, tailor 5, team 3, this 2, those 2, towel 5, tower 5, town 3, unloose 6, we 1, welfare 6

Homonyms

ate 3, be 3, eight 2, for 2, in 1, isle 6, made 3, not 2, our 2, some 2, their 2, there 2, through 3, to 2, too 2

Snurks

are 2, blood 5, flood 6, height 6, most 3, of 2, others 2, should 2, tough 3

> * The Mastery Test for Unit 28 also includes the new basic unit words, which are not shown on this chart. The numeral following a word indicates the level at which that word is introduced. Underscored words are those that appear in the unit Study Chart as review words.

UNIT 29　Diagnostic Chart of Test Words*

Regular Spellings	allow 6, astounded 6, boiler 2, bowl 4, brightness 6, but 1, came 2, can 2, choice 4 clean 2, comet 6, cooked 3, cowboys 4, dentist 6, employment 5, enjoyable 5 flowers 3, had 2, jingle 5, join 2, lace 3, make 3, mansion 5, moist 5, my 2, next 3 noisy 4, oily 4, on 2, platter 5, pocket 4, pointer 2, poison 4, power 6, rejoin 5 roundup 6, royal 5, splendor 6, that 2, this 2, towel 5, trousers 6, under 2 unemployment 5, us 1, use 2, voyage 5, we 1, western 6
Homonyms	be 3, for 2, hear 2, here 2, hours 3, I 1, I'll 3, in 1, isles 6, no 2, our 2, see 2, seems 5 so 3, some 2, to 2, two 2, week 3
Snurks	cough 6, have 2, of 2, put 2, they 2, tough 3, you 2, your 2

* The Mastery Test for Unit 29 also includes the new basic unit words, which are not shown on this chart The numeral following a word indicates the level at which that word is introduced. Underscored words are those that appear in the unit Study Chart as review words.

UNIT 30　Diagnostic Chart of Test Words*

Regular Spellings	agreeable 6, agreement 5, always 3, asked 2, astronauts 5, author 4, avoidable 6 before 3, beggar 5, between 4, birds 2, broiler 6, broke 3, clothes 6, counter 5 countries 4, daughter 4, dinosaur 5, disagreements 4, displayed 6, each 3, eagles 4 famous 4, faucet 5, flight 5, football 4, had 2, halt 4, haunt 4, hawks 6, her 2, his 2 hydrant 5, lady's 4, leaks 5, look 2, naughty 5, on 2, oyster 6, player 2, poor 5, raw 5 recall 4, rejoice 6, sausage 5, store 2, take 3, treaty 6, trousers 6, us 1
Homonyms	for 2, I 1, not 2, our 2, prey 6, to 2, two 2
Snurks	among 3, are 2, both 2, friends 2, guide 5, many 2, of 2, was 2, watch 2, weird 6, were 2

* The Mastery Test for Unit 30 also includes the new basic unit words, which are not shown on this chart. The numeral following a word indicates the level at which that word is introduced. Underscored words are those that appear in the unit Study Chart as review words.

UNIT 31   Diagnostic Chart of Test Words*

Regular Spellings

arctic 5, army 3, autograph 6, <u>barbers</u> 5, <u>barnyard</u> 5, before 3, book 2, can 2, <u>carnival</u> 5, <u>carpenters</u> 5, <u>carton</u> 5, <u>carved</u> 5, cedar 6, clever 6, display 6, drew 4, excellent 5, fables 6, famous 4, farmer 2, <u>harbor</u> 5, <u>harmful</u> 5, high 3, humorous 6, lost 2, <u>marble</u> 5, <u>marvel</u> 5, metal 3, museum 4, mushrooms 6, must 2, on 2, oyster 6, <u>party</u> 2, perched 3, precaution 6, raising 3, <u>remarked</u> 5, saucer 6, scissors 6, sculptors 6, <u>sharp</u> 3, tables 3, that 2, this 2, those 2, tie 4, wallet 6, walruses 6, wrens 4

Homonyms

be 3, cord 6, for 2, four 2, in 1, knots 3, mail 2, male 4, not 2, pieces 2, seas 3, see 2, their 2, two 2, vane 6, wood 2, would 2

Snurks

are 2, build 2, field 4, from 2, have 2, live 2, many 2, of 2, weather 4, works 2, you 2

> * The Mastery Test for Unit 31 also includes the new basic unit words, which are not shown on this chart. The numeral following a word indicates the level at which that word is introduced. Underscored words are those that appear in the unit Study Chart as review words.

UNIT 32   Diagnostic Chart of Test Words*

Regular Spellings

agreement 4, <u>armchair</u> 5, artist 6, at 1, barbers 5, <u>bareback</u> 5, barn 2, <u>beware</u> 5, came 2, cardinal 6, <u>careless</u> 4, cartoon 6, cautious 6, coin 6, customer 4, <u>dairy</u> 5, <u>dare</u> 2, day 2, good 2, <u>haircuts</u> 5, he 2, her 2, is 1, <u>library</u> 4, lonely 4, man 2, marvelous 6, ninety 6, on 2, pioneer 5, plywood 6, prefers 6, <u>preparation</u> 5, ran 2, remarked 5, <u>repair</u> 4, retire 6, ride 2, <u>scarecrow</u> 4, she 1, snarled 6, store 2, swiftly 6, that 2, that's 4, weary 6, went 2, will 2

Homonyms

aunt's 3, buy 2, by 2, cents 3, <u>fair</u> 2, <u>fare</u> 5, for 2, hear 2, here 2, I 1, I'll 3, it's 3, know 2, male 4, night 2, our 2, read 2, red 2, <u>stairs</u> 3, <u>their</u> 2, to 2

Snurks

another 3, give 2, of 2, said 2, wash 2

> * The Mastery Test for Unit 32 also includes the new basic unit words, which are not shown on this chart. The numeral following a word indicates the level at which that word is introduced. Underscored words are those that appear in the unit Study Chart as review words.

UNIT 33   Diagnostic Chart of Test Words*

Regular Spellings	addresses 3, as 2, basketball 6, careful 6, chestnut 6, contrary 6, cookies 4 declared 4, down 2, elect 5, explore 5, factory 4, foreman 5, glory 5, high 3 important 4, includes 5, insects 3, is 1, marvelous 6, much 2, normal 5, old 2, on 2 orchard 5, order 5, original 5, orphan 5, parcel 6, peach 5, pounds 4, prairie 6 president 4, scorecard 5, scores 5, silver 3, sport 5, swooped 6, teacher 4, territory 5 that 2, these 3, think 3, this 2, told 2, tree 2, use 2, voice 3, we 1, years 2
Homonyms	do 2, for 2, hoarse 5, in 1, pole 5, polled 6, scene 4, seen 4, to 2, too 2, two 2
Snurks	builders 2, business 4, cough 6, Father's 2, have 2, of 2, people 3, put 2, they 2 was 2, were 2, you 2, your 2

* The Mastery Test for Unit 33 also includes the new basic unit words, which are not shown on this chart The numeral following a word indicates the level at which that word is introduced. Underscored words are those that appear in the unit Study Chart as review words.

UNIT 34   Diagnostic Chart of Test Words*

Regular Spellings	around 3, audience 5, blurt 5, burglar 5, campers 5, careful 6, coat 2, conference 5 deserves 3, dirty 3, farmland 6, flows 5, forbid 6, giant 4, hardware 6, her 2, is 1 judge 3, king 2, laundry 6, like 2, loudly 3, loyal 6, make 3, mirror 5, motion 5 murmured 5, my 2, nervous 4, public 6, purple 3, purpose 5, raising 3, she 1, squirt 6 stern 5, terrible 4, that 2, these 3, this 2, treatment 4, trees 2, twirled 5, upstairs 6 used 2, warm 3, whirlpool 6
Homonyms	be 3, fir 5, for 2, fur 5, hear 2, here 2, I 1, in 1, read 2, so 3, through 3, to 2, too 2 vain 6, veins 6
Snurks	blood 5, child 3, could 2, dead 3, friend 2, front 3, heart 3, heavy 3, of 2, said 2 should 2, watch 2, wear 3, you 2, your 2

* The Mastery Test for Unit 34 also includes the new basic unit words, which are not shown on this chart The numeral following a word indicates the level at which that word is introduced. Underscored words are those that appear in the unit Study Chart as review words.

UNIT 35   Diagnostic Chart of Test Words*

Regular Spellings

across 4, boss 5, certain 4, <u>companion</u> 5, <u>confident</u> 5, corridor 6, curtain 6, demanded 4, deportment 6, <u>descendant</u> 5, <u>disgraceful</u> 5, dog 2, down 2, <u>enjoyable</u> 5, <u>expression</u> 5, favorite 4, flowers 3, gave 2, go 2, has 1, hurdle 6, included 5, <u>invisible</u> 5, is 1, library 4, men 2, my 2, nerve 6, owner 6, photo 6, <u>prediction</u> 5, project 6, <u>protection</u> 5, <u>replacement</u> 4, slowly 2, this 2, those 2, trip 3, <u>when</u> 2

Homonyms

aisle 6, be 3, doing 2, for 2, I 1, I'll 3, its 4, it's 3, scent 5, sent 3, to 2, two 2

Snurks

are 2, friend 2, having 2, love 3, moved 2, of 2, who 2, you 2

    * The Mastery Test for Unit 35 also includes the new basic unit words, which are not shown on this chart. The numeral following a word indicates the level at which that word is introduced. Underscored words are those that appear in the unit Study Chart as review words.

UNIT 36   Diagnostic Chart of Test Words*

Regular Spellings

about 3, address 3, all 2, <u>alligators</u> 5, <u>arithmetic</u> 5, as 2, at 1, boasted 6, buckles 6, continent 6, convenient 6, conversation 6, days 2, degrees 4, <u>evaporate</u> 5, finish 3, fuzzy 6, <u>geography</u> 5, getting 2, has 1, <u>independence</u> 5, is 1, known 6, lake 4, large 3, leaves 3, <u>manufacture</u> 5, marvelous 6, men 2, near 2, <u>necessary</u> 5, on 2, <u>ordinary</u> 5, parcel 6, <u>particular</u> 5, pets 2, previous 6, project 6, responsible 6, scholar 6, school 2, spent 3, that 2, <u>thermometer</u> 5, this 2, up 1, us 1, vegetables 4, we 1, went 2, wore 2

Homonyms

ate 3, bough 6, eight 2, for 2, in 1, inn 4, it's 3, nights 2, not 2, our 2, right 2, their 2, there 2, to 2, too 2, two 2

Snurks

are 2, enough 4, having 2, many 2, put 2, shoe 2, soup 3, they 2, who 2, young 2

    * The Mastery Test for Unit 36 also includes the new basic unit words, which are not shown on this chart. The numeral following a word indicates the level at which that word is introduced. Underscored words are those that appear in the unit Study Chart as review words.

SPELLING ALPHABET

The letters of the alphabet are written symbols which we use to spell words. There are twenty-six letters in our alphabet. Each letter of the alphabet has a capital and a lower-case form.

a b c d e f g h i

j k l m n o p q r

s t u v w x y z

A B C D E F G H I

J K L M N O P Q R

S T U V W X Y Z

SOUND-SPELLING ALPHABET

We show the pronunciation of a word by using special symbols inside slant marks. There are forty-four sound-spelling symbols, one for each of the dictionary sounds. A sound-spelling symbol always stands for the same sound, no matter how the sound is spelled in a word.

Consonant Symbols

/b/ big	/n/ noon	/ch/ <u>ch</u>ur<u>ch</u>
/d/ did	/p/ pop	/hw/ <u>wh</u>en
/f/ fife	/r/ rare	/ng/ si<u>ng</u>
/g/ gag	/s/ sense	/sh/ <u>sh</u>ip
/h/ hot	/t/ tot	/ᵺ/ <u>th</u>is
/j/ judge	/v/ valve	/th/ <u>th</u>in
/k/ kick	/w/ wet	/zh/ vi<u>s</u>ion
/l/ lull	/y/ yes	
/m/ mum	/z/ zoo	

Vowel Symbols

/a/ ran	/o/ not	/ə/ <u>a</u>bout
/ā/ rain	/ō/ no	tak<u>e</u>n
/ã/ care	/ô/ off	penc<u>i</u>l
/ä/ car		lem<u>o</u>n
	/u/ us	circ<u>u</u>s
/e/ hen	/ū/ use	
/ē/ he	/ü/ tool	
/ėr/ her	/ù/ took	
/i/ in	/ou/ cow	
/ī/ ice	/oi/ boy	

Answers

1a patch, badge, damp,
   snatch, trash, brand
 b chest, strength, pledge,
   smell, flesh, dent
 c whiz, pink, film, thrill,
   swift, whisk
 d lock, loss, broth, dodge,
   tongs, bomb
 e shrug, thumb, stuck,
   punch, junk, numb

Study Chart

Vowel Sounds	Review Words	Sound-Spellings	Spelling Cues
/a/	patch badge	/pach/ /baj/	How do we usually spell /a/?
/e/	chest strength	/chest/ /strength/	How do we usually spell /e/?
/i/	whiz pink	/hwiz/ /pingk/	How do we usually spell /i/?
/o/, /ô/	lock loss	/lok/ /lôs/	How do we spell /o/ or /ô/ with one letter?
/u/	shrug thumb	/shrug/ /thum/	How do we usually spell /u/?

New Words

damp	stuck	thrill	flesh	brand
pledge	smell	punch	swift	bomb
film	snatch	junk	trash	whisk
broth	dodge	tongs	dent	numb

1 Write six words from the new and review lists for each of
the following. Write the words in which
 a *a* spells /a/ **d** *o* spells /o/ or /ô/
 b *e* spells /e/ **e** *u* spells /u/
 c *i* spells /i/

2

Teaching Suggestions

In this series pupils are repeatedly made aware
of the four basic categories of sound-symbol relationships: (1) short-vowel syllables; (2) long-
vowel syllables; (3) digraphic-vowel syllables;
and (4) vowel-*r* syllables. Pupils are also alerted
to the idiosyncrasies of consonant spellings
that appear in conjunction with the four vowel-
spelling groups. Unit 1 of this text summarizes
the spelling pattern of using the letters *a, e, i, o,*
and *u* to represent the short vowel sounds in the
medial position of syllables and monosyllabic
words.

Use the Study Chart to introduce the uni
Elicit from the pupils the appropriate response
to the questions in the Spelling Cues colum
Have the pupils apply the generalizations t
the new words.

● These exercises are a written reinforce
ment of the generalizations developed throug
the use of the Study Chart. Exercise 1 cause
pupils to write the words according to the
vowel sounds. Exercises 2 and 3 call attentio
to consonant characteristics of the words.

Handwriting Models

damp	*stuck*	*thrill*	*flesh*	*brand*
pledge	*smell*	*punch*	*swift*	*bomb*
film	*snatch*	*junk*	*trash*	*whisk*
broth	*dodge*	*tongs*	*dent*	*numb*

2 Write the new and review words in which

a *tch* spells /ch/   **e** *mb* spells /m/
b *ch* spells /ch/   **f** *ng* spells /ng/
c *sh* spells /sh/   **g** *n* spells /ng/
d *th* spells /th/   **h** *dge* spells /j/

3 Write the new and review words in which

a /j/ is spelled *j*   **d** one consonant sound
b /hw/ is spelled *wh*   is spelled by the
c /k/ is spelled *ck*   same two letters

1 Write the new and review words for these sound-spellings.

a /plej/   **e** /stuk/   **i** /smel/
b /snach/   **f** /doj/   **j** /thril/
c /jungk/   **g** /bom/   **k** /hwisk/
d /num/   **h** /thum/   **l** /baj/

2 A *synonym* is a word that means the same or nearly the same as another word. Write synonyms from the list of new words for *clamps, soup, wet,* and *hit.*

3 Write the *ing* forms of /brand/, /snach/, /film/, and /smel/.

4 Write the *ing* forms of /doj/ and /plej/.

5 Write in alphabetical order the new and review words that begin with the letter *b.* Remember to use the third letter in alphabetizing if the second letter is the same in two different words.

3

2a patch, snatch
 b chest, punch
 c shrug, flesh, trash
 d strength, thumb, broth, thrill
 e thumb, bomb, numb
 f strength, tongs
 g pink, junk
 h badge, pledge, dodge
3a junk
 b whiz, whisk
 c lock, stuck
 d loss, smell, thrill

●● **Answers**

1a pledge   **g** bomb
 b snatch   **h** thumb
 c junk   **i** smell
 d numb   **j** thrill
 e stuck   **k** whisk
 f dodge   **l** badge
2 tongs, broth, damp, punch
3 branding, snatching, filming, smelling
4 dodging, pledging
5 badge, bomb, brand, broth

●● The exercises in this section cause the pupils to write the new and review words again without invoking the generalizations.

● The Read and Spell list consists of thirty words that illustrate the same sound-symbol relationships as those of the words in the Study Chart. The first use of these words should be a diagnostic decoding test for as many individual pupils as possible. See page T-8 for suggestions. Exercises 2 through 5 focus on the spelling of the words.

●● This section begins with a proofreading exercise. Have the pupils find the errors before writing the story. The correct exercise, with corrected errors underscored, is as follows:

The word junk *was once used to mean "old, useless* bits *of rope." The word came to be used for other useless things like rags, trash, and old paper.*

Junk is the name of a kind of boat, too. A junk is a Chinese boat with a flat bottom and sails to which strips of wood have been nailed.

The second exercise in this section is de-

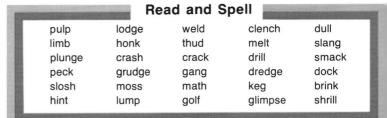

Read and Spell

pulp	lodge	weld	clench	dull
limb	honk	thud	melt	slang
plunge	crash	crack	drill	smack
peck	grudge	gang	dredge	dock
slosh	moss	math	keg	brink
hint	lump	golf	glimpse	shrill

1 We write letters to spell sounds. We can also sound ou
words when we see the letters. We say the sounds softly to
gether without stopping between sounds.

Write any Read and Spell word that you cannot read o
any word for which you do not know the meaning.

2 Write the Read and Spell words for these sound-spellings
a /gruj/ **d** /drej/ **g** /plunj/
b /loj/ **e** /krak/ **h** /shril/
c /môs/ **f** /glimps/ **i** /bringk/

3 Write the Read and Spell words in which *ck* spells /k/.

4 *Antonyms* are words that have opposite or nearly opposit
meanings. Write antonyms from the Read and Spell list fo
freeze, sharp, and *break*.

5 Write the Read and Spell words for these pictures.

1 Dan's class wrote stories about interesting words. Proo
read what Dan wrote about the word *junk* at the top of th
next page. You should find three spelling mistakes and thre
mistakes in capitalization and punctuation. After you hav
found the mistakes, write the word story correctly.

4

voted to dictionary instruction and practice.
Encourage the pupils to perform the exercise
conscientiously.

Each unit in this text concludes with a
story and exercise about one or more words ex-
tracted from another language. This feature is
designed to stimulate pupils' interest in words
and in the sources of English words.

The two parts of the unit test follow. See
pages T-9–T-11 for a description of the testing
program and directions for using the test.

The word junk was once used to mean "old, useless bites of rope." The word came to be used for other useless things like rags, trash, and old paper.

Junk is the name of a kind of boat, to. A junk is a chinese boat with a flat bottom and sails too which strips of wood have been nailed.

2 A *lexicographer* /lek′ sə kog′ rə fər/ is a dictionary maker. A lexicographer usually does the things shown below.

Write the entry word.	Show the sound-spelling.	Use an abbreviation for the part of speech.

• **badge** /baj/ *n.* Something that persons wear to show that they belong to a certain club, team, or occupation: *Police officers wear badges.*

Define the entry word.
Use the word in a sentence.

Do the lexicographer's five jobs for the entry word *broth.* Use your own words to write a definition and a sample sentence. When you have finished, compare your work with the entry in the Spelling Dictionary.

A Word from the Greeks

We have over 600,000 words in our language. One reason we have so many words is because we have taken thousands of words from other languages.

The word part *tele* comes from a Greek word that means "far." The word part *phone* comes from a Greek word that means "sound." We put the two word parts together to make the word *telephone*, an instrument that brings "sound from far away."

Write the definition of the word *telegraph*. Write your definition so it shows the Greek meaning of the two word parts. You may use the Spelling Dictionary for help.

5

/tôngz/. It's best to lift hot *brands* with long *tongs.*

14 The two lids with /dents/ are just /jungk/. The two lids with *dents* are just *junk.*

Mastery Test 1b

1 /lok/ *lock*
2 /thril/ *thrill*
3 /lôs/ *loss*
4 /bom/ *bomb*
5 /shrug/ *shrug*
6 /stuk/ *stuck*
7 /damp/ *damp*
8 /bôs/ *boss*
9 /skrub/ *scrub*
10 /hej/ *hedge*

11 I want some of that hot /brôth/ that I

/smel/. I want some of that hot *broth* that I *smell.*

12 The /thum/ on Betty's left hand is /num/. The *thumb* on Betty's left hand is *numb.*

13 "/doj/ this /punch/ if you can!" yelled Tom. "*Dodge* this *punch* if you can!" yelled Tom.

14 Most of the plums in this dish have soft /pingk/ /flesh/. Most of the plums in this dish have soft *pink flesh.*

2 Long-Vowel **Words**

Study Chart

We can spell each long vowel sound several different ways.

Vowel Sounds	Review Words	Sound-Spellings	Spelling Cues
/ā/	faint bathe bay	/fānt/ /bāᴛʜ/ /bā/	Which three options do we use to spell /ā/?
/ē/	cheese squeal	/chēz/ /skwēl/	Which two options do we use to spell /ē/?
/ī/	slice sly	/slīs/ /slī/	Which two options do we use to spell /ī/?
/ō/	goal phone row	/gōl/ /fōn/ /rō/	Which three options do we use to spell /ō/?
/ū/, /ü/	huge knew	/hūj/ /nü/	Which two options do we use to spell /ū/ or /ü/?

New Words

grace	roast	chime	phrase	bray
steep	plume	grease	clothe	known
quite	pose	quail	dune	cure
	hew	feast	spry	

6

Teaching Suggestions

Unit 2 summarizes the common long-vowel spelling patterns of *ai, a*-consonant-*e,* and *ay* for /ā/; *ee* and *ea* for /ē/; *i*-consonant-*e* and *y* for /ī/; *oa, o*-consonant-*e,* and *ow* for /ō/; and *u*-consonant-*e* and *ew* for /ū/ or /ü/. Several long-vowel spelling patterns are not included here because they do not appear frequently in vocabulary lists for this level. Thus, final /ē/ spelled *e (me)*, final /ō/ spelled *o (so)*, final /ī/ spelled *ie (pie)*, and /ū/ or /ü/ spelled *ue (blue)* are not included in this level of study.

Use the Study Chart to present the long-vowel generalizations. This can best be don through a discussion of the questions in th Spelling Cues column. Have the pupils appl the generalizations to the new words. You ma also use the Study Chart to preview the conso nant-spelling generalizations that pupils wi encounter in this unit.

● Supervise the writing of the new and re view words in this section.

●● Exercise 1 of this section requires the pu

Handwriting Models

grace	roast	chime	phrase	bray
steep	plume	grease	clothe	known
quite	pose	quail	dune	cure
	hew	feast	spry	

1 Write the new and review words in which

a /ā/ is spelled *ai*

b /ā/ is spelled *a*-consonant-*e*

c /ā/ is spelled *ay*

d /ē/ is spelled *ee*

e /ē/ is spelled *ea*

f /ī/ is spelled *i*-consonant-*e*

g /ī/ is spelled *y*

h /ō/ is spelled *oa*

i /ō/ is spelled *o*-consonant-*e*

j /ō/ is spelled *ow*

k /ū/ or /ü/ is spelled *u*-consonant-*e*

l /ū/ or /ü/ is spelled *ew*

2 Write the new and review words in which

a /ŦH/ is spelled *th*

b /z/ is spelled *s*

c /kw/ is spelled *qu*

d /f/ is spelled *ph*

e /s/ is spelled *c*

f /k/ is spelled *c*

g /j/ is spelled *g*

h /n/ is spelled *kn*

1 Write the new words for these sound-spellings.

a /nōn/

b /fēst/

c /plüm/

d /kūr/

e /frāz/

f /pōz/

g /sprī/

h /grēs/

i /kwīt/

j /brā/

k /kwāl/

l /rōst/

m /klōŦH/

n /hū/

o /grās/

p /dün/

q /chīm/

r /stēp/

2 Write the *ing* forms of *pose, clothe, bathe, cure, grease,* and *slice.*

3 Write synonyms from the new and review lists for *feather, heal, chop, wash, dress,* and *sneaky.*

7

● **Answers**

1a faint, quail

b bathe, grace, phrase

c bay, bray

d cheese, steep

e squeal, grease, feast

f slice, quite, chime

g sly, spry

h goal, roast

i phone, pose, clothe

j row, known

k huge, plume, dune, cure

l knew, hew

2a bathe, clothe

b cheese, pose, phrase

c squeal, quite, quail

d phone, phrase

e slice, grace

f clothe, cure

g huge

h knew, known

●● **Answers**

1a known

b feast

c plume

d cure

e phrase

f pose

g spry

h grease

i quite

j bray

k quail

l roast

m clothe

n hew

o grace

p dune

q chime

r steep

2 posing, clothing, bathing, curing, greasing, slicing

3 plume, cure, slice, bathe, clothe, sly

●ils to read sound-spellings. Some pupils may ●eed help doing this in these early units.

●●
The Read and Spell words reiterate the ●ng-vowel spelling patterns. Any pupil who ●ails to sound out these words may have de-●oding problems with other textbooks and ●ay need help in mastering sound-blending ●echniques.

It is important for pupils to identify those ●ords whose meanings are not known and to ●ave the meaning of those words clarified.

●●
●● The pupils' work in Exercise 1 should be carefully checked. The correct exercise, with corrected errors underscored, is as follows:

Quails are shy birds that do not like to fly. They make nests on the ground and run in the fields to find a <u>feast</u> of seeds<u>,</u> weeds<u>,</u> and bugs.

Quails can hide <u>quite</u> well just by standing still. Their black, tan, and white feathers look like the grass and twigs around them.

Quails are <u>known</u> as bobwhites in <u>A</u>merica. Their song <u>seems</u> to say, "Bob White."

2a screech   **d** cube
 b crease   **e** prune
 c spray   **f** oath
3 /plēd/, /rōp/, /kwōt/,
   /stü/, /strān/, /dēl/
4a faith, strain
 b spray, fray
 c beef, seek, screech
 d plead, crease, deal
 e spy
 f toad, oath
5a crane
 b spruce
 c dome

Read and Spell

faith	rope	seek	cube	brew
slime	quake	dome	spruce	crease
spray	spy	blow	oath	screech
plead	prune	toad	fray	deal
quote	rice	spine	crane	strain
beef	duke	stew	vine	tribe

1 Write any Read and Spell word that you cannot read or any word for which you do not know the meaning.

2 Write the Read and Spell words for these sound-spellings.
a /skrēch/   **c** /sprā/   **e** /prün/
b /krēs/   **d** /kūb/   **f** /ōth/

3 Write the sound-spellings for the Read and Spell words *plead, rope, quote, stew, strain,* and *deal.*

4 Write the Read and Spell words in which
a /ā/ is spelled *ai*   **d** /ē/ is spelled *ea*
b /ā/ is spelled *ay*   **e** /ī/ is spelled *y*
c /ē/ is spelled *ee*   **f** /ō/ is spelled *oa*

5 Write the Read and Spell words for these pictures.

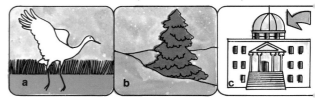

1 Jean wrote a report about quails for her science class. Proofread her work at the top of the next page. You should find three spelling mistakes and three mistakes in capitalization and punctuation. After you have proofread Jean's work, write the report correctly.

8

If Exercise 2 in this section of each unit is taken seriously, checked carefully, and discussed, pupils will be provided with a thorough study of dictionary conventions.

Regarding the word *bouquet,* you may want to point out that the *ou* spelling of /ü/ or /ō/ is typical of French words. The exercise after the word story is intended to oblige pupils to use the Spelling Dictionary.

The two parts of the unit test follow. See pages T-9–T-11 for a description of the testing program and directions for using the test.

1 /frāz/ *phrase*   **6** /rō/ *row*
2 /gōl/ *goal*   **7** /brā/ *bray*
3 /grās/ *grace*   **8** /damp/ *damp*
4 /fōn/ *phone*   **9** /smel/ *smell*
5 /kwāl/ *quail*   **10** /num/ *numb*
11 I had a /slīs/ of /chēz/ and two cups of /brôth/ for lunch.   I had a *slice* of *cheese* and two cups of *broth* for lunch.
12 "Those girls want to /fēst/ on /rōst/ beef," said Dad.   "Those girls want to *feast* on *roast* beef," said Dad.
13 A young child should not /skwēl/ when

> *Quails are shy birds that do not like to fly. They make nests on the ground and run in the fields to find a feast of seeds weeds and bugs.*
>
> *Quails can hide quit well just by standing still. Their black, tan, and white feathers look like the grass and twigs around them.*
>
> *Quails are known as bobwhites in america. Their song seams to say, "Bob White."*

 2 A lexicographer does these things for many entry words.

Write more than one definition, and number the definitions.	Write more than one sample sentence if the word has more than one definition.

- **bathe** /bāᴛʜ/ *v.* **1.** Take a bath: *I bathe every morning.* **2.** Give a bath to: *They have to bathe the dog.* **bathed, bathing.**

  Show the *ed* and *ing* forms of verbs that drop final *e*.

Write a complete entry for the word *clothe*. Use your own words to write at least two definitions and two sample sentences. When you have finished, compare your work with the entry in the Spelling Dictionary.

A Word from the French

The word *bouquet,* which we pronounce /bü kā′/ or /bō kā′/, means "a bunch of flowers." It comes from the French word for forest. Many French words have the *quet* spelling of /kā/.

There are two ways to pronounce *bouquet.* Find *plume, dune, hew,* and *quail* in the Spelling Dictionary. Write the word for which there are two pronunciations. After the word, write the sound-spelling for the pronunciation you use.

9

---

1 (See Teaching Suggestions.)
2 (See the entry for *clothe* in the Spelling Dictionary as a model answer.)

A Word from the French
dune /dūn/ or /dün/

Mastery Test

For complete directions and an explanation of the testing program, see the Introduction to this Teacher's Edition.

---

ou /bāᴛʜ/ him.   A young child should not *squeal* when you *bathe* him.
14 I bought a new hat with /hūj/ /pingk/ plümz/.   I bought a new hat with *huge pink plumes.*

Mastery Test 2b

1 /grēs/ *grease*	**6** /hū/ *hew*
2 /sprī/ *spry*	**7** /hwisk/ *whisk*
3 /pōz/ *pose*	**8** /doj/ *dodge*
4 /klōᴛʜ/ *clothe*	**9** /tôngz/ *tongs*
5 /kūr/ *cure*	**10** /pach/ *patch*

11 The fox is /nōn/ to be /kwīt/ /slī/ and /swift/.   The fox is *known* to be *quite sly* and *swift.*
12 The road to the /bā/ runs through /stēp/ sand /dūnz/.   The road to the *bay* runs through *steep* sand *dunes.*
13 He /nü/ that a /chest/ should have a strong /lok/.   He *knew* that a *chest* should have a strong *lock.*
14 I think the /chīm/ on my old clock is too /fānt/.   I think the *chime* on my old clock is too *faint.*

10

● **Answers**

1a smooth, loop, booth, stoop, groove, troop

b poor, crook, soot, nook

c noun, sprout, ounce, bough, drought

d scowl, browse

e moist, broil, foil, toil

f joy

g caught, clause

h claw, hawk, sprawl, drawl

i salt, squall

3 Two-Letter Vowels

Study Chart

We spell some vowel sounds with two letters.

Vowel Sounds	Review Words	Sound-Spellings	Spelling Cues
/ü/	smooth	/smüᴛʜ/	How do we spell /ü/ in this word?
/u̇/	poor crook	/pu̇r/ /kru̇k/	How do we spell /u̇/ in these words?
/ou/	noun scowl	/noun/ /skoul/	Which two options do we use to spell /ou/?
/oi/	moist joy	/moist/ /joi/	Which two options do we use to spell /oi/?
/ô/	caught claw salt	/kôt/ /klô/ /sôlt/	Which three options do we use to spell /ô/?

New Words

loop	soot	booth	sprawl	drought
sprout	ounce	stoop	groove	troop
broil	foil	bough	drawl	squall
clause	hawk	toil	nook	browse

1 Write the new and review words in which

a *oo* spells /ü/

b *oo* spells /u̇/

c *ou* spells /ou/

d *ow* spells /ou/

e *oi* spells /oi/

f *oy* spells /oi/

g *au* spells /ô/

h *aw* spells /ô/

i *a(l)* spells /ô/

10

Teaching Suggestions

This unit centers attention on the third large group of syllable spellings, the digraphic vowels. As in the first two units, the spelling of these monosyllabic words will not cause serious problems. The most important function of these first four units is to help pupils to understand that our syllable spellings fall into four basic categories and that within a category each vowel sound has several spelling options.

Use the Study Chart to review the digraphic-vowel generalizations. These generalizations may be applied to the list of new words.

We commonly use the *oo* spelling to represen /ü/ and /u̇/. We always spell /ou/ with *ou* c *ow* (although *ou* is often used to spell othe vowel sounds and *ow* is also used to spell /ō/ /oi/ is regularly spelled *oi* or *oy*. /ô/ is usual spelled *au, aw,* or *a(l)*.

● Exercise 1 causes pupils to write the ne and review words according to their vowe sounds.

●● The first exercise in this section provide

10

Handwriting Models

loop   soot   booth   sprawl   drought
sprout   ounce   stoop   groove   troop
broil   foil   bough   drawl   squall
clause   hawk   toil   nook   browse

2 Write the new and review words in which

a *s* spells /z/
b *qu* spells /kw/
c *th* spells /ᵀH/
d *th* spells /th/

1 Write the new words for these sound-spellings.

a /skwôl/   **f** /trüp/   **k** /drôl/
b /sprôl/   **g** /stüp/   **l** /büth/
c /hôk/   **h** /foil/   **m** /ouns/
d /sút/   **i** /klôz/   **n** /broil/
e /sprout/   **j** /lüp/   **o** /nük/

2 Write synonyms from the new list for *work, furrow, corner,* and *dryness.*

3 Write antonyms from the review list for *rough, dry, rich, gloom, smile,* and *released.*

4 *Homonyms* are words that sound alike but have different meanings and different spellings. Write the pair of homonyms from the new and review lists. (You will have to add *s* to one word in order to do this.)

5 Write the *ing* form of a new or review word to show what each person below is doing.

11

2a clause, browse
b squall
c smooth
d booth

●● **Answers**

1a squall   **i** clause
b sprawl   **j** loop
c hawk   **k** drawl
d soot   **l** booth
e sprout   **m** ounce
f troop   **n** broil
g stoop   **o** nook
h foil
2 toil, groove, nook, drought
3 smooth, moist, poor, joy, scowl, caught
4 claws, clause
5a stooping
b broiling
c salting

---

n opportunity for pupils to interpret sound-pellings and to translate them into standard pellings. Exercises 2, 3, and 4 deal with syn-nyms, antonyms, and homonyms. The last xercise causes pupils to write *ing* forms.

● Again, the Read and Spell list should be sed first to identify specific disabilities in de-oding. Pupils who have trouble sounding out hese monosyllabic words should have imme-iate help. Some pupils may also need help vith the word meanings.

Exercises 2 through 5 focus on the spelling and meaning of the words.

●●
●● The correct proofreading exercise, with corrected errors underscored, is as follows:

Do you know why the abbreviation for ounce is oz? Some people say that the abbreviation was once just an o. Printers put a crooked little mark at the end of many shortened nouns. The looping mark looked like the letter z. It made the abbreviation seem to be oz.

The dictionary work in Exercise 2 may be

Answers

2a mood   **g** flaw
 b vow   **h** spoon
 c cause   **i** snout
 d scoot   **j** toy
 e hood   **k** bald
 f coil   **l** staunch
3 /lüm/, /stüd/, /nôt/
4a trout   **f** flaw
 b vow   **g** ooze
 c prow   **h** waltz
 d pounce   **i** naught
 e bald
5   brook, vow, slouch, soil

Read and Spell

loom	roost	prow	cause	brook
stood	spoon	hood	toy	staunch
mood	scoot	bald	ooze	slouch
waltz	naught	wool	boil	fool
soil	point	coil	spoil	pounce
trout	vow	snout	flaw	stool

1 Write any Read and Spell word that you cannot read or any word for which you do not know the meaning.

2 Write the Read and Spell words for these sound-spellings.

a /müd/   **e** /hůd/   **i** /snout/
b /vou/   **f** /koil/   **j** /toi/
c /kôz/   **g** /flô/   **k** /bôld/
d /sküt/   **h** /spün/   **l** /stônch/

3 Write the sound-spellings for the Read and Spell words *loom*, *stood*, and *naught*.

4 Write the Read and Spell words that mean

a a fish   **d** to jump and grab   **g** to leak out
b to promise   **e** without hair   **h** a dance
c a ship's bow   **f** a fault   **i** nothing

5 Write synonyms from the Read and Spell list for *stream*, *oath*, *slump*, and *dirt*.

1 The pupils in Paula's class wrote short reports on abbreviations that they found in their math books. Paula wrote her report about the abbreviation for *ounce*. Proofread her work at the top of the next page. You should find two mistakes in spelling and three mistakes in capitalization and punctuation. After you have found the mistakes that Paula made, write the report correctly.

12

---

supplemented by having pupils check all the new and review words to see which ones may be used as both a noun and a verb.

In addition to *raccoon*, there are many other American Indian words in our language. Some of them are *caribou, chipmunk, skunk, squash, persimmon, hominy, moose,* and *muskrat.*

The unit test that follows, like all the others, includes snurks (unexpected spellings) and homonyms. These tests thus provide a review of many frequently misspelled words.

Mastery Test 3a

1 /skwôl/ *squall*   **6** /chīm/ *chime*
2 /noun/ *noun*   **7** /trüp/ *troop*
3 /nůk/ *nook*   **8** /grās/ *grace*
4 /skoul/ *scowl*   **9** /sprôl/ *sprawl*
5 /drôl/ *drawl*   **10** /broil/ *broil*

11 I /nü/ those seeds would not /sprout/ in this /drout/. I *knew* those seeds would not *sprout* in this *drought.*

12 /hwisk/ the /sůt/ from the /chest/ with a /moist/ cloth. *Whisk* the *soot* from the *chest* with a *moist* cloth.

13 She gave a /skwēl/ of /joi/ when the /fōn/ rang. She gave a *squeal* of *joy* when the

Do you know why the abbreviation for ounce is oz. Some people say that the abbreviation was once just an o. Printers put a crooked little mark at the end of many shortened nouns. The looping mark looked like the letter z; it made the abbreviation seem to be oz.

2 A lexicographer often shows that an entry word may be used as more than one part of speech.

Write one or more noun definitions after the abbreviation *n.*, meaning *noun*.	Write one or more verb definitions after the abbreviation *v.*, meaning *verb*.

- **sprout** /sprout/ *n.* A shoot of a plant: *The farmer is setting out sprouts.* —*v.* **1.** Begin to grow. **2.** Cause to grow: *The sunlight sprouted our lettuce seeds.*

Write a complete entry for the word *troop*. Do all of the dictionary jobs that a lexicographer would. Use your own words to write noun and verb definitions and sample sentences. When you have finished, compare your work with the entry in the Spelling Dictionary.

A Word from the Indians of Virginia

When white people first came to this continent, they saw plants and animals they had never seen before. Having no names of their own for the new plants and animals, the white people used the Indian names and spelled them as they sounded.

One of these animals was a small gray creature with a bushy, ringed tail. The Virginia Indians' word for the animal became the English word *raccoon.*

Write the two spellings that are shown in the Spelling Dictionary for the word *raccoon.*

13

●● **Answers**
1 (See Teaching Suggestions.)
2 (See the entry for *troop* in the Spelling Dictionary as a model answer.)

A Word from the Indians of Virginia
raccoon, racoon

Mastery Test
For complete directions and an explanation of the testing program, see the Introduction to this Teacher's Edition.

phone rang.
14 The /brôth/ needs an /ouns/ or two of /sôlt/. The *broth* needs an *ounce* or two of *salt.*
15 I have a new /pingk/ /plüm/ on my hat. I have a new *pink plume* on my hat.

Mastery Test 3b

1 /toil/ *toil*	**6** /nōn/ *known*
2 /lüp/ *loop*	**7** /büth/ *booth*
3 /smüᴛн/ *smooth*	**8** /klôz/ *clause*
4 /thril/ *thrill*	**9** /stēp/ *steep*
5 /grüv/ *groove*	**10** /krùk/ *crook*

11 You must /stüp/ a bit when you /brouz/ in this small shed. You must *stoop* a bit when you *browse* in this small shed.
12 Who has the /strength/ to /hū/ down this /hūj/ /bou/? Who has the *strength* to *hew* down this *huge bough?*
13 Put /foil/ in your pan when you bake a /rōst/. Put *foil* in your pan when you bake a *roast.*
14 A /hôk/ /kôt/ a /pùr/ /kwāl/ in its /klôz/. A *hawk caught* a *poor quail* in its *claws.*
15 This plate with a /dent/ is just /jungk/. This plate with a *dent* is just *junk.*

4 Vowel-r Words

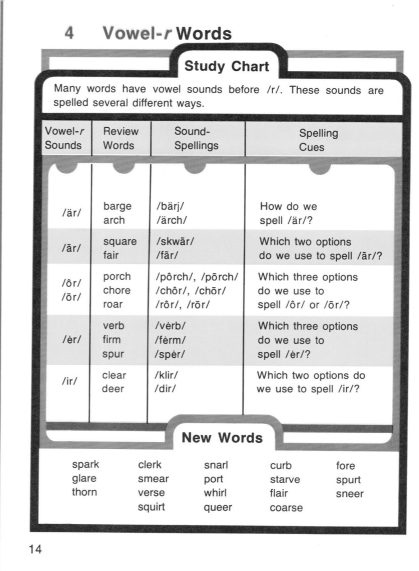

Study Chart

Many words have vowel sounds before /r/. These sounds are spelled several different ways.

Vowel-r Sounds	Review Words	Sound-Spellings	Spelling Cues
/är/	barge arch	/bärj/ /ärch/	How do we spell /är/?
/ãr/	square fair	/skwãr/ /fãr/	Which two options do we use to spell /ãr/?
/ôr/ /ōr/	porch chore roar	/pôrch/, /pōrch/ /chôr/, /chōr/ /rôr/, /rōr/	Which three options do we use to spell /ôr/ or /ōr/?
/ėr/	verb firm spur	/vėrb/ /fėrm/ /spėr/	Which three options do we use to spell /ėr/?
/ir/	clear deer	/klir/ /dir/	Which two options do we use to spell /ir/?

New Words

spark	clerk	snarl	curb	fore
glare	smear	port	starve	spurt
thorn	verse	whirl	flair	sneer
	squirt	queer	coarse	

14

Teaching Suggestions

This unit summarizes the common spelling options of the fourth basic category of sound-symbol relationships, the vowel-r syllables. As the Study Chart indicates, there are five groups of sounds in this category. We commonly spell /är/ with *ar*. /ãr/ is usually spelled *are* or *air*. Because /ôr/ is pronounced /ōr/ in some regions, we show the two as alternate pronunciations. The sounds are regularly spelled *or, ore,* or *oar*. The standard spellings of /ėr/ are *er, ir,* or *ur*. /ir/ is usually spelled *ear* or *eer*.

Use the Study Chart as usual to introduce the unit. Discuss the questions in the Spelling Cues column and apply the spelling generalizations to the list of new words.

● Exercise 1 causes the pupils to write the new and review words according to their vowel-r spelling patterns. Exercise 2 calls attention to some consonant characteristics.

●● Three homonyms in Exercise 1 are not in the vocabulary lists of this unit. Those words, however, have been taught in earlier levels.

Handwriting Models

spark clerk snarl curb fore
glare smear port starve spurt
thorn verse whirl flair sneer
squirt queer coarse

1 Write the new and review words in which

a /är/ is spelled *ar*
b /ãr/ is spelled *are*
c /ãr/ is spelled *air*
d /ôr/ or /ōr/ is spelled *or*
e /ôr/ or /ōr/ is spelled *ore*
f /ôr/ or /ōr/ is spelled *oar*
g /èr/ is spelled *er*
h /èr/ is spelled *ir*
i /èr/ is spelled *ur*
j /ir/ is spelled *ear*
k /ir/ is spelled *eer*

2 Write the three new and review words in which /kw/ is spelled *qu* and the new word in which /th/ is spelled *th.*

1 Homonyms are words that sound alike but have different meanings and different spellings. Write the correct homonym for each of these sentences. (Some words you will write are not in the new and review lists.)

a The sun is shining, and the day is ____ /fãr/.
b Did you pay your ____ /fãr/ on the bus?
c The hunter shot a ____ /dir/.
d She is a ____ /dir/ friend.
e The captain stood in the ____ /fôr/ part of the ship.
f We saw ____ /fôr/ ships sail by.

2 Write the *ing* forms of the words /skwãr/, /glãr/, and /stärv/.

3 Write the word for each of these sound-spellings.

a /kwir/
b /glãr/
c /kèrb/
d /vèrs/
e /snärl/
f /hwèrl/
g /thôrn/
h /skwèrt/
i /snir/

15

●● The Read and Spell list should first be used to identify pupils who have trouble decoding vowel-*r* words. Exercises 2 through 4 are devoted to spellings and meanings.

●● You may want to review the dual use of the apostrophe before pupils do the proofreading exercise. The correct exercise, with corrected errors underscored, is as follows:

Snarl *means to growl in a gruff and harsh way. A snarling dog bares its teeth. A snarling person <u>scowls</u> and frowns when speaking. Have you ever heard of a snarling letter? That's what people once called the letter* r. *They said that* r *had the sharp sound of a dog's snarl.*

The dictionary exercise will be most profitable if pupils do all of their work before consulting the Spelling Dictionary.

To supplement the Japanese word story, pupils may learn about such words as *geisha, hara-kiri, sake, sukiyaki,* and *tycoon.*

Answers

2 warmth, merge, snare, peer

3 quartz, curve, tear, stair

4a share, fare

 b board, ford

Read and Spell

starch	merge	ford	snore	beer
curve	stair	fare	lurk	dirt
snare	quartz	core	swore	wharf
peer	lair	hoarse	warmth	fear
dwarf	share	jeer	term	tear
hair	spear	board	skirt	earn

1 Write any Read and Spell word that you cannot read or any word for which you do not know the meaning.

2 Write Read and Spell synonyms for *heat, join, trap,* and *stare.*

3 Write the Read and Spell words for the sound-spellings /kwärtz/, /kėrv/, /tir/, and /stār/.

4 Write two Read and Spell words that rhyme for each sentence below.

a He is going to pay his ____ of the ____.

b She's using a ____ to help her ____ the stream.

1 Carlos had to write an interesting word story. Proofread his work. You should find one spelling mistake, one mistake in punctuation at the end of a sentence, and two apostrophe mistakes. (Remember that apostrophes are used to show ownership and to stand for missing letters in contractions.) After you have found the mistakes, write the word story correctly.

16

Mastery Test 4a

1 /ärch/ *arch*

2 /glãr/ *glare*

3 /rôr/ *roar*

4 /spärk/ *spark*

5 /fėrm/ *firm*

6 /drôl/ *drawl*

7 /klėrk/ *clerk*

8 /sprôl/ *sprawl*

9 /vėrs/ *verse*

10 /trüp/ *troop*

11 It's a /chôr/ to drag trash from the /pôrch/. It's a *chore* to drag trash from the *porch.*

12 "I /stuk/ a /thôrn/ in my /thum/," /snärld/ the boy. "I *stuck* a *thorn* in my *thumb,*" *snarled* the boy.

13 Some /dir/ /stärv/ when there's a long /drout/. Some *deer starve* when there's a long *drought.*

14 The wall at the /fôr/ part of that /pùr/ house needs paint. The wall at the *fore* part of that *poor* house needs paint.

15 The sun was too warm for that /rō/ of /sprouts/. The sun was too warm for that *row* of *sprouts.*

Mastery Test 4b

1 /spėrt/ *spurt*

2 /spėr/ *spur*

3 /hwėrl/ *whirl*

16

Snarl means to growl in a gruff and harsh way. A snarling dog bares its teeth. A snarling person scowls and frowns when speaking. Have you ever heard of a snarling letter. That's what people once called the letter r. They said that r had the sharp sound of a dog's snarl.

2 Read the dictionary entry below for the word *coarse.*

The lexicographer may write only a phrase, or part of a sentence, to show how an entry word is used.	The lexicographer shows the *er* and *est* forms of adjectives that drop final *e* before the endings.

• **coarse** /kôrs/ *adj.* **1.** Not fine: *coarse hair.* **2.** Rough: *coarse cloth.* **3.** Poor: *coarse food.* **4.** Crude: *coarse manners.* **coarser, coarsest.**

Write a complete dictionary entry for the word *hoarse.* Give two meanings. Write a sample sentence for one meaning and a phrase for the other meaning. Show the *er* and *est* endings. When you have finished, compare your work with the entry in the Spelling Dictionary.

A Word from the Japanese

The Japanese method of defending oneself without using weapons is called *karate* /kə rä′ tē/. In Japanese, the word *karate* means "empty hands." Many Americans have become interested in karate and have mastered the skills.

Write only the one sentence from the two below that is true. Spell all the words correctly.

a The word *karate* /mā/ /bē/ /ūzd/ /az/ /ā/ /noun/.
b The word *karate* /mā/ /bē/ /ūzd/ /az/ /ā/ /vėrb/.

:: **Answers**
1 (See Teaching Suggestions.)
2 (See the entry for *hoarse* in the Spelling Dictionary as a model answer.)

A Word from the Japanese
a The word *karate* may be used as a noun.

Mastery Test
For complete directions and an explanation of the testing program, see the Introduction to this Teacher's Edition.

4 /snir/ *sneer*
5 /toil/ *toil*
6 /smir/ *smear*
7 /ouns/ *ounce*
8 /kėrb/ *curb*
9 /nùk/ *nook*
10 /skwėrt/ *squirt*
11 A /bärj/ came to /pôrt/ with its load of /kôrs/ sand.   A *barge* came to *port* with its load of *coarse* sand.
12 Some words are /nōn/ as /nounz/ and some as /vėrbz/.   Some words are *known*

as *nouns* and some as *verbs.*
13 /kwālz/ are /kwir/ birds that don't fly much.   *Quails* are *queer* birds that don't fly much.
14 Your drawings at the /fãr/ show /kwīt/ a /flãr/ for art.   Your drawings at the *fair* show *quite* a *flair* for art.
15 Is it /klir/ that a /skwãr/ must have four sides?   Is it *clear* that a *square* must have four sides?

● **Answers**

1 tid/bit, hand/cuff, drum/stick, chest/nut, off/spring
2 grape/vine, bee/hive, fire/place, stage/coach, yule/tide, drive/way

5 Long and Short Vowels in Compounds

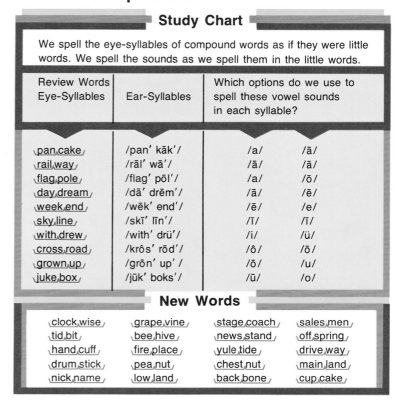

Study Chart

We spell the eye-syllables of compound words as if they were little words. We spell the sounds as we spell them in the little words.

Review Words Eye-Syllables	Ear-Syllables	Which options do we use to spell these vowel sounds in each syllable?	
pan‚cake‚	/pan' kāk'/	/a/	/ā/
rail‚way‚	/rāl' wā'/	/ā/	/ā/
flag‚pole‚	/flag' pōl'/	/a/	/ō/
day‚dream‚	/dā' drēm'/	/ā/	/ē/
week‚end‚	/wēk' end'/	/ē/	/e/
sky‚line‚	/skī' līn'/	/ī/	/ī/
with‚drew‚	/with' drü'/	/i/	/ü/
cross‚road‚	/krôs' rōd'/	/ô/	/ō/
grown‚up‚	/grōn' up'/	/ō/	/u/
juke‚box‚	/jūk' boks'/	/ū/	/o/

New Words

clock‚wise‚	grape‚vine‚	stage‚coach‚	sales‚men‚
tid‚bit‚	bee‚hive‚	news‚stand‚	off‚spring‚
hand‚cuff‚	fire‚place‚	yule‚tide‚	drive‚way‚
drum‚stick‚	pea‚nut‚	chest‚nut‚	main‚land‚
nick‚name‚	low‚land‚	back‚bone‚	cup‚cake‚

1 Write the five new compound words in which both vowel sounds are short. Draw lines between the eye-syllables.

2 Write the six new compound words in which both vowel sounds are long. Draw lines between the eye-syllables.

18

Teaching Suggestions

Unit 5 is the first of three units dealing with compound words. In this unit the short- and long-vowel spelling patterns appear again. Most two-syllable compounds have secondary stress on the softer syllable and thus have a clear vowel sound in both syllables. Pupils can apply to both syllables the spelling generalizations learned in monosyllabic spelling.

Since this is the first unit of multisyllabic words, eye-syllables are marked for the first time in the Study Chart. See page T-7 for a discussion of the eye-syllable concept.

Use the Study Chart to demonstrate that the spelling of long words is easier if each syllable is spelled as if it were a "little" (i.e., monosyllabic) word. A discussion of the phonemes in the last column may be used to review the short- and long-vowel spelling patterns as they pertain to the review words. Pupils should then apply these generalizations to the list of new words.

● Some pupils may require guidance from you in doing the exercises in this section.

Handwriting Models

clockwise   grapevine   stagecoach   salesmen
tidbit   beehive   newsstand   offspring
handcuff   fireplace   yuletide   driveway
drumstick   peanut   chestnut   mainland
nickname   lowland   backbone   cupcake

3 Write the four new compound words in which the vowel sound is short in the first eye-syllable and long in the second. Draw lines between the eye-syllables.

4 Write the five new compound words in which the vowel sound is long in the first eye-syllable and short in the second. Draw lines between the eye-syllables.

5 Write the eye-syllables of the review words with these vowel sounds. Write the whole word next to its eye-syllables.

a /i/ and /ü/   **d** /ū/ and /o/   **g** /ô/ and /ō/
b /ā/ and /ē/   **e** /ā/ and /ā/   **h** /a/ and /ō/
c /a/ and /ā/   **f** /ō/ and /u/   **i** /ī/ and /ī/

1 Copy these sound-spellings. Place the primary (′) and secondary (′) accent marks to show the loud and half-loud syllables. Then write the correct spelling for each word.

a /klok wīz /   **c** /mān land /   **e** /wēk end /
b /ôf spring /   **d** /tid bit /   **f** /with drü /

2 Write the correct spelling for each sound-spelling below. Draw a line between the eye-syllables of each word.

a /stāj′ kōch′/   **e** /fīr′ plās′/   **i** /drum′ stik′/
b /hand′ kuf′/   **f** /nüz′ stand′/   **j** /drīv′ wā′/
c /kup′ kak′/   **g** /bak′ bōn′/   **k** /pē′ nut′/
d /grāp′ vīn′/   **h** /bē′ hīv′/   **l** /lō′ land′/

19

3 clock/wise, nick/name, back/bone, cup/cake
4 pea/nut, low/land, news/stand, sales/men, main/land
5a with drew   withdrew
 b day dream   daydream
 c pan cake   pancake
 d juke box   jukebox
 e rail way   railway
 f grown up   grownup
 g cross road   crossroad
 h flag pole   flagpole
 i sky line   skyline

●●   **Answers**
1a /klok′ wīz′/ clockwise
 b /ôf′ spring′/ offspring
 c /mān′ land′/ mainland
 d /tid′ bit′/ tidbit
 e /wēk′ end′/ weekend
 f /with′ drü′/ withdrew
2a stage/coach   **g** back/bone
 b hand/cuff   **h** bee/hive
 c cup/cake   **i** drum/stick
 d grape/vine   **j** drive/way
 e fire/place   **k** pea/nut
 f news/stand   **l** low/land

●●   Before the pupils do Exercise 1, you may want to use the Study Chart to review the use of primary and secondary accent marks.

●●
●●   The Read and Spell list is an important test of the pupils' ability to decode compounds. Exercises 2 and 3 are designed to compel pupils to apply the sound-symbol generalizations.

●●   The correct proofreading exercise, with corrected errors underscored, is as follows:

The <u>noun</u> chestnut *has one queer meaning. America<u>ns</u> call an old, stale joke a chestnut. No one seems to know why the word came to be used this way, but many people have tried to track down the reason. Don't tell an old and dull joke or someone may <u>squeal</u>, "What a chestnut!"*

In addition to *rhinoceros,* numerous other words have been made from such Greek word parts as *bio* (life), *chron* (time), *graph* (writing), *log* (study), and *phon* (sound).

Answers

2a hitch/hike   **d** pad/lock
  b home/made   **e** oat/meal
  c fuse/box   **f** rain/drop

3a flake, scape, made
  b hail, rain, rail
  c way
  d stone, bone, home
  e toe
  f oat
  g snow
  h meal, steam, stream
  i side, pipe, lime, line,
     hike, like, wise
  j fuse

Read and Spell

upkeep	inside	handbag	tiptoe	pipeline
hillside	handspring	landscape	midway	hitchhike
hailstone	pathway	offside	indent	uphill
thumbtack	steamship	beside	midstream	homemade
oatmeal	snowflake	bagpipe	wishbone	padlock
fusebox	raindrop	limestone	handrail	likewise

1 Write any Read and Spell word that you cannot read or any word for which you do not know the meaning.

2 Write the Read and Spell word for each sound-spelling below. Draw a line between the eye-syllables of each word.
a /hich′ hīk′/   **c** /fūz′ boks′/   **e** /ōt′ mēl′/
b /hōm′ mād′/   **d** /pad′ lok′/   **f** /rān′ drop′/

3 Write eye-syllables only from the Read and Spell list for the exercises below. Write each eye-syllable only once.
a Write three eye-syllables in which /ā/ is spelled with the letters *a*-consonant-*e*.
b Write three eye-syllables in which /ā/ is spelled *ai*.
c Write one eye-syllable in which /ā/ is spelled *ay*.
d Write three eye-syllables in which *o*-consonant-*e* spells /ō/.
e Write one eye-syllable in which *oe* spells /ō/.
f Write one eye-syllable in which *oa* spells /ō/.
g Write one eye-syllable in which *ow* spells /ō/.
h Write three eye-syllables in which *ea* spells /ē/.
i Write seven eye-syllables in which *i*-consonant-*e* spells /ī/.
j Write the eye-syllable in which *u*-consonant-*e* spells /ū/.

1 Maryann wrote a paragraph about the word *chestnut*. Proofread her work. You should find two spelling mistakes, one capitalization mistake, and one apostrophe mistake. Then write the paragraph correctly.

20

Mastery Test 5a

1 /stärv/ *starve*
2 /kwir/ *queer*
3 /thôrn/ *thorn*
4 /nik′ nām′/ *nickname*
5 /flag′ pōl′/ *flagpole*
6 /pan′ kāk′/ *pancake*
7 /lō′ land′/ *lowland*
8 /tid′ bit′/ *tidbit*
9 /nüz′ stand′/ *newsstand*
10 /rāl′ wā′/ *railway*
11 We'll /rōst/ /ches′ nuts′/ in the /fīr′ plās′/ at /ūl′ tīd′/.   We'll *roast chestnuts* in the *fireplace* at *yuletide*.

12 Some /grōn′ ups′/ like to hear tunes on the /jūk′ boks′/.   Some *grownups* like to hear tunes on the *jukebox*.
13 The /sālz′ mən/ leaped from the /stāj′ kōch′/ at the /krôs′ rōd′/.   The *salesmen* leaped from the *stagecoach* at the *crossroad*.
14 Those /klėrks/ have a lot for sale at the /fãr/.   Those *clerks* have a lot for sale at the *fair*.
15 They brought the ship to /pôrt/ in spite of a bad /skwôl/.   They brought the ship to *port* in spite of a bad *squall*.

The noun chestnut has one queer meaning. Americans call an old, stale joke a chestnut. No one seems to know why the word came to be used this way, but many people have tried to track down the reason. Don't tell an old and dull joke or someone may squeal, "what a chestnut!"

2 Read the dictionary entry below for the word *chestnut*.

The lexicographer uses a primary accent mark to show the loud ear-syllable.	The lexicographer uses a secondary accent mark to show the half-loud ear-syllable.

- **chestnut** /ches′ nut′/ *n.* **1.** Small, sweet nut in a prickly burr. **2.** Tree on which a chestnut grows. **3.** Wood from the chestnut tree: *The table is made of chestnut.* —*adj.* Reddish brown: *chestnut hair.*

Write a dictionary entry for the word *grownup*. Show the sound-spelling of the word. Use your own words to give a noun definition and an adjective definition of the word. Write sample sentences or phrases to make your definitions clear. When you have finished, compare your work with the entry in the Spelling Dictionary.

Another Word from the Greeks

Rhin is a Greek word part that means "nose." *Keras* is a Greek word part that means "horn." Because the huge animal we see at the zoo has one or two horns on the snout, *rhinoceros* is the name we have given to it.

Write the two plural forms the Spelling Dictionary shows for the word *rhinoceros.*

21

●● **Answers**
1 (See Teaching Suggestions.)
2 (See the entry for *grownup* in the Spelling Dictionary as a model answer.)

Another Word from the Greeks
rhinoceroses, rhinoceros

Mastery Test
For complete directions and an explanation of the testing program, see the Introduction to this Teacher's Edition.

Mastery Test 5b
1 /bak′ bōn′/ *backbone*
2 /klok′ wīz′/ *clockwise*
3 /drīv′ wā′/ *driveway*
4 /dā′ drēm′/ *daydream*
5 /bärj/ *barge*
6 /hand′ kuf′/ *handcuff*
7 /skī′ līn′/ *skyline*
8 /skwėrt/ *squirt*
9 /drum′ stik′/ *drumstick*
10 /with′ drü′/ *withdrew*
11 Sometimes a cook puts /pē′ nuts′/ on /kup′ kāks′/.   Sometimes a cook puts *peanuts* on *cupcakes.*

12 A long /grāp′ vīn′/ grew near the base of the /bē′ hīv′/.   A long *grapevine* grew near the base of the *beehive.*
13 /ôf′ spring′/ of cows are called calves. *Offspring* of cows are called calves.
14 The sailors spent a /wēk′ end′/ on the /mān′ land′/.   The sailors spent a *weekend* on the *mainland.*
15 Don't /smir/ that /pach/ of /pingk/ paint on the /pôrch/.   Don't *smear* that *patch* of *pink* paint on the *porch.*

1a teaspoon, toothbrush, uproot, footstool

b textbook, falsehood, fishhook, footstool, plywood

c outfit, blowout, roundhouse, roundup, household

d downtown, snowplow, cowbell, downstream, downfall

e soybean, joyride

f oilskin, oilcan, pointblank

g causeway, dauntless

h sawmill, strawstack, crawfish

i hallway, falsehood, softball, downfall

6 Two-Letter Vowels in Compounds

Study Chart

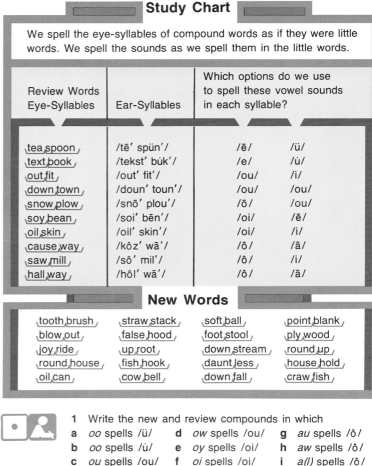

We spell the eye-syllables of compound words as if they were little words. We spell the sounds as we spell them in the little words.

Review Words Eye-Syllables	Ear-Syllables	Which options do we use to spell these vowel sounds in each syllable?	
tea spoon	/tē′ spün′/	/ē/	/ü/
text book	/tekst′ bŭk′/	/e/	/ù/
out fit	/out′ fit′/	/ou/	/i/
down town	/doun′ toun′/	/ou/	/ou/
snow plow	/snō′ plou′/	/ō/	/ou/
soy bean	/soi′ bēn′/	/oi/	/ē/
oil skin	/oil′ skin′/	/oi/	/i/
cause way	/kôz′ wā′/	/ô/	/ā/
saw mill	/sô′ mil′/	/ô/	/i/
hall way	/hôl′ wā′/	/ô/	/ā/

New Words

tooth brush	straw stack	soft ball	point blank
blow out	false hood	foot stool	ply wood
joy ride	up root	down stream	round up
round house	fish hook	daunt less	house hold
oil can	cow bell	down fall	craw fish

1 Write the new and review compounds in which

a *oo* spells /ü/ **d** *ow* spells /ou/ **g** *au* spells /ô/
b *oo* spells /ù/ **e** *oy* spells /oi/ **h** *aw* spells /ô/
c *ou* spells /ou/ **f** *oi* spells /oi/ **i** *a(l)* spells /ô/

22

Teaching Suggestions

In this unit the digraphic-vowel spellings that were presented in Unit 3 are recycled through compound words. Included are the *oo* spellings of /ü/ and /ù/; the *ou* and *ow* spellings of /ou/; the *oy* and *oi* spellings of /oi/; and the *au, aw,* and *a(l)* spellings of /ô/.

Use the Study Chart to introduce the unit. The eye-syllable markings should remind pupils that we spell the parts of compounds as if they were little words. The ear-syllables column may be used to review the sound symbols and the primary and secondary accent marks. The spell-ing generalizations may be reviewed by a dis-cussion of the phonemes in the third column, and they should then be applied to the new words.

● The exercises in this section utilize the spelling generalizations which appear in the Study Chart.

●● Exercises 1 and 2 of this section cause pupils to examine the sound-symbol relation-ships again, eye-syllable by eye-syllable.

Handwriting Models

toothbrush *strawstack* *softball* *pointblank*
blowout *falsehood* *footstool* *plywood*
joyride *uproot* *downstream* *roundup*
roundhouse *fishhook* *dauntless* *household*
oilcan *cowbell* *downfall* *crawfish*

2 Write the sound-spellings for *footstool, plywood,* and *joyride.* Be sure to place the accent marks correctly.

3 Write the compound words for these sound-spellings.
a /strô′ stak′/   **c** /sôft′ bôl′/   **e** /blō′ out′/
b /point′ blangk′/   **d** /doun′ strēm′/   **f** /up′ rüt′/

1 Write the eye-syllables of the new and review words in which you hear the vowel sounds /ü/, /u̇/, /ou/, /oi/, and /ô/. Do not write the same eye-syllable more than once.

2 Write the eye-syllables of the new and review words in which you hear the vowel sounds shown below. The numerals in parentheses show how many eye-syllables to write for each sound. Do not write the same eye-syllable more than once.
a /a/ (3)   **d** /u/ (2)   **g** /ī/ (2)
b /e/ (3)   **e** /ā/ (1)   **h** /ō/ (3)
c /i/ (4)   **f** /ē/ (3)

3 Write the compound words that these pictures suggest.

23

2 /fu̇t′ stül′/, /plī′ wu̇d′/, /joi′ rīd′/
3a strawstack   **d** downstream
   b pointblank   **e** blowout
   c softball   **f** uproot

●● **Answers**
1 /ü/ spoon, tooth, root, stool
   /u̇/ book, hood, hook, foot, wood
   /ou/ out, down, town, plow, round, house, cow
   /oi/ soy, oil, joy, point
   /ô/ cause, saw, hall, straw, false, soft, ball, daunt, fall, craw
2a can, stack, blank
   b text, bell, less
   c fit, skin, mill, fish
   d brush, up
   e way
   f tea, bean, stream
   g ride, ply
   h snow, blow, hold
3a toothbrush   **d** oilcan
   b cowbell   **e** footstool
   c fishhook   **f** crawfish

●● Exercise 1 once more causes pupils to relate their encoding skills to the process of decoding compound words. Pupils should be taught to separate the compounds into eye-syllables and to blend the sounds of each eye-syllable.

●● The correct proofreading exercise, with the corrected errors underscored, is as follows:
Softball is a game something like baseball. However, a softball is usually larger than a baseball. The pitcher <u>throws</u> underhand in <u>softball</u> and overhand in <u>baseball</u>. The batter <u>tries</u> to hit the ball and get on base in both games. Three strikes make an out in both games.

For the dictionary exercise, it may be profitable to expand the explanation about the formation of plurals. Pupils may use the Spelling Dictionary to observe which plurals are shown and discuss why they are shown.

In addition to *kindergarten,* pupils may investigate other words from the Germans, such as *liverwurst, pretzel, pumpernickel, rathskeller, sauerkraut, snorkel,* and *yodel.*

Answers

2a mothball **d** lawsuit
 b fireproof **e** sawdust
 c loophole **f** backwoods
3 broom, proof, noon, room, loose, loop, fool
4 /bel′ boi′/, /drift′ wůd′/, /pôn′ shop′/

Answers

1 (See Teaching Suggestions.)

Read and Spell

outlook	dugout	noonday	backwoods	hothouse
whiskbroom	downstairs	sawdust	rawhide	toyland
cowboy	lawsuit	drawstring	ballroom	drawback
saltbox	woodchuck	windfall	outlaw	driftwood
mothball	fireproof	proofread	looseleaf	loophole
lawnmower	pawnshop	bellboy	outcast	foolproof

1 Write any Read and Spell word that you cannot read or any word for which you do not know the meaning.

2 Write the Read and Spell words for these sound-spellings.
a /môth′ bôl′/ **c** /lüp′ hōl′/ **e** /sô′ dust′/
b /fīr′ prüf′/ **d** /lô′ süt′/ **f** /bak′ wůdz′/

3 Write the seven Read and Spell eye-syllables in which /ü/ is spelled *oo*. Do not write the same one more than once.

4 Write the sound-spellings for the Read and Spell words *bellboy*, *driftwood*, and *pawnshop*.

1 Gina wrote this paragraph about the games of baseball and softball. She made two mistakes in the facts she wrote. She also misspelled two words. Proofread Gina's paragraph. The Spelling Dictionary will help you check the facts. After you have found the mistakes, write the paragraph correctly.

> Softball is a game something like baseball. However, a softball is usually larger than a baseball. The pitcher throse underhand in baseball and overhand in softball. The batter trys to hit the ball and get on base in both games. Three strikes make an out in both games.

24

Mastery Test 6a

1 /tē′ spün′/ *teaspoon*
2 /oil′ kan′/ *oilcan*
3 /soi′ bēn′/ *soybean*
4 /grāp′ vīn′/ *grapevine*
5 /doun′ fôl′/ *downfall*
6 /ôf′ spring′/ *offspring*
7 /hôl′ wā′/ *hallway*
8 /stāj′ kōch′/ *stagecoach*
9 /strô′ stak′/ *strawstack*
10 /kou′ bel′/ *cowbell*
11 A /blō′ out′/ spoiled our /joi′ rīd′/ and picnic. A *blowout* spoiled our *joyride* and picnic.

12 You do not need /fish′ hůks′/ to catch /krô′ fish′/. You do not need *fishhooks* to catch *crawfish*.
13 /swift/ cars drive /doun′ toun′/ on the wide /kôz′ wā′/. *Swift* cars drive *downtown* on the wide *causeway*.
14 /dônt′ les′/ /trüps/ marched out to meet the foe. *Dauntless troops* marched out to meet the foe.
15 Each child /plejd/ to use a /tüth′ brush′/ twice a day. Each child *pledged* to use a *toothbrush* twice a day.

2 Read the dictionary entries below for the words *falsehood* and *firefly*.

The lexicographer arranges words in alphabetical order according to the first letter of each word. Words that have the same first letter are listed alphabetically according to their second letters. Words that have the same first two letters are listed alphabetically according to their third letters.

- **falsehood** /fôls′ hùd′/ *n.* False statement; lie: *The reason they gave for being late is a falsehood.*

- **firefly** /fīr′ flī′/ *n.* A small insect that gives off flashes of light at night. *pl.* **fireflies.**

The lexicographer shows the plural form of entry words that are not formed simply by adding *s* or *es* to the singular.

Write dictionary entries for *crawfish* and *cowbell*. Use your own words to write the definitions and the sample sentences or phrases. When you have finished, compare your work with the entries in the Spelling Dictionary.

A Word from the Germans

The German word for children is *Kinder*. The German word for garden is *Garten*. These two words have been put together to make the compound word *Kindergarten*—a "garden for children." The first kindergartens appeared in Germany. They were thought of as places where children could grow and learn as plants grow in a garden. Children below the age of six now attend kindergartens in many countries.

Write the words for the sound-spellings below. Draw a ring around the words that come before *kindergarten* in a dictionary.

a /kou′ bel′/   b /krô′ fish′/   c /oil′ kan′/

25

---

2 (See the entries for *cowbell* and *crawfish* in the Spelling Dictionary as model answers.)

A Word from the Germans
a (cowbell)
b (crawfish)
c oilcan

Mastery Test
For complete directions and an explanation of the testing program, see the Introduction to this Teacher's Edition.

Mastery Test 6b
1 /up′ rüt′/ *uproot*
2 /plī′ wùd′/ *plywood*
3 /round′ up′/ *roundup*
4 /tekst′ bùk′/ *textbook*
5 /oil′ skin′/ *oilskin*
6 /pē′ nut′/ *peanut*
7 /out′ fit′/ *outfit*
8 /fôls′ hùd′/ *falsehood*
9 /hous′ hōld′/ *household*
10 /mān′ land′/ *mainland*
11 I told you /point′ blangk′/ not to play /sôft′ bôl′/.   I told you *pointblank* not to play *softball.*
12 Let's row /doun′ strēm′/ past the /sô′ mil′/. Let's row *downstream* past the *sawmill.*
13 There are two /fùt′ stülz′/ near the /fīr′ plās′/.   There are two *footstools* near the *fireplace.*
14 All trains in the /round′ hous′/ run /klok′ wīz′/.   All trains in the *roundhouse* run *clockwise.*
15 A /snō′ plou′/ cleaned the snow from their /drīv′ wā′/.   A *snowplow* cleaned the snow from their *driveway.*

7 Vowel-*r* Compound Words

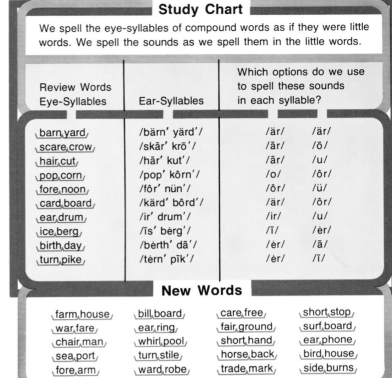

Study Chart

We spell the eye-syllables of compound words as if they were little words. We spell the sounds as we spell them in the little words.

Review Words Eye-Syllables	Ear-Syllables	Which options do we use to spell these sounds in each syllable?	
barn‚yard	/bärn′ yärd′/	/är/	/är/
scare‚crow	/skär′ krō′/	/är/	/ō/
hair‚cut	/här′ kut′/	/är/	/u/
pop‚corn	/pop′ kôrn′/	/o/	/ôr/
fore‚noon	/fôr′ nün′/	/ôr/	/ü/
card‚board	/kärd′ bôrd′/	/är/	/ôr/
ear‚drum	/ir′ drum′/	/ir/	/u/
ice‚berg	/īs′ bėrg′/	/ī/	/ėr/
birth‚day	/bėrth′ dā′/	/ėr/	/ā/
turn‚pike	/tėrn′ pīk′/	/ėr/	/ī/

New Words

farm‚house bill‚board care‚free short‚stop
war‚fare ear‚ring fair‚ground surf‚board
chair‚man whirl‚pool short‚hand ear‚phone
sea‚port turn‚stile horse‚back bird‚house
fore‚arm ward‚robe trade‚mark side‚burns

1 Write the new and review compounds in which

a *ar* spells /är/
b *are* spells /är/
c *air* spells /är/
d *or* spells /ôr/ or /ōr/
e *ore* spells /ôr/ or /ōr/
f *oar* spells /ôr/ or /ōr/
g *ear* spells /ir/
h *er* spells /ėr/
i *ir* spells /ėr/
j *ur* spells /ėr/

26

Teaching Suggestions

In this third unit of compound words, the vowel-*r* spellings introduced in Unit 4 are featured again. We commonly spell /är/ with *ar*; /är/ with *are* or *air*; /ôr/ or /ōr/ with *or*, *ore*, or *oar*; /ėr/ with *er*, *ir*, or *ur*; and /ir/ with *ear* or *eer*. One or two of these sounds are found in each compound.

As usual, the Study Chart may be used to introduce the unit. The eye-syllable markings will again establish the usefulness of separating compounds into their component parts for ease of spelling. The ear-syllables column will pro-vide more practice with sound symbolization and accent marks. The spelling options used for the vowel sounds shown in the third column of the Study Chart may be discussed. The spelling generalizations should then be applied to the new words.

● Exercise 1 reiterates the vowel-*r* generalizations which appear in the Study Chart and provides a written reinforcement of the understanding of them. Exercises 2 and 3 involve the use of *c* to spell /s/ or /k/.

Handwriting Models

farmhouse   billboard   carefree   shortstop
warfare   earring   fairground   surfboard
chairman   whirlpool   shorthand   earphone
seaport   turnstile   horseback   birdhouse
forearm   wardrobe   trademark   sideburns

2 Write the five new and review words in which *c* before *a, o, u,* or a consonant letter spells /k/.

3 Write the word from the review list in which *c* before *e, i,* or *y* spells /s/.

1 Write the eight eye-syllables of the new and review words in which you hear /är/.

2 Write the six eye-syllables in which you hear /âr/.

3 Write the six eye-syllables in which you hear /ôr/ or /ōr/. Do not write the same one more than once.

4 Write the one eye-syllable in which you hear /ir/.

5 Write the seven eye-syllables in which you hear /ėr/. Do not write the same one more than once.

6 Write the two eye-syllables in which *ou* spells /ou/.

7 Write the two eye-syllables in which *oo* spells /ü/.

8 Write the eye-syllables in which you hear the vowel sounds shown below. The numerals in parentheses show how many eye-syllables to write for each sound.

a /a/ (3)	**d** /u/ (2)	**g** /ī/ (4)
b /i/ (2)	**e** /ā/ (2)	**h** /ō/ (3)
c /o/ (2)	**f** /ē/ (2)	

27

2 scarecrow, haircut, popcorn, cardboard, carefree

3 iceberg

●● **Answers**

1 barn, yard, card, farm, war, arm, ward, mark

2 scare, hair, fare, chair, care, fair

3 corn, fore, board, port, short, horse

4 ear

5 berg, birth, turn, whirl, surf, bird, burns

6 house, ground

7 noon, pool

8a man, hand, back
 b bill, ring
 c pop, stop
 d cut, drum
 e day, trade
 f sea, free
 g ice, pike, stile, side
 h crow, robe, phone

●● The exercises in this section again focus attention on the eye-syllables.

●
●● The Read and Spell words illustrate the same generalizations as the unit spelling words. As usual, they may be used to diagnose pupils' decoding and meaning problems.

●●
●● The correct proofreading exercise, with the corrected errors underscored, is as follows:

A trademark *is a picture, word, or symbol that a manufacturer uses to mark his own* goods. The manufacturer owns the trademark. No one else may use it without permission.

A turnstile *is a post with bars that turn. One person at a time may go through. A turnstile is used at places where* fares *are paid.*

Sideburns are hair on the sides of a man's face. Gen. Ambrose Burnside first wore them.

In addition to *pianoforte,* we use many other musical terms from the Italian language. Among those that pupils might investigate are *concerto, contralto, oboe, opera, piccolo, sonata, soprano, trombone,* and *violin.*

2a streetcar **d** rainstorm
 b storeroom **e** forewarn
 c shirttail **f** barefoot
3 bare, air
4 tear, fear, gear
5a birdbath **d** stockyards
 b dashboard **e** corkscrew
 c pitchfork **f** airport

Read and Spell

streetcar	marksman	stockyards	bareback	airport
corkscrew	forbid	pitchfork	rainstorm	storeroom
forewarn	dashboard	fearless	germproof	foresee
bluebird	birdbath	turnout	birthplace	outburst
teardrop	shirttail	paydirt	blackboard	gearshift
barefoot	passport	foreman	springboard	uproar

1 Write any Read and Spell word that you cannot read or any word for which you do not know the meaning.

2 Write the Read and Spell words for these sound-spellings.
a /strēt′ kär′/ **c** /shėrt′ tāl′/ **e** /fôr′ wärn′/
b /stôr′ rüm′/ **d** /rān′ stôrm′/ **f** /bãr′ fùt′/

3 Write the two Read and Spell eye-syllables with /ãr/.

4 Write the three Read and Spell eye-syllables with /ir/.

5 Write the Read and Spell words for these pictures.

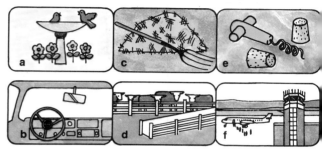

1 Doug's assignment was to write definitions for three words from the list of new words. Proofread his work. You should find five mistakes, including one incorrect fact. After you have found the mistakes, write the definitions correctly. The Spelling Dictionary will help you check the facts.

28

Mastery Test 7a
1 /pop′ kôrn′// *popcorn*
2 /bėrd′ hous′// *birdhouse*
3 /shôrt′ hand′// *shorthand*
4 /nik′ nām′// *nickname*
5 /fôr′ nün′// *forenoon*
6 /ūl′ tīd′// *yuletide*
7 /ir′ fōn′// *earphone*
8 /kärd′ bôrd′// *cardboard*
9 /wär′ fãr′// *warfare*
10 /īs′ bėrg′// *iceberg*
11 There's a /skãr′ krō′/ near the /strô′ stak′/ in the /bärn′ yärd′/. There's a *scarecrow* near the *strawstack* in the *barnyard*.

12 You can't hear well if you harm your /ir′ drum′/. You can't hear well if you harm your *eardrum*.
13 A small fish in a /hwėrl′ pül′/ is the /trād′ märk′/ on my /sėrf′ bôrd′/. A small fish in a *whirlpool* is the *trademark* on my *surfboard*.
14 I'll hang your /oil′ skin′/ /kōt′/ in the /wôrd′ rōb′/. I'll hang your *oilskin coat* in the *wardrobe*.
15 Let's row /doun′ strēm′/ past the /sô′ mil′/. Let's row *downstream* past the *sawmill*.

A trademark is a picture, word, or symbol that a manu-facturer uses to mark his own goods. The manufacturer owns the trademark no one else may use it without per-mission.

A turnstile is a post with bars that turn. One person at a time may go through. A turnstile is used at places where fairs are paid.

Sideburns are hair on the sides of a mans face. Gen. Ambrose Sideburns first wore them.

 2 Read the dictionary entry below for the word *forearm*.

> A lexicographer sometimes uses a drawing to show the exact meaning of an entry word.

* **forearm** /fôr′ ärm′/ *n.* The part of the arm between the wrist and the elbow.

Use your own words and a drawing of your own to show the meaning of the entry word *earring*. When you have finished, compare your work with the Spelling Dictionary.

A Word from the Italians

Many of our musical terms and our names for musical instruments come from the Italian language. *Piano,* for example, is a short form of *piano-forte. Pianoforte* comes from the Italian *piano* ("soft") and *forte* ("strong"). It was so named because the tones of a piano could be made softer or stronger than those of a similar musical instrument called a spinet.

Write the words and their plural forms for the sound-spellings below. Draw a ring around each of the plural forms that is shown in the Spelling Dictionary.

a /pē an′ ō/   **b** /pop′ kôrn′/   **c** /fôr′ man′/

29

●● **Answers**
1 (See Teaching Suggestions.)
2 (See the entry and drawing for *earring* in the Spelling Dictionary as a model answer.)

A Word from the Italians
a piano, ⟨pianos⟩
b popcorn, popcorns
c foreman, ⟨foremen⟩

Mastery Test
For complete directions and an explanation of the testing program, see the Introduction to this Teacher's Edition.

Mastery Test 7b

1 /bil′ bôrd′/ *billboard*
2 /chār′ man′/ *chairman*
3 /bėrth′ dā′/ *birthday*
4 /point′ blangk′/ *pointblank*
5 /fôr′ ärm′/ *forearm*
6 /ir′ ring′/ *earring*
7 /kār′ frē′/ *carefree*
8 /sē′ pôrt′/ *seaport*
9 /färm′ hous′/ *farmhouse*
0 /tėrn′ pīk′/ *turnpike*
1 /kou′ boiz′/ ride /hôrs′ bak′/ in a round′ up′/.   *Cowboys* ride *horseback* in a *roundup.*

12 She's the best /shôrt′ stop′/ on our /sôft′ bôl′/ team.   She's the best *shortstop* on our *softball* team.
13 Pay your fare here as you go through the /tėrn′ stīl′/.   Pay your fare here as you go through the *turnstile.*
14 Will you have your /sīd′ bėrnz′/ trimmed when you get a /hār′ kut′/?   Will you have your *sideburns* trimmed when you get a *haircut?*
15 Take this /chēz/ to the /fār′ ground′/ to sell at the /fār/.   Take this *cheese* to the *fairground* to sell at the *fair.*

8 Snurks

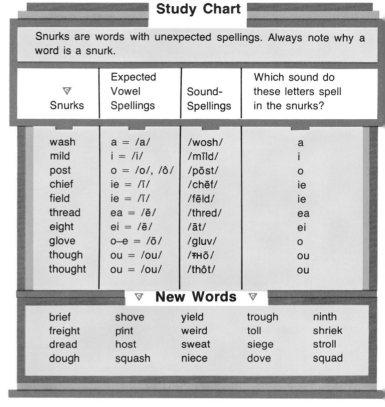

Study Chart

Snurks are words with unexpected spellings. Always note why a word is a snurk.

▽ Snurks	Expected Vowel Spellings	Sound-Spellings	Which sound do these letters spell in the snurks?
wash	a = /a/	/wosh/	a
mild	i = /i/	/mīld/	i
post	o = /o/, /ô/	/pōst/	o
chief	ie = /ī/	/chēf/	ie
field	ie = /ī/	/fēld/	ie
thread	ea = /ē/	/thred/	ea
eight	ei = /ē/	/āt/	ei
glove	o–e = /ō/	/gluv/	o
though	ou = /ou/	/ŦHō/	ou
thought	ou = /ou/	/thôt/	ou

▽ New Words ▽

brief	shove	yield	trough	ninth
freight	pint	weird	toll	shriek
dread	host	sweat	siege	stroll
dough	squash	niece	dove	squad

1 The letter *a* usually spells /a/. Write the three new and re‑ view words in which *a* spells /o/.

2 The letter *i* usually spells /i/. Write the three words in which *i* spells /ī/.

30

Teaching Suggestions

In this unit attention is focused on spellings that are in violation of regular sound-symbol relationships. Throughout this series pupils have been alerted to these violators, which we have designated as *snurks*. A snurk is a word with an unexpected or irregular spelling.

Snurks appear frequently in our writing. In fact, there are 115 monosyllabic snurks among the one thousand most frequently used English words. In order to master these snurks, pupils must learn the expected sound-symbol relationships so as to detect the deviations.

Use the Study Chart to introduce the unit. For each snurk in the list, pupils should observe the sound-symbol relationship that is expected and the nature of the deviation. In the word *wash,* for example, the *a* is in medial position, so we expect it to represent /a/. It does not

● The eight exercises in this section serve as a written reinforcement of the concepts and skills discussed in the Study Chart.

Handwriting Models

brief   shove   yield   trough   ninth
freight   pint   weird   toll   shriek
dread   host   sweat   siege   stroll
dough   squash   niece   dove   squad

3   post, host, toll, stroll
4   chief, field, brief, yield, niece, siege, shriek
5   thread, dread, sweat
6   eight, freight, weird
7   glove, shove, dove
8   though, dough, thought, trough

●●   **Answers**

1a dough		**k** sweat	
b trough		**l** pint	
c squad		**m** toll	
d shove		**n** host	
e shriek		**o** squash	
f dread		**p** freight	
g yield		**q** ninth	
h niece		**r** brief	
i weird		**s** dove	
j stroll		**t** siege	
2a field		**d** glove	
b though		**e** thread	
c eight		**f** post	

3   The letter *o* usually spells /o/ or /ô/. Write the four words in which *o* spells /ō/.

4   The letters *ie* together usually spell /ī/. Write the seven words in which *ie* spells /ē/.

5   The letters *ea* together usually spell /ē/. Write the three words in which *ea* spells /e/.

6   The letters *ei* often spell /ē/. Write the two words in which *ei* spells /ā/ and the one word in which *ei* spells /i/.

7   The letter *o* usually spells /ō/ in the *o*-consonant-*e* pattern. Write the three words in which *o* spells /u/.

8   The letters *ou* usually spell /ou/. Write the two words in which *ou* spells /ō/ and the two words in which *ou* spells /ô/.

1   Write the new words for these sound-spellings.

a /dō/		**h** /nēs/		**o** /skwosh/
b /trôf/		**i** /wird/		**p** /frāt/
c /skwod/		**j** /strōl/		**q** /nīnth/
d /shuv/		**k** /swet/		**r** /brēf/
e /shrēk/		**l** /pīnt/		**s** /duv/
f /dred/		**m** /tōl/		**t** /sēj/
g /yēld/		**n** /hōst/		

2   Write a review word that rhymes with each of these words.

a yield	**c** freight	**e** dread
b dough	**d** shove	**f** host

31

●●   Note that Exercise 2 illustrates spelling patterns of snurks that are analogous.

●   The Read and Spell list consists of thirty monosyllabic snurks that have been introduced in earlier levels of this series. The snurks are troublesome in reading as well as in spelling. They must be dealt with as sight words in reading and as words to memorize in spelling. It may be well to print the words on cards for the poor readers to use with one another as a drill activity.

●●   The correct proofreading exercise is:
The words host *and* guest *have opposite meanings. They are* <u>antonyms</u>. *A host is a person who has another person as a visitor or for a meal. A guest is the person who comes to the host's house or table. The odd part of the story is that the word* host *comes from a word that once meant "guest." I* <u>guess</u> *we could say that* host *and* guest *are related words.*

Bolshevik, borsch, czar, mammoth, parka, and *vodka* are more Russian words.

3 niece, siege, squash, squad

4 shriek, dread, shove, stroll, weird, brief

5 thought, mild

 Answers

2a eye	**g** head
b ache	**h** death
c breath	**i** built
d guard	**j** key
e worm	**k** some
f tongue	**l** month

3 worst, work, health

4 guide, thief, earth

---

3 Write the new word in which *c* spells /s/, the new wor[d] in which *g* spells /j/, and the two words in which *qu* spells /kw[/.

4 Write synonyms from the new list for *scream, fear, pus[h], walk, strange,* and *short.*

5 Write the words /thôt/ and /mīld/.

Read and Spell

guide	view	door	thief	tongue
pour	death	ton	month	earth
built	wealth	head	worm	some
ache	work	meant	eye	breath
veil	key	court	worst	worth
soul	health	blood	guard	rein

1 The Read and Spell words are snurks that you have ha[d] before. Write any Read and Spell snurk that you do not recog[-]nize as a sight word or any word for which you do not kno[w] the meaning.

2 Write the Read and Spell words for these sound-spelling[s]

a /ī/	**e** /wėrm/	**i** /bilt/
b /āk/	**f** /tung/	**j** /kē/
c /breth/	**g** /hed/	**k** /sum/
d /gärd/	**h** /deth/	**l** /munth/

3 Write antonyms from the Read and Spell list for *best, pla[y]* and *sickness.*

4 Write synonyms from the Read and Spell list for *steer, rob[-] ber,* and *soil.*

1 John wrote an interesting word story for a spelling assig[n]ment. Proofread his work. You should find three mistake[s]. After you have found the mistakes, write the story correctly.

32

Mastery Test 8a

1 /chēf/ *chief*

2 /kãr′ frē′/ *carefree*

3 /ŦHō/ *though*

4 /trôf/ *trough*

5 /nēs/ *niece*

6 /swet/ *sweat*

7 /hwėrl′ pül′/ *whirlpool*

8 /skwosh/ *squash*

9 /dred/ *dread*

10 /shuv/ *shove*

11 Each /skwod/ of /āt/ boys has two /brēf/ /chôrz/. Each *squad* of *eight* boys has two *brief chores.*

12 /wosh/ these new /gluvz/ with /mīld/ soap[.] *Wash* these new *gloves* with *mild* soap.

13 I need blue /thred/ to /pach/ this shirt. I need blue *thread* to *patch* this shirt.

14 /stüp/ down or that /bou/ will hit your head. *Stoop* down or that *bough* will hit your head.

15 A /hūj/ tree /shēldz/ the /bē′ hīv′/ from the sun. A *huge* tree *shields* the *beehive* from the sun.

Mastery Test 8b

1 /fôls′ hùd′/ *falsehood*

The words host and guest have opposite meanings. They are antonyms. A host is a person who has another person as a visitor or for a meal. A guest is the person who comes to the host's house or table. The odd part of the story is that the word host comes from a word that once meant "guest." I guess we could say that host and guest are related words.

2 When two or more different words are spelled the same way, each word is shown as a separate entry in a dictionary.

| A lexicographer uses numerals after the entry words to show that there are different words spelled the same. | • **toll¹** /tōl/ *v:* Sound with single strokes, slowly and regularly: *Bells tolled on Sunday morning.*—*n.* Sound of a bell being tolled. |
| | • **toll²** /tōl/ *n.* Charge for a certain right or service: *a toll on long-distance telephone calls.* |

Write two complete dictionary entries for *squash*. Number the entries. Compare your work with the Spelling Dictionary.

A Word from the Russians

The Russian word for "self" is *samo*. The Russian word for "boil" is *varit*. A compound of the two words, meaning "self-boiler," became the English word *samovar* /sam′ ə vär/. A samovar is an urn with a faucet at the base that is used to boil water for tea.

Write only the one sentence below that is true. Spell all the words correctly.

a A samovar is an /ėrn/ /with/ /ə/ /fô′ sət/.
b A samovar is an /ėrn/ /with/ /tü/ /fô′ səts/.
c A samovar is a /kīnd/ /uv/ /kup/ /fôr/ /tē/.

33

2 /pōst/ *post*
3 /wird/ *weird*
4 /nīnth/ *ninth*
5 /grēs/ *grease*
6 /sēj/ *siege*
7 /frāt/ *freight*
8 /hōst/ *host*
9 /hôrs′ bak′/ *horseback*
10 /strōl/ *stroll*
11 Did you hear that /shrēk/ from the old /ärm′ hous′/? Did you hear that *shriek* from the old *farmhouse?*
12 She /thôt/ that the /duv/ was a /kwāl/.

She *thought* that the *dove* was a *quail.*
13 We pay /tōl/ when we drive on some /kôz′ wāz′/ and /tėrn′ pīks′/. We pay *toll* when we drive on some *causeways* and *turnpikes.*
14 I bought a /pīnt/ of cream to use for the /kup′ kāk′/ /dō/. I bought a *pint* of cream to use for the *cupcake dough.*
15 He had a good /yēld/ from his /fēld/ of /soi′ bēnz′/. He had a good *yield* from his *field* of *soybeans.*

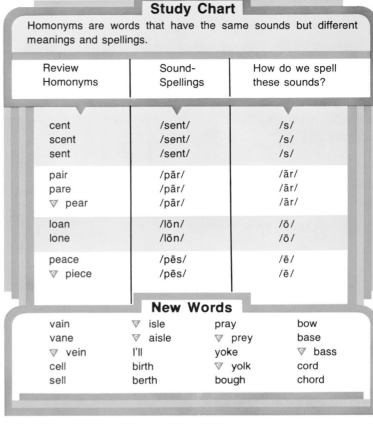

9 Homonyms

Study Chart

Homonyms are words that have the same sounds but different meanings and spellings.

Review Homonyms	Sound-Spellings	How do we spell these sounds?
cent	/sent/	/s/
scent	/sent/	/s/
sent	/sent/	/s/
pair	/pãr/	/ãr/
pare	/pãr/	/ãr/
▽ pear	/pãr/	/ãr/
loan	/lōn/	/ō/
lone	/lōn/	/ō/
peace	/pēs/	/ē/
▽ piece	/pēs/	/ē/

New Words

vain	▽ isle	pray	bow
vane	▽ aisle	▽ prey	base
▽ vein	I'll	yoke	▽ bass
cell	birth	▽ yolk	cord
sell	berth	bough	chord

1 Look at the words in which you hear /s/.
a Write the word in which /s/ is spelled *sc*.
b Write the four words in which /s/ is spelled *c*.

34

Teaching Suggestions

There are more than 2,000 sets of homonyms in English spelling. Each set provides a special problem in spelling. In order to help pupils with these problems, homonym units appear in each level of this series. Also, homonyms reappear regularly in the end-of-the-unit tests.

Some of the words in this unit have appeared singly in the word lists of earlier levels. However, homonym pairs and trios are presented only after all of the words have a likelihood of appearing in pupils' reading books.

Use the Study Chart to highlight the dif-

ferences in spelling for each set of homonyms. Follow the same procedure for the new homonyms. It is essential that the meaning of each word be clarified during the discussion. The Spelling Dictionary may be used for this purpose. As in any group of homonyms, there are a fair number of snurks presented here. Pupils should have a chance to discuss the snurks.

● Exercises 1 through 4 deal with specific spelling problems of the words. Exercises and 6 involve the use of words in context.

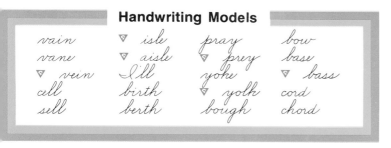

Handwriting Models

vain	▽ isle	pray	bow
vane	▽ aisle	▽ prey	base
▽ vein	I'll	yoke	▽ bass
cell	birth	▽ yolk	cord
sell	berth	bough	chord

2 Look at the words in which you hear /ãr/.

a Write the word in which /ãr/ is spelled *air*.

b Write the word in which /ãr/ is spelled *are*.

c Write the /ãr/ word that is a snurk.

3 Look at the words in which you hear /ā/.

a Write the word in which /ā/ is spelled *ai*.

b Write the two words in which /ā/ is spelled *a*-consonant-*e*.

c Write the word in which /ā/ is spelled *ay*.

d Write the three /ā/ words that are snurks.

4 We usually spell /ī/ with *ie* or *i*-consonant-*e*. Write the two /ī/ snurks and the /ī/ contraction.

5 Write the correct homonyms for these sentences. Use the Spelling Dictionary for help if you need it.

a We smelled the sweet ____ /sent/ of roses.

b She ____ /sent/ me a note.

c I did not have a ____ /sent/ in my pocket.

6 Write the correct homonyms for these sentences.

a I have a new ____ /pãr/ of shoes.

b The ____ /pãr/ was too ripe to eat.

c ____ /pãr/ the apple so the child can eat it.

 Write the correct homonyms for the sentences below and on the next page. Use the Spelling Dictionary for help.

1 He lay in the upper ____ /bẽrth/ of the jail ____ /sel/.

2 He played a ____ /kôrd/ and sang in a ____ /bãs/ voice.

35

2a pair
 b pare
 c pear
3a vain
 b vane, base
 c pray
 d vein, prey, bass
4 isle, aisle, I'll
5a scent
 b sent
 c cent
6a pair
 b pear
 c Pare

●● **Answers**
1 berth, cell
2 chord, bass

The exercises in this section continue the study of words in context.

The Read and Spell list consists of fifteen pairs of monosyllabic homonyms. All of these words have been introduced in the earlier levels of this series. Again, it is vital that pupils know the meaning of each of the words.

The correct proofreading exercise, with corrected spelling errors underscored and corrected list errors starred, is as follows:

Antonyms
sell-buy
foul-fair
dear-cheap
peace-war
* *some-none*

Synonyms
base-bottom
main-<u>chief</u>
pray-beg
cord-rope
* *vain-proud*

You may want to support the dictionary exercise with some additional comment.

In addition to the word *yacht*, some other words from the Dutch that are in our language are *decoy, easel, etch, frolic, harpoon, knuckle,* and *landscape.*

3 sell, loan
4 yoke, cord
5 lone, prey
6 bough
7 piece
8 yolk
9 bow, pray
10 birth

 Answers
2a dye, fur
b steal, fowl
c flee, night
d seem, fair
e Some, read
f sum, fare
g knight, steel
3 wring

3 If we can't ____ /sel/ our house, we'll need a ____ /lōn/.
4 They tied the ____ /yōk/ on the oxen with a ____ /kôrd/.
5 A ____ /lōn/ hawk swooped down on its ____ /prā/.
6 The bird flew from a ____ /bou/ of the tree.
7 The wolf chewed a ____ /pēs/ of meat.
8 The cook needs the ____ /yōk/ of an egg for a cake.
9 The people will ____ /bou/ down to ____ /prā/.
10 The ____ /bėrth/ of the child brought great joy.

Read and Spell

creek	knight	die	ring	fowl
creak	night	dye	wring	foul
fur	main	read	sum	soul
fir	mane	reed	some	sole
seam	rap	fare	flee	steal
seem	wrap	fair	flea	steel

 1 The Read and Spell list is 15 pairs of homonyms you have seen before. Write any word you cannot read or any word for which you do not know the meaning.

2 Write Read and Spell homonyms for these sentences.
a She plans to ____ /dī/ the ____ /fėr/ black.
b The sly fox will ____ /stēl/ our ____ /foul/.
c It will ____ /flē/ into the ____ /nīt/.
d That doesn't ____ /sēm/ ____ /fār/ to us.
e ____ /sum/ children ____ /rēd/ more often than others.
f Have the right ____ /sum/ of money to pay your ____ /fār/.
g The ____ /nīt/ was dressed all in ____ /stēl/.

3 Write the Read and Spell word that means "to squeeze."

 1 Nan made a list of antonyms and a list of synonyms. Proofread her work. You should find four mistakes, including two pairs of words in the wrong list. After you have found the mistakes, write the two lists correctly.

36

For the suggested end-of-the-unit test that follows, note that the format is slightly different than in the previous tests. There are only five isolated sound-spellings for each part. However, each sound-spelling requires the writing of two or three homonyms.

Mastery Test 9a
1 /vān/ *vain, vane, vein*
2 /lōn/ *loan, lone*
3 /sel/ *cell, sell*
4 /bās/ *base, bass*

5 /fār/ *fair, fare*
6 /īl/ eat a /pēs/ of the /pār/ you've /pārd/. *I'll eat a piece of the pear you've pared.*
7 /hôks/ /prā/ on game birds like /kwālz/. *Hawks prey on game birds like quails.*
8 The /tü/ men /mād/ deep /bouz/ /tü/ /ᵺār/ /hōst/. *The two men made deep bows to their host.*
9 /wùd/ you like /tü/ /strōl/ through the /fēld/ /ᵺār/ by the /färm′ hous′/? *Would you like to stroll through the field there by the farmhouse?*

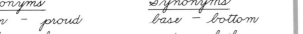

Antonyms		*Synonyms*	
vain	– proud	base	– bottom
sell	– buy	main	– chief
foul	– fair	pray	– beg
dear	– cheap	cord	– rope
piece	– war	some	– none

 2 English verbs are classed as "regular" or "irregular." We form the past tense of a regular verb by adding *d* or *ed* to the root *(walk, walked; pare, pared)*. We change the spelling of irregular verbs in some other way to form the past tense *(see, saw; steal, stole).*

> A lexicographer shows the past tense of irregular verbs.

• **send** /send/ *v.* **1.** Cause to go or come. **2.** Drive; throw: *send a ball; send clouds of smoke into the air.* → **sent, sending.**

Write a complete dictionary entry for the verb *sell*. Show the form for the past tense and the *ing* form. When you have finished, compare your work with the Spelling Dictionary.

A Word from the Dutch

An old Dutch compound word was *jachtschiff*. *Jacht* meant "hunt," and *schiff* meant "ship." A jachtschiff was a hunting ship, or one that hunted enemies. The Dutch pronounced the first sound in the word *jacht* as the first sound in *yes* is pronounced, and so we spell the word *yacht*. Since English speakers have a hard time saying the Dutch sound that *ch* is used for in that language, we skip that sound and pronounce the word /yot/. A yacht is now a ship used for pleasure or racing.

For each sound-spelling below, write a word that has one or more silent consonants.

a /yot/   **b** /yōk/   **c** /bou/

37

 Answers

1 (See Teaching Suggestions.)
2 (See the entry for *sell* in the Spelling Dictionary as a model answer.)

A Word from the Dutch
a yacht
b yolk
c bough

Mastery Test
For complete directions and an explanation of the testing program, see the Introduction to this Teacher's Edition.

---

0 They /āt/ all the /kup′ kāks′/ and pan′ kāks′/ they could /sē/.   They *ate* all the *cupcakes* and *pancakes* they could *see*.

Mastery Test 9b
1 /bėrth/ *berth, birth*
2 /kôrd/ *chord, cord*
3 /fôr/ *fore, four, for*
4 /yōk/ *yoke, yolk*
5 /sent/ *cent, scent, sent*
6 We tried /tü/ find /pēs/ /hir/ on this /īl/ n the /sē/.   We tried *to* find *peace here* on

this *isle* in the *sea*.
   7 /āt/ /grōn′ ups′/ went down the church /īl/ /tü/ /prā/.   *Eight grownups* went down the church *aisle to pray*.
   8 A /pār/ of /duvz/ flew /tü/ the /bou/ of the tree.   A *pair* of *doves* flew *to* the *bough* of the tree.
   9 Did you /hir/ the /wird/ /shrēk/ from the /wüdz/?   Did you *hear* the *weird shriek* from the *woods*?
10 Let's /shuv/ the /trôf/ into the /bärn′ yärd′/.   Let's *shove* the *trough* into the *barnyard*.

- **Answers**

1a clumsy, weary, greasy, husky

b turkey, honey

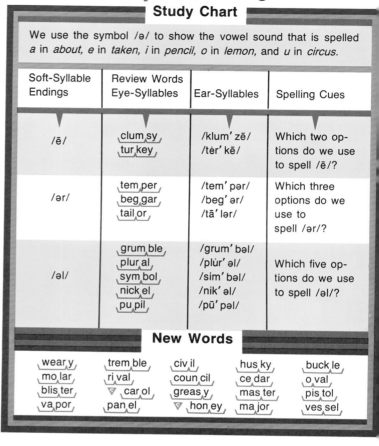

Study Chart

We use the symbol /ə/ to show the vowel sound that is spelled *a* in *about,* *e* in *taken,* *i* in *pencil,* *o* in *lemon,* and *u* in *circus.*

Soft-Syllable Endings	Review Words Eye-Syllables	Ear-Syllables	Spelling Cues
/ē/	clum sy tur key	/klum′ zē/ /tėr′ kē/	Which two options do we use to spell /ē/?
/ər/	tem per beg gar tail or	/tem′ pər/ /beg′ ər/ /tā′ lər/	Which three options do we use to spell /ər/?
/əl/	grum ble plur al sym bol nick el pu pil	/grum′ bəl/ /plur′ əl/ /sim′ bəl/ /nik′ əl/ /pū′ pəl/	Which five options do we use to spell /əl/?

New Words

wear y	trem ble	civ il	hus ky	buck le
mo lar	ri val	coun cil	ce dar	o val
blis ter	▽ car ol	greas y	mas ter	pis tol
va por	pan el	▽ hon ey	ma jor	ves sel

1 We can spell the soft-syllable /ē/ ending with *y* or *ey.*
a Write the four new and review words in which *y* spells /ē/.
b Write the two new and review words in which *ey* spells /ē/.

38

Teaching Suggestions

This unit focuses attention on the three common unstressed-syllable endings that occur in thousands of English words: /ē/, /ər/, and /əl/. The soft-syllable /ē/ ending is usually spelled *y* or *ey.* The soft-syllable /ər/ ending is usually spelled *er, ar,* or *or.* The soft-syllable /əl/ ending is spelled *le, al, ol, el,* or *il.*

Use the Study Chart to introduce the three soft-syllable endings. The questions in the last column will help pupils to understand that there are several spelling options for each ending. You may also use the Study Chart to introduce

or review the concept of the schwa sound, its symbol (/ə/), and its various spellings. As indicated, /ə/ can be spelled with *a, e, i, o,* and *u.* Many spelling problems exist because of this blurred vowel sound that is heard in so many unstressed syllables.

Some lexicographers have a tendency to omit the schwa symbol and to show only consonant symbols in certain syllables. Thus, you might find *cotton* shown as /kot′ n/ in some dictionaries and /kot′ ən/ in others. We show the schwa sound in all unstressed syllables.

Handwriting Models

weary   tremble   civil   husky   buckle
molar   rival   council   cedar   oval
blister   ▽ carol   greasy   master   pistol
vapor   panel   ▽ honey   major   vessel

2 We can spell the soft-syllable /ər/ ending with *er, ar,* or *or.*

a Write the three words in which *er* spells /ər/.

b Write the three words in which *ar* spells /ər/.

c Write the three words in which *or* spells /ər/.

3 We can spell the soft-syllable /əl/ ending with *le, al, el, il,* or *ol.*

a Write the three words in which *le* spells /əl/.

b Write the three words in which *al* spells /əl/.

c Write the three words in which *el* spells /əl/.

d Write the three words in which *il* spells /əl/.

e Write the three words in which *ol* spells /əl/.

4 Write the eye-syllables of the review words in which you hear the vowel sounds shown below. The numerals in parentheses show how many eye-syllables to write for each sound.

a /u/ (2)   **c** /i/ (2)   **e** /ū/ (1)
b /ů/ (1)   **d** /e/ (2)   **f** /ā/ (1)

1 Write the new words for these sound-spellings.

a /koun′ səl/   **e** /ō′ vəl/   **i** /pan′ əl/
b /hun′ ē/   **f** /ves′ əl/   **j** /trem′ bəl/
c /mas′ tər/   **g** /blis′ tər/   **k** /buk′ əl/
d /pis′ təl/   **h** /sē′ dər/   **l** /mō′ lər/

2 When we write the *er* and *est* forms of adjectives that end in *y*, we change the final *y* to *i* and add the ending. Write the *er* and *est* forms of *weary, greasy,* and *husky.*

39

2a temper, blister, master
b beggar, molar, cedar
c tailor, vapor, major
3a grumble, tremble, buckle
b plural, rival, oval
c nickel, panel, vessel
d pupil, civil, council
e symbol, carol, pistol
4a clum, grum
b plur
c sym, nick
d tem, beg
e pu
f tail

●● **Answers**

1a council   **g** blister
b honey   **h** cedar
c master   **i** panel
d pistol   **j** tremble
e oval   **k** buckle
f vessel   **l** molar
2 wearier, weariest, greasier, greasiest, huskier, huskiest

The exercises in this section, as usual, serve as a written reinforcement of the concepts developed through the Study Chart.

●● Note the structural generalizations in Exercises 2 and 3.

●● The Read and Spell list is again specifically diagnostic.

●● The correct proofreading exercise, with corrected errors underscored, is as follows:

Nickel is a hard metal that looks like silver and is something like iron. It is a useful metal that is easy to <u>shine</u> and does not rust. It can be made into thin <u>sheets</u> or stretched into long wires. A pound of pure nickel can make a wire 80 miles long.

Nickel has been mixed with copper for the coin we call a nickel in the <u>United States</u> and <u>Canada</u>.

For the suggested end-of-the-unit test that follows, note that all the words are in sound-spelling. This is the recommended format.

3 rivaling, caroling, paneling

4 greasy, carol, vapor, civil

5 rival, major, husky, weary

6 civil, council, cedar, carol, council, buckle

 Answers

2a collar   **d** suitor
 b easel   **e** pickle
 c traitor   **f** vocal

3 pedaling, yodeling, stenciling

4 gulleys, donkeys, mercies

3 When /əl/-ending words end with *one* vowel letter and *or* consonant letter, we do not double the final consonant lett before we add the *ing* ending. Write the *ing* forms of *riva carol,* and *panel*.

4 Write synonyms from the list of new words for *oily, son steam,* and *polite*.

5 Write antonyms from the list of new words for *helper, mind tiny,* and *fresh*.

6 Write three new words in which *c* spells /s/, two new word in which *c* spells /k/, and a new word in which *ck* spells /k*

Read and Spell

gully	peril	coastal	scribble	parsley
yodel	pickle	suitor	tutor	idol
traitor	freezer	alcohol	pedal	lumber
barley	stencil	humble	poplar	mercy
easel	shower	donkey	anvil	parasol
collar	gaudy	weasel	vocal	vulgar

1 Write any Read and Spell word that you cannot read any word for which you do not know the meaning.

2 Write the Read and Spell words for these sound-spellings
a /kol′ ər/   **c** /trā′ tər/   **e** /pik′ əl/
b /ē′ səl/   **d** /sü′ tər/   **f** /vō′ kəl/

3 Write the *ing* forms of the words /ped′ əl/, /yō′ dəl/, an /sten′ səl/.

4 Write the plural forms of the nouns /gul′ ē/, /dong′ kē/ and /mer′ sē/.

 1 Tina wrote a report for her science class. Proofread he report. You should find five mistakes. After you have found th mistakes, write the report correctly.

40

Mastery Test 10a

1 /grē′ sē/ *greasy*

2 /ter′ kē/ *turkey*

3 /mō′ lər/ *molar*

4 /tem′ pər/ *temper*

5 /vā′ pər/ *vapor*

6 /hus′ kē/ *husky*

7 /pū′ pəl/ *pupil*

8 /mas′ tər/ *master*

9 /swet/ *sweat*

10 /sēj/ *siege*

11 /bãrz/ /got/ /ᵮʜə/ /sent/ /uv/ /hun′ ē/ /frum/ /ᵮʜat/ /trē/   *Bears got the scent of honey from that tree.*

12 /sum/ /sē′ dər/ /trēz/ /är/ /grōn/ /fôr/ /lum′ bər/   *Some cedar trees are grown for lumber.*

13 /ᵮʜə/ /klum′ zē/ /fôr′ man′/ /got/ /ə/ /blis′ tər/ /ôn/ /hiz/ /thum/   *The clumsy foreman got a blister on his thumb.*

14 /ᵮʜis/ /shü/ /buk′ əl/ /haz/ /ə/ /kwir/ /ō′ vəl/ /shāp/   *This shoe buckle has a queer oval shape.*

15 /ᵮʜə/ /tā′ lər/ /sent/ /us/ /ᵮʜis/ /pēs/ /uv/ /red/ /wül/ /fôr/ /ə/ /süt/   *The tailor sent us this piece of red wool for a suit.*

Mastery Test 10b

1 /grum′ bəl/ *grumble*

2 /trem′ bəl/ *tremble*

Nickel is a hard metal that looks like silver and is something like iron. It is a useful metal that is easy to skin and does not rust. It can be made into thin sheets or stretched into long wires. A pound of pure nickel can make a wire 80 miles long.

Nickel has been mixed with copper for the coin we call a nickel in the united states and canada.

2 We drop the final *e* in verbs that end with *le* before adding an *ed* or *ing*.

> A lexicographer shows the *ed* and *ing* forms of *le*-ending verbs.

- **tremble** /trem′ bəl/ *v.* **1.** Shake because of fear, cold, weakness, etc.: *Her hands trembled.* **2.** Move gently: *The leaves trembled.* **trembled, trembling.** ◄

Write a complete dictionary entry for the word *buckle.* Show the word as a noun and as a verb. Show the *ed* and *ing* forms after the verb definition. When you have finished, compare your work with the entry in the Spelling Dictionary.

Two Words from the Australians

When explorers first saw the strange leaping animals in Australia, they had no name for them. They took the native name *kangaroo* and gave it the spelling we now use. A related word from Australia is *wallaby,* the name of the smaller, brightly colored kangaroo.

Write only the sentence below that is true. Spell the words correctly. You may use the Spelling Dictionary for help.

a /ə/ /kang′ gə rü′/ /haz/ /smôl/ /hīnd/ /legz/.
b /ə/ /kang′ gə rü′/ /haz/ /strông/ /fôr′ legz′/.
c /ə/ /kang′ gə rü′/ /haz/ /strông/ /hīnd/ /legz/.

41

●● **Answers**
1 (See Teaching Suggestions.)
2 (See the entry for *buckle* in the Spelling Dictionary as a model answer.)

Two Words from the Australians
c A kangaroo has strong hind legs.

Mastery Test
For complete directions and an explanation of the testing program, see the Introduction to this Teacher's Edition.

3 /plür′ əl/ *plural*
4 /rī′ vəl/ *rival*
5 /sim′ bəl/ *symbol*
6 /pis′ təl/ *pistol*
7 /pan′ əl/ *panel*
8 /siv′ əl/ *civil*
9 /skwosh/ *squash*
0 /tōl/ *toll*
1 /ə/ /skül′ boi′/ /gāv/ /ᴛнə/ /pùr/ /beg′ ər/ /tü/ /nik′ əlz/   *A schoolboy gave the poor beggar two nickels.*
2 /wir′ ē/ /sā′ lərz/ /rōd/ /ᴛнār/ /ves′ əl/ /frum/ /ᴛнə/ /mān′ land′/ /with/ /ᴛнēz/ /ôrz/   *Weary sailors rowed their vessel from the mainland with these oars.*
13 /its/ /wel/ /nōn/ /ᴛнat/ /wē/ /sing/ /kar′ əlz/ /at/ /ül′ tīd′/   *It's well known that we sing carols at yuletide.*
14 /ᴛнə/ /toun/ /koun′ səl/ /plejd/ /tü/ /rē pār′/ /ôl/ /mā′ jər/ /strēts/   *The town council pledged to repair all major streets.*
15 /mom/ /pùt/ /āt/ /eg/ /yōks/ /in/ /ᴛнə/ /kup′ kāk′/ /dō/   *Mom put eight egg yolks in the cupcake dough.*

11   VCCV and VCCCV Patterns

Study Chart

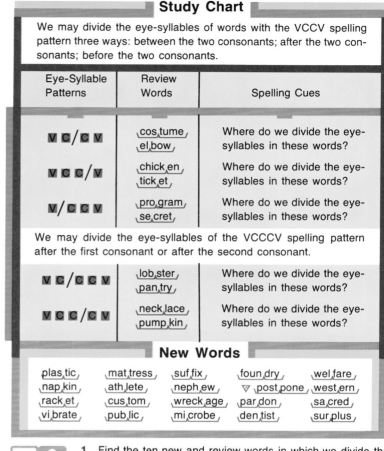

We may divide the eye-syllables of words with the VCCV spelling pattern three ways: between the two consonants; after the two consonants; before the two consonants.

Eye-Syllable Patterns	Review Words	Spelling Cues
V C / C V	cos,tume, el,bow,	Where do we divide the eye-syllables in these words?
V C C / V	chick,en, tick,et,	Where do we divide the eye-syllables in these words?
V / C C V	pro,gram, se,cret,	Where do we divide the eye-syllables in these words?

We may divide the eye-syllables of the VCCCV spelling pattern after the first consonant or after the second consonant.

V C / C C V	lob,ster, pan,try,	Where do we divide the eye-syllables in these words?
V C C / C V	neck,lace, pump,kin,	Where do we divide the eye-syllables in these words?

New Words

plas,tic,	mat,tress,	suf,fix,	foun,dry,	wel,fare,
nap,kin,	ath,lete,	neph,ew,	▽ post,pone,	west,ern,
rack,et,	cus,tom,	wreck,age,	par,don,	sa,cred,
vi,brate,	pub,lic,	mi,crobe,	den,tist,	sur,plus,

1 Find the ten new and review words in which we divide the eye-syllables VC/CV. For each word, write the eye-syllables as if they were little words. Then write the whole word.

42

Teaching Suggestions

This unit deals with the VCCV and VCCCV spelling patterns. In earlier levels of this series we have alerted pupils to these patterns. In so doing, we have attempted to keep the points of syllabication flexible. For example, the majority of words in which the VCCV pattern occurs can most sensibly be divided between the two consonants. Pupils should try that division first. If the VC/CV division does not work, they can try VCC/V and V/CCV.

If pupils learn to syllabicate multisyllabic words, they will not find it necessary to memorize long spelling sequences. Syllabication allows pupils to separate multisyllabic words into parts visually and to deal with the parts as if they were monosyllabic words. When one uses the eye-syllables of *necklace* and thinks /nek/ and /lās/, the spelling becomes much easier to remember.

Use the Study Chart to remind pupils that long words are easier to spell when they are spelled by syllables. When equal stress is placed on all syllables, the four basic sound-symbol relationships can be applied.

Handwriting Models

plastic mattress suffix   foundry   welfare
napkin athlete   nephew ▽ postpone western
racket custom   wreckage pardon   sacred
vibrate public   microbe   dentist   surplus

2 Find the six new and review words in which we divide the eye-syllables VCC/V. For each word, write the eye-syllables. Then write the whole word.

3 Find the five new and review words in which we divide the eye-syllables V/CCV. For each word, write the eye-syllables. Then write the whole word.

4 Find the five new and review words in which we divide the eye-syllables VC/CCV. For each word, write the eye-syllables. Then write the whole word.

5 Find the four new and review words in which we divide the eye-syllables VCC/CV. For each word, write the eye-syllables. Then write the whole word.

1 Write the new and review words for the sound-spellings /kus′ təm/, /nap′ kin/, and /ath′ lēt/.

2 Write these sentences.
a /den′ tists/ /māk/ /plas′ tic/ /tēth/.
b /mī/ /nef′ ū/ /brōk/ /hiz/ /rak′ ət/.
c /wē/ /found/ /our/ /mat′ rəs/ /in/ /ᴛʜat/ /rek′ ij/.

3 Write the plural forms of the nouns *pantry, foundry,* and *suffix*.

4 From the list of new words, write two in which you hear /ī/ in the loud syllable, one in which you hear /ā/ in the loud syllable, and one in which you hear /ėr/ in the loud syllable.

43

2 chick en chicken
  tick et ticket
  rack et racket
  neph ew nephew
  wreck age wreckage
  west ern western
3 pro gram program
  se cret secret
  vi brate vibrate
  mi crobe microbe
  sa cred sacred
4 lob ster lobster
  pan try pantry
  mat tress mattress
  foun dry foundry
  sur plus surplus
5 neck lace necklace
  pump kin pumpkin
  ath lete athlete
  post pone postpone

●● **Answers**
1 custom, napkin, athlete
2a Dentists make plastic teeth.
 b My nephew broke his racket.
 c We found our mattress in that wreckage.
3 pantries, foundries, suffixes
4 /ī/ vibrate, microbe
  /ā/ sacred
  /ėr/ surplus

● The exercises in this section are designed to cause pupils to make use of the eye-syllables.

●● Note the structural generalizations that are reviewed in Exercise 3 of this section.

●
●● The Read and Spell list offers pupils an opportunity to apply syllabication techniques in sounding out the words.
  For Exercise 3, be sure pupils understand that eye-syllables are simply a visual grouping of letters into manageable word parts.

●●
●● The correct proofreading exercise is:
  1. A suffix is added to the beginning of a word. false
  2. A synonym for <u>racket</u> *is* noise. *true*
  3. Vibrate means "to <u>tremble</u>." *true*
  4. Pardon means "to forgive." true
  5. An uncle may have nephews and <u>nieces</u>. *true*
  6. An antonym for public *is* private. *true*
  Some words from the Irish, in addition to *shamrock,* that pupils might learn about are *colleen, leprechaun, limerick,* and *shillelagh.*

Answers

2 ant/lers, trum/pet, lock/et,
em/blem, a/pron,
sand/wich

3 short age, muf fin,
east ern

4 canvas, nugget, advance,
rascal, muffin, banjo,
piston, trumpet, common,
victim

Read and Spell

canvas	antlers	district	empty	eclipse
empress	muffin	banjo	puncture	sandwich
nugget	monster	improve	emblem	employ
bucket	bushel	degree	eastern	common
advance	shortage	locket	piston	package
rascal	apron	hyphen	trumpet	victim

1 We divide the eye-syllables of the Read and Spell words in the same five patterns you see in the Study Chart. Write any Read and Spell word that you cannot read or any word for which you do not know the meaning.

2 Write a Read and Spell word for each picture. Draw a line between the eye-syllables of each word.

3 Write the eye-syllables of the Read and Spell words /shôr′ tij/, /muf′ ən/, and /ē′ stərn/.

4 Write the ten Read and Spell words in which we divide the eye-syllables VC/CV.

1 Henry wrote these sentences for a true-false test. Proof-read his work. You should find three spelling mistakes. After you have found the mistakes, write the sentences correctly. Also, mark each sentence *true* or *false*.

44

Mastery Test 11a

1 /kos′ tüm/ *costume*
2 /suf′ iks/ *suffix*
3 /pärd′ ən/ *pardon*
4 /el′ bō/ *elbow*
5 /den′ tist/ *dentist*
6 /lob′ stər/ *lobster*
7 /mat′ rəs/ *mattress*
8 /wir′ ē/ *weary*
9 /rak′ ət/ *racket*
10 /pan′ əl/ *panel*

11 /its/ /ŦHə/ /kus′ təm/ /tü/ /hav/ /nap′ kinz/ /hwen/ /ū/ /dīn/   *It's the custom to have napkins when you dine.*

12 /ī/ /gāv/ /mī/ /nēs/ /ə/ /nek′ ləs/ /mād/ /uv/ /plas′ tik/ /bēdz/   *I gave my niece a necklace made of plastic beads.*

13 /wē/ /thôt/ /wē/ /kùd/ /pōst′ pōn′/ /our/ /prō′ gram/ /fôr/ /an/ /our/   *We thought we could postpone our program for an hour.*

14 /ŦHə/ /ves′ əl/ /sāld/ /past/ /ŦHə/ /rek′ ij/ /uv/ /tü/ /ships/ *The vessel sailed past the wreckage of two ships.*

15 /much/ /frāt/ /iz/ /hōld/ /hir/ /at/ /ŦHis/ /sē′ pôrt′/   *Much freight is hauled here at this seaport.*

Mastery Test 11b

1 /wel′ fãr′/ *welfare*
2 /chik′ ən/ *chicken*
3 /vī′ brāt/ *vibrate*
4 /mī′ krōb/ *microbe*

44

> *1. A suffix is added to the beginning of a word.*
> *2. A synonym for <u>rackit</u> is <u>noise</u>.*
> *3. <u>Vibrate</u> means "to <u>trembel</u>."*
> *4. <u>Pardon</u> means "to <u>forgive</u>."*
> *5. An uncle may have <u>nephews</u> and <u>neices</u>.*
> *6. An antonym for <u>public</u> is <u>private</u>.*

 2 Some plural forms have a special meaning of their own. Read the dictionary entry below for the word *common*.

A lexicographer shows the plural form of an entry word when the plural has a special meaning.	• **common** /kom′ ən/ *adj.* **1.** Belonging equally to each or all of a group: *The house was the common property of the three brothers.* **2.** Often met with; usual; familiar: *Snow is common in cold countries.* **commons** *n. pl.* A dining hall or building where food is served to a large group at common tables.

Write a complete dictionary entry for the word *custom*. Show one or more special meanings of the plural form. You may use the Spelling Dictionary for help. When you have finished, check your work with the Spelling Dictionary.

A Word from the Irish

A shamrock is a three-leaved plant that looks like clover. The green shamrock is the symbol, or emblem, of Ireland. We got the word *shamrock* from the Irish word *seamrog,* which means "having three leaves." The shamrock is proudly worn by Irishmen all over the world on St. Patrick's Day, March 17.

Write the two-syllable word from the story above that has the VCCCV spelling pattern.

45

●● **Answers**
1 (See Teaching Suggestions.)
2 (See the entry for *custom* in the Spelling Dictionary as a model answer.)

A Word from the Irish
emblem

Mastery Test
For complete directions and an explanation of the testing program, see the Introduction to this Teacher's Edition.

5 /sē′ krət/ *secret*
6 /pīnt/ *pint*
7 /pump′ kin/ *pumpkin*
8 /sē′ dər/ *cedar*
9 /ath′ lēt/ *athlete*
10 /buk′ əl/ *buckle*
11 /ᴛHār/ /iz/ /sėr′ pləs/ /füd/ /in/ /ᴛHār/ /pan′ trē/ *There is surplus food in their pantry.*
12 /ᴛHə/ /krôs/ /iz/ /ə/ /sā′ krəd/ /sim′ bəl/ /in/ /sum/ /chėr′ chəz/ *The cross is a sacred symbol in some churches.*
13 /ᴛHə/ /foun′ drē/ /wuz/ /bilt/ /in/ /ᴛHə/ /wes′ tərn/ /pärt/ /uv/ /toun/ *The foundry was built in the western part of town.*
14 /mī/ /yung/ /nef′ ū/ /iz/ /ə/ /pū′ pəl/ /in/ /ᴛHə/ /nīnth/ /grād/ *My young nephew is a pupil in the ninth grade.*
15 /tik′ əts/ /fôr/ /ᴛHə/ /sôft′ bôl′/ /gām/ /är/ /ôn/ /sāl/ /tü/ /ᴛHə/ /pub′ lik/ *Tickets for the softball game are on sale to the public.*

● **Answers**
1 slo/gan, do/nate, o/mit,
   stu/pid, so/da, vi/rus,
   pho/to, tu/na, a/gent,
   u/nite

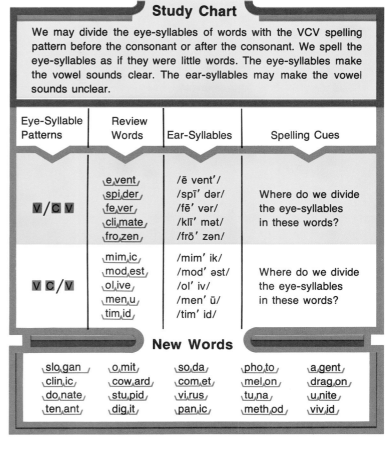

12 VCV Patterns

Study Chart

We may divide the eye-syllables of words with the VCV spelling pattern before the consonant or after the consonant. We spell the eye-syllables as if they were little words. The eye-syllables make the vowel sounds clear. The ear-syllables may make the vowel sounds unclear.

Eye-Syllable Patterns	Review Words	Ear-Syllables	Spelling Cues
V/C V	e‿vent‿ spi‿der‿ fe‿ver‿ cli‿mate‿ fro‿zen‿	/ē vent'/ /spī' dər/ /fē' vər/ /klī' mət/ /frō' zən/	Where do we divide the eye-syllables in these words?
V C/V	mim‿ic‿ mod‿est‿ ol‿ive‿ men‿u‿ tim‿id‿	/mim' ik/ /mod' əst/ /ol' iv/ /men' ū/ /tim' id/	Where do we divide the eye-syllables in these words?

New Words

slo‿gan‿	o‿mit‿	so‿da‿	pho‿to‿	a‿gent‿
clin‿ic‿	cow‿ard‿	com‿et‿	mel‿on‿	drag‿on‿
do‿nate‿	stu‿pid‿	vi‿rus‿	tu‿na‿	u‿nite‿
ten‿ant‿	dig‿it‿	pan‿ic‿	meth‿od‿	viv‿id‿

 1 Write the ten new words in which we divide the eye-syllables *before* the consonant letter (V/CV). Draw a line between the eye-syllables of each word.

46

Teaching Suggestions

This unit deals with the VCV spelling pattern, and the words illustrate both the V/CV and VC/V syllabic divisions. The V/CV division ends with a vowel letter which regularly spells a long vowel sound. The VC/V division indicates that the first vowel letter is in an initial or medial position and, therefore, regularly spells a short vowel sound. The former of these two divisions occurs somewhat more frequently than does the latter. Pupils have been alerted in earlier levels of this series to try first the V/CV separation and then the VC/V.

Use the Study Chart to introduce pupils to this unit of two-syllable words. A discussion of the questions in the last column will assist pupils to understand the syllabication of the V/CV and VC/V words. The Study Chart may also be used to illustrate that the spelling of words by eye-syllables causes stress to be placed on the soft syllables and, thus, provides cues for the vowel spellings.

● The exercises in this section offer a written reinforcement of the Study Chart.

Handwriting Models

slogan   omit   soda   photo   agent
clinic   coward   comet   melon   dragon
donate   stupid   virus   tuna   unite
tenant   digit   panic   method   vivid

2 Write the new words for the sound-spellings /dij' it/, /meth' əd/, /kou' ərd/, and /vī' rəs/.

3 Write the ten new words in which we divide the eye-syllables *after* the consonant letter (VC/V). Draw a line between the eye-syllables of each word.

4 Write both eye-syllables of the review words in which you hear these vowel sounds in the loud syllable. (The numerals in parentheses show how many words have the vowel sound.)

a /e/ (2)   **c** /i/ (2)   **e** /ō/ (1)
b /o/ (2)   **d** /ī/ (2)   **f** /ē/ (1)

1 Some words, like *panic,* may be used both as nouns and as verbs. For verbs that end with *ic,* like *panic,* we add a *k* before the *ed* and *ing* when writing those forms. Write the *ed* and *ing* forms of *panic* and *mimic.*

2 Find three other verbs in the list of new words. Write the *ing* form of each verb.

3 Write a noun from the list of new words for each of these clues.

a a motto   **d** one who acts   **g** a germ
b a numeral   for you   **h** a picture
c a snakelike   **e** a renter   **i** a place for
   monster   **f** a fish   medical aid

4 Write the new and review words for the sound-spellings /frō' zən/, /mod' əst/, and /viv' id/.

47

---

2 digit, method, coward, virus

3 clin/ic, ten/ant, cow/ard, dig/it, com/et, pan/ic, mel/on, meth/od, drag/on, viv/id

4a e vent, men u
b mod est, ol ive
c mim ic, tim id
d spi der, cli mate
e fro zen
f fe ver

●● **Answers**

1 panicked, panicking, mimicked, mimicking

2 donating, omitting, uniting

3a slogan   **f** tuna
b digit   **g** virus
c dragon   **h** photo
d agent   **i** clinic
e tenant

4 frozen, modest, vivid

●● Note the structural generalization taught in Exercise 1.

●
●● The Read and Spell list is again a useful check on the ability of pupils to use syllabic divisions to simplify decoding. Some of this vocabulary may pose meaning problems.

●● For this proofreading exercise, pupils are given no clues as to the kind or number of errors to be found. This procedure will be used for most of the remainder of this text.

The correct proofreading exercise, with corrected errors underscored, is as follows:

A star that has a tail may not be a star at all. It may be a ball of gas and rocks called a comet. A comet <u>whizzes</u> toward the sun from outer space. It <u>whirls</u> around the sun in a long <u>oval</u>.

Some people say that a comet's <u>tail</u> looks like long, flowing hair. <u>It</u> is really gas and bits of the comet's head that have broken off.

The dictionary exercise is very important and should be supplemented for many pupils.

2a te/pee **d** si/lo
 b ca/boose **e** so/fa
 c bea/con **f** rob/in
3 rigid, talent, comic, vacant, legend, basic
4a A critic is not always polite.
 b Put my china in her closet.
 c A poor widow won that award.

Read and Spell

polite	rigid	sofa	china	wagon
beacon	chorus	talent	vacant	critic
award	lilac	seven	tepee	widow
legend	human	civic	arouse	robin
closet	basic	deepen	item	caboose
madam	cocoon	comic	credit	silo

1 The Read and Spell words all have the VCV spelling pattern. Write any Read and Spell word that you cannot read or any word for which you do not know the meaning.

2 Write a Read and Spell word for each picture. Draw a line between the eye-syllables of each word.

3 Write synonyms from the Read and Spell list for *stiff, skill, funny, empty, story,* and *important.*

4 Write these sentences. Spell all the words correctly.
a /ə/ /krit′ ik/ /iz/ /not/ /ôl′ wiz/ /pə līt′/.
b /pùt/ /mī/ /chī′ nə/ /in/ /hèr/ /kloz′ ət/.
c /ə/ /pùr/ /wid′ ō/ /wun/ /ᵺat/ /ə wärd′/.

1 Susan wrote this report for her science notebook. Proofread her work. After you have found the mistakes, write the report correctly.

48

Mastery Test 12a
 1 /ē vent′/ *event*
 2 /slō′ gən/ *slogan*
 3 /sō′ də/ *soda*
 4 /meth′ əd/ *method*
 5 /spī′ dər/ *spider*
 6 /ū nīt′/ *unite*
 7 /plas′ tik/ *plastic*
 8 /mod′ əst/ *modest*
 9 /ten′ ənt/ *tenant*
 10 /rī′ vəl/ *rival*
11 /ol′ ivz/ /grō/ /in/ /ə/ /wärm/ /klī′ mət/
Olives grow in a warm climate.
12 /ə/ /slīs/ /uv/ /mel′ ən/ /iz/ /ôn/ /our/ /men′ ū/ /fôr/ /lunch/ *A slice of melon is on our menu for lunch.*
13 /hav/ /ū/ /hèrd/ /ᵺə/ /wird/ /tāl/ /uv/ /ᵺə/ /drag′ ən/ /hü/ /wuz/ /ə/ /kou′ ərd/

Have you heard the weird tale of the dragon who was a coward?
14 /wē/ /nü/ /wē/ /kùd/ /foil/ /ᵺə/ /planz/ /uv/ /ᵺə/ /stü′ pid/ /thēf/ *We knew we could foil the plans of the stupid thief.*
15 /ᵺə/ /toun/ /koun′ səl/ /met/ /ᵺə/ /ath′ lēts/ /hü/ /wun/ /ᵺə/ /gām/ *The town council met the athletes who won the game.*

Mastery Test 12b
 1 /frō′ zən/ *frozen*
 2 /mim′ ik/ *mimic*
 3 /pōst′ pōn′/ *postpone*
 4 /dij′ it/ *digit*

A star that has a tail may not be a star at all. It may be a ball of gas and rocks called a comet. A comet whizes toward the sun from outer space. It wherls around the sun in a long ovel.

Some people say that a comet's tale looks like long, flowing hair it is really gas and bits of the comet's head that have broken off.

2 We double the final consonant before adding *ed* and *ing* when a one-syllable word ends in one vowel followed by one consonant: *whiz, whizzed, whizzing.*

We double the final consonant before adding *ed* and *ing* when a two-syllable word has the accent on the second ear-syllable and ends in one vowel followed by one consonant: *admit, admitted, admitting.*

- **admit** /ad mit′/ *v.* **1.** Say something is real or true: *admit making a mistake.* **2.** Allow to enter: *Do not admit strangers.* **admitted, admitting.** ◄———

A lexicographer shows the *ed* and *ing* forms of verbs when the final consonant is doubled.

Write a complete dictionary entry for the word *omit.* Show the *ed* and *ing* forms of the verb. Compare your work with the entry in the Spelling Dictionary.

A Word from the Hawaiians

Aloha! That word is pronounced /ə lō′ ə/ or /ä lō′ hä/. *Aloha* is the well-known greeting given by Hawaiians to the visitors to their beautiful islands. *Aloha* means "love" in Hawaiian, but it is also used to mean "hello" or "good-bye."

Write the plural forms of *soda, tuna, tepee, menu, aloha,* and *photo.*

49

---

5 /fō′ tō/ *photo*
6 /ō mit′/ *omit*
7 /kus′ təm/ *custom*
8 /pan′ ik/ *panic*
9 /nef′ ū/ *nephew*
10 /tim′ id/ *timid*
11 /hėr/ /fē′ vər/ /wuz/ /kôzd/ /bī/ /ə/ /vī′ rəs/ *Her fever was caused by a virus.*
12 /ə/ /kom′ əts/ /tāl/ /māks/ /ə/ /viv′ id/ /path/ /in/ /ŦHə/ /skī/ *A comet's tail makes a vivid path in the sky.*
13 /ŦHat/ /tī′ nē/ /fish/ /iz/ /ŦHə/ /trād′ märk′/ /uv/ /wun/ /brand/ /uv/ /kand/ /tü′ nə/ *That tiny fish is the trademark of one brand of canned tuna.*
14 /kash/ /ū/ /dō′ nāt/ /wil/ /help/ /tü/ /bild/ /ə/ /nü/ /klin′ ik/ *Cash you donate will help to build a new clinic.*
15 /it/ /tůk/ /an/ /our/ /fôr/ /ŦHə/ /ā′ jənt/ /tü/ /sel/ /tü/ /färm′ hou′ zəz/ *It took an hour for the agent to sell two farmhouses.*

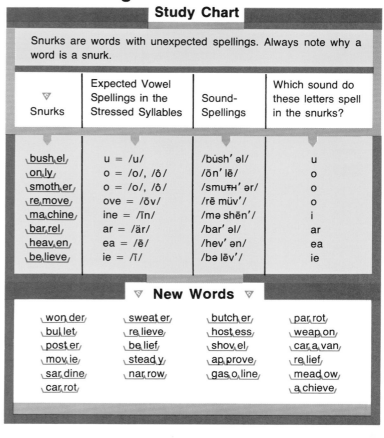

13 Longer Snurks

Study Chart

Snurks are words with unexpected spellings. Always note why a word is a snurk.

▽ Snurks	Expected Vowel Spellings in the Stressed Syllables	Sound-Spellings	Which sound do these letters spell in the snurks?
bush‚el	u = /u/	/bȯsh′ əl/	u
on‚ly	o = /o/, /ô/	/ōn′ lē/	o
smoth‚er	o = /o/, /ô/	/smuᴛʜ′ ər/	o
re‚move	ove = /ōv/	/rē müv′/	o
ma‚chine	ine = /īn/	/mə shēn′/	i
bar‚rel	ar = /är/	/bar′ əl/	ar
heav‚en	ea = /ē/	/hev′ ən/	ea
be‚lieve	ie = /ī/	/bə lēv′/	ie

▽ New Words ▽

won‚der	sweat‚er	butch‚er	par‚rot
bul‚let	re‚lieve	host‚ess	weap‚on
post‚er	be‚lief	shov‚el	car‚a‚van
mov‚ie	stead‚y	ap‚prove	re‚lief
sar‚dine	nar‚row	gas‚o‚line	mead‚ow
car‚rot			a‚chieve

1 The letter *u* usually spells /u/. Write the three new and review words in which *u* spells /ȯ/. Draw lines between the eye-syllables.

Teaching Suggestions

This unit presents a group of multisyllabic snurks in which the stressed syllables are irregularly spelled and are, therefore, likely to be the source of spelling errors.

Use the Study Chart as usual to introduce the unit. Pupils should observe that the expected spellings of the stressed vowel sounds are in the second column. The last column causes pupils to decide what sounds the vowel letters actually represent in the snurks. Thus, we expect the *u* in *bushel* to spell /u/, not /ȯ/. Conversely, we expect /ȯ/ to be spelled with

oo, not with *u*. The snurky spellings of the eight review words are generally repeated in the new words. Through a discussion, pupils should identify the reason why each of the new words is a snurk.

● The seven exercises in this section draw attention, one at a time, to the seven snurky elements presented in the second column of the Study Chart. As usual, this written work is a reinforcement of the understandings gained in the previous discussion of the Study Chart.

Handwriting Models

wonder   sweater   butcher   parrot
bullet   relieve   hostess   weapon
poster   belief   shovel   caravan
movie   steady   approve   relief
sardine   narrow   gasoline   meadow
carrot   achieve

2 The letter *o* usually spells /o/ or /ô/.

a Write the three words in which *o* spells /ō/. Draw lines between the eye-syllables.

b Write the three words in which *o* spells /u/. Draw lines between the eye-syllables.

3 We expect *ove* to spell /ōv/. Write the two words in which *ove* spells /üv/. Draw lines between the eye-syllables.

4 We expect *ine* to spell /īn/. Write the three words in which *ine* spells /ēn/. Draw lines between the eye-syllables.

5 We expect *ar* to spell /är/. Write the five words in which *ar* spells /ar/. Draw lines between the eye-syllables.

6 We expect *ea* to spell /ē/. Write the five words in which *ea* spells /e/. Draw lines between the eye-syllables.

7 We expect *ie* to spell /ī/. Write the six words in which *ie* spells /ē/. Draw lines between the eye-syllables.

1 Write words from the list of new words to complete the sentences below and on the next page.

a If he'd remove his ____, he'd get some ____.

51

2a on/ly, post/er, host/ess
  b smoth/er, won/der, shov/el
3 re/move, ap/prove
4 ma/chine, sar/dine, gas/o/line
5 bar/rel, car/rot, nar/row, par/rot, car/a/van
6 heav/en, sweat/er, stead/y, weap/on, mead/ow
7 be/lieve, mov/ie, re/lieve, be/lief, re/lief, a/chieve

●● **Answers**
1a sweater, relief

●● These exercises are routine and can be done independent of supervision.

●● The Read and Spell list consists of a group of snurks that have appeared in earlier levels of this series and in earlier units of this text. As the spellings are irregular, this group of words is a sight-word list. Those pupils who perform poorly on the oral decoding activity will undoubtedly benefit from additional practice in using these words. The two writing exercises should present no problems.

●● The correct proofreading exercise is:
I visited my aunt in England last year. One afternoon she said, "Would you enjoy a biscuit?"

"No, thank you," I <u>replied</u>.

"I thought you were hungry," my aunt said. "What <u>would</u> you like for a treat<u>?</u>"

"Those cookies look good. May I have one?"

My aunt laughed. "Cookies are called biscuits in <u>England</u>. Please have several biscuits, <u>dear</u>."

b hostess, sardines, shovel
c bullets, poster, weapon

2a parrot   **f** carrot
  b caravan   **g** butcher
  c narrow   **h** approve
  d meadow   **i** movie
  e steady

● ●
●● **Answers**

2a among   **f** sugar
  b busy   **g** worry
  c shoulder   **h** money
  d enough   **i** ocean
  e police
3 couple, pleasant, marry,
   during, dozen, earnest

b The ____ is serving ____ with a ____.

c He's shooting ____ at the ____ with his
   ____.

2 Write the new words for these sound-spellings.
a /par′ ət/   **d** /med′ ō/   **g** /bủch′ ər/
b /kar′ ə van/ **e** /sted′ ē/   **h** /ə prüv′/
c /nar′ ō/   **f** /kar′ ət/   **i** /mü′ vē/

Read and Spell

welcome	usual	beauty	reindeer	shoulder
busy	ocean	threaten	earnest	sugar
enough	double	early	dozen	instead
earthquake	business	money	garage	already
worry	among	pleasant	forehead	marry
couple	police	during	danger	neighbor

1 Write any Read and Spell word that you cannot read or
any word for which you do not know the meaning.

2 Write the Read and Spell words for these sound-spellings.
a /ə mung′/   **d** /ə nuf′/   **g** /wėr′ ē/
b /biz′ ē/   **e** /pə lēs′/   **h** /mun′ ē/
c /shōl′ dər/   **f** /shủg′ ər/ **i** /ō′ shən/

3 Write synonyms from the Read and Spell list for *pair, nice,
wed, while, twelve,* and *sincere.*

1 Chet wrote a short story about an experience he had on
a trip. Proofread his work. You should find five mistakes. After
you have found the mistakes, write the story correctly.

52

Mastery Test 13a

1 /smuᵵн′ ər/ *smother*   **6** /kom′ ət/ *comet*
2 /rē lēf′/ *relief*   **7** /yēld/ *yield*
3 /wep′ ən/ *weapon*   **8** /nar′ ō/ *narrow*
4 /mə shēn′/ *machine*   **9** /nīnth/ *ninth*
5 /ə prüv′/ *approve*   **10** /par′ ət/ *parrot*
11 /ī/ /wun′ dər/ /if/ /ᵵнə/ /bủch′ ər/ /wil/
/rē müv′/ /ᵵнə/ /fat/ /frum/ /ᵵнə/ /rōst/
*I wonder if the butcher will remove the fat
from the roast.*
12 /ī/ /bə lēv′/ /ᵵнat/ /hun′ ē/ /tāsts/ /gủd/
/ôn/ /mel′ ən/   *I believe that honey tastes
good on melon.*

13 /hē/ /brôt/ /ə/ /bủsh′ əl/ /uv/ /kar′ əts/
/tü/ /toun/ /tü/ /sel/ /last/ /wēk′ end′/   *He
brought a bushel of carrots to town to sell
last weekend.*
14 /ᵵнə/ /hōst/ /and/ /hō′ stəs/ /shōd/ /grāt/
/on′ ər/ /tü/ /ᵵнâr/ /viz′ ə tərz/   *The host and
hostess showed great honor to their visitors.*
15 /tāk/ /ᵵнə/ /bủl′ ət/ /frum/ /yủr/ /pis′ təl/
/tü/ /bē/ /sāf/   *Take the bullet from your
pistol to be safe.*

I visited my aunt in England last year. One afternoon she said, "Would you enjoy a biscuit?"

"No, thank you," I replyed.

"I thought you were hungry," my aunt said. "What wood you like for a treat."

"Those cookies look good. May I have one?"

My aunt laughed. "Cookies are called biscuits in england. Please have several biscuits, deer."

2 For words like *turkey* that end in a vowel letter and *y,* we do not change the *y* to *i* before adding *es* to form the plural.

For words like *foundry* that end in a consonant letter and *y,* we change the *y* to *i* before adding *es* to form the plural.

• **turkey** /tėr′ kē/ *n.* **1.** A large North American bird. **2.** Flesh of the turkey, used as food. *pl.* **turkeys.** ◄———

> A lexicographer shows the plural form of an entry word if we do not change final *y* to *i* before adding *es.*

Write a complete dictionary entry for the word *journey.* Show the plural form of the noun. When you have finished, compare your work with the entry in the Spelling Dictionary.

Two Words from the Scotch

The word *plaid* comes from the Scotch word *plaide.* A plaid is a rectangle of cloth worn over the left shoulder by men and women as part of the Scotch costume. This plaid has a striped design of different colors and widths that is called a *tartan.* We now call any such pattern of crossing stripes a *plaid.*

Write sound-spellings for *stripe, costume, plaid,* and *cloth.*

53

●● **Answers**
1 (See Teaching Suggestions.)
2 (See the entry for *journey* in the Spelling Dictionary as a model answer.)

Two Words from the Scotch
/strīp/, /kos′ tüm/, /plad/, /klôth/

Mastery Test
For complete directions and an explanation of the testing program, see the Introduction to this Teacher's Edition.

Mastery Test 13b

1 /mü′ vē/ *movie*
2 /gas′ ə lēn/ *gasoline*
3 /med′ ō/ *meadow*
4 /sär dēn′/ *sardine*
5 /rē lēv′/ *relieve*
6 /sted′ ē/ *steady*
7 /viv′ id/ *vivid*
8 /mel′ ən/ *melon*
9 /pō′ stər/ *poster*
10 /hev′ ən/ *heaven*
11 /ŦHə/ /jėr′ nē/ /uv/ /ŦHə/ /kar′ ə van/ /las′ təd/ /ōn′ lē/ /tü/ /wēks/ *The journey of the caravan lasted only two weeks.*
12 /ŦHə/ /pur/ /chīld/ /wuz/ /tü/ /wēk/ /tü/ /tāk/ /ôf/ /hiz/ /ōn/ /swet′ ər/ *The poor child was too weak to take off his own sweater.*
13 /its/ /mī/ /bə lēf′/ /ŦHat/ /fū/ /ath′ lēts/ /ə chēv′/ /welth/ *It's my belief that few athletes achieve wealth.*
14 /lets/ /shuv′ əl/ /ŦHə/ /trash/ /in′ tü′/ /ŦHis/ /bar′ əl/ *Let's shovel the trash into this barrel.*
15 /wùd/ /ū/ /līk/ /tü/ /kut/ /tü/ /kôrdz/ /uv/ /wùd/ /in/ /wun/ /dā/ *Would you like to cut two cords of wood in one day?*

● **Answers**

1 pre/dict, pre/fer, pre/view
2 re/turn, re/duce, re/fuse
3 dis/please, un/kind, dis/gust, un/able, dis/miss
4 pro/duce, pro/ceed, pro/claim

━━━━━ Study Chart ━━━━━

We spell prefixes and roots as if they were little words.

Prefixes	Eye-Syllables	Ear-Syllables	Spelling Cues
re (back, again)	re‚turn‚	/rē tėrn′/	
ex (out, from)	ex‚change‚	/eks chānj′/	
com con (together, with)	com‚plain‚ con‚vince‚	/kəm plān′/ /kən vins′/	How do we spell the prefixes and roots as little words in each of these words?
en (in, make)	en‚joy‚	/en joi′/	
in im (in, not)	in‚clude‚ im‚press‚	/in klüd′/ /im pres′/	
pre (before)	pre‚dict‚	/prē dikt′/	
pro (for, onward)	pro‚duce‚	/prō düs′/	
de (from, down)	de‚stroy‚	/dē stroi′/	
dis un (opposite, not)	dis‚please‚ un‚kind‚	/dis plēz′/ /un kīnd′/	

New Words

re‚duce‚	con‚dense‚	pre‚fer‚	un‚able‚	pre‚view‚
ex‚ert‚	en‚gage‚	pro‚ceed‚	re‚fuse‚	pro‚claim‚
com‚pose‚	in‚fect‚	de‚cay‚	ex‚tend‚	dis‚miss‚
	im‚port‚	dis‚gust‚	com‚merce‚	

1 Write the three new and review words with the prefix *pre.*

2 Write the three words that have the prefix *re.*

54

Teaching Suggestions

The twelve prefixes presented in this unit were first introduced in the Level 5 text. These prefixes are not serious spelling problems because they form convenient eye-syllables.

The more common meanings of the prefixes are included in the Study Chart. Effective use of the meanings is limited, however, because the prefixes are often affixed to Latin roots that have little meaning for pupils at this level. It is quite obvious in the word *return* that the *re* prefix means "back" and that it affects directly the meaning of the root. Similarly, the function of *dis* in *displease* and *un* in *unkind* is evident to pupils because the roots, *please* and *kind,* have meaning for them. On the other hand, Latin roots like *dict, duce, pose,* and *port* are not used as English words, and so the effect of the prefixes is hard for pupils to perceive.

Use the Study Chart to introduce the prefixes. A discussion of the question in the last column as it pertains to each word will focus attention on the eye-syllables of each word.

● The exercises in this section review the

Handwriting Models

reduce condense prefer unable preview
exert engage proceed refuse proclaim
compose infect decay extend dismiss
import disgust commerce

3 Write the five words that have the prefixes *dis* and *un*.

4 Write the three words that have the prefix *pro*.

5 Write the four words that have the prefixes *in* and *im*.

6 Write the three words that have the prefix *ex*.

7 Write the two words that have the prefix *de*.

8 Write the five words that have the prefixes *com* and *con*.

9 Write the two words that have the prefix *en*.

10 Draw a line between the prefix and the root in each word in Exercises 1–9.

11 Write the meaning of each of the prefixes in the words in Exercises 1–9.

1 The sound-spellings of the new-word roots are shown below. Find the right prefix for the root and write the correct spelling of each word.

a /pôrt/	**g** /gāj/	**m** /tend/
b /mis/	**h** /vū/	**n** /fūz/
c /dens/	**i** /kā/	**o** /fekt/
d /mėrs/	**j** /sēd/	**p** /fėr/
e /ėrt/	**k** /ā′ bəl/	**q** /gust/
f /pōz/	**l** /düs/	**r** /klām/

2 Write the *ing* forms of *prefer, include, condense, produce, engage,* and *exchange.*

55

5 in/clude, im/press, in/fect, im/port
6 ex/change, ex/ert, ex/tend
7 de/stroy, de/cay
8 com/plain, con/vince, com/pose, con/dense, com/merce
9 en/joy, en/gage
10 (See answers 1–9.)
11 pre "before"
re "back, again"
dis, un "opposite, not"
pro "for, onward"
in, im "in, not"
ex "out, from"
de "from, down"
com, con "together, with"
en "in, make"

●● **Answers**

1a import	**j** proceed
b dismiss	**k** unable
c condense	**l** reduce
d commerce	**m** extend
e exert	**n** refuse
f compose	**o** infect
g engage	**p** prefer
h preview	**q** disgust
i decay	**r** proclaim

2 preferring, including, condensing, producing, engaging, exchanging

---

information presented in the Study Chart.

●● Exercise 1 in this section centers attention on the root word spellings. Exercise 2 deals with the structural generalizations about adding *ing* to roots.

●● The twelve prefixes appear again in the words of the Read and Spell list. Pupils will probably have more trouble with the meanings than they will with decoding the words. The written work involves the *ing* forms of the words.

●● The correct proofreading exercise, with corrected spelling errors underscored and corrected list errors starred, is as follows:

Synonyms	Antonyms
commerce-business	*import-export*
refuse-trash	*unkind-kind*
exert-use	*reduce-enlarge*
predict-foretell	*please-displease*
proclaim-declare	*refuse-accept*
* *destroy-spoil*	* *unable-able*

Answers

2a prescribing **g** discarding
  b competing **h** dethroning
  c imploring **i** examining
  d conducting **j** inflating
  e depositing **k** undressing
  f connecting **l** recalling

Read and Spell

reflect	dethrone	enlist	undress	procure
propel	connect	discard	prevail	prepaid
compete	deposit	impair	inflate	examine
prolong	endure	enrich	recall	prescribe
conduct	combine	uncommon	implore	exist
export	disable	incline	resist	dissolve

1 The Read and Spell words have the same prefixes as those shown in the Study Chart. Write any Read and Spell word that you cannot read or any word for which you do not know the meaning.

2 What are they doing? Write the *ing* form of a word from the Read and Spell list for each picture below.

56

1 Ruth made lists of synonyms and antonyms. Proofread her work. Write the lists correctly.

Synonyms	Antonyms
commerce – business	import – export
refuse – trash	unkind – kind
exert – use	reduse – enlarge
predict – foretell	please – displease
proclame – declare	refuse – accept
unable – able	destroy – spoil

2 In two-syllable words, we double the final consonant before the *ed* and *ing* endings when (1) the accent is on the last syllable and (2) the word ends in one vowel letter followed by one consonant letter.

- **omit** /ō mit′/ *v.* **1.** Leave out: *Some spelling mistakes are made by omitting letters.* **2.** Neglect: *She omitted doing the dishes.* **omitted, omitting.**

> A lexicographer often uses the *ed* or *ing* form in a sample sentence or phrase.

Write a dictionary entry for the word *prefer*. Use the *ed* and *ing* forms in sample sentences. When you have finished, compare your work with the Spelling Dictionary.

Another Word from the Dutch

Anything that is used to lure people or other creatures into danger may be called a *decoy*. One kind of decoy is a wooden bird used to attract other birds so that they can be trapped or shot. The word *decoy* comes from the Dutch *de kooi*, which means "the cage."

Write the words from the list below that are shown in the Spelling Dictionary as both nouns and verbs.

a enjoy   **b** decay   **c** decoy   **d** destroy

57

Answers

1 (See Teaching Suggestions.)

2 (See the entry for *prefer* in the Spelling Dictionary as a model answer.)

Another Word from the Dutch
b decay   **c** decoy

Mastery Test
For complete directions and an explanation of the testing program, see the Introduction to this Teacher's Edition.

Mastery Test 14b

1 /ə chēv′/ *achieve*
2 /rē tėrn′/ *return*
3 /dē stroi′/ *destroy*
4 /eg zėrt′/ *exert*
5 /kən dens′/ *condense*
6 /prō klām′/ *proclaim*
7 /gas′ ə lēn/ *gasoline*
8 /dis gust′/ *disgust*
9 /un kīnd′/ *unkind*
10 /dē kā′/ *decay*
11 /ī/ /wuz/ /un ā′ bəl/ /tü/ /eks chānj′/ /ᵺə/ /shuv′ əl/ /ī/ /bôt/ /at/ /ᵺə/ /stôr/ *I was unable to exchange the shovel I bought at the store.*
12 /wē/ /en gāj′/ /in/ /kom′ ərs/ /with/ /men′ ē/ /uᵺ′ ər/ /landz/ *We engage in commerce with many other lands.*
13 /ᵺə/ /men′ ū/ /in klüdz′/ /mel′ ən/ /and/ /hun′ ē/ *The menu includes melon and honey.*
14 /ī/ /wun′ dər/ /hü/ /kəm pōzd′/ /ᵺēz/ /vėr′ səz/ *I wonder who composed these verses.*
15 /hē/ /prē fėrz′/ /wes′ tərn/ /mü′ vēz/ *He prefers western movies.*

15 Root-Suffix **Words**

Study Chart

We spell roots and suffixes as if they were little words.

Suffixes	Eye-Syllables	Ear-Syllables	How do we spell these suffixes?
ness (n.)	wit,ness	/wit' nəs/	/nəs/
ment (n.)	set,tle,ment	/set' əl mənt/	/mənt/
tion (n.) sion (n.)	col,lec,tion	/kə lek' shən/	/shən/
ance (n.) ence (n.)	am,bu,lance au,di,ence	/am' bū ləns/ /ô' dē əns/	/əns/ /əns/
ful (adj.)	faith,ful	/fāth' fəl/	/fəl/
less (adj.)	reck,less	/rek' ləs/	/ləs/
ant (adj.) ent (adj.)	el,e,gant fre,quent	/el' ə gənt/ /frē' kwənt/	/ənt/ /ənt/
ous (adj.)	gen,er,ous	/jen' ər əs/	/əs/
able (adj.) ible (adj.)	hon,or,able vis,ible	/on' ər ə bəl/ /viz' ə bəl/	/ə bəl/ /ə bəl/

New Words

dark,ness	match,less	weak,ness	pa,tience
ail,ment	at,tend,ant	judg,ment	fright,ful
fric,tion	hu,mor,ous	pen,sion	law,less
an,noy,ance	rea,son,able	fash,ion	op,po,nent
help,ful			di,vis,ible

Teaching Suggestions

The common suffixes presented in this unit as a group were all introduced in earlier levels of this series. In those earlier levels, pupils have been alerted to the difference in function of prefixes and suffixes. Prefixes affect directly the meaning of roots. Suffixes are normally employed to change words from one part of speech to another. (Some suffixes, like *ful* and *less*, do directly affect root meanings.)

Suffixes cause some spelling problems. For example, the /shən/ suffix is spelled either *tion* or *sion*. Likewise, /əns/ is spelled *ance* or *ence*, /ənt/ is spelled *ant* or *ent*, and /ə bəl/ is spelled *able* or *ible*.

Use the Study Chart to introduce the unit. Pupils should become aware of the difference in function of suffixes and prefixes. The material in the first column may be used to identify the suffixes as noun or adjective suffixes. Again, the eye-syllables column may be used to demonstrate that root-suffix words may be separated into visible units as an aid to spelling. Note that although *able* and *ible* have two ear-syllables, we show them as single eye-syllables.

Handwriting Models

darkness   matchless   weakness   patience
ailment   attendant   judgment   frightful
friction   humorous   pension   lawless
annoyance   reasonable   fashion   opponent
helpful   divisible

1 Suffixes change words from one part of speech to another. Write the six common noun suffixes shown in the Study Chart.

2 Write the seven adjective suffixes in the Study Chart.

3 Write the three words that have the /nəs/ suffix.

4 Write the four words that have the /shən/ suffix.

5 Write the three words that have the /mənt/ suffix.

6 Write the words that have the roots /lô/, /frīt/, /mach/, and /rek/.

7 Write the words for these sound-spellings.

a /jen′ ər əs/   **f** /am′ bū ləns/
b /hū′ mər əs/   **g** /on′ ər ə bəl/
c /el′ ə gənt/   **h** /rē′ zən ə bəl/
d /ə ten′ dənt/   **i** /viz′ ə bəl/
e /frē′ kwənt/   **j** /də viz′ ə bəl/

1 Write new or review words to complete these sentences.

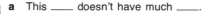

a This ____ doesn't have much ____.

b The lawman is facing a ____ ____.

59

Answers

Answers
1 ness, ment, tion, sion, ance, ence
2 ful, less, ant, ent, ous, able, ible
3 witness, darkness, weakness
4 collection, friction, pension, fashion
5 settlement, ailment, judgment
6 lawless, frightful, matchless, reckless
7a generous   **f** ambulance
  b humorous   **g** honorable
  c elegant   **h** reasonable
  d attendant   **i** visible
  e frequent   **j** divisible

Answers
1a audience, patience
  b lawless (reckless, frightful), opponent

The first five exercises in this section review the information about suffixes.

The exercises in this section require a knowledge of the meanings of the words. Note that alternate answers are possible for several of the exercises.

The Read and Spell vocabulary repeats the root-suffix patterns of the words in the Study Chart. Pupils should separate these words into eye-syllables and apply sound-blending skills to decode the roots and suffixes. Exercises 2 through 5 center attention on suffixes.

The correct proofreading exercise, with correct errors underscored, is as follows:
Sale — Joan's Dress Shop
Gowns and Tailored Suits at
Reasonable Prices!
See a collection of elegant fashions. Let our helpful attendants show you our display of dresses. Our clothes have a matchless quality.

c attendant, helpful
d judgment, reasonable
e collection, elegant
 (matchless)
2 annoyance, humorous,
 ailment, faithful

 Answers
2 eagerness, sickness
3 agreement, treatment,
 performance
4 forcible, suitable,
 sensible, portable
5 hopeful, fruitful,
 lawful

 c This ____ is very ____.

 d In his ____ the policewoman is not being
____.

 e She has a ____ of ____ jewels.

2 Write synonyms from the new and review lists for *irritation, funny, illness,* and *loyal.*

Read and Spell

eagerness	treatment	election	mansion	ignorance
hopeful	countless	vacant	marvelous	sensible
suction	sickness	agreement	fiction	tension
evidence	fruitful	faultless	gallant	silent
suitable	lotion	performance	residence	lawful
fragrant	accident	tremendous	portable	forcible

1 Write any Read and Spell word that you cannot read or any word for which you do not know the meaning.

2 Write Read and Spell words by adding a noun suffix to the adjectives *eager* and *sick.*

3 Write Read and Spell words by adding a noun suffix to the verbs *agree, treat,* and *perform.*

4 Write Read and Spell words by adding an adjective suffix to the words *force, suit, sense,* and *port.*

5 Write antonyms from the Read and Spell list by changing the suffix of the adjectives *hopeless, fruitless,* and *lawless.*

60

Mastery Test 15a
1 /därk′ nəs/ *darkness* **2** /dē kā′/ *decay*
3 /frik′ shən/ *friction* **4** /mach′ ləs/ *matchless*
5 /set′ əl mənt/ *settlement* **6** /ə pō′ nənt/
opponent **7** /prē fėr′/ *prefer* **8** /prō sēd′/
proceed **9** /kə lek′ shən/ *collection*
10 /jen′ ər əs/ *generous.*
11 /it/ /tāks/ /pā′ shəns/ /tü/ /fash′ ən/ /ə/
/wúd/ /kärv′ ing/   *It takes patience to fashion
a wood carving.*
12 /sum/ /āl′ mənts/ /kôz/ /ū/ /tü/ /fēl/ /grāt/
/wēk′ nəs/   *Some ailments cause you to feel
great weakness.*

13 /ᵺə/ /ô′ dē əns/ /shōd/ /ə noi′ əns/
/hwen/ /ᵺə/ /mim′ ik/ /fāld/ /tü/ /pər fôrm′/
*The audience showed annoyance when the
mimic failed to perform.*
14 /ī/ /went/ /tü/ /sē/ /ə/ /prē′ vū′/ /uv/
/ᵺat/ /hū′ mər əs/ /mü′ vē/ /last/ /nīt/
*I went to see a preview of that humorous
movie last night.*
15 /an/ /out′ lô′/ /iz/ /wun/ /hü/ /iz/ /lô′ ləs/
An outlaw is one who is lawless.

1 Each person in Joan's class wrote a sample newspaper ad. Proofread the ad that Joan wrote. Write the ad correctly.

> *Sale — Joans Dress Shop*
> *Gowns and Tailered Suits at Reasonable Prices!*
> *See a collection of elegent fashions. Let our helpful*
> *attendants show you our display of dresses. Our*
> *clothes have a matchless quality.*

2 Read the dictionary entries below for the words *honor* and *honorable*. Notice that we add the suffix *able* to the noun or verb *honor* to form the adjective *honorable*.

A lexicographer uses the abbreviations *n.* and *v.* to stand for *noun* and *verb*.	• **honor** /on′ ər/ *n.* Glory; fame: *She had the honor of being elected president.* —*v.* Think highly of: *We honor Washington on his birthday.*

A lexicographer uses the abbreviation *adj.* to stand for *adjective*.	• **honorable** /on′ ər ə bəl/ *adj.* **1.** Honest: *Cheating is not honorable.* **2.** Noble: *an hon-. orable deed.*

Write dictionary entries for the words *reason* and *reasonable*. Compare your work with the Spelling Dictionary.

Another Word from the Russians

The word *sputnik* has become widely known because of space exploration. The Russians use the word *sputnik* to refer to their man-made satellites that orbit around the earth or other heavenly bodies. The word, made from two Russian word parts, means "a traveling companion."

Write the two words from the story above that have the *ion* or *tion* suffix.

61

●● **Answers**
1 (See Teaching Suggestions.)
2 (See the entries for *reason* and *reasonable* in the Spelling Dictionary as model answers.)

Another Word from the Russians
exploration, companion

Mastery Test
For complete directions and an explanation of the testing program, see the Introduction to this Teacher's Edition.

Mastery Test 15b
1 /am′ bū ləns/ *ambulance* **2** /help′ fəl/ *helpful* **3** /kar′ ət/ *carrot* **4** /im′ pôrt/ *import* **5** /dis mis′/ *dismiss* **6** /də viz′ ə bəl/ *divisible* **7** /pen′ shən/ *pension* **8** /frīt′ fəl/ *frightful* **9** /el′ ə gənt/ *elegant* **10** /viz′ ə bəl/ *visible.* **11** /rek′ ləs/ /drī′ vərz/ /shō/ /pür/ /juj′ mənt/ *Reckless drivers show poor judgment.* **12** /ŦHə/ /brāv/ /nīt/ /wuz/ /ə/ /fāth′ fəl/ /ə ten′ dənt/ /uv/ /ŦHə/ /ōld/ /king/ *The brave knight was a faithful attendant of the old king.* **13** /round′ ups′/ /är/ /frē′ kwənt/ /ē vents′/

/at/ /our/ /ranch/ *Roundups are frequent events at our ranch.* **14** /ŦHā/ /bôt/ /gluvz/ /doun′ toun′/ /at/ /ə/ /rē′ zən ə bəl/ /prīs/ *They bought gloves downtown at a reasonable price.* **15** /an/ /on′ ər ə bəl/ /wit′ nəs/ /wüd/ /not/ /tel/ /ə/ /fôls′ hüd′/ *An honorable witness would not tell a falsehood.*

Answers

1 reg u lar regular
cal en dar calendar
e qua tor equator
cu cum ber cucumber

Study Chart

We spell each eye-syllable as if it were a little word in order to remember how to spell /ə/.

Eye-Syllable Vowels			Eye-Syllables	Ear-Syllables	Spelling Cues
e	u	a(r)	reg u lar	/reg′ yə lər/	Say the first
a(r)	i	a	car niv al	/kär′ nə vəl/	eye-syllable
e	i	a	hes it ate	/hez′ ə tāt/	of each word
e	e(r)	a	des per ate	/des′ pər ət/	as if it were
a	i	y	sat is fy	/sat′ is fī/	a little word.
o	a	i	moc cas in	/mok′ ə sən/	Then spell it.
o	a	o	vol ca no	/vol kā′ nō/	Do the same
i	o	ee	pi o neer	/pī′ ə nir′/	for the second
a	o(r)	y	fac tor y	/fak′ tər ē/	and the third
o	i	ue	con tin ue	/kən tin′ ū/	eye-syllables.

New Words

cal en dar	oc cu py	av en ue	es tim ate
nu mer al	▽ bul let in	e qua tor	vi ta min
hi ber nate	to bac co	at mo sphere	cel er y
sac rif ice	vol un teer	dy na mite	cu cum ber
ab so lute	en er gy	mi cro phone	ob stin ate

Soft syllables are hard to spell because their vowel sound is usually /ə/. You can best remember which vowel letter to use if you will think of the syllables as little words.

1 Write the eye-syllables of the four new and review words that have the /ər/ ending. After the eye-syllables of each word, write the whole word.

62

Teaching Suggestions

This unit on three-syllable words is presented in order to focus attention again on the vowel spellings in unstressed syllables. Most of the words have a heavily stressed syllable in which the vowel spelling cue is audible and two soft syllables in which the vowel spelling cues are absent. Some of these words, such as *mocca-sin* and *tobacco,* contain doubled consonants, another source of spelling errors.

Words like *volcano* /vol kā′ nō/, in which the vowel spelling cues are audible in all three syllables, are rare. In most words, like *obstinate*

/ob′ stə nət/, the vowel spelling cue is audible only in the stressed syllable. The technique of separating the word into eye-syllables and then treating each eye-syllable as a monosyllabic word allows pupils to hear a vowel spelling cue in each syllable. Thus, *obstinate* can be thought of as the three monosyllables /ob/, /stin/, and /āt/.

Use the Study Chart to provoke another discussion about the merits of using eye-syllables as an aid to spelling. Continue the same procedure for the new words.

Handwriting Models

calendar occupy avenue estimate
numeral ▽ bulletin equator vitamin
hibernate tobacco atmosphere celery
sacrifice volunteer dynamite cucumber
absolute energy microphone obstinate

2 Write the eye-syllables and the two whole words that have the /əl/ ending.

3 Write the eye-syllables and the three whole words that have the /ət/ ending.

4 Write the eye-syllables and the two whole words that have the /ī/ ending.

5 Write the eye-syllables and the three whole words that have the /ē/ ending.

6 Write the eye-syllables and the three whole words that have the /ir/ ending.

1 Write the eye-syllables of the three words that have the /in/ or /ən/ ending. Then write the whole words.

2 Write the two words in which *ph* spells /f/. Draw lines between the eye-syllables.

3 Write the words for these sound-spellings. Draw lines between the eye-syllables.

a	/hez′ ə tāt/	**d**	/dī′ nə mīt/	**g**	/tə bak′ ō/
b	/hī′ bər nāt/	**e**	/ab′ sə lüt/	**h**	/kən tin′ ū/
c	/sak′ rə fīs/	**f**	/vol kā′ nō/	**i**	/av′ ə nū/

4 Write the word that means "to sleep all winter" and the two words that are names of vegetables.

63

2 car niv al carnival
nu mer al numeral
3 des per ate desperate
es tim ate estimate
ob stin ate obstinate
4 sat is fy satisfy
oc cu py occupy
5 fac tor y factory
en er gy energy
cel er y celery
6 pi o neer pioneer
vol un teer volunteer
at mo sphere atmosphere

●● **Answers**
1 moc cas in moccasin
bul let in bulletin
vi ta min vitamin
2 at/mo/sphere,
mi/cro/phone
3a hes/it/ate **f** vol/ca/no
b hi/ber/nate **g** to/bac/co
c sac/rif/ice **h** con/tin/ue
d dy/na/mite **i** av/en/ue
e ab/so/lute
4 hibernate, celery,
cucumber

● The exercises in this section require pupils to concentrate on the eye-syllables of each word as well as the entire words.

●● These exercises are routine and should require very little supervision from you.

● The Read and Spell list consists of thirty more three-syllable words. It is provided to give pupils practice in isolating the three eye-syllables of each word and in decoding the syllabic parts.

●● The correct proofreading exercise, with corrected errors underscored, is as follows:

Animals that hibernate spend the winter in an inactive state. Hibernating animals hardly seem to be alive. Their body temperatures drop and their hearts beat slowly. They use almost no energy and need almost no food. They use the fat that is stored in their bodies.

Pupils may supplement the work in the dictionary exercise by compiling lists of words whose plurals are formed by adding *s*, by adding *es*, and by adding either *s* or *es*.

Answers

2a violin **f** announcer
  b engineer **g** messenger
  c microscope **h** delegate
  d general **i** hospital
  e buffalo

3 ancestor, origin,
  fortunate, notify,
  peculiar, terrify

Read and Spell

ancestor	announcer	hospital	celebrate	hemisphere
exercise	microscope	substitute	delegate	notify
origin	buffalo	engineer	property	barbecue
peculiar	messenger	general	civilize	fortunate
simplify	conference	violin	delicate	tornado
sympathy	chocolate	melody	century	terrify

1 Write any Read and Spell word that you cannot read or any word for which you do not know the meaning.

2 Write the Read and Spell word suggested by each picture.

3 Write synonyms from the Read and Spell list for the words *forefather, beginning, lucky, inform, strange,* and *frighten.*

1 Proofread the report on the next page that Carl wrote for his science class. After you have found all the mistakes, write the report correctly.

64

Mastery Test 16a

1 /en′ ər jē/ *energy* **2** /vol kā′ nō/ *volcano*
3 /ob′ stə nət/ *obstinate* **4** /es′ tə māt/
estimate **5** /ab′ sə lüt/ *absolute* **6** /ə pō′ nənt/
opponent **7** /rē fūz′/ *refuse* **8** /rē′ zən ə bəl/
reasonable **9** /nü′ mər əl/ *numeral*
10 /hez′ ə tāt/ *hesitate.*
11 /sel′ ə rē/ /and/ /kū′ kum bərz/ /hav/
/men′ ē/ /vī′ tə minz/ *Celery and cucumbers
have many vitamins.*
12 /leᴛH′ ər/ /mok′ ə sənz/ /är/ /mād/ /ᴛHār/
/in/ /ᴛHat/ /fak′ tər ē/ *Leather moccasins are
made there in that factory.*

13 /ᴛHə/ /pī′ ə nirz′/ /sak′ rə fīst/ /kum′ fərt/
/and/ /plezh′ ər/ /in/ /ᴛHār/ /jér′ nēz/ *The
pioneers sacrificed comfort and pleasure in
their journeys.*
14 /dī′ nə mīt/ /māks/ /ə/ /frīt′ fəl/ /blast/
Dynamite makes a frightful blast.
15 /ə/ /kôrd/ /haz/ /at/ /lēst/ /thrē/ /nōts/
A chord has at least three notes.

Mastery Test 16b

1 /kən tin′ ū/ *continue* **2** /mī′ krə fōn/
microphone **3** /at′ mə sfir/ *atmosphere*

> *Animals that hibernate spend the winter in an inactive state. Hibernateing animals hardly seem to be alive. There body temperatures drop and there hearts beat slowly. They use almost no energy and need almost no food. They use the fat that is stored in their bodys.*

2 We form the plural of *o*-ending words by adding *s* (*solo, solos*), by adding *es* (*hero, heroes*), or by adding either *s* or *es* (*tobacco, tobaccos, tobaccoes*).

• **tobacco** /tə bak′ ō/ *n.* **1.** The leaves of certain plants, prepared and used for smoking or chewing or for snuff. **2.** One of these plants. *pl.* **tobaccos** or **tobaccoes.** ◄

> A lexicographer shows the plural form or forms of words that end in *o*.

Write a complete dictionary entry for the word *volcano*. Show the two plural forms of the entry word and everything else that a lexicographer would. When you have finished writing your entry, compare your work with the entry in the Spelling Dictionary.

A Word from the Algonquian Indians

Moccasin is from the Indian word *mokkussin,* which means "shoe." A moccasin is a soft leather shoe or sandal. The sole of a moccasin is brought up and sewed to a leather strip that fits over the top of the foot. A *water moccasin* is a poisonous snake that looks something like a moccasin shoe.

Write these words from the story above: the homonym of *soul;* an adjective with the *ous* suffix; a snurk in which *ea* spells /e/; a snurk in which *oe* spells /ü/.

65

Answers
1 (See Teaching Suggestions.)
2 (See the entry for *volcano* in the Spelling Dictionary as a model answer.)

A Word from the Algonquian Indians
sole, poisonous, leather, shoe

Mastery Test
For complete directions and an explanation of the testing program, see the Introduction to this Teacher's Edition.

4 /hī′ bər nāt/ *hibernate* **5** /juj′ mənt/ *judgment* **6** /wēk′ nəs/ *weakness*
7 /kal′ ən dər/ *calendar* **8** /vol′ ən tir′/ *volunteer* **9** /sat′ is fī/ *satisfy* **10** /des′ pər ət/ *desperate.*
11 /chil′ drən/ /māk/ /reg′ yə lər/ /viz′ its/ /tü/ /kär′ nə vəlz/ *Children make regular visits to carnivals.*
12 /tə bak′ ō/ /iz/ /rāzd/ /ôn/ /färmz/ /in/ /ə/ /wärm/ /klī′ mət/ *Tobacco is raised on farms in a warm climate.*
13 /wē/ /ok′ yə pī/ /ə/ /hous/ /ôn/ /ŦHə/

/mān/ /av′ ə nū/ *We occupy a house on the main avenue.*
14 /it/ /tāks/ /pā′ shəns/ /tü/ /rēd/ /ŦHis/ /fash′ ən/ /bùl′ ə tən/ *It takes patience to read this fashion bulletin.*
15 /ŦHōz/ /ves′ əlz/ /krôs/ /ŦHə/ /ē kwā′ tər/ /ōn′ lē/ /ə/ /fū/ /tīmz/ /ə/ /munth/ *Those vessels cross the equator only a few times a month.*

17 Combinations with /a/

Study Chart

Word Types		Review Words	Sound-Spellings	How do we spell these sounds?
■	1 syllable	grasp	/grasp/	/a/
◀	y / ey /ē/ ending	fan‚cy / al‚ley	/fan' sē/ / /al' ē/	/a/ /ē/ / /a/ /ē/
◀	er / or / ar /ər/ ending	plat‚ter / an‚chor / gram‚mar	/plat' ər/ / /ang' kər/ / /gram' ər/	/a/ /ər/ / /a/ /ər/ / /a/ /ər/
■	le / el / al /əl/ ending	scram‚ble / trav‚el / sand‚al	/skram' bəl/ / /trav' əl/ / /san' dəl/	/a/ /əl/ / /a/ /əl/ / /a/ /əl/
■■	compound	grand‚stand	/grand' stand'/	/a/ /a/
■■	2 syllables	at‚tract	/ə trakt'/	/ə/ /a/
■■■	3 syllables	ba‚nan‚a	/bə nan' ə/	/ə/ /a/ /ə/
◀■	prefix-root	com‚mand / con‚stant	/kə mand'/ / /kon' stənt/	/kəm/ /a/ / /kon/ /ə/
■▶	root-suffix	ac‚tion	/ak' shən/	/a/ /shən/

New Words

clamp	plas‚ter	tack‚le	grass‚land	com‚pact
craf‚ty	act‚or	mam‚mal	at‚las	con‚tract
val‚ley	hang‚ar	cam‚el	pa‚jam‚as	frac‚tion

Teaching Suggestions

The preceding sixteen units have presented the basic generalizations of English spelling. The units were designed to cause pupils to apply the generalizations to homogeneously grouped spelling vocabulary. In order to provide pupils with opportunities to observe and to practice variable applications of the generalizations in heterogeneous spelling contexts, the remaining twenty units of this text offer a different scheme of word groupings and a different format for the study charts.

In this and the following units, the basic sound-symbol generalizations are applied, one at a time, to all of the word types that exist in our English vocabulary. As the Study Chart indicates, these word types are monosyllabic words, words with the three common unstressed endings, compounds, two-syllable words, three-syllable words, and words with prefix-root-suffix structures. Also included, from time to time, will be new snurks and homonyms. The purpose of this organization is to help pupils apply their previous learnings to the wide variety of spelling contexts that exist.

Handwriting Models

clamp   *actor*   *camel*   *compact*
crafty   *hangar*   *grassland*   *contract*
valley   *tackle*   *atlas*   *fraction*
plaster   *mammal*   *pajamas*

1 Write the two new and review one-syllable words in which /a/ is spelled *a*.

2 We spell /a/ with *a* in the loud syllables of the new and review words that have the soft /ē/ ending. Write the two words in which *y* spells the /ē/ ending and the two words in which *ey* spells the /ē/ ending.

3 We spell /a/ with *a* in the loud syllables of the new and review words that have the soft /ər/ ending. Write the two words in which *er* spells the /ər/ ending, the two words in which *or* spells the /ər/ ending, and the two words in which *ar* spells the /ər/ ending.

4 We spell /a/ with *a* in the loud syllables of the new and review words that have the soft /əl/ ending. Write the two words in which *le* spells the /əl/ ending, the two words in which *al* spells the /əl/ ending, and the two words in which *el* spells the /əl/ ending.

5 We spell the eye-syllables of compounds as if they were little words. Write the eye-syllables of the two compounds.

6 We spell the eye-syllables of two- and three-syllable words as if they were little words. Write the eye-syllables of /ə trakt′/, /at′ ləs/, /bə nan′ ə/, and /pə jä′ məz/.

7 We spell the /kəm/, or /kom/, prefix with *com*. Write the two words that have this prefix.

67

Attention in this unit is focused on the *a* spelling of /a/ in the various word types. Use the Study Chart to acquaint pupils with the various word types that appear. These word types will reappear in subsequent study charts. Pupils should observe that structural elements are symbolized by a small square to represent a syllable and a small triangle to represent an affix. Pupils should also observe that the spelling options are shown for the three soft-syllable endings. Through a discussion, help pupils identify the word type of each new word.

For each word in the Study Chart, pupils should determine how the sounds shown in the last column are spelled. These generalizations should then be applied to each of the fifteen new words.

●   The exercises in this section require the pupils to attend to the various spelling generalizations of the words as they occur by word types. Many pupils, especially those who have not participated in the previous discussion of the Study Chart, will need your support.

8 constant, contract
9 action, fraction

●● **Answers**

1a sandal   **i** compact
 b fraction   **j** banana
 c hangar   **k** platter
 d contract   **l** atlas
 e valley   **m** clamp
 f anchor   **n** camel
 g pajamas   **o** grandstand
 h actor
2 craftier, craftiest,
   fancier, fanciest
3 scrambling, tackling,
   traveling
4 travel, constant,
   grassland

8 We spell the /kən/, or /kon/, prefix with *con.* Write the two words that have this prefix.

9 We spell the /shən/ noun suffix with *tion* or *sion.* Write the two words that have this suffix.

1 Write the words suggested by these pictures.

2 Write the *er* and *est* forms of *crafty* and *fancy.*

3 Write the *ing* forms of *scramble, tackle,* and *travel.*

4 Write synonyms for *movement, faithful,* and *pasture.*

●● These exercises should be done independently by the pupils. Exercises 2 and 3 require the application of structural generalizations.

●
●● The Read and Spell words illustrate the various spelling patterns and word types presented in the Study Chart. The list constitutes a useful word perception test that requires pupils to apply a variety of decoding skills. As usual, pupils who have difficulty in decoding these words should have some extra help. The spelling work in Exercises 2, 3, and 4 should

be done independently by the pupils.

●●
●● The corrected proofreading exercise is:
   An atlas is a book of maps of many countries. Atlases are named for a giant who appeared in Greek legends. The giant was said to hold the heavens on his mighty shoulders. When a collection of maps was brought out in the sixteenth century, a picture of Atlas was used on the cover. The same kind of picture was used for centuries on books of maps, so the books were called "atlases."

Read and Spell

snack	tractor	channel	madam	compass
raft	master	panel	adapt	company
gasp	factor	handbag	attack	commander
galley	saddle	knapsack	avalanche	contractor
scanty	rascal	bandstand	contact	caption
dancer	angle	sandbag	combat	attraction

1 The Read and Spell words have all the spelling combinations with /a/. Write any word that you cannot read or any word for which you do not know the meaning.

2 Write the Read and Spell words for these pictures.

3 Write Read and Spell synonyms for *change, strip,* and *title.*

4 Write antonyms for *plentiful, slave,* and *retreat.*

1 Reggie wrote an interesting word story for his English class. Proofread his work. Write the story correctly.

69

Answers

2a sandbag
b compass
c knapsack
d saddle
e handbag
f bandstand
g tractor
h galley
i dancer

3 adapt, panel, caption

4 scanty, master, attack

Mastery Test 17a

1 /grasp/ *grasp* **2** /kraf′ tē/ *crafty* **3** /al′ ē/ *alley* **4** /plas′ tər/ *plaster* **5** /ang′ kər/ *anchor*
6 /hang′ ər/ *hangar* **7** /gram′ ər/ *grammar*
8 /san′ dəl/ *sandal* **9** /bu̇l′ ə tən/ *bulletin*
10 /dī′ nə mīt/ *dynamite.*
11 /ūz/ /yu̇r/ /at′ ləs/ /tü/ /fīnd/ /landz/ /nir/ /ŦHə/ /ē kwā′ tər/ *Use your atlas to find lands near the equator.*
12 /bə nan′ əz/ /är/ /found/ /in/ /klī′ məts/ /ŦHat/ /är/ /mīld/ *Bananas are found in climates that are mild.*
13 /ŦHãr/ /iz/ /much/ /gras′ land′/ /in/ /ŦHis/ /kwī′ ət/ /val′ ē/ *There is much grassland in this quiet valley.*
14 /kam′ əlz/ /är/ /mam′ əlz/ /ŦHat/ /trav′ əl/ /fôr/ /dāz/ /with′ out′/ /wô′ tər/ *Camels are mammals that travel for days without water.*
15 /ī/ /en joi′/ /ŦHə/ /el′ ə gənt/ /at′ mə sfir/ /uv/ /ŦHə/ /man′ shən/ *I enjoy the elegant atmosphere of the mansion.*

Mastery Test 17b

1 /skram′ bəl/ *scramble* **2** /klamp/ *clamp*

1 (See Teaching Suggestions.)
2 (See the entry and drawing for *sandal* in the Spelling Dictionary as a model answer.)

Another Word from the Scotch
antonym, synonym, synonym

Mastery Test
For complete directions and an explanation of the testing program, see the Introduction to this Teacher's Edition.

An atlas is a book of maps of many country. Atlas are named for a giant who appeared in greek legends. The giant was said to hold the heavens on his mighty shoulders. When a collection of maps was brought out in the sixteenth century, a picture of Atlas was used on the cover. The same kind of picture was used for century on books of maps, so the books were called "atlases."

2 Read the dictionary entry below for the word *camel*.

A lexicographer sometimes gives information in a short paragraph or with a picture.

• **camel** /kam′ əl/ *n.* A large, four-footed mammal with cushioned feet and a long neck. It is used as a beast of burden in the deserts of northern Africa and central Asia.

Camel
8 feet long
7½ feet high

Write a complete dictionary entry for the word *sandal*. Draw an illustration and include information next to it. You may need to use the Spelling Dictionary for help.

Another Word from the Scotch

In the highlands of Scotland, families with the same ancestor have united. Such a group of families is called a *clann*. We have adopted the word as *clan*. We use it to mean any group of people who stick together for a common purpose.

Use the Spelling Dictionary if you need to and write *synonym* or *antonym* for each of these pairs of words: *ancestor-descendant; clan-group; unite-join.*

70

3 /kon′ stənt/ *constant* 4 /tak′ əl/ *tackle*
5 /kə mand′/ *command* 6 /ə ten′ dənt/
attendant 7 /frak′ shən/ *fraction*
8 /āl′ mənt/ *ailment* 9 /ok′ yə pī/ *occupy*
10 /kom′ pakt/ *compact.*
11 /ŦHat/ /ak′ tər/ /ə trakts′/ /lärj/
/ô′ dē ən səz/ *That actor attracts large audiences.*
12 /wē/ /kůd/ /sē/ /ôl/ /uv/ /ŦHə/ /ak′ shən/
/frum/ /ŦHə/ /grand′ stand′/ *We could see all of the action from the grandstand.*
13 /dü/ /ū/ /prē fėr′/ /fan′ sē/ /pə jä′ məz/
/ôr/ /plān/ /wunz/ *Do you prefer fancy pajamas or plain ones?*
14 /plat′ ərz/ /uv/ /sel′ ə rē/ /and/ /ol′ ivz/
/wėr/ /set/ /ôn/ /ŦHə/ /tā′ bəl/ *Platters of celery and olives were set on the table.*
15 /ŦHə/ /ā′ jənt/ /gāv/ /ŦHə/ /ten′ ənt/ /ə/
/kon′ trakt/ /tü/ /rent/ /ŦHə/ /hous/ *The agent gave the tenant a contract to rent the house.*

Combinations with /e/

Study Chart

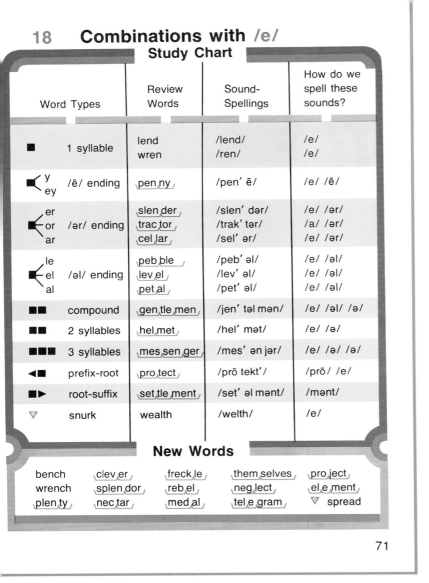

Word Types		Review Words	Sound-Spellings	How do we spell these sounds?
■	1 syllable	lend wren	/lend/ /ren/	/e/ /e/
y ey	/ē/ ending	pen ny	/pen' ē/	/e/ /ē/
er or ar	/ər/ ending	slen der trac tor cel lar	/slen' dər/ /trak' tər/ /sel' ər/	/e/ /ər/ /a/ /ər/ /e/ /ər/
le el al	/əl/ ending	peb ble lev el pet al	/peb' əl/ /lev' əl/ /pet' əl/	/e/ /əl/ /e/ /əl/ /e/ /əl/
■■	compound	gen tle men	/jen' təl mən/	/e/ /əl/ /ə/
■■	2 syllables	hel met	/hel' mət/	/e/ /ə/
■■■	3 syllables	mes sen ger	/mes' ən jər/	/e/ /ə/ /ə/
◄■	prefix-root	pro tect	/prō tekt'/	/prō/ /e/
■►	root-suffix	set tle ment	/set' əl mənt/	/mənt/
▽	snurk	wealth	/welth/	/e/

New Words

bench	clev er	freck le	them selves	pro ject
wrench	splen dor	reb el	neg lect	el e ment
plen ty	nec tar	med al	tel e gram	▽ spread

71

Teaching Suggestions

In this unit the *e* spelling of /e/ is revolved through the various word-type patterns. The review and new words illustrate monosyllabic words; words with the soft /ē/, the soft /ər/, and the soft /əl/ endings; compounds; two-syllable words; three-syllable words; prefix-root words; root-suffix words; and snurks. All of the words except one have the vowel sound /e/. *Tractor* is used as the review example of a word with the *or* spelling of the soft /ər/ ending because no suitable word with /e/ is available from previous levels.

Use the Study Chart to discuss the review words one by one. Pupils should note the word type of each word and the spellings used for the sounds shown in the last column of the Study Chart. Call attention again to the spelling options shown for the three soft-syllable endings. Pupils should develop the habit of thinking of these spelling options whenever they hear these soft syllables. Help pupils to identify the word type of each new word and to apply the spelling generalizations discussed in the Study Chart to the new words.

● **Answers**
1 lend, wren, bench, wrench
2 wren, wrench
3 penny, plenty
4a slender, messenger, clever
 b tractor, splendor
 c cellar, nectar
5a pebble, freckle
 b level, rebel
 c petal, medal
6 gen tle men, them selves

●● **Answers**
1 hel met, neg lect

Handwriting Models

bench   *nectar*   *neglect*
wrench   *freckle*   *telegram*
plenty   *rebel*   *project*
clever   *medal*   *element*
splendor   *themselves*   ▽ *spread*

1 We expect to spell /e/ with *e*. Write the four new and re-view one-syllable words in which /e/ is spelled *e*.

2 Write the two words in which /r/ is spelled *wr*.

3 We spell /e/ with *e* in the loud syllables of the new and review words that end with /ē/. Write the two words in which the soft /ē/ ending is spelled *y*.

4 We spell /e/ with *e* in the loud syllables of the new and review words that end with /ər/.
a Write the three words in which the soft /ər/ ending is spelled *er*.
b Write the two words in which /ər/ is spelled *or*.
c Write the two words in which /ər/ is spelled *ar*.

5 We spell /e/ with *e* in the loud syllables of the new and review words that end with /əl/.
a Two words that have the soft /əl/ ending spelled *le* are /peb′ əl/ and /frek′ əl/. Write those two words.
b Write the two words in which /əl/ is spelled *el*.
c Write the two words in which /əl/ is spelled *al*.

6 We spell the eye-syllables of compounds as if they were little words. Write the eye-syllables of the two compounds.

1 Write the eye-syllables of the two-syllable words /hel′ mət/ and /nə glekt′/.

72

● The exercises in this section require the pupils to attend to the spelling generalizations of the words for the first six word types. Some pupils will need your support, especially if they have not participated in a previous discussion of the Study Chart.

●● Exercises 1 through 5 in this section require the pupils to attend to the spelling generalizations for the last five word types. Again, some pupils will need your support in order to perform satisfactorily.

●● The Read and Spell words illustrate the *e* spelling of /e/. All of the word types found in the Study Chart are included in this list. After using the list as a word perception test, you will probably need to spend some time clarifying the meanings. If you do so, Exercises 2, 3, and 4 should offer few problems.

●● The correct proofreading exercise, with corrected errors underscored, is as follows:
1. A wrench is used to smooth rough lumber.   false

2 Write the eye-syllables of the three-syllable review word /mes′ ən jər/ and the three-syllable new word /tel′ ə gram/.

3 Write the eye-syllables and the whole word for each of the two prefix-root words.

4 We spell the /mənt/ suffix with *ment*.

a Write the eye-syllables of /set′ əl mənt/. Then write the whole word.

b Write the eye-syllables of /el′ ə mənt/. Then write the whole word.

5 Write the two snurks in which *ea* spells /e/.

6 Write new words to complete these sentences.

a One of the simple substances from which all other things are made is an _____.

b A tool to turn nuts and bolts is a _____.

c A sweet liquid in flowers is _____.

Read and Spell

clench	jelly	wrestle	anthem	protest
crept	member	pedal	tenant	professor
melt	senator	kettle	patent	segment
flesh	elector	kennel	telecast	tenement
messy	beggar	eggplant	telegraph	amendment
entry	tremble	bedspread	propel	twenty

 1 The Read and Spell words have spelling combinations with /e/. Write any Read and Spell word that you cannot read or any word for which you do not know the meaning.

2 Write a Read and Spell word to complete each sentence.

 a They're singing the national _____.

73

2 mes sen ger, tel e gram
3 pro tect protect
  pro ject project
4a set tle ment settlement
 b el e ment element
5 wealth, spread
6a element
 b wrench
 c nectar

 Answers
2a anthem

---

2. *The word* themselves *is a plural pronoun.* true

3. *Hibernating animals need* plenty *of food.* false

4. *A helmet can be used to* protect *one's head.* true

5. *The words* slim *and* slender *are antonyms.* false

6. *The words* clever *and* stupid *are antonyms.* true

7. *All* telegrams *are delivered by messengers.* false

Mastery Test 18a
1 /set′ əl mənt/ *settlement*
2 /rench/ *wrench*
3 /nek′ tər/ *nectar*
4 /frek′ əl/ *freckle*
5 /lend/ *lend*
6 /slen′ dər/ *slender*
7 /welth/ *wealth*
8 /drīv′ wā′/ *driveway*
9 /pə jä′ məz/ *pajamas*
10 /kam′ əl/ *camel*
11 /ŦHār/ /wėr/ /plen′ tē/ /uv/ /pan′ kāks′/ /tü/ /ēt/ /with/ /hun′ ē/ *There were plenty*

b telecast
c patent
d messy

3a pedal   **d** bedspread
  b telegraph   **e** beggar
  c kennel   **f** kettle

4 professor, tenant, propel

b She's doing a _____.

c He wants a _____ for his invention.

d He is a _____ cook.

3 Write the Read and Spell words suggested by the pictures below.

4 Write the Read and Spell words that mean "college teacher," "rent payer," and "to send forward."

1 Alice wrote the sentences at the top of the next page for a true-false test. Proofread her work for spelling mistakes and write the sentences correctly. Also, mark each sentence *true* or *false*.

74

---

of pancakes to eat with honey.

12 /jen′ təl mən/ /är/ /help′ fəl/ /tü/ /ŦHōz/ /hü/ /kant/ /prō tekt′/ /ŦHem′ selvz′/
Gentlemen are helpful to those who can't protect themselves.

13 /ŦHə/ /bōld/ /nīt/ /wôr/ /ə/ /hev′ ē/ /stēl/ /hel′ mət/ *The bold knight wore a heavy steel helmet.*

14 /ŦHə/ /fôr′ man′/ /ploud/ /ŦHə/ /lev′ əl/ /fēld/ /with/ /hiz/ /nü/ /trak′ tər/ *The foreman plowed the level field with his new tractor.*

15 /ū/ /kan/ /sē/ /ŦHə/ /splen′ dər/ /uv/ /ŦHə/ /kom′ ət/ /in/ /ŦHə/ /skī/ /at/ /nīt/ *You can see the splendor of the comet in the sky at night.*

Mastery Test 18b

1 /med′ əl/ *medal*
2 /prō jekt′/ *project*
3 /ren/ *wren*
4 /kū′ kum bər/ *cucumber*
5 /pen′ ē/ *penny*
6 /peb′ əl/ *pebble*

1. A wrench is used to smooth rough lumber.
2. The word _themselves_ is a plural pronoun.
3. Hibernating animals need plentey of food.
4. A helmet can be used to portect one's head.
5. The words _slim_ and _slender_ are antonyms.
6. The words _clever_ and _stupid_ are antonyms.
7. All telagrams are delivered by messengers.

2 Some entry words have two pronunciations.

A lexicographer shows both pronunciations for different parts of speech.	• **rebel** /reb′ əl/ *n.* Person who resists or fights against authority instead of obeying. —*adj.* Fighting against law or authority. /rē bel′/ *v.* Resist or fight against law or authority. **rebelled, rebelling.**

Write a complete dictionary entry for the word *project*. Show the pronunciations and meanings of *project* as a noun and as a verb. Use sample sentences or phrases. When you have finished, compare your work with the Spelling Dictionary.

Another Word from the Germans

A *delicatessen* is a store where we can buy prepared foods like cooked meats, smoked fish, pickles, and salads. The old German word for a tasty food, a delicacy, was *delicatesse*. The German word came from Latin.

Which of the items below would you expect to buy at a delicatessen? Write the correct spellings for your answers.

a /sal′ əd/   **c** /jel′ ē/   **e** /bred/
b /chēz/   **d** /shuv′ əlz/   **f** /lum′ bər/

75

---

7 /tə bak′ ō/ *tobacco*
8 /av′ ə nū/ *avenue*
9 /el′ ə mənt/ *element*
10 /bench/ *bench*
11 /klev′ ər/ /pū′ pəlz/ /wil/ /not/ /nə glekt′/ /ᵼHār/ /tekst′ bŭks′/   *Clever pupils will not neglect their textbooks.*
12 /ə/ /swift/ /mes′ ən jər/ /brôt/ /ᵼHə/ /tel′ ə gram/   *A swift messenger brought the telegram.*
13 /flou′ ər/ /pet′ əlz/ /wėr/ /spred/ /ə round′/ /ᵼHə/ /sel′ ər/ /uv/ /ᵼHə/ /hous/   *Flower petals were spread around the cellar of the house.*
14 /ᵼHə/ /reb′ əlz/ /fôt/ /ᵼHār/ /ə pō′ nəntz/ /fôr/ /munths/   *The rebels fought their opponents for months.*
15 /wē/ /āt/ /āt/ /hōl/ /mel′ ənz/ /fôr/ /en′ ər jē/   *We ate eight whole melons for energy.*

19

Combinations with /i/

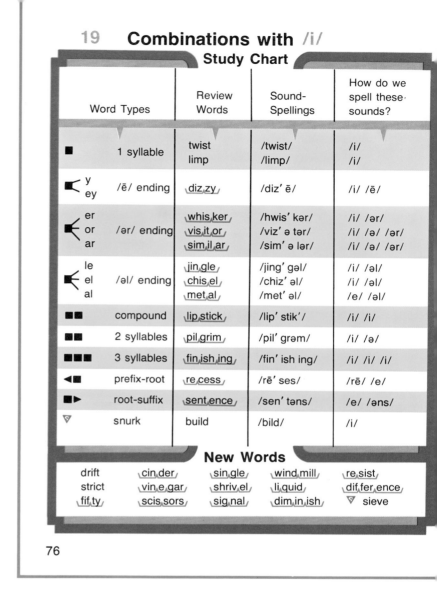

Study Chart

Word Types		Review Words	Sound-Spellings	How do we spell these sounds?
■	1 syllable	twist limp	/twist/ /limp/	/i/ /i/
◀ y ey	/ē/ ending	diz͵zy͵	/diz' ē/	/i/ /ē/
◀ er or ar	/ər/ ending	whis͵ker͵ vis͵it͵or͵ sim͵il͵ar͵	/hwis' kər/ /viz' ə tər/ /sim' ə lər/	/i/ /ər/ /i/ /ə/ /ər/ /i/ /ə/ /ər/
◀ le el al	/əl/ ending	jin͵gle͵ chis͵el͵ met͵al͵	/jing' gəl/ /chiz' əl/ /met' əl/	/i/ /əl/ /i/ /əl/ /e/ /əl/
■■	compound	lip͵stick͵	/lip' stik'/	/i/ /i/
■■	2 syllables	pil͵grim͵	/pil' grəm/	/i/ /ə/
■■■	3 syllables	fin͵ish͵ing͵	/fin' ish ing/	/i/ /i/ /i/
◀■	prefix-root	re͵cess͵	/rē' ses/	/rē/ /e/
■▶	root-suffix	sent͵ence͵	/sen' təns/	/e/ /əns/
▽	snurk	build	/bild/	/i/

New Words

drift	cin͵der͵	sin͵gle͵	wind͵mill͵	re͵sist͵
strict	vin͵e͵gar͵	shriv͵el͵	li͵quid͵	dif͵fer͵ence͵
fif͵ty͵	scis͵sors͵	sig͵nal͵	dim͵in͵ish͵	▽ sieve

76

Teaching Suggestions

In this unit the *i* spelling of /i/ is illustrated in the various word-type patterns, except for a few instances in the review list where a suitable word with /i/ is not available. Two snurks, in which /i/ is spelled irregularly, are included for study.

As usual, the best way to introduce the unit is with the Study Chart. Pupils should discuss the review words according to the word types that they represent and identify the word type of each of the new words. Pupils should also discuss the spellings used for the sounds shown in the last column of the Study Chart and apply these generalizations to the new words. There is a new word that is analogous to each review word in the Study Chart. Particular attention should be given to the spelling options used in the words with the three soft-syllable endings. Pupils might also discuss why *build* and *sieve* are snurks.

Handwriting Models

drift	*vinegar*	*signal*	*resist*
strict	*scissors*	*windmill*	*difference*
fifty	*single*	*liquid*	▽ *sieve*
cinder	*shrivel*	*diminish*	

1 We expect to spell /i/ with *i*. Write the four new and review one-syllable words in which /i/ is spelled *i*.

2 Write the two words in which the soft /ē/ ending is spelled with *y*.

3 We can spell the soft /ər/ ending with *er, or,* or *ar*. Write the two words in which the /ər/ ending is spelled *er,* the two words in which /ər/ is spelled *or,* and the two words in which /ər/ is spelled *ar*.

4 We can spell the soft /əl/ ending with *le, el,* or *al*. Write the two words in which the /əl/ ending is spelled *le,* the two words in which /əl/ is spelled *el,* and the two words in which /əl/ is spelled *al*.

5 Write the five words in which /s/ is spelled *c* or *sc*.

6 Write the eye-syllables and the whole words for these sound-spellings.
a /lip′ stik′/   **c** /pil′ grəm/   **e** /fin′ ish ing/
b /wind′ mil′/   **d** /lik′ wid/   **f** /də min′ ish/

7 Write the eye-syllables for these prefix-root and root-suffix words. Then write the whole words.
a /rē′ ses/   **c** /sen′ təns/
b /rē zist′/   **d** /dif′ ər əns/

8 Write the snurk in which *ui* spells /i/ and the snurk in which *ie* spells /i/.

77

● These exercises cause pupils to write all of the review and new words. In so doing, pupils receive a written reinforcement of the understandings developed through the previous discussion of the Study Chart. This work should be done independently by pupils.

●● The exercises in this section are routine and should be done independently by the pupils.

●● The Read and Spell words illustrate the various word-type patterns. The *i* spelling of /i/ is featured in nearly all of the words. Be sure to attend to the word meanings while listening to the pupils decode. These words will appear in the pupils' reading materials, but many of them may not be in pupils' speaking vocabularies. The written work in Exercise 2 will cause some trouble if pupils do not know the meaning of the words to be written.

●● **Answers**

1a diz/zy   **f** jin/gle
 b sieve   **g** whis/ker
 c shriv/el   **h** vin/e/gar
 d cin/der   **i** sin/gle
 e build
2a signal   **d** fifty
 b lipstick   **e** chisel
 c pilgrim   **f** scissors
3a liquid, sieve
 b diminish, windmill
 c visitor, similar

1 Write the words for these sound-spellings. Draw a line between the eye-syllables of each word.

a /diz′ ē/   **d** /sin′ dər/   **g** /hwis′ kər/
b /siv/   **e** /bild/   **h** /vin′ ə gər/
c /shriv′ əl/   **f** /jing′ gəl/   **i** /sing′ gəl/

2 Write the new or review word suggested by each of these pictures.

3 Complete the sentences below with words from the new and review lists.

a She's pouring a ___ through a ___.

b If the wind doesn't ___, the ___ may break.

c The ___ and the host look very ___.

78

●●
The correct proofreading exercise, with corrected spelling errors underscored and suggested corrected definition errors starred, is as follows:

1. twist-wind
2. _visitor_-guest
3. single-lone
4. strict-harsh
5. wealth-riches
6. _splendor_-glory

* 7. neglect-ignore
8. penny-_cent_
9. level-flat
10. pilgrim-traveler
11. similar-alike
*12. crafty-sly

Mastery Test 19a

1 /limp/ *limp*
2 /strikt/ *strict*
3 /siz′ ərz/ *scissors*
4 /diz′ ē/ *dizzy*
5 /shriv′ əl/ *shrivel*
6 /hwis′ kər/ *whisker*
7 /spred/ *spread*
8 /nə glekt′/ *neglect*
9 /jing′ gəl/ *jingle*
10 /bild/ *build*

Read and Spell

chill	windy	cripple	critic	tennis
film	blister	scribble	bandit	citizen
quiz	liver	kindle	attic	criminal
dingy	litter	tidbit	magic	restrict
giddy	filter	ashpit	splendid	react
silly	brittle	pickax	indignant	repent

2a films, bandits (criminals)
 b splendid, tennis
 c criminal, repented
 d citizen, indignant, litter
 e tidbits, liver, litter

1 Write any Read and Spell word that you cannot read or any word for which you do not know the meaning.

2 Write Read and Spell words to complete these sentences.

a He likes ____ about ____.

b She's a ____ ____ player.

c The ____ has really ____.

d This good ____ is ____ about the ____.

e He's feeding ____ of ____ to the ____ of kittens.

79

---

11 /ᵺǝ/ /pil′grǝmz/ /mād/ /ᵺār/ /fėrst/ /set′ǝl mǝnt/ /nir/ /ᵺǝ/ /sē/ *The pilgrims made their first settlement near the sea.*
12 /ᵺis/ /met′ǝl/ /iz/ /nōn/ /tü/ /rē zist′/ /rust/ *This metal is known to resist rust.*
13 /fif′ tē/ /pū′ pǝlz/ /wėr/ /dis mist′/ /fôr/ /rē′ ses/ /at/ /wun/ /ǝ klok′/ *Fifty pupils were dismissed for recess at one o'clock.*
14 /ᵺǝ/ /lik′ wid/ /in/ /ᵺǝ/ /jug/ /iz/ /vin′ ǝ gǝr/ *The liquid in the jug is vinegar.*

15 /ᵺǝ/ /vėrb/ /in/ /ᵺis/ /sen′ tǝns/ /shōz/ /ak′ shǝn/ *The verb in this sentence shows action.*

Mastery Test 19b
 1 /twist/ *twist*
 2 /sim′ ǝ lǝr/ *similar*
 3 /strōl/ *stroll*
 4 /plen′ tē/ *plenty*
 5 /chiz′ ǝl/ *chisel*
 6 /siv/ *sieve*

1 (See Teaching Suggestions.)

2 (See the entries for *dizzy* and *strict* in the Spelling Dictionary as model answers.)

Another Word from the Japanese
volcanoes or volcanos, tornados or tornadoes, patios, tobaccos or tobaccoes, kimonos, solos, zeros or zeroes, potatoes

Mastery Test
For complete directions and an explanation of the testing program, see the Introduction to this Teacher's Edition.

1 Ted wrote one-word definitions for twelve words. Proofread his work for spelling mistakes and incorrect definitions. Write the words and their definitions correctly.

1. twist – wind
2. visiter – guest
3. single – lone
4. strict – harsh
5. wealth – riches
6. splender – glory
7. neglect – include
8. penny – scent
9. level – flat
10. pilgrim – traveler
11. similar – alike
12. crafty – shy

2 Read the dictionary entries below for *crafty* and *limp*.

- **crafty** /kraf′ tē/ *adj.* Skillful in deceiving others: *The crafty fox caught the hen at the henhouse.* **craftier, craftiest.**

  A lexicographer shows the *er* and *est* forms of adjectives only when there is a change in the spelling of the root word.

- **limp** /limp/ *adj.* Lacking stiffness: *This collar is limp.*

Write complete dictionary entries for the adjectives *dizzy* and *strict*. Show the *er* and *est* forms, if necessary. Compare your work with the Spelling Dictionary.

Another Word from the Japanese

A kimono /kə mō′ nə/ is a loose garment with wide sleeves worn with a broad sash. Many Japanese wear it as an outer coat. It is popular in the United States as a woman's dressing gown. The word *kimono* appears in many tricky spelling lists.

Use the Spelling Dictionary for help if you need it and write the plural form or forms of *volcano, tornado, patio, tobacco, kimono, solo, zero,* and *potato*.

80

---

7 /welth/ *wealth*
8 /drift/ *drift*
9 /fin′ ish ing/ *finishing*
10 /lip′ stik′/ *lipstick*
11 /ᵺə/ /viz′ ə tərz/ /kùd/ /not/ /sē/ /ə/ /sing′ gəl/ /wind′ mil′/ /ôn/ /ᵺə/ /färm/ *The visitors could not see a single windmill on the farm.*
12 /ᵺār/ /är/ /ruf/ /sin′ dərz/ /ôn/ /ᵺār/ /drīv′ wā′/ *There are rough cinders on their driveway.*
13 /noiz/ /in/ /ᵺə/ /ô′ dē əns/ /də min′ isht/ /hwen/ /ᵺə/ /ak′ tər/ /spōk/ *Noise in the audience diminished when the actor spoke.*
14 /shē/ /gāv/ /ə/ /sig′ nəl/ /and/ /ᵺə/ /skwod/ /hôl′ təd/ *She gave a signal, and the squad halted.*
15 /hwot/ /iz/ /ᵺə/ /dif′ ər əns/ /in/ /ᵺə/ /wāt/ /uv/ /ᵺēz/ /bar′ əlz/ *What is the difference in the weight of these barrels?*

Study Chart

Word Types		Review Words	Sound-Spellings	How do we spell these sounds?
■	1 syllable	plot boss	/plot/ /bôs/	/o/ /ô/
◄	y ey /ē/ ending	cop̲y̲ jock̲ey̲	/kop′ ē/ /jok′ ē/	/o/ /ē/ /o/ /ē/
◄	er or /ər/ ending ar	both̲er̲ doc̲tor̲ dol̲lar̲	/boŦH′ ər/ /dok′ tər/ /dol′ ər/	/o/ /ər/ /o/ /ər/ /o/ /ər/
◄	le el /əl/ ending al	bot̲tle̲ mod̲el̲	/bot′ əl/ /mod′ əl/	/o/ /əl/ /o/ /əl/
■■	compound	top̲notch̲	/top′ noch′/	/o/ /o/
■■	2 syllables	bot̲tom̲	/bot′ əm/	/o/ /ə/
■■■	3 syllables	moc̲ca̲sin̲	/mok′ ə sən/	/o/ /ə/ /ə/
◄■	prefix-root	in̲come̲	/in′ kum/	/in/ /u/
■►	root-suffix	soft̲ness̲	/sôft′ nəs/	/ô/ /nəs/
◄■►	prefix-root-suffix	im̲poss̲ible̲	/im pos′ ə bəl/	/ə bəl/

New Words

blond	hock̲ey̲	schol̲ar̲	hop̲scotch̲	▽ im̲prove̲
moth	soc̲cer̲	hob̲ble̲	cot̲ton̲	in̲volve̲
hob̲by̲	spon̲sor̲	nov̲el̲	pol̲it̲ics̲	fond̲ness̲

81

Teaching Suggestions

In this unit the o spelling of /o/ and /ô/ is illustrated in the various word-type contexts. Note that for the first time the prefix-root-suffix word type is illustrated. Note, too, that the review word *income,* although shown as an example of a prefix-root word, is also a snurk. *Improve* is presented as a new snurk.

Use the Study Chart in the usual manner to introduce the unit. Pupils should discuss the word types of both the review words and the new words. Pupils should also discuss the spellings used for the sounds shown in the last column of the Study Chart and apply these generalizations to the new words. It might be valuable to review the device of marking eye-syllables as a way of visually grouping letters so as to make the spellings easier to remember.

● As usual, these exercises cause pupils to write all of the words according to their

Answers

1 plot, blond, boss, moth
2 copy, hobby, jockey, hockey
3 bother, soccer, doctor, sponsor, dollar, scholar
4 bottle, hobble, model, novel
5a hop scotch hopscotch
 b top notch topnotch
 c cot ton cotton
 d pol it ics politics
 e moc ca sin moccasin
 f bot tom bottom
6 in/come, im/prove, in/volve
7 soft/ness, fond/ness
8 im/poss/ible
9 copies, hobbies, jockeys

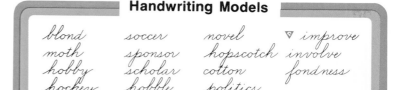

Handwriting Models

blond   soccer   novel   ▽ improve
moth   sponsor   hopscotch   involve
hobby   scholar   cotton   fondness
hockey   hobble   politics

1 Write the two one-syllable words in which *o* spells /o/ and the two one-syllable words in which *o* spells /ô/.

2 Write the two words in which the /ē/ ending is spelled *y* and the two words in which the /ē/ ending is spelled *ey*.

3 We can spell the soft /ər/ ending with *er, or,* or *ar.* Write the two words in which /ər/ is spelled *er,* the two words in which /ər/ is spelled *or,* and the two words in which /ər/ is spelled *ar.*

4 We can spell the soft /əl/ ending with *le* or *el.* Write the two two-syllable words in which /əl/ is spelled *le* and the two words in which /əl/ is spelled *el.*

5 Write the eye-syllables and then the whole words for these sound-spellings.
a /hop′ skoch′/   c /kot′ ən/   e /mok′ ə sən/
b /top′ noch′/   d /pol′ ə tiks/   f /bot′ əm/

6 Write the three prefix-root words. Draw a line between the eye-syllables of each word.

7 Write the two root-suffix words. Draw a line between the eye-syllables of each word.

8 Write the prefix-root-suffix word. Draw lines between the eye-syllables.

9 Write the plural forms of the /ē/-ending words *copy, hobby,* and *jockey.*

82

word-type patterns. This written work should be done independently by the pupils.

●● The exercises in this section follow familiar patterns. Note that Exercise 2 deals with synonyms, Exercise 3 deals with antonyms, and Exercise 4 deals with the structural generalization of adding *ing* to words.

●● The Read and Spell vocabulary is essentially another list of words with /o/ or /ô/. Some words contain /a/, /e/, or /i/. Pupils should first be required to apply the short-vowel generalizations to the decoding of these words. Exercises 3 and 4 review familiar structural generalizations.

●● Note that the proofreading exercise has an error of fact as well as the usual kinds of errors. The correct exercise, with corrected errors underscored, is as follows:
   Ice hockey is one of the fastest games you

1 Complete the sentences below with new and review words.

a That is a ＿＿ playing ＿＿.

b That old ＿＿ will sell for ten ＿＿.

c This ＿＿ player is quite a ＿＿.

d This ＿＿ goes in for ＿＿.

e She always loses her ＿＿ when she plays ＿＿.

2 Write synonyms from the new and review lists for *scheme*, *supporter*, *liking*, and *limp*.

3 Write antonyms from the new and review lists for *hardness*, *expense*, *possible*, and *worsen*.

4 Write the *ing* forms of the words *hobble*, *involve*, and *plot*.

5 Write the correct spellings for these sound-spellings.
a /dok′ tər/   **b** /môth/   **c** /blond/

83

can imagine. It is played by two teams of <u>six</u> players each. The teams have cages made of strong net at <u>opposite</u> ends of the ice. Players on skates flash across the ice with sticks that curve at the <u>bottom</u>. They try to push a flat disk, or puck, into <u>their</u> opponent's net. It's a <u>thrill</u> to watch them.

Mastery Test 20a
1 /in volv′/ *involve*
2 /pol′ ə tiks/ *politics*
3 /nov′ əl/ *novel*
4 /plot/ *plot*
5 /kom′ ərs/ *commerce*
6 /hob′ əl/ *hobble*
7 /dif′ ər əns/ *difference*
8 /mod′ əl/ *model*
9 /kop′ ē/ *copy*
10 /spon′ sər/ *sponsor*
11 /ŦHə/ /chil′ drən/ /fin′ isht/ /gāmz/ /uv/

2a hammock **d** otter
  b nozzle **e** padlock
  c cobweb **f** collar
3 foggier, foggiest,
  soggier, soggiest
4 chopping, toppling,
  wobbling
5 He is taking a snapshot
  of a witness.

Read and Spell

chop	otter	cobweb	blossom	impress
shock	nozzle	snapshot	indent	hotness
foggy	topple	hilltop	insist	madness
holly	wobble	hammock	immense	witness
soggy	padlock	gossip	index	sickness
proper	collar	pocket	impact	sadness

1 Write any Read and Spell word you cannot read or any word for which you do not know the meaning.

2 Write the Read and Spell words for these pictures.

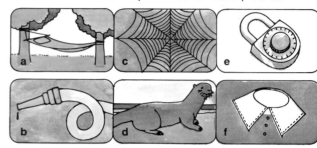

3 Write the *er* and *est* forms of the words *foggy* and *soggy*.

4 Write the *ing* forms of the words *chop*, *topple*, and *wobble*.

5 Write this sentence correctly:
  /hē/ /iz/ /tāk′ ing/ /ə/ /snap′ shot′/ /uv/ /ə/ /wit′ nəs/.

1 Robert wrote a paragraph about ice hockey. Proofread his work. The entry for *hockey* in the Spelling Dictionary will help you check the facts of the paragraph. After you have found the mistakes, write the paragraph correctly.

84

/hok′ ē/ /and/ /sok′ ər/ /at/ /rē′ ses/ *The children finished games of hockey and soccer at recess.*
12 /its/ /im pos′ ə bəl/ /tü/ /plā/ /hop′ skoch′/ /with′ out′/ /thrō′ ing/ /peb′ əlz/ /doun/ /hir/ *It's impossible to play hopscotch without throwing pebbles down here.*
13 /ŦHə/ /bot′ əm/ /uv/ /mī/ /mok′ ə sən/ /iz/ /mād/ /uv/ /leŦH′ ər/ *The bottom of my moccasin is made of leather.*
14 /īv/ /ə/ /fond′ nəs/ /fôr/ /ē′ ting/ /kū′ kum bərz/ /with/ /sôlt/ /and/ /vin′ ə gər/ *I've a fondness for eating cucumbers with salt and vinegar.*
15 /ŦHə/ /mat′ rəs/ /ôn/ /ŦHat/ /bėrth/ /haz/ /tü/ /much/ /sôft′ nəs/ *The mattress on that berth has too much softness.*

Mastery Test 20b
 1 /siv/ *sieve*
 2 /boŦH′ ər/ *bother*
 3 /bot′ əm/ *bottom*
 4 /skol′ ər/ *scholar*
 5 /bild/ *build*

Ice hockey is one of the fastest games you can imagine. It is played by two teams of eight players each. The teams have cages made of strong net at opposite ends of the ice. Players on skates flash across the ice with sticks that curve at the bottom. They try to push a flat disk, or puck, into there opponents net. It's a thrill to watch them.

2 Read the dictionary entries below.

- **weak** /wēk/ *adj.* Not strong.

- **weakness** /wēk′ nəs/ *n.* Lack of strength or power.

> A lexicographer shows the *ness* form of some words as a separate entry.

- **soft** /sôft/ *adj.* **1.** Not hard or stiff. **2.** Gentle: *a soft voice.* **3.** Smooth: *soft as silk.* **4.** Pleasant: *soft light.* —*n.* **softness.**

> A lexicographer shows the *ness* form of some words at the end of the entry.

Write a complete entry for the adjective *fond.* Show the noun form of the word at the end of the entry. When you have finished, compare your work with the Spelling Dictionary.

A Word from the Arabs

The English word *alcohol* comes from the Arabs' *al-kuhl.* Arabs first used the word to mean the black powder that Arabian women put on their eyelids to make them more attractive. We use the word to mean the colorless liquid that makes people drunk. Alcohol is also used in medicines and as a fuel.

Write the correct spellings of these words from the Arabs: /ôr′ ənj/, /lem′ ən/, /mag′ ə zēn′/.

85

●● Answers
1 (See Teaching Suggestions.)
2 (See the entry for *fond* in the Spelling Dictionary as a model answer.)

A Word from the Arabs
orange, lemon, magazine

Mastery Test
For complete directions and an explanation of the testing program, see the Introduction to this Teacher's Edition.

6 /bôs/ *boss*
7 /hob′ ē/ *hobby*
8 /welth/ *wealth*
9 /môth/ *moth*
10 /blond/ *blond*
11 /ᵺə/ /dok′ tər/ /gāv/ /mē/ /tü/ /bot′ əlz/ /uv/ /vī′ tə minz/ /tü/ /im prüv′/ /mī/ /helth/ *The doctor gave me two bottles of vitamins to improve my health.*
12 /ə/ /top′ noch′/ /jok′ ē/ /mā/ /ėrn/ /ə/ /hūj/ /in′ kum/ *A topnotch jockey may earn a huge income.*

13 /fif′ tē/ /dol′ ərz/ /iz/ /ə/ /dir/ /prīs/ /fôr/ /ə/ /kot′ ən/ /dres/ *Fifty dollars is a dear price for a cotton dress.*
14 /ū/ /kant/ /kut/ /ᵺis/ /pēs/ /uv/ /met′ əl/ /with/ /yùr/ /siz′ ərz/ *You can't cut this piece of metal with your scissors.*
15 /wē/ /kùd/ /hir/ /much/ /rak′ ət/ /frum/ /ᵺə/ /foun′ drē/ *We could hear much racket from the foundry.*

21 Combinations with /u/

Study Chart

Word Types		Review Words	Sound-Spellings	How do we spell these sounds?
■	1 syllable	bunch	/bunch/	/u/
y ey	/ē/ ending	clum,sy stud,y	/klum′ zē/ /stud′ ē/	/u/ /ē/ /u/ /ē/
er or ar	/ər/ ending	but,ter hon,or	/but′ ər/ /on′ ər/	/u/ /ər/ /o/ /ər/
le el al	/əl/ ending	tum,ble tun,nel	/tum′ bəl/ /tun′ əl/	/u/ /əl/ /u/ /əl/
■■	compound	bath,tub	/bath′ tub′/	/a/ /u/
■■	2 syllables	pump,kin	/pump′ kin/	/u/ /i/
■■■	3 syllables	cus,tom,er	/kus′ təm ər/	/u/ /ə/ /ə/
◀■	prefix-root	un,luck,y	/un luk′ ē/	/un/ /u/ /ē/
■▶	root-suffix	trust,ful	/trust′ fəl/	/u/ /fəl/
▽	snurk	ton	/tun/	/u/
Ⓗ	homonyms	some-sum	/sum/	/u/

New Words

drug	thun,der	fun,nel	um,brel,la	▽ sponge
fuz,zy	sculp,tor	thumb,tack	un,just	rung
bulk,y	mus,cle	pup,pet	thought,ful	wrung

86

Teaching Suggestions

This is the last of the five units in which the short-vowel spellings are recycled through the various spelling contexts. The *u* spelling of /u/ is featured in this unit. Among the word types illustrated are review and new snurks with /u/. Included also in this unit of study are review and new homonyms.

Use the Study Chart to introduce the unit in the same manner as was suggested in the previous four units. In addition, it would be worthwhile to again call attention to the usefulness of spelling eye-syllables as if they were little words. For example, spelling *pump* and *kin* as eye-syllables is certainly helpful to the pupils who would otherwise be obliged to memorize a long sequence of unrelated letters in order to spell *pumpkin*.

● These writing exercises should be done independently by the pupils.

Handwriting Models

drug   muscle   unjust

fuzzy   funnel   thoughtful

bulky   thumbtack   ▽ sponge

thunder   puppet   rung

sculptor   umbrella   wrung

1 We expect to spell /u/ with *u*. Write the two new and review one-syllable words in which /u/ is spelled *u*.

2 Write the four new and review two-syllable words in which the soft /ē/ ending is spelled *y*.

3 We can spell the soft /ər/ ending with *er* or *or*. Write the three words in which /ər/ is spelled *er* and the two words in which /ər/ is spelled *or*.

4 We can spell the soft /əl/ ending with *le* or *el*. Write the two words in which /əl/ is spelled *le* and the two words in which /əl/ is spelled *el*.

5 Write the eye-syllables of the two compounds.

6 Write the eye-syllables and the whole words of these two- and three-syllable words.

a /pump' kin/   **c** /kus' təm ər/

b /pup' ət/   **d** /um brel' ə/

7 Write the two words that have the /un/ prefix.

8 Write the two words that have the /fəl/ suffix.

9 Write the two snurks in which /u/ is spelled *o*.

10 Write the two homonyms that are pronounced /sum/ and the two homonyms that are pronounced /rung/.

87

● **Answers**

1 bunch, drug

2 clumsy, study, fuzzy, bulky

3 butter, customer, thunder, honor, sculptor

4 tumble, muscle, tunnel, funnel

5 bath tub, thumb tack

6a pump kin   pumpkin

b pup pet   puppet

c cus tom er   customer

d um brel la   umbrella

7 unlucky, unjust

8 trustful, thoughtful

9 ton, sponge

10 some, sum, rung, wrung

●● These exercises are routine and should be done independently by the pupils.

●

●● Nearly all of the Read and Spell words have the /u/ vowel sound. Pupils should first decode these words by applying the generalizations. Exercises 2, 3, and 4 are routine.

●● Note that the proofreading exercise has improper listing errors as well as spelling errors.

The correct exercise, with corrected spelling errors underscored and corrected listing errors starred, is as follows:

Nouns	Adjectives
customer	*fuzzier*
thumbtack	*clumsiest*
sculptor	*unjust*
puppet	*unlucky*
umbrella	**bulky*
*muscle	*trustful*

Answers

1a sum
 b some
 c rung
 d wrung
 e rung
2 unlucky, unjust, clumsy, fuzzy
3a butter **g** pumpkin
 b funnel **h** sponge
 c thumbtack **i** muscle
 d umbrella **j** bathtub
 e sculptor **k** puppet
 f tunnel **l** customer
4a tumble **d** trustful
 b ton **e** study
 c thunder **f** thoughtful

1 Write the correct homonym for each of these sentences.
a The ____ /sum/ of 2 and 3 is 5.
b We need ____ /sum/ money.
c The bell has ____ /rung/.
d He has ____ /rung/ out his wet clothes.
e She broke a ____ /rung/ on the ladder.

2 Write antonyms from the new and review lists for *lucky, just, nimble,* and *smooth.*

3 Write the new or review word suggested by each of these pictures.

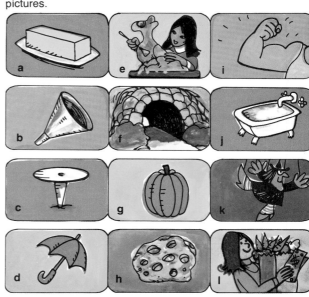

4 Write the new or review word for each of these sound-spellings.
a /tum′ bəl/ **c** /thun′ dər/ **e** /stud′ ē/
b /tun/ **d** /trust′ fəl/ **f** /thôt′ fəl/

88

A considerable number of Mexican-Spanish words are in our language in addition to *mustang* and *bronco.* Some of them are *adobe, arroyo, hacienda, lariat, lasso, mesa, patio, pinto, plaza, pueblo, sierra, taco, tamale,* and *tortilla.*

Mastery Test 21a
 1 /klum′ zē/ *clumsy*
 2 /but′ ər/ *butter*
 3 /thum′ tak′/ *thumbtack*
 4 /fun′ əl/ *funnel*
 5 /bul′ kē/ *bulky*
 6 /thôt′ fəl/ *thoughtful*
 7 /sing′ gəl/ *single*
 8 /tum′ bəl/ *tumble*
 9 /vol′ ən tir′/ *volunteer*
 10 /hok′ ē/ *hockey*
 11 /dok′ tərz/ /and/ /den′ tists/ /stud′ ē/ /fôr/ /men′ ē/ /yirz/ *Doctors and dentists*

Read and Spell

husky	drummer	handcuff	mutton	unfasten
sunny	gutter	humbug	nutmeg	unhappy
stubby	knuckle	humdrum	uncommon	unravel
gully	rumble	sudden	unpack	skillful
lumber	buckle	button	unbuckle	thankful
number	chestnut	muffin	unbutton	trunkful

1 Write any Read and Spell word that you cannot read or any word for which you do not know the meaning.

2 Write the Read and Spell word suggested by each of these pictures.

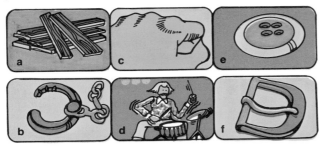

3 Write the words for these sound-spellings. Then write their antonyms by using the /un/ prefix.

a /kom′ ən/   **c** /hap′ ē/   **e** /but′ ən/
b /buk′ əl/   **d** /fas′ ən/   **f** /rav′ əl/

4 Write synonyms from the Read and Spell list for *big, short,* and *ordinary.*

1 Brigit made a list of nouns and a list of adjectives that she found in this unit. Proofread her work. After you have found the mistakes, write the two lists correctly.

89

study for many years.
12 /ᵮHə/ /sālz′ mən/ /sōld/ /hiz/ /kus′ təm ər/ /ə/ /blü/ /um brel′ ə/ *The salesman sold his customer a blue umbrella.*
13 /sum/ /belz/ /wėr/ /rung/ /tü/ /sig′ nəl/ /ᵮHə/ /bėrth/ /uv/ /ᵮHə/ /kingz/ /sun/ *Some bells were rung to signal the birth of the king's son.*
14 /pump′ kənz/ /grü/ /in/ /ᵮHə/ /fēld/ /nir/ /ᵮHār/ /färm′ hous′/ *Pumpkins grew in the field near their farmhouse.*
15 /ᵮHārz/ /ə/ /wet/ /spunj/ /in/ /ᵮHə/

/bath′ tub′/ /tü/ *There's a wet sponge in the bathtub, too.*

Mastery Test 21b
 1 /tun′ əl/ *tunnel*
 2 /drug/ *drug*
 3 /un luk′ ē/ *unlucky*
 4 /thun′ dər/ *thunder*
 5 /un just′/ *unjust*
 6 /fuz′ ē/ *fuzzy*
 7 /trust′ fəl/ *trustful*
 8 /hob′ ē/ *hobby*

Nouns	Adjectives
customer	fuzzier
thumbtack	clumsiest
sculptor	unjust
puppet	unluckier
umbrella	muscle
bulky	trustful

Answers

1 (See Teaching Suggestions.)
2 (See the entries for *wring* and *wrung* in the Spelling Dictionary as model answers.)

Two Words from the Mexicans

a A mustang is a small, tough, western horse.

b The word *bronco* means "rough" or "wild."

c Mustangs and broncos are range horses.

Mastery Test
For complete directions and an explanation of the testing program, see the Introduction to this Teacher's Edition.

2 The form of the verb *ring* that is used with "helping" words like *was, were, have,* and *has* is *rung.* Verb forms such as *rung* usually receive a separate entry in a dictionary.

- **ring** /ring/ *v.* Give forth a clear sound as bells do: *Did the telephone ring?* **rang, rung, ringing.**

- **rung** /rung/ *v. See* **ring.** *The telephone has not rung.*

> A lexicographer shows that we can find the meaning of *rung* by reading the entry for *ring.*

Write dictionary entries for the word *wrung* and the verb of which *wrung* is a form. Compare your work with the Spelling Dictionary.

Two Words from the Mexicans

Mustang is our name for the small, tough, western horse that is descended from the horses brought to Mexico by the Spaniards. *Mustang* comes from the Spanish word *mestengo.* Another name for the range horse that is not broken is *bronco. Bronco* comes from a Mexican-Spanish word that means "rough" or "wild."

Write only the sentences below that are true. Spell the words correctly. Use capital letters and punctuation marks.

a /ə/ /mus′ tang/ /iz/ /ə/ /smôl/ /tuf/ /wes′ tərn/ /hôrs/.

b /ᵮᴴə/ /werd/ /brong′ kō/ /mēnz/ /ruf/ /ôr/ /wīld/.

c /mus′ tangz/ /and/ /brong′ kōz/ /är/ /rānj/ /hôr′ səz/.

90

---

9 /kot′ ən/ *cotton*

10 /tun/ *ton*

11 /ᵮᴴə/ /ô′ dē əns/ /en joid′/ /ᵮᴴə/ /pup′ ət/ /shō/ /tü/ /tīmz/ *The audience enjoyed the puppet show two times.*

12 /shē/ /haz/ /rung/ /ᵮᴴə/ /rag/ /drī/ /with/ /her/ /bār/ /handz/ *She has wrung the rag dry with her bare hands.*

13 /ᵮᴴə/ /skulp′ tər/ /wuz/ /on′ ərd/ /fôr/ /hiz/ /proj′ ekt/ /in/ /mōl′ ding/ /klā/ *The sculptor was honored for his project in molding clay.*

14 /shē/ /haz/ /strength/ /in/ /ᵮᴴə/ /mus′ əlz/ /uv/ /hėr/ /ärmz/ *She has strength in the muscles of her arms.*

15 /ī/ /bôt/ /ə/ /bunch/ /uv/ /flou′ ərz/ /fôr/ /ᵮᴴə/ /sum/ /uv/ /ten/ /sents/ *I bought a bunch of flowers for the sum of ten cents.*

Study Chart

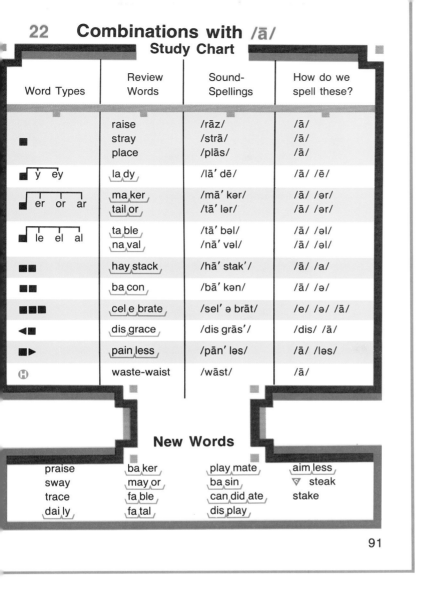

Word Types	Review Words	Sound-Spellings	How do we spell these?
■	raise	/rāz/	/ā/
	stray	/strā/	/ā/
	place	/plās/	/ā/
■ y ey	la dy	/lā′ dē/	/ā/ /ē/
■ er or ar	ma ker	/mā′ kər/	/ā/ /ər/
	tail or	/tā′ lər/	/ā/ /ər/
■ le el al	ta ble	/tā′ bəl/	/ā/ /əl/
	na val	/nā′ vəl/	/ā/ /əl/
■ ■	hay stack	/hā′ stak′/	/ā/ /a/
■ ■	ba con	/bā′ kən/	/ā/ /ə/
■ ■ ■	cel e brate	/sel′ ə brāt/	/e/ /ə/ /ā/
◀ ■	dis grace	/dis grās′/	/dis/ /ā/
■ ▶	pain less	/pān′ ləs/	/ā/ /ləs/
Ⓗ	waste-waist	/wāst/	/ā/

New Words

praise	ba ker	play mate	aim less
sway	may or	ba sin	▽ steak
trace	fa ble	can did ate	stake
dai ly	fa tal	dis play	

91

Teaching Suggestions

In this unit the three familiar spellings of /ā/, ai, ay, and a-consonant-e, are recycled through the various word-type contexts. Pupils are again reminded that what they learned in monosyllabic spelling continues to apply to multisyllabic spelling.

Use the Study Chart to review with the pupils the generalization that we customarily spell /ā/ in words and syllables with ai, ay, or a-consonant-e. A discussion of the spellings of the sounds shown in the last column is a good way to accomplish the review. The generalizations should be applied to the new words. Discuss also the eye-syllable markings for the review and new words.

● The exercises in this section involve the writing of all the words according to their word types. Note that two pairs of homonyms are included. One new homonym is also a snurk.

Handwriting Models

praise   baker   playmate aimless
sway   mayor   basin   ▽ steak
trace   fable   candidate stake
daily   fatal   display

1   We can spell /ā/ with *ai, ay,* or *a*-consonant-*e.* Write the two one-syllable words in which /ā/ is spelled *ai,* the two one-syllable words in which /ā/ is spelled *ay,* and the two one-syllable words in which /ā/ is spelled *a*-consonant-*e.*

2   Write the two words in which *y* spells the soft /ē/ ending.

3   We can spell the soft /ər/ ending with *er* or *or.* Write the two words in which /ər/ is spelled *er* and the two words in which /ər/ is spelled *or.*

4   We can spell the soft /əl/ ending with *le* or *al.* Write the two words in which /əl/ is spelled *le* and the two words in which /əl/ is spelled *al.*

5   Write the compounds /hā′ stak′/ and /plā′ māt′/. Draw a line between the eye-syllables of each word.

6   Write these two- and three-syllable words. Draw lines between the eye-syllables of each word.

  a /bā′ kən/   **c** /sel′ ə brāt/

  b /bā′ sən/   **d** /kan′ də dāt/

7   Write these prefix and suffix words. Draw a ring around the prefix or suffix of each word.

  a /dis grās′/   **c** /pān′ ləs/

  b /dis plā′/   **d** /ām′ ləs/

8   Write the two homonyms pronounced /wāst/ and the two homonyms pronounced /stāk/.

92

●● These exercises follow the usual pattern and should be done independently by the pupils. Exercise 2 repeats the familiar *ing* generalization. Exercise 4 involves word meanings.

●● The Read and Spell words offer another opportunity for pupils to practice word perception skills. All of these words contain /ā/. The writing exercises are routine and should be done independently by the pupils.

●● The errors in the proofreading exercise are ones of spelling, capitalization, and punctuation. The correct exercise, with corrected errors underscored, is as follows:

A fable is a story that is made up to teach a lesson. Animals behave like human beings in many fables. Some are wise. Others are stupid. The sly fox, the carefree grasshopper, and the vain crow are characters in fables that are known in many countries.

1 Write the correct homonym to complete each of the sentences below.

a Do not _____ /wāst/ your time.
b She wore a belt around her _____ /wāst/.
c He drove a _____ /stāk/ into the ground.
d They bought a _____ /stāk/ at the meat market.

2 Write the *ing* form of each of these words.

a /rāz/　　**c** /plās/　　**e** /sel′ ə brāt/
b /prāz/　　**d** /trās/　　**f** /wāst/

3 Write the new or review word suggested by each of these pictures.

4 Write a word from the new or review list for each clue below.

a deadly
b without pain
c move back and forth
d every day
e shame
f move up
g story
h wander
i having no purpose
j to show
k of the navy
l woman

93

●● **Answers**

1a waste
b waist
c stake
d steak

2a raising
b praising
c placing
3a candidate
b haystack
c bacon
d mayor
e table

d tracing
e celebrating
f wasting
f baker
g tailor
h playmate
i basin

4a fatal
b painless
c sway
d daily
e disgrace
f raise

g fable
h stray
i aimless
j display
k naval
l lady

A Greek slave named *Aesop* wrote many of the fables more than twenty-five hundred years ago. Isn't it remarkable that we can still enjoy them?(!)

Other words from the Latin language, in addition to *alias*, that we use are *alibi*, *nil*, *per*, *quorum*, *quota*, *status*, and *via*. Pupils could investigate Latin phrases, such as *ad hoc*, *alma mater*, *bona fide*, *corpus delicti*, *de facto*, *per annum*, *per capita*, and *status quo*.

Mastery Test 22a

1 /bā′ sən/ *basin*
2 /dis plā′/ *display*
3 /dis grās′/ *disgrace*
4 /plās/ *place*
5 /trās/ *trace*
6 /fā′ təl/ *fatal*
7 /lā′ dē/ *lady*
8 /um brel′ ə/ *umbrella*
9 /spunj/ *sponge*
10 /mā′ kər/ *maker*

Answers

2 praying, braying,
  complaining
3a landscape
  b estate
  c gravy, drain
4 major, cradle, inhale,
  labor

Read and Spell

grain	shady	cradle	dismay	unsafe
drain	gravy	salesman	complain	painful
pray	waiter	landscape	contain	pavement
bray	major	estate	relay	station
blaze	labor	agent	invade	shameless
flame	maple	estimate	inhale	plainness

1 Write any Read and Spell word that you cannot read or any word for which you do not know the meaning.

2 Write the *ing* forms of the Read and Spell words /prā/, /brā/, and /kəm plān′/.

3 Write Read and Spell words to complete these sentences.

a She's painting a _____.

b She sells real _____.

c He's pouring _____ down the _____.

4 Write the Read and Spell words /mā′ jər/, /krā′ dəl/, /in hāl′/, and /lā′ bər/.

1 Proofread the paragraphs Jane wrote about fables. Find her mistakes and write the paragraphs correctly.

94

---

11 /lets/ /not/ /wāst/ /ᵮнis/ /pēs/ /uv/ /bā′ kən/ /sed/ /ᵮнə/ /kůk/ *"Let's not waste this piece of bacon," said the cook.*
12 /wē/ /sel′ ə brāt/ /ūl′ tīd′/ /bī/ /sing′ ing/ /kar′ əlz/ *We celebrate yuletide by singing carols.*
13 /ᵮнə/ /tā′ lər/ /sōd/ /ᵮнə/ /wāst/ /tü/ /ᵮнə/ /skėrt/ /with/ /blü/ /thred/ *The tailor sewed the waist to the skirt with blue thread.*
14 /hav/ /ᵮнōz/ /tü/ /plā′ māts′/ /had/ /ᵮнār/ /dā′ lē/ /gām/ /uv/ /hop′ skoch′/

Have those two playmates had their daily game of hopscotch?
15 /ᵮнə/ /ak′ tərz/ /boud/ /az/ /ᵮнə/ /līts/ /ôn/ /ᵮнə/ /stāj/ /wėr/ /rāzd/ *The actors bowed as the lights on the stage were raised.*

Mastery Test 22b
 1 /nā′ vəl/ *naval*
 2 /prāz′ əz/ *praises*
 3 /skulp′ tər/ *sculptor*
 4 /hā′ stak′/ *haystack*

A fable is a story that is made up to teach a lesson. Animals behave like human beings in many fables. Some are wise. Others are stuped. The sly fox the carefree grasshopper and the vain crow are characters in fables that are known in many country.

A Greek slave named aesop wrote many of the fables more than twenty-five hundred years ago. Isn't it remarkable that we can still enjoy them.

2 When two different words are spelled the same way, each word is given a separate dictionary entry.

A lexicographer uses the numerals *1* and *2* to show that there are two different words spelled *base*.	• **base**[1] /bās/ *n.* **1.** The bottom: *the base of the statue.* **2.** Starting place. **3.** Goal in a game. • **base**[2] /bās/ *adj.* Mean and low: *base deeds.* **baser, basest.**

Write two complete entries for the words spelled *stake*. Compare your work with the entries in the Spelling Dictionary.

A Word from the Romans

More of our English words have come from Latin than from any other language. Our word *alias* /ā′ lē əs/ comes from the Romans' Latin word *alius,* meaning "other." We use it to mean "a false name." We might say: *James Johnson, the spy, used "John Harrison" as an alias.*
Write only the true sentence below. Spell the words correctly.
a /an/ /ā′ lē əs/ /iz/ /ə/ /spī/.
b /an/ /ā′ lē əs/ /iz/ /ə/ /fôls/ /nām/.
c /an/ /ā′ lē əs/ /iz/ /ə/ /pèr′ sənz/ /rē′ əl/ /nām/.

95

Answers
1 (See Teaching Suggestions.)
2 (See the entries for *stake* in the Spelling Dictionary as model answers.)

A Word from the Romans
b An alias is a false name.

Mastery Test
For complete directions and an explanation of the testing program, see the Introduction to this Teacher's Edition.

5 /thum′ tak′/ *thumbtack*
6 /pān′ ləs/ *painless*
7 /strā/ *stray*
8 /spon′ sər/ *sponsor*
9 /fā′ bəl/ *fable*
10 /ām′ ləs/ *aimless*
11 /ᵺār/ /wėr/ /tü/ /kan′ də dāts/ /fôr/ /mā′ ər/ /uv/ /our/ /sit′ ē/ *There were two candidates for mayor of our city.*
12 /plēz/ /set/ /ᵺis/ /plat′ ər/ /uv/ /stāk/ /ôn/ /ᵺə/ /tā′ bəl/ *Please set this platter of steak on the table.*
13 /bouz/ /uv/ /trēz/ /swād/ /hwen/ /sôft/ /brē′ zəz/ /blü/ *Boughs of trees swayed when soft breezes blew.*
14 /ᵺə/ /bāk′ ər/ /let/ /hiz/ /bred/ /dō/ /rīz/ /fôr/ /wun/ /our/ *The baker let his bread dough rise for one hour.*
15 /its/ /im pos′ ə bəl/ /tü/ /rench/ /ᵺis/ /stāk/ /frum/ /ᵺə/ /ground/ *It's impossible to wrench this stake from the ground.*

95

23 Combinations with /ē/

Study Chart

Word Types	Review Words	Sound-Spellings	How do we spell these?
■	peach greet these	/pēch/ /grēt/ /ᵀHēz/	/ē/ /ē/ /ē/
■< y ey	needy	/nē' dē/	/ē/ /ē/
■< er or ar	fever	/fē' vər/	/ē/ /ər/
■< le el al	needle eagle	/nē' dəl/ /ē' gəl/	/ē/ /əl/ /ē/ /əl/
■■	daydream seaweed	/dā' drēm'/ /sē' wēd'/	/ā/ /ē/ /ē/ /ē/
■■	season	/sē' zən/	/ē/ /ə/
■■■	appealing	/ə pēl' ing/	/ə/ /ē/ /i/
◄■	explain	/eks plān'/	/eks/ /ā/
■►	readable	/rēd' ə bəl/	/ē/ /ə bəl/
Ⓗ	piece-peace	/pēs/	/ē/

New Words

cheat	treaty	legal	vehicle	agreeable
sleet	eager	teammate	extreme	▽ grief
scheme	steeple	reason	exceed	▽ shield

96

Teaching Suggestions

The *ee, ea,* and *e*-consonant-*e* spellings of /ē/ are illustrated by the words in this unit. Many spelling errors result from confusion over whether to use *ee* or *ea* in specific instances. For that reason, these two spelling patterns dominate in the words of this unit. Note that three words, *fever, legal,* and *vehicle,* are examples of words with /ē/ at the end of a syllable spelled *e.* Two review homonyms are included, as are two new snurks.

Use the Study Chart in the usual manner to introduce the unit. Have the pupils discuss the spelling generalizations illustrated by the words in the Study Chart and in the list of new words. Regular attention to the sound-spellings in the Study Chart will enable pupils to use dictionary pronunciations with confidence.

● These exercises provide, as usual, a written reinforcement of the Study Chart.

Handwriting Models

cheat	*eager*	*reason*	*agreeable*
sleet	*steeple*	*vehicle*	▽ *grief*
scheme	*legal*	*extreme*	▽ *shield*
treaty	*teammate*	*exceed*	

● **Answers**
1 peach, peace, cheat, greet, sleet, these, scheme
2 needy, treaty
3 fever, eager
4 needle, eagle, steeple, legal
5 day dream, sea weed, team mate
6 sea son, rea son, ap peal ing
7 ex plain, ex treme, ex ceed
8 read able, a gree able
9 piece, grief, shield, ie

1 We can spell /ē/ with *ea, ee,* or *e*-consonant-*e.* Write the three one-syllable words in which *ea* spells /ē/, the two one-syllable words in which *ee* spells /ē/, and the two one-syllable words in which *e*-consonant-*e* spells /ē/.

2 Write the two new and review words in which *y* spells the soft /ē/ ending.

3 Write the two new and review words in which *er* spells the /ər/ ending.

4 We can spell the soft /əl/ ending with *le* or *al.* Write the three two-syllable words in which *le* spells /əl/ and the word in which *al* spells /əl/.

5 Write the eye-syllables of the three new and review compound words.

6 Write the eye-syllables of the two-syllable words /sē′ zən/ and /rē′ zən/ and the three-syllable word /ə pēl′ ing/.

7 Write the eye-syllables of the prefix-root words /eks plān′/, /eks trēm′/, and /ek sēd′/.

8 Write the eye-syllables of the root-suffix words /rēd′ ə bəl/ and /ə grē′ ə bəl/.

9 Write one review-word snurk and two new-word snurks. These words are snurks because /ē/ is spelled ____, instead of one of the expected ways.

97

●● It will be helpful for pupils if you run through these sentences orally before the written work is assigned. The vocabulary at this level is becoming increasingly abstract. Many of the words that regularly appear in the pupils' reading material, and therefore in this spelling text, are not part of their normal speech.

●● The Read and Spell list is again a good word perception test. The word meanings are becoming a formidable factor of difficulty in this section, also. You may need to make an increased effort to help pupils identify and learn those words with which they are not thoroughly familiar. As usual, many of the writing exercises that follow require familiarity with the meanings of the words.

●● The correct proofreading exercise, with corrected errors underscored, is as follows:

Write words from the new and review lists to complete the sentences below and on the next page. You will have to change the form of some words to fit the sentences.

1 He sure does ＿＿ his ＿＿ in height!

2 That's an ＿＿ sitting on a ＿＿.

3 He found out it's not ＿＿ to ＿＿.

4 ＿＿ children are showing ＿＿ ＿＿.

5 That's a clever ＿＿ to make people ＿＿ to help the ＿＿.

6 She's trying to ＿＿ her ＿＿ from the ＿＿.

98

The bald eagle with its wings *spread* out is the symbol of the United States. The famous Benjamin Franklin would have *preferred* to use the turkey instead. He explained that the wild turkey was a native of the *fields* and woods of North America.

What do you think about having a turkey on the official seal used for legal papers and *treaties?* Perhaps it would not seem odd if we had never thought of the great eagle at all.

Mastery Test 23a

1 /rēd′ ə bəl/ *readable*
2 /lē′ gəl/ *legal*
3 /tēm′ māt′/ *teammate*
4 /rē′ zən/ *reason*
5 /pēch/ *peach*
6 /eks trēm′/ *extreme*
7 /ə pēl′ ing/ *appealing*
8 /swet′ ər/ *sweater*
9 /bə lēf′/ *belief*
10 /kan′ də dāt/ *candidate*

7 She is ____ for the winter ____ to end.

Read and Spell

scream	beagle	beacon	proceed	evidence
bleed	steamship	succeed	disease	weakness
eve	midstream	female	exchange	heedless
greasy	peanut	arena	release	reasonable
beaver	athlete	concrete	completion	indeed
feeble	tepee	compete	treatment	uneven

1 Write any Read and Spell word that you cannot read or any word for which you do not know the meaning.

2 Write the Read and Spell words for these pictures.

3 Write synonyms from the Read and Spell list for *oily, weak, illness,* and *trade.*

4 Write antonyms from the Read and Spell list for *fail, capture, attentive,* and *even.*

1 Kip wrote two paragraphs for a social studies assignment. Proofread his work. Write the paragraphs correctly.

99

7 eager, season

●● **Answers**

2a beaver   **d** beacon
  b beagle   **e** arena
  c steamship   **f** peanut
3 greasy, feeble, disease, exchange
4 succeed, release, heedless, uneven

1 /wē/ /hav/ /dā′lē/ /slēt/ /stôrmz/ /at/ /ŦHis/ /sē′zən/ *We have daily sleet storms at this season.*

2 /its/ /not/ /on′ ər ə bəl/ /tü/ /chēt/ /ôn/ /tests/ *It's not honorable to cheat on tests.*

3 /ə/ /bôld/ /ē′gəl/ /flü/ /tü/ /ŦHə/ /top/ /uv/ /ŦHə/ /stē′pəl/ *A bald eagle flew to the top of the steeple.*

4 /tā′lərz/ /ūz/ /hūj/ /nē′dəlz/ /tü/ /sō/ /kot′ən/ /klôth/ *Tailors use huge needles to sew cotton cloth.*

15 /ə/ /pēs/ /uv/ /sē′ wēd′/ /drif′ təd/ /tôrd/ /shôr/ *A piece of seaweed drifted toward shore.*

Mastery Test 23b
1 /ek sēd′/ *exceed*
2 /grēt/ *greet*
3 /grēf/ *grief*
4 /shēld/ *shield*

The bald eagle with its wings spred out is the symbol of the United States. The famous Benjamin Franklin would have prefered to use the turkey instead. He explained that the wild turkey was a native of the feilds and woods of North America.

What do you think about having a turkey on the official seal used for legal papers and treatys. Perhaps it would not seem odd if we had never thought of the great eagle at all.

2 Some dictionaries give synonyms for some entry word
Read the dictionary entry below for the word *grief.*

● **grief** /grēf/ *n.* Great sadness
caused by trouble or loss: *Her
grief was caused by the death of
a friend. syn.* **sorrow.** ◄——

> A lexicographer ma
> show one or more
> synonyms for the
> entry word.

Write a complete dictionary entry for the word *agreeabl*
Include several synonyms at the end of the entry. Compa
your work with the entry in the Spelling Dictionary.

=== **A Word from the Norwegians** ===

The word *ski* is pronounced /skē/ in America. It is pronounced /shē/
in England. *Ski* comes from a Norwegian word meaning "a stick of
wood." Skis are narrow strips of wood, metal, or plastic that are used
to slide over snow.

Write only the sentences below that are true. Spell the words correctly. Use capital letters and punctuation marks.
a /skēz/ /är/ /wīd/ /pē′ səz/ /uv/ /wùd/.
b /skēz/ /är/ /ūzd/ /tü/ /slīd/ /ō′ vər/ /snō/.
c /skēz/ /kan/ /bē/ /mād/ /uv/ /met′ əl/.

100

Study Chart

Word Types	Review Words	Sound-Spellings	How do we spell these?
■	shy glide flight	/shī/ /glīd/ /flīt/	/ī/ /ī/ /ī/
y ey	ti ny	/tī' nē/	/ī/ /ē/
er or ar	spi der	/spī' dər/	/ī/ /ər/
le el al	ri fle fi nal	/rī' fəl/ /fī' nəl/	/ī/ /əl/ /ī/ /əl/
■■	fire fly	/fīr' flī'/	/ī/ /ī/
■■	si ren hy drant	/sī' rən/ /hī' drənt/	/ī/ /ə/ /ī/ /ə/
◀■	re cite	/rē sīt'/	/rē/ /ī/
■▶	like ness	/līk' nəs/	/ī/ /nəs/
Ⓗ	die-dye	/dī/	/ī/
▽	guide	/gīd/	/ī/

New Words

pry	nine ty	ti tle	ny lon	i dol
crime	mi ser	like wise	re tire	i dle
blight	vi sor	rep tile	bright ness	▽ height

101

Teaching Suggestions

This unit features three spellings of /ī/ recycled through the various word-type patterns. The three spellings of /ī/ are *y*, *i*-consonant-*e*, and *gh*. Of course, spellings of /ī/ from the earlier levels are shown also. For example, the *i* spelling of /ī/ when it is in the terminal position of a syllable is common. Pupils might recall, also, that the *ie* spelling of /ī/ is common in earlier levels because of the heavy occurrence of words like *die*, *lie*, *pie*, and *tie*. Unfortunately, *ie* frequently spells /ē/ in words at this level such as *field*, *yield*, *shield*, *niece*, and *piece*. Another spelling of /ī/ much used in earlier level vocabulary, namely *i* in the *ind* family of words (*bind*, *find*, *mind*, etc.), is not considered to be a problem at this level and is not included in this unit.

Introduce the unit by using the Study Chart as a discussion vehicle. Pupils should discuss the spelling generalizations in the usual manner and apply them to the new words. You may need to make a special effort to help pupils understand that final *y* spells /ē/ in unstressed syl-

1 shy, dye, pry, flight, blight, glide, crime

2 tiny, ninety

3 spider, miser, visor

4 rifle, title, idle, final

5 fire fly firefly
like wise likewise

6 recite, retire, likeness, brightness

7 guide, height

8a die

 b dye

 c idle

 d idols

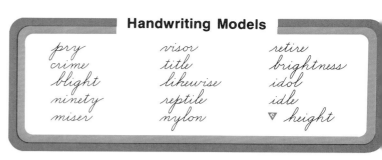

Handwriting Models

pry   visor   retire
crime   title   brightness
blight   likewise   idol
ninety   reptile   idle
miser   nylon   ▽ height

1 We can spell /ī/ with *y*, *igh*, or *i-consonant-e*. Write the three one-syllable words in which *y* (or *ye*) spells /ī/, the two one-syllable words in which *igh* spells /ī/, and the two one-syllable words in which *i-consonant-e* spells /ī/.

2 Write the two words in which *y* spells the soft /ē/ ending.

3 We can spell the soft /ər/ ending with *er* or *or*. Write the two words in which *er* spells /ər/ and the word in which *or* spells /ər/.

4 We can spell the soft /əl/ ending with *le* or *al*. Write the three words in which *le* spells /əl/ and the word in which *al* spells /əl/.

5 Write the eye-syllables of the two compounds. Write the whole word after the eye-syllables.

6 Write the two prefix-root words and the two root-suffix words.

7 Write the snurk in which /ī/ is spelled *ui* and the snurk in which /ī/ is spelled *ei*.

8 Write the correct homonym for each of these sentences.
a In winter the flowers ____ /dī/.
b We ____ /dī/ our clothes.
c Lazy people are often ____ /ī′ dəl/.
d Long ago people made ____ /ī′ dəlz/ into gods.

102

lables and that it spells /ī/ in stressed syllables. (In words of Greek origin, *y* is also used to spell /i/ or /ī/, as in *cyclone, cylinder, dynamite, hyphen,* and *syllable.*) Note that the Study Chart contains a pair of review homonyms and a review snurk.

● As usual, pupils should do these exercises independently, unless they have not participated in a previous discussion of the Study Chart.

●● These exercises are routine.

●
●● The Read and Spell words serve as a diagnostic probe into the word perception skills centered on words with /ī/. As suggested in the last unit, it is increasingly important that extra time and effort be spent on clarifying the meanings of these words.

●●
●● The correct proofreading exercise, with corrected errors underscored, is as follows:

1 Write a word from the new or review list for each of these pictures.

2 Write synonyms from the review list for the words *bashful, little,* and *last.*

3 Write the *ing* forms of the review words /glīd/, /gīd/, and /rē sīt′/.

4 Write the new and review words that mean "to move by force," "not busy," and "to color."

5 Write the words for these sound-spellings.

a	/krīm/	**d**	/flīt/	**g**	/blīt/
b	/hīt/	**e**	/brīt′ nəs/	**h**	/līk′ nəs/
c	/līk′ wīz′/	**f**	/rē tīr′/	**i**	/tī′ təl/

6 Write the two new and review words that have the /nəs/ noun suffix.

7 Write the two new and review words that have the /rē/ prefix.

103

1. The words weight *and* height *are homonyms.* false

2. A spider is a kind of reptile. false

3. The final syllable of the word nylon has a long vowel sound. false

4. A miser spends his money in a carefree way. false

5. Fireflies are tiny birds. false

6. The sum of fifty and twenty is less than ninety. true

7. A rifle is a kind of pistol. false

Mastery Test 24a
1 /rē tīr′/ *retire*
2 /rī′ fəl/ *rifle*
3 /shī/ *shy*
4 /rep′ tīl/ *reptile*
5 /līk′ wīz′/ *likewise*
6 /glīd/ *glide*
7 /vī′ zər/ *visor*
8 /shēld/ *shield*
9 /skēm/ *scheme*
10 /flīt/ *flight*
11 /ŦHə/ /mī′ zər/ /hid/ /hiz/ /welth/ /in/ /ə/

Read and Spell

sly	bridle	lightning	imply	assignment
quite	pipeline	frighten	inside	silence
slight	grapevine	python	unwind	blindness
spicy	daylight	revise	profile	frightful
diver	beehive	confide	excite	sightless
glider	entire	combine	vibration	likable

1 The Read and Spell words have all the combinations with /ī/. Write any word that you cannot read or any word for which you do not know the meaning.

2 Write the Read and Spell words for these pictures.

3 Write the *ing* forms of the Read and Spell words /rē vīz′/, /kən fīd′/, and /un wīnd′/.

4 Write the Read and Spell words that are formed by adding a noun suffix to the words /blīnd/, /ə sīn′/, and /vī′ brāt/.

5 Write the Read and Spell words that are formed by adding an adjective suffix to the words /sīt/, /līk/, and /frīt/.

1 Mike wrote ten sentences for a true-false test. Proofread his work for spelling. After you have found his mistakes, write the sentences correctly. Also, write *true* or *false* after each sentence.

104

/chest/ *The miser hid his wealth in a chest.*
12 /duz/ /ə/ /tī′ nē/ /spī′ dər/ /hav/ /six/
/legz/ /ôr/ /āt/ *Does a tiny spider have six legs or eight?*
13 /hwot/ /kôz′ əz/ /such/ /splen′ dər/ /in/
/ə/ /fīr′ flīz′/ /tāl/ *What causes such splendor in a firefly's tail?*
14 /our/ /dônt′ les′/ /gīd/ /led/ /ᵺ Hə/ /wā/
/thrü/ /ᵺ Hə/ /därk′ nəs/ *Our dauntless guide led the way through the darkness.*

15 /shē/ /dīd/ /hėr/ /nī′ lon/ /dres/ /red/
She dyed her nylon dress red.

Mastery Test 24b
 1 /fī′ nəl/ *final*
 2 /brīt′ nəs/ *brightness*
 3 /prī/ *pry*
 4 /prāz′ əz/ *praises*
 5 /sī′ rən/ *siren*
 6 /eks trēm′/ *extreme*

1. *The words wright and height are homonyms.*
2. *A spider is a kind of reptile.*
3. *The final syllable of the word nylon has a long vowel sound.*
4. *A mizer spends his money in a carefree way.*
5. *Fireflys are tiny birds.*
6. *The sum of fifty and twenty is less than ninty.*
7. *A rifle is a kind of pistle.*

2 Antonyms are given for some words in some dictionaries. Read the dictionary entry below for the word *tiny*.

- **tiny** /tī′ nē/ *adj.* Very small: *a tiny baby duck.* **tinier, tiniest.** *ant.* **huge, large.** ◄——

> A lexicographer may show one or more antonyms for the entry word after the abbreviation *ant.*

Write a complete dictionary entry for the word *idle*. Use a sample sentence or phrase to make the meaning clear. Show the *er* and *est* forms of the word. Give one or more antonyms for the word. When you have finished, compare your work with the entry in the Spelling Dictionary.

A Word from the Icelanders

The Icelandic word *geysir,* meaning "gusher," has become the English word *geyser* /gī′ zər/. A geyser is a spring that throws out jets of hot water and steam at regular times.

Write only the rhyming words in this list. Spell all of the rhyming words correctly.

a /mī′ zər/　　**c** /vī′ zər/　　**e** /gī′ zər/
b /ī′ dəl/　　　**d** /wī′ zər/　　**f** /nī′ lon/

105

Answers
1 (See Teaching Suggestions.)
2 (See the entry for *idle* in the Spelling Dictionary as a model answer.)

A Word from the Icelanders
a miser
c visor
d wiser
e geyser

Mastery Test
For complete directions and an explanation of the testing program, see the Introduction to this Teacher's Edition.

---

7 /grēf/ *grief*
8 /hī′ drənt/ *hydrant*
9 /krīm/ *crime*
10 /līk′ nəs/ *likeness*
11 /ᵻHə/ /ī′ dəl/ /iz/ /mād/ /uv/ /gōld/ /sil′ vər/ /and/ /led/ *The idol is made of gold, silver, and lead.*
12 /hwots/ /ᵻHə/ /tī′ təl/ /uv/ /ᵻHə/ /vèrs/ /ūl/ /rē sīt′/ *What's the title of the verse you'll recite?*

13 /ᵻHə/ /hīt/ /uv/ /ᵻHə/ /stē′ pəl/ /ek sēdz′/ /nīn′ tē/ /fēt/ *The height of the steeple exceeds ninety feet.*
14 /ᵻHə/ /lā′ zē/ /chīld/ /past/ /ᵻHə/ /tīm/ /in/ /ī′ dəl/ /dā′ drē′ ming/ *The lazy child passed the time in idle daydreaming.*
15 /ə/ /sir′ ē əs/ /blīt/ /kôzd/ /ôl/ /ᵻHə/ /trēz/ /tü/ /dī/ *A serious blight caused all the trees to die.*

Combinations with /ō/
Study Chart

Word Types	Review Words	Sound-Spellings	How do we spell these?
■	throat	/thrōt/	/ō/
	flow	/flō/	/ō/
	globe	/glōb/	/ō/
y / ey	lone ly	/lōn' lē/	/ō/ /ē/
er / or / ar	clo ver	/klō' vər/	/ō/ /ər/
	mo tor	/mō' tər/	/ō/ /ər/
	po lar	/pō' lər/	/ō/ /ər/
le / el / al	to tal	/tō' təl/	/ō/ /əl/
■ ■	rail road	/rāl' rōd'/	/ā/ /ō/
■ ■	cy clone	/sī' klōn/	/ī/ /ō/
	lo cate	/lō' kāt/	/ō/ /ā/
◀ ■	pro mote	/prō mōt'/	/prō/ /ō/
■ ▶	mo tion	/mō' shən/	/ō/ /shən/
⊕	roll-role	/rōl/	/ō/

New Words

boast	ho ly	so lar	rain bow	lo ca tion
growth	own er	no ble	co coa	▽ poll
clothes	o dor	lo cal	pro pose	pole

106

Teaching Suggestions

This unit features three spellings of /ō/ recycled through the various word-type patterns. The three spellings of /ō/ are *oa, ow,* and *o*-conso-nant-*e*. The *o* spelling of /ō/ when it is in the terminal position of a syllable, a generalization introduced in earlier levels, is also illustrated by many of the words in this unit. The *o* spelling of /ō/ in the *old* family of words (*bold, cold, fold,* etc.) is a familiar spelling pattern in earlier level vocabulary. However, it is not considered to be a problem at this level and is not, therefore, included in this unit.

Introduce the unit with a discussion of the Study Chart. You may want to spend some time discussing with pupils the ambiguity of the *ow* spelling. As used in the words of this unit, *ow* spells /ō/. However, it is also a common spelling of /ou/. Note, too, that there are a pair of review homonyms and an analogous pair of new homonyms. One in each pair is a snurk.

Handwriting Models

boast   owner   local   location
growth   odor   rainbow   ▽ poll
clothes   solar   cocoa   pole
holy   noble   propose

1 Write the two one-syllable words in which *oa* spells /ō/, the two one-syllable words in which *ow* spells /ō/, and the four one-syllable words in which *o-consonant-e* spells /ō/.

2 Write the two words in which *y* spells the soft /ē/ ending.

3 Write the two words in which *er* spells the /ər/ ending, the two words in which *or* spells /ər/, and the two words in which *ar* spells /ər/.

4 Write the word in which *le* spells the /əl/ ending and the two words in which *al* spells the /əl/ ending.

5 Write the eye-syllables of /rāl′ rōd′/, /rān′ bō′/, /sī′ klōn/, /lō′ kāt/, and /kō′ kō/.

6 Write the eye-syllables of /prō mōt′/ and /mō′ shən/.

7 Write the correct homonym for each of these sentences.
a We called the ____ /rōl/ of names.
b We took a ____ /pōl/ of the class.
c He played the ____ /rōl/ of the prince.
d She broke her fishing ____ /pōl/.

1 Write the new and review words for these sound-spellings.
a /thrōt/   **c** /flō/   **e** /tō′ təl/
b /bōst/   **d** /grōth/   **f** /lō′ kəl/

2 Write the *ing* forms of /lō′ kāt/, /prō pōz′/, and /prō mōt′/.

3 Write the *er* and *est* forms of *lonely* and *holy*.

107

●   The exercises in this section focus on the spelling generalizations of the words according to their word-type patterns.

●●   Exercises 2 and 3 of this section cause pupils to apply structural generalizations.

●
●●   The Read and Spell list can again be used as a decoding test. The meanings of some words may require clarification.

●●
●●   There are no errors of fact in the proof-reading exercise. The correct exercise, with corrected errors underscored, is as follows:

A rainbow is a band of colors arching across the sky. It forms when sunshine and drops of rain are in the sky at the same time. The sunlight <u>*breaks*</u> *up when it passes* <u>*through*</u> *the raindrops. The light scatters into bands of red,* <u>*orange,*</u> *yellow,* <u>*green,*</u> *blue,* <u>*indigo,*</u> *and violet. The seven colors always appear in this order.*

4a cyclone, railroad
 b polar, solar
 c role, noble

4 Write new and review words to complete these sentences.

a The ____ blew the roof off of the ____ station.

b This ____ bear didn't expect a ____ eclipse.

c She's playing the ____ of a ____ queen.

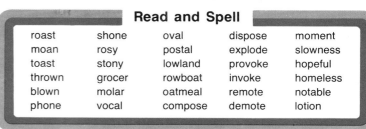

Read and Spell

roast	shone	oval	dispose	moment
moan	rosy	postal	explode	slowness
toast	stony	lowland	provoke	hopeful
thrown	grocer	rowboat	invoke	homeless
blown	molar	oatmeal	remote	notable
phone	vocal	compose	demote	lotion

1 Write any Read and Spell word that you cannot read or any word for which you do not know the meaning.

2 Write Read and Spell words to complete the sentences below and on the next page.

a He likes to ____ music on a ____ island.

108

A morning rainbow in the western sky means that rain will soon begin. An evening rainbow in the eastern sky means that rain has passed.

In addition to *kosher*, some other words from the Hebrews that pupils may investigate are *behemoth, hallelujah, hosanna, leviathan, manna,* and *shibboleth.* Hebrew has, of course, been revived in modern Israel. Most of our borrowed Hebrew words come from the Bible and have English spellings.

Mastery Test 25a
1 /pō′ lər/ *polar*
2 /lōn′ lē/ *lonely*
3 /thrōt/ *throat*
4 /flō/ *flow*
5 /glōb/ *globe*
6 /nō′ bəl/ *noble*
7 /lō′ kəl/ *local*
8 /tī′ təl/ *title*
9 /vī′ tə min/ *vitamin*
10 /lik′ wid/ *liquid*
11 /hwot/ /rōl/ /duz/ /ŦHat/ /ak′ tər/ /plā/ /in/

b This ____ worker seems to ____ the dog.

c He's very ____ when he's on the ____.

d He's a ____ eater of ____.

e The dog is ____, but ____ of finding a home.

f This ____ must have a very sore ____.

g She wants to ____ of her bottles of beauty ____ in a hurry.

b postal, provoke
c vocal, phone
d notable, oatmeal
e homeless, hopeful
f grocer, molar
g dispose, lotion

1 Rosa wrote the short report on the next page for her science class. Proofread her work for mistakes in spelling and punctuation and for incorrect facts. You may need to use the Spelling Dictionary to check the facts. After you have found her mistakes, write the report correctly.

109

/ᵮHə/ /nü/ /mü′ vē/   *What role does that actor play in the new movie?*
12 /ū/ /kan/ /sē/ /ə/ /rān′ bō′/ /in/ /ᵮHə/ /wes′ tərn/ /skī/ /frum/ /ᵮHis/ /lō kā′ shən/ *You can see a rainbow in the western sky from this location.*
13 /ᵮHārz/ /ə/ /thik/ /grōth/ /uv/ /klō′ vər/ /in/ /mī/ /frunt/ /yärd/   *There's a thick growth of clover in my front yard.*
14 /ᵮHə/ /tō′ təl/ /kôst/ /uv/ /ə/ /mō′ tər/ /fôr/ /yůr/ /vē′ ə kəl/ /iz/ /nīn′ tē/ /dol′ ərz/   *The*

total cost of a motor for your vehicle is ninety dollars.
15 /ə/ /pōl/ /shōd/ /ᵮHat/ /mōst/ /pē′ pəl/ /prē fer′/ /tü/ /rēd/ /nov′ əlz/   *A poll showed that most people prefer to read novels.*

Mastery Test 25b
  1 /hīt/ *height*
  2 /mō′ shən/ *motion*
  3 /rāl′ rōd′/ *railroad*
  4 /lō′ kāt/ *locate*

A rainbow is a band of colors arching across the sky. It forms when sunshine and drops of rain are in the sky at the same time. The sunlight break up when it passes though the raindrops. The light scatters into bands of red orange yellow green blew indigo and violet. The seven colors always appear in this order.

A morning rainbow in the westren sky means that rain will soon begin. An evening rainbow in the eastern sky means that rain has passed.

2 Read the dictionary entry below for the word *holy*.

• **holy** /hō′ lē/ *adj.* **1.** Belonging to God; sacred: *the Holy Bible.* **2.** Like a saint; pure in heart: *a holy person.* **3.** Worthy of honor: *The grave of the unknown soldier is a holy place.* **holier, holiest.**

> A lexicographer shows the *er* and *est* forms of adjectives in which we change the final *y* to *i* before adding *er* and *est*.

Write a complete dictionary entry for the word *lonely*. Compare your work with the entry in the Spelling Dictionary.

A Word from the Hebrews

The word *kosher* /kō′ shər/ comes from the Hebrew word *kasher*, meaning "right" or "proper." Food is kosher when it is prepared according to the Jewish law. Stores often advertise such food as kosher food. We often use the word *kosher* to mean "something that is right, lawful, or genuine."

Write only the true sentence below. Spell the words correctly.
a A homonym of the word *kosher* is /prop′ ər/.
b An antonym of the word *kosher* is /rīt/.
c A synonym of the word *kosher* is /lô′ fəl/.

110

---

5 /prō mōt′/ *promote*
6 /hō′ lē/ *holy*
7 /ō′ nər/ *owner*
8 /sō′ lər/ *solar*
9 /ō′ dər/ *odor*
10 /hī′ bər nāt/ *hibernate*
11 /ŦHə/ /sī′ klōn/ /blü/ /doun/ /āt/ /pōlz/ *The cyclone blew down eight poles.*
12 /ī/ /wu̇d/ /līk/ /tü/ /ēt/ /ə/ /swēt/ /rōl/ /with/ /ŦHis/ /kō′ kō/ *I would like to eat a sweet roll with this cocoa.*

13 /sum/ /ath′ lēts/ /är/ /tü/ /shī/ /tü/ /bōst/ /uv/ /ŦHār/ /skil/ /in/ /pub′ lik/ *Some athletes are too shy to boast of their skill in public.*
14 /ôl/ /ŦHə/ /klōz/ /in/ /ŦHis/ /süt′ kās′/ /är/ /mād/ /uv/ /blü/ /nī′ lon/ /and/ /kot′ ən/ *All the clothes in this suitcase are made of blue nylon and cotton.*
15 /shē/ /prō pōzd′/ /tü/ /rē tīr′/ /at/ /ŦHə/ /āj/ /uv/ /fif′ tē/ *She proposed to retire at the age of fifty.*

Combinations with /ū/ and /ü/

Study Chart

Word Types	Review Words	Sound-Spellings	How do we spell these?
■	rude	/rüd/	/ü/
	glue	/glü/	/ü/
	bruise	/brüz/	/ü/
	drew	/drü/	/ü/
■ y ey	du ty	/dū′ tē/	/ū/ /ē/
■ er or ar	ru ler	/rü′ lər/	/ü/ /ər/
	hu mor	/hū′ mər/	/ū/ /ər/
■ le el al	fu el	/fū′ əl/	/ū/ /əl/
■ ■	news reel	/nüz′ rēl′/	/ü/ /ē/
■ ■	mu sic	/mū′ zik/	/ū/ /i/
■ ■ ■	mu se um	/mū zē′ əm/	/ū/ /ē/ /ə/
◀ ■	con fuse	/kən fūz′/	/kən/ /ū/
■ ▶	suit able	/sü′ tə bəl/	/ü/ /ə bəl/
◀ ■ ▶	con fu sion	/kən fū′ zhən/	/zhən/
▽	truth	/trüth/	/ü/

New Words

crude	brew	ru mor	hu mid	us able
hue	tru ly	jew el	lat it ude	con clu sion
cruise	su per	screw driv er	con sume	▽ youth

Teaching Suggestions

This is the last of the five units in which the long-vowel spellings are recycled through the various spelling contexts. The *ue, ui, ew,* and *u*-consonant-*e* spellings of /ū/ or /ü/ are featured in this unit. In addition, several words illustrate a familiar pattern from earlier levels in which /ū/ or /ü/ at the end of a syllable is spelled *u.* The *ue* and *ui* spellings occur less frequently than do the *u*-consonant-*e* and *ew* spellings.

Use the Study Chart to introduce the unit as usual, exercising whatever preference may locally prevail between the /ū/ and /ü/ pronunciations. Note that the Study Chart contains a prefix-root-suffix word and a snurk from an earlier level. The list of new words contains an analogous word for each of these two review words. Once again, help the pupils to observe how the act of separating multisyllabic words into eye-syllables helps with the spellings.

● The exercises in this section provide the usual written reinforcement of the Chart.

112

Answers

1 rude, crude, glue, hue, bruise, cruise, drew, brew
2 truth, youth
3 duty, truly
4 ruler, super, humor, rumor
5 fuel, jewel
6a screw driv er
b mu sic
c mu se um
d news reel
e hu mid
f lat it ude
7 con sume, con fuse
8 confusion, conclusion

●● Answers

1 latitude
2 hue

Handwriting Models

crude   *super*   *latitude*
hue   *rumor*   *consume*
cruise   *jewel*   *usable*
brew   *screwdriver*   *conclusion*
truly   *humid*   ▽ *youth*

1 Write the two one-syllable words in which *u*-consonant-*e* spells /ü/, the two one-syllable words in which *ue* spells /ū/ or /ü/, the two one-syllable words in which *ui* spells /ü/, and the two one-syllable words in which *ew* spells /ü/.

2 Write the snurk in which /ü/ is spelled *u* and the snurk in which /ü/ is spelled *ou*.

3 Write the two words in which *y* spells the /ē/ ending.

4 Write the two words in which the /ər/ ending is spelled *er* and the two words in which it is spelled *or*.

5 Write the two words in which /əl/ is spelled *el*.

6 Write the eye-syllables for these new and review words.
a /skrü′ drī′ vər/   **d** /nūz′ rēl′/
b /mū′ zik/   **e** /hū′ mid/
c /mū zē′ əm/   **f** /lat′ ə tüd/

7 Write the eye-syllables for /kən süm′/ and /kən füz′/.

8 Write the two prefix-root-suffix words.

Write words from the new and review lists to complete the sentences below and on the next page.

1 One degree of ____ is about 69 miles.

2 A synonym for the word *color* is ____.

●● The exercises in this section stress the meanings of the words. It may be necessary for you to provide some help with the meanings, either before or during the time the pupils do the written work.

● ●● Use the Read and Spell list as a decoding test as usual. A discussion of the word meanings will probably be needed for the benefit of some of the pupils. Exercises 2 and 4 require pupils to know the meanings.

●● The correct proofreading exercise, with corrected spelling errors underscored and corrected adjective errors starred, follows:

1. ruder   6. humid   11. super
2. suitable   7. crudest   12. <u>humorous</u>
3. <u>stupid</u>   8. useful   *13. renewable
4. youthful   * 9. truthful   14. unused
5. crueler   10. usable   15. hugest

3 A pleasure voyage is a ____.

4 Many ____ (/krüd/) people have ____ (/rüd/) manners.

5 The *ing* form of /brüz/ is ____, of /krüz/ is ____, of /kən füz'/ is ____, of /kən süm'/ is ____.

6 The plural form of /dū' tē/ is ____.

7 A ____ is ____ for measuring.

8 Idle gossip is called ____ and is not always the ____.

9 A ____ is highly ____ to remove screws.

10 An antonym for the word *dry* is ____.

11 ____ and ____ are the noun forms of *confuse* and *conclude.*

12 If you can spell *rumor,* you can easily spell ____.

13 The four words that rhyme are ____, ____, ____, and ____.

14 A diamond is a ____, but coal is a ____.

15 The two compounds in the lists are ____ and ____.

16 People often close their letters with "Yours ____."

17 The alphabetical order of the words that begin with *m* is ____ and ____.

Read and Spell

brute	suitor	suitcase	unused	unsuitable
truce	cruiser	salute	dispute	renewable
cue	brutal	stupid	nuisance	untruthful
fruit	cruel	computer	amusement	recruitment
shrewd	newsstand	produce	usefulness	endurance
puny	blueprint	refuse	fruitful	execution

 1 Write any Read and Spell word that you cannot read or any word for which you do not know the meaning.

113

---

3 cruise
4 crude, rude
5 bruising, cruising, confusing, consuming
6 duties
7 ruler, suitable (usable)
8 rumor, truth
9 screwdriver, usable (suitable)
10 humid
11 confusion, conclusion
12 humor
13 glue, drew, hue, brew
14 jewel, fuel
15 newsreel, screwdriver
16 truly
17 museum, music

The dictionary exercise should be supported by some guidance from you. Pupils might be directed to observe in the Spelling Dictionary other words that have inflectional endings.

Mastery Test 26a
1 /krüz/ *cruise*
2 /sü' pər/ *super*
3 /lat' ə tüd/ *latitude*
4 /kən süm'/ *consume*
5 /kən füz'/ *confuse*
6 /nūz' rēl'/ *newsreel*
7 /hū' mər/ *humor*
8 /fū' əl/ *fuel*
9 /mō' shən/ *motion*
10 /sī' klōn/ *cyclone*

2 Write synonyms from the Read and Spell list for *hint, fun*
clever, and *weak.*

3 Add a prefix and a suffix to the roots *suit, new,* and *truth*
to form Read and Spell words.

4 Write words from the Read and Spell list to complete the
sentences below.

a He wants a _____ to end their _____.

b She needs great _____ to carry that _____

c The _____ can really _____ information.

d He shouldn't _____ to _____ the general.

e A _____ of a house has great _____.

1 Dirk wrote a list of words he thought could be used as adjectives. Proofread his work. Write the list correctly. Add adjective suffixes to the words that are not adjectives.

114

---

11 /wē/ /must/ /chüz/ /süt′ ə bəl/ /mū′ zik/
/hwen/ /wē/ /sel′ ə brāt/   *We must choose*
suitable music when we celebrate.
12 /its/ /kwīt/ /hū′ mid/ /nir/ /ɍHə/ /ē kwā′ tər/
It's quite humid near the equator.
13 /shē/ /rē sīts′/ /trü′ lē/ /hū′ mər əs/
/vėr′ səz/   *She recites truly humorous verses.*
14 /hav/ /ū/ /hėrd/ /ɍHə/ /rü′ mər/ /uv/ /ɍHə/
/mī′ zərz/ /welth/   *Have you heard the rumor*
of the miser's wealth?

15 /ɍHārz/ /nō/ /kən fū′ zhən/ /hwen/ /ə/
/wit′ nəs/ /telz/ /ɍHə/ /trüth/   *There's no*
confusion when a witness tells the truth.

Mastery Test 26b
 1 /ūz′ ə bəl/ *usable*
 2 /kən klü′ zhən/ *conclusion*
 3 /dū′ tē/ *duty*
 4 /drü/ *drew*
 5 /brüz/ *bruise*

114

1. ruder	6. humid	11. super
2. suitable	7. crudest	12. humerous
3. stuipid	8. useful	13. renew
4. youthful	9. truth	14. unused
5. crueler	10. usable	15. hugest

2 The *er* and *est* endings that are added to adjectives like *rude* are called *inflectional endings*. Words with inflectional endings are not entry words in a dictionary.

> A lexicographer shows *ruder* and *rudest* as forms of the entry.
>
> A lexicographer shows words with suffixes as separate entries.

- **rude** /rüd/ *adj.* **1.** Not courteous. **2.** Roughly made: *a rude cabin of logs.* → **ruder, rudest.**

- **truthful** /trüth′ fəl/ *adj.* **1.** Telling the truth: *a truthful person.* **2.** Agreeing with the facts: *a truthful report.*

Write a complete dictionary entry for the word below that does not have an inflectional ending. When you have finished, compare your work with the entry in the Spelling Dictionary.

crudest   youthful   newer

Another Word from the Hebrews

Jubilee comes from the old Hebrew word *yobhel*. A yobhel was a ram's horn, which would often be blown at celebrations. The Jewish people used to have a year of jubilee, or celebration, every 50 years. We now use *jubilee* to mean "a time of rejoicing or great joy." People may celebrate a wedding jubilee.

Write the two words from this list that have the /ū/ or the /ü/ sound: *jubilee, liquid, museum, build.*

115

Answers

1 (See Teaching Suggestions.)

2 (See the entry for *youthful* in the Spelling Dictionary as a model answer.)

Another Word from the Hebrews
jubilee, museum

Mastery Test
For complete directions and an explanation of the testing program, see the Introduction to this Teacher's Edition.

---

6 /glü/ *glue*
7 /rüd/ *rude*
8 /mō′ tər/ *motor*
9 /strōl/ *stroll*
10 /nüz′ stand′/ *newsstand*
11 /ᵺär/ /wėr/ /jü′ əlz/ /uv/ /men′ ē/ /hūz/ /in/ /ᵺə/ /rü′ lərz/ /kroun/ *There were jewels of many hues in the ruler's crown.*
12 /ə/ /krüd/ /ī′ dəl/ /iz/ /lō′ kāt əd/ /in/ /ə/ /mū zē′ əm/ /ôn/ /fifth/ /av′ ə nū/ *A crude idol is located in a museum on Fifth Avenue.*
13 /tülz/ /līk/ /rench′ əz/ /and/ /skrü′ drī′ vərz/ /är/ /fôr/ /sāl/ /hir/ *Tools like wrenches and screwdrivers are for sale here.*
14 /in/ /hiz/ /ūth/ /hē/ /sāld/ /tü/ /pôrts/ /in/ /ôl/ /pärts/ /uv/ /ᵺə/ /wėrld/ *In his youth he sailed to ports in all parts of the world.*
15 /ī/ /kant/ /rē zist′/ /ə/ /tāst/ /uv/ /ᵺis/ /brü/ *I can't resist a taste of this brew.*

Study Chart

Word Types	Review Words	Sound-Spellings	How do we spell these?
■	bloom	/blüm/	/ü/
	scoop	/sküp/	/ü/
	hood	/hùd/	/ù/
■ y ey	cook y	/kùk′ ē/	/ù/ /ē/
■ er or ar	roost er	/rü′ stər/	/ü/ /ər/
	cook er	/kùk′ ər/	/ù/ /ər/
■ le el al	poo dle	/pü′ dəl/	/ü/ /əl/
■■	school room	/skül′ rüm′/	/ü/ /ü/
	proof read	/prüf′ rēd′/	/ü/ /ē/
	tool box	/tül′ boks′/	/ü/ /o/
■■	bal loon	/bə lün′/	/ə/ /ü/
	fool ish	/fü′ lish/	/ü/ /i/
◄■	un hook	/un hùk′/	/un/ /ù/
■►	good ness	/gùd′ nəs/	/ù/ /nəs/
▽	blood	/blud/	/u/

New Words

proof	gloom y	noo dle	mush room	un loose
swoop	boost er	cook book	bam boo	smooth ness
hoof	scoot er	foot step	rac coon	▽ flood

116

Teaching Suggestions

This is the first of four units that present the digraphic-vowel spellings in conjunction with the various word-type patterns. In this unit the *oo* spelling of /ü/ and /ù/ is featured. The *oo* spells either /ü/ or /ù/ in fifty-nine of the sixty-two words in which it occurs in elementary monosyllabic vocabulary. Note, however, that /ü/ and /ù/ have other spellings that are not treated in this unit. The most notable of these other spellings is *ou.*

Use the Study Chart in the usual manner to introduce the unit. Use the last column to help the pupils hear the /ü/ and /ù/ sounds in the words and to distinguish between them. Follow the same procedures of identification and discrimination with the words in the new list. Pupils should also observe the review and new snurks and discuss the fact that they are snurks because the *oo* does not spell /ü/ or /ù/ in either of the words.

Handwriting Models

proof   *scooter*   *bamboo*
swoop   *noodle*   *raccoon*
hoof   *cookbook*   *unloose*
gloomy   *footstep*   *smoothness*
booster   *mushroom*   ▽ *flood*

1 Write the two one-syllable review words and the eight eye-syllables of the review words in which *oo* spells /ü/.

2 Write the one-syllable review word and the four eye-syllables of the review words in which *oo* spells /ù/.

3 Write the two one-syllable new words and the nine eye-syllables of the new words in which *oo* spells /ü/. (Do not include the word *hoof.*)

4 Write the one-syllable new word and the three eye-syllables of the new words in which *oo* spells /ù/.

5 Write the two snurks in which *oo* spells /u/.

1 Write the new and review words for these sound-spellings.

a /fü′ lish/	**e** /blud/	**i** /prüf/
b /bü′ stər/	**f** /nü′ dəl/	**j** /kùk′ bùk′/
c /fùt′ step′/	**g** /bam bü′/	**k** /flud/
d /blüm/	**h** /swüp/	**l** /prüf′ rēd′/

2 Write the singular and plural forms of /kùk′ ē/.

3 Write the *er* and *est* forms of /glüm′ ē/.

4 Write the antonyms of /hùk/ and /lüs/.

5 Write the noun forms of /gùd/ and /smü̦ŦH/ by adding a noun suffix to each.

117

● For the exercises in this section, pupils are to write only the monosyllables and the eye-syllables of multisyllabic words. The emphasis is on the spelling generalizations within the stressed syllables rather than on the various word-type patterns.

●● The exercises in this section are routine. Note that Exercises 2, 3, and 5 cause the pupils to apply structural generalizations.

●● The words in the Read and Spell list are further illustrations of the /ü/ and /ù/ sounds spelled *oo*.

●● The correct proofreading exercise, with corrected errors underscored, is as follows:

    1. You're unlikely to see a rainbow on a gloomy day. true
    2. A scoop is like a small shovel. true
    3. The words wise *and* foolish *are*

6a raccoon   **g** mushroom
  b balloon   **h** toolbox
  c schoolroom **i** scoop
  d hood   **j** cooker
  e scooter   **k** hoof
  f rooster   **l** poodle

6 Write the new or review word suggested by each of these pictures.

Read and Spell

soothe	nook	fireproof	firewood	uncooked
groom	woolly	uproot	papoose	retool
noose	roomer	fishhook	igloo	coolness
shook	doodle	moonlight	cuckoo	gloominess
soot	broomstick	loophole	kangaroo	rootless
moose	toothpaste	bedroom	reproof	roomful

1 The Read and Spell words have all the *oo* spelling combinations. Write any word that you cannot read or any word for which you do not know the meaning.

---

homonyms. *false*

    4. You would expect to find a <u>screwdriver</u> *in a toolbox.* true

    5. A hoof is a kind of head covering. false

    6. A <u>raccoon</u> *is an animal with a bushy* <u>tail</u>. true

    7. The words rough *and* smooth *are synonyms.* false

    8. A scooter is a <u>vehicle</u> *with two wheels under a board.* true

Mastery Test 27a
 1 /prüf/ *proof*
 2 /blüm/ *bloom*
 3 /hůf/ *hoof*
 4 /skůp/ *scoop*
 5 /bü′ stər/ *booster*
 6 /hůd/ *hood*
 7 /skůt′ ər/ *scooter*
 8 /hū′ mid/ *humid*
 9 /kůk′ ər/ *cooker*
10 /kən fū′ zhən/ *confusion*
11 /půt/ /ŦнƏ/ /rench/ /and/ /chiz′ əl/ /in/

2 .Write Read and Spell words to complete these sentences.

a That's not good _____, is it?

b That's a big _____, isn't it?

c What's a _____ doing near an _____?

d This _____ got caught in a _____.

e Why would she bring _____ into a _____?

f The _____ she's riding isn't _____, is it?

1 Sandy wrote true-false statements using words from the new and review lists. Proofread her work. After you have found her mistakes, write the statements correctly. Also, write *true* or *false* after each statement.

119

Answers

2a toothpaste
 b fishhook
 c kangaroo, igloo
 d moose, noose
 e firewood, bedroom
 f broomstick, fireproof

/yuṙ/ /tül′ boks′/ *Put the wrench and chisel in your toolbox.*
12 /an/ /ē′ gəl/ /swüpt/ /down/ /and/ /kôt/ /ŦHə/ /rü′ stər/ /in/ /hiz/ /klôz/ *An eagle swooped down and caught the rooster in his claws.*
13 /it/ /iz/ /fü′ lish/ /not/ /tü/ /prüf′ rēd′/ /yuṙ/ /wėrk/ *It is foolish not to proofread your work.*
14 /ŦHə/ /ra kün′/ /left/ /ə/ /trāl/ /uv/ /blud/ /ôn/ /ŦHə/ /snō/ *The raccoon left a trail of blood on the snow.*
15 /ŦHə/ /hōl/ /wuz/ /tü/ /dēp/ /fôr/ /ŦHə/ /tent/ /stāk/ *The hole was too deep for the tent stake.*

Mastery Test 27b
 1 /nü′ dəl/ *noodle*
 2 /bə lün′/ *balloon*
 3 /kuk′ buk′/ *cookbook*
 4 /un huk′/ *unhook*
 5 /un lüs′/ *unloose*

119

1 (See Teaching Suggestions.)

2 (See the entries for *cookie* and *cooky* in the Spelling Dictionary as model answers.)

A Word from the Eskimos
bamboo, mushroom, whirlpool, igloo

Mastery Test
For complete directions and an explanation of the testing program, see the Introduction to this Teacher's Edition.

---

1. Your unlikely to see a rainbow on a gloomey day.
2. A scoop is like a small shovel.
3. The words <u>wise</u> and <u>foolish</u> are homonyms.
4. You would expect to find a scroodriver in a toolbox.
5. A hoof is a kind of head covering.
6. A rackoon is an animal with a bushy tale.
7. The words <u>rough</u> and <u>smooth</u> are synonyms.
8. A scooter is a vehical with two wheels under a board.

 2 Some words can be spelled more than one way. Each spelling of such words is shown as a separate entry in most dictionaries.

A lexicographer usually gives the definition of a word with the more common spelling.	→	• **raccoon** /ra kün′/ *n.* **1.** Small, grayish animal with a bushy, ringed tail, that lives in wooded areas. **2.** Its fur. (Also spelled **racoon**.)

• **racoon** /ra kün′/ *n.* Raccoon.

The word /kük′ ē/ may be spelled *cookie* or *cooky*. Write the two entries for this word. Show the plural form if necessary. When you have finished, compare your work with the entries in the Spelling Dictionary.

A Word from the Eskimos

The word *igloo* comes from the Eskimo word *iglu,* which simply means "house." An igloo is often made of snow blocks in the shape of a dome. Eskimos live in northern Canada, Alaska, Greenland, and in eastern Siberia.

Write the four words from this group that have the /ü/ vowel sound: *bamboo, Eskimo, mushroom, tobacco, whirlpool, photo, igloo,* and *equator.*

120

---

6 /jü′ əl/ *jewel*
7 /smüŦH′ nəs/ *smoothness*
8 /gu̇d′ nəs/ *goodness*
9 /kən klü′ zhən/ *conclusion*
10 /lat′ ə tüd/ *latitude*
11 /sum/ /mush′ rümz′/ /är/ /gu̇d/ /tü/ /ēt/ /with/ /stāk/ *Some mushrooms are good to eat with steak.*
12 /mā/ /ī/ /bring/ /mī/ /smȯl/ /pü′ dəl/ /in′ tü/ /ŦHə/ /skül′ rüm′/ /af′ tər/ /rē′ ses/

May I bring my small poodle into the schoolroom after recess?
13 /bam bü′/ /hōmz/ /wėr/ /dē stroid′/ /in/ /ŦHə/ /grāt/ /flud/ *Bamboo homes were destroyed in the great flood.*
14 /wē/ /ku̇d/ /hir/ /fu̇t′ steps′/ /in/ /ŦHə/ /glüm′ ē/ /mü zē′ əm/ *We could hear footsteps in the gloomy museum.*
15 /did/ /ü/ /kən süm′/ /ŦHə/ /hōl/ /ku̇k′ ē/ *Did you consume the whole cooky?*

Study Chart

Word Types	Review Words	Sound-Spellings	How do we spell these?
■	scout prowl	/skout/ /proul/	/ou/ /ou/
y ey	count y drow sy	/koun' tē/ /drou' zē/	/ou/ /ē/ /ou/ /ē/
er or ar	tow er flow er count er	/tou' ər/ /flou' ər/ /koun' tər/	/ou/ /ər/ /ou/ /ər/ /ou/ /ər/
le el al	tow el	/tou' əl/	/ou/ /əl/
■ ■	snow plow	/snō' plou'/	/ō/ /ou/
■ ■	a bout a round	/ə bout'/ /ə round'/	/ə/ /ou/ /ə/ /ou/
◄■	dis mount	/dis mount'/	/dis/ /ou/
■►	bal ance fa mous	/bal' əns/ /fā' məs/	/a/ /əns/ /ā/ /əs/
▽	tough	/tuf/	/u/

New Words

pound	row dy	trou sers	al low	al low ance
vow	pow er	vow el	a stound	moun tain ous
grouch y	pow der	count down	dis count	▽ cough

121

Teaching Suggestions

This unit deals with the second of the digraphic-vowel spellings, the *ou* and *ow* spellings of /ou/. The *ou* spelling of /ou/ is the least reliable of the digraphic spellings. There are about seventy-five monosyllabic *ou* spellings in our elementary vocabulary, of which only forty-one spell /ou/. Monosyllables that contain an *ou* spelling account for many of the spelling snurks. These include *brought, could, course, court, four, group, ought, should, soul, though,* *thought, through, touch, would, you, young, your,* and *youth.* The *ow* spelling is much more reliable. However, it too is ambiguous in that it is used to spell both /ou/ and /ō/.

Use the Study Chart to promote a discussion of the spelling generalizations illustrated by the review words. Help the pupils apply the generalizations to the new words. Discuss with the pupils the fact that *tough* and *cough* are snurks because *ou* spells /u/ and /ô/.

1 scout, pound, prowl, vow
2 count, drow, grouch, row
3 tow, flow, count, pow, pow, trou
4 tow, vow
5 plow, count, down
6 bout, round, low, stound
7 mount, count
8 bal/ance, al/low/ance, fa/mous, moun/tain/ous
9 tough, cough

1a drowsy, drowsier, drowsiest
 b grouchy, grouchier, grouchiest
 c rowdy, rowdier, rowdiest
2 tough, cough
3 snowplow

Handwriting Models

pound   powder   astound
vow   trousers   discount
grouchy   vowel   allowance
rowdy   countdown   mountainous
power   allow   ▽ cough

1 We can spell /ou/ with *ou* or with *ow*. Write the two one-syllable words in which *ou* spells /ou/ and the two one-syllable words in which *ow* spells /ou/.

2 Write the /ou/ eye-syllables of the four /ē/-ending words

3 Write the five /ou/ eye-syllables of the six /ər/-ending words.

4 Write the /ou/ eye-syllables of the two /əl/-ending words

5 Write the three /ou/ eye-syllables of the compound words

6 Write the /ou/ eye-syllables of /ə bout'/, /ə round', /ə lou'/, and /ə stound'/.

7 Write the /ou/ eye-syllables of the two words with the /dis prefix.

8 Write the four words that have the /əns/ and /əs/ suffixes Draw lines between the eye-syllables of each word.

9 Write the snurk in which *ou* spells /u/ and the snurk i which *ou* spells /ô/.

1 Write these words and their *er* and *est* forms.
 a /drou' zē/   **b** /grouch' ē/   **c** /rou' dē/

2 Write the two words in which *gh* spells /f/.

3 Write the word in which *ow* spells both /ō/ and /ou/.

122

● Again, these exercises concentrate on the monosyllabic words and on the eye-syllables of the multisyllabic words. The pupils should be able to do the exercises independently and with a great deal of ease.

●● These exercises focus on the whole words and cause pupils to apply their knowledge of structural generalizations, spelling generalizations, word meanings, and sound-spelling.

●● The Read and Spell list presents mor words in which /ou/ is spelled *ou* and *ow*. Us the list as a decoding test and as an opportunit to enrich the pupils' vocabularies. The writing exercises are routine and should be easy for th pupils to do independently.

●● The correct proofreading exercise, wit corrected spelling errors underscored and cor rected list errors starred, is as follows:

4 Write synonyms from the list of new words for *surprise, permit, strength,* and *pants*.

5 Write antonyms from the new and review lists for *tender, unknown, mount,* and *flat*.

6 Write these new and review words.

a /ə lou′ əns/ c /flou′ ər/ e /koun′ tē/

b /ə round′/ d /tou′ ər/ f /skout/

7 Write words from the new and review lists to complete the sentences below.

a They want to get the ＿＿ on ＿＿ at the bargain ＿＿.

b He needs three ＿＿ of ＿＿ to make the scale ＿＿.

c She's ＿＿ to make a ＿＿ to tell the truth.

d He needs the /ē/, /ü/, and /u/ ＿＿ sounds to make that ＿＿.

e It is ＿＿ to ＿＿ an animal like this.

123

---

4 astound, allow, power, trousers

5 tough, famous, dismount, mountainous

6a allowance **d** tower

  b around **e** county

  c flower **f** scout

7a discount, towels, counter

  b pounds, powder, balance

  c about, vow

  d vowel, countdown

  e tough, dismount

Synonyms	Antonyms
flower-bloom	truth-*falsehood*
color-hue	youth-age
suitable-right	rude-polite
drowsy-sleepy	*crude-fine
vow-*pledge*	power-*weakness*

Some other words from the Chinese that are in use in our language, in addition to kow-ow, are *chop suey, chow mein, kumquat, oo-ong,* and *tong*.

Mastery Test 28a

1 /pou′ dər/ *powder*

2 /vou′ əl/ *vowel*

3 /skout/ *scout*

4 /flud/ *flood*

5 /un lüs′/ *unloose*

6 /kount′ doun′/ *countdown*

7 /ə stound′/ *astound*

8 /koun′ tē/ *county*

9 /drou′ zē/ *drowsy*

10 /ra kün′/ *raccoon*

Answers

2 couch, blouse, crown, foundation

3a flounders, drown

b doubtful, rebounds

c aroused, announcement

d scowl, pronounce

Read and Spell

lounge	loudly	flounder	southwest	rebound
couch	proudly	trowel	arouse	disallow
blouse	foundry	outwit	fountain	announcement
scowl	outer	downstream	compound	foundation
crown	shower	roundup	unwound	countless
drown	chowder	playground	pronounce	doubtful

1 Write any Read and Spell word that you cannot read or any word for which you do not know the meaning.

2 Write the Read and Spell words for the sound-spellings /kouch/, /blous/, /kroun/, and /foun dā′ shən/.

3 Write Read and Spell words to complete these sentences

a If she ____ much more, she'll ____.

b It's ____ if number 7 will get many ____

c Paul ____ the colonists with that ____.

d You'd ____, too, if you had to ____ that word.

124

---

11 /ᵺə/ /hīt/ /uv/ /ᵺə/ /fā′ məs/ /tou′ ər/ /iz/ /āt/ /hun′ drəd/ /fēt/ *The height of the famous tower is eight hundred feet.*
12 /wē/ /āt/ /ə bout′/ /ə/ /pound/ /uv/ /kük′ ēz/ *We ate about a pound of cookies.*
13 /dôgz/ /shüd/ /not/ /bē/ /ə loud′/ /tü/ /proul/ /thrü/ /ᵺə/ /toun/ /at/ /nīt/ *Dogs should not be allowed to prowl through the town at night.*
14 /snō′ plouz′/ /är/ /nēd′ əd/ /in/ /moun′ tən əs/ /plās′ əs/ *Snowplows are*

needed in mountainous places.
15 /ᵺār/ /iz/ /ə/ /les′ ən/ /at/ /ᵺə/ /kən klü′ zhən/ /uv/ /mōst/ /fā′ bəlz/ *There is a lesson at the conclusion of most fables.*

Mastery Test 28b
 1 /kôf/ *cough*
 2 /prüf/ *proof*
 3 /blud/ *blood*
 4 /tou′ əl/ *towel*
 5 /ə round′/ *around*

1 Howard wrote lists of synonyms and antonyms. Proofread his work and write the two lists correctly.

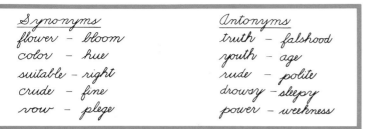

Synonyms
flower – bloom
color – hue
suitable – right
crude – fine
vow – plege

Antonyms
truth – falshood
youth – age
rude – polite
drowsy – sleepy
power – weekness

2 Many words have the same spelling as other words.

A lexicographer gives a separate entry for each spelled-alike word, and numbers each entry.	• **counter**¹ /koun′ tər/ *n.* Long table in a store, restaurant, or bank.
	• **counter**² /koun′ tər/ *n.* Person or thing that counts.
	• **counter**³ /koun′ tər/ *adv.* Contrary; opposed: *He acted counter to my wishes. —v.* Oppose.

Write a dictionary entry for each of the three words spelled *pound.* When you have finished, compare your work with the entries in the Spelling Dictionary.

A Word from the Chinese

The word *kowtow* is made from Chinese words meaning "to bump the head." We use *kowtow* to mean "to kneel and touch the forehead to the ground in a show of respect." If you go out of your way to make someone feel important, you kowtow to that person.

Write a sentence of your own using the words /klèrk/ and /man′ ə jər/ and the *ed* or *ing* form of *kowtow.*

125

Answers
1 (See Teaching Suggestions.)
2 (See the entries for *pound* in the Spelling Dictionary as model answers.)

A Word from the Chinese
The clerk kowtowed to his manager. (Answers will vary.)

Mastery Test
For complete directions and an explanation of the testing program, see the Introduction to this Teacher's Edition.

---

6 /ə lou′ əns/ *allowance*
7 /koun′ tər/ *counter*
8 /dis mount′/ *dismount*
9 /bal′ əns/ *balance*
10 /dis′ kount/ *discount*
11 /ə/ /help′ fəl/ /tā′ lər/ /mād/ /ᵀʜōz/ /trou′ zərz/   *A helpful tailor made those trousers.*
12 /sum/ /boiz/ /ôn/ /ᵀʜə/ /hok′ ē/ /tēm/ /är/ /tuf/ /and/ /rou′ dē/   *Some boys on the hockey team are tough and rowdy.*

13 /ī/ /voud/ /not/ /tü/ /bē/ /tü/ /grouch′ ē/ /ôn/ /our/ /krüz/   *I vowed not to be too grouchy on our cruise.*
14 /sum/ /rü′ lərz/ /eg zėrt′/ /ᵀʜār/ /pou′ ər/ /fôr/ /ᵀʜə/ /wel′ fār′/ /uv/ /uᵀʜ′ ərz/   *Some rulers exert their power for the welfare of others.*
15 /flou′ ərz/ /är/ /nou/ /in/ /blüm/ /ôn/ /ᵀʜis/ /lōn′ lē/ /īl/   *Flowers are now in bloom on this lonely isle.*

Study Chart

Word Types	Review Words	Sound-Spellings	How do we spell these?
■	moist	/moist/	/oi/
	join	/join/	/oi/
	choice	/chois/	/oi/
◀ y / ey	oil y	/oi' lē/	/oi/ /ē/
	noi sy	/noiz' ē/	/oi/ /ē/
◀ er / or / ar	point er	/poin' tər/	/oi/ /ər/
	boil er	/boi' lər/	/oi/ /ər/
◀ le / el / al	roy al	/roi' əl/	/oi/ /əl/
■ ■	cow boy	/kou' boi'/	/ou/ /oi/
■ ■	poi son	/poi' zən/	/oi/ /ə/
	voy age	/voi' ij/	/oi/ /ij/
◀ ■	re join	/rē join'/	/rē/ /oi/
■ ▶	en joy able	/en joi' ə bəl/	/en/ /oi/ /ə bəl/
	em ploy ment	/em ploi' mənt/	/em/ /oi/ /mənt/
◀ ◀ ■ ▶	un em ploy ment	/un' em ploi' mənt/	/un/ /mənt/

New Words

hoist	doi ly	broil er	an noy	ap point ment
coin	noi si ly	loy al	ap point	a void able
poise	oy ster	tin foil	re joice	un a void able

126

Teaching Suggestions

This is the third unit of digraphic-vowel spellings presented in conjunction with the various word-type patterns. The *oi* and *oy* spellings of /oi/ are featured in this unit. The /oi/ vowel sound is invariably spelled *oi* or *oy*. For the first time, the prefix-prefix-root-suffix word type is illustrated by the review word *unemployment* and by the new word *unavoidable*.

Use the Study Chart as usual to establish the spelling generalizations of /oi/ in each of the review words. Help the pupils to apply the generalizations to the list of new words. You might also demonstrate again how much easier the syllable spellings become when some stress is placed on each eye-syllable. Thus *cowboy*, like most compounds, has secondary stress on the second syllable and the vowel-spelling clue is easy to hear. In *poison* /poi' zən/, there is no auditory clue to the vowel spelling in the unstressed syllable. The simple device of saying

Handwriting Models

hoist　　*oyster*　　*appoint*
coin　　*broiler*　　*rejoice*
poise　　*loyal*　　*appointment*
doily　　*tinfoil*　　*avoidable*
noisily　　*annoy*　　*unavoidable*

1 We can spell /oi/ with ＿＿ or with ＿＿. Write the six one-syllable words in which *oi* spells /oi/.

2 We can spell the soft /ē/ ending with ＿＿ or with ＿＿. Write the four words in which *y* spells the /ē/ ending.

3 We can spell the soft /ər/ ending with ＿＿, ＿＿, or ＿＿. Write the four words in which *er* spells the /ər/ ending.

4 We can spell the soft /əl/ ending with ＿＿, ＿＿, or ＿＿. Write the two words in which *al* spells the /əl/ ending.

5 Write the eye-syllables of the two compound words.

6 Write the eye-syllables of the two-syllable words /poi′ zən/, /voi′ ij/, /ə noi′/, and /ə point′/.

7 We spell the /rē/ prefix with ＿＿. Write the roots of the two words with the /rē/ prefix.

8 We spell the /em/ prefix with ＿＿, the /en/ prefix with ＿＿, and the /un/ prefix with ＿＿. We spell the /mənt/ suffix with ＿＿ and the /ə bəl/ suffix with ＿＿ or ＿＿. Write the six words that have any of these prefixes or suffixes.

1 Write synonyms from the new and review lists for *work, balance, faithful, lift, loud,* and *wet.*

2 Write antonyms from the new and review lists for *please, grieve, avoidable, quietly, unpleasant,* and *separate.*

127

● **Answers**

1 oi, oy, moist, join, choice, hoist, coin, poise

2 y, ey, oily, noisy, doily, noisily

3 er, or, ar, pointer, boiler, oyster, broiler

4 le, el, al, royal, loyal

5 cow boy, tin foil

6 poi son, voy age, an noy, ap point

7 re, join, joice

8 em, en, un, ment, able, ible, enjoyable, employment, unemployment, appointment, avoidable, unavoidable

●● **Answers**

1 employment, poise, loyal, hoist, noisy, moist

2 annoy, rejoice, unavoidable, noisily, enjoyable, join

---

the eye-syllables as if they were "little" words causes stress to be placed on each syllable and, therefore, provides a spelling clue.

● These exercises should, by now, be routine and can be done independently.

●● The exercises involve synonyms, antonyms, suffixes, sound-spellings, and word meanings.

●● The Read and Spell list provides a decoding test. All of the words contain /oi/ spelled *oi* or *oy.*

The writing exercises require knowledge of the word meanings.

●● Note the error of fact in the last sentence of the proofreading exercise. The correct exercise, with corrected errors underscored, is:

Oysters are found along the seacoasts

3 boiler, broiler, pointer
4 employment, appointment
5 coin, choice, oyster, royal
6a This was a famous voyage.
 b You can tell that is poison.
 c That doily will be very oily.
 d This cowboy does not
    enjoy his unemployment.
 e That animal is not easy to
    hoist.

3 Write three nouns by adding the /ər/ ending to the words /boil/, /broil/, and /point/.

4 Write two nouns by adding the /mənt/ suffix to the words /em ploi′/ and /ə point′/.

5 Write the words for the sound-spellings /koin/, /chois/, /oi′ stər/, and /roi′ əl/.

6 Write the sentences below using the correct spelling of the words. Complete the sentences by writing words from the new and review lists.

 a /ᵺis/ /wuz/ /ə/ /fā′ məs/ ____.

 b /ū/ /kan/ /tel/ /ᵺat/ /iz/ ____.

 c /ᵺat/ ____ /wil/ /bē/ /ver′ ē/ ____.

 d /ᵺis/ ____ /duz/ /not/ /en joi′/ /hiz/
____.

 e /ᵺat/ /an′ ə məl/ /iz/ /not/ /ē′ zē/ /tü/
____.

128

in many parts of the world. Most people consume oysters because they taste good. People
<u>know</u> that oysters are rich in <u>vitamins</u>, too.

Pearls are produced inside some oysters.
The pearl forms on the inside shell around a
tiny grain of sand. Drops of liquid from the
oyster's body trickle around the grain of sand
and harden. Little by little, as the drops harden,
a smooth and shiny pearl is formed.

The best pearls are found in oysters that
live in the <u>warm</u> waters of the <u>southern</u> latitudes.

Mastery Test 29a
 1 /hoist/ *hoist*
 2 /poiz/ *poise*
 3 /loi′ əl/ *loyal*
 4 /ə lou′/ *allow*
 5 /tuf/ *tough*
 6 /trou′ zərz/ *trousers*
 7 /poin′ tər/ *pointer*
 8 /oi′ lē/ *oily*
 9 /noiz′ ē/ *noisy*
10 /boi′ lər/ *boiler*
11 /ᵺā/ /had/ /an/ /en joi′ ə bəl/ /voi′ ij/

Read and Spell

toil	spoil	topsoil	alloy	poisonous
coy	loyalty	pinpoint	convoy	joyful
foil	royalty	oilcloth	exploit	annoyance
void	jointly	newsboy	recoil	enjoyment
joist	cloister	adjoin	unspoiled	voiceless
voice	oilskin	boycott	disjoint	moistness

Answers

2a newsboy   **d** joist(s)
 b foils   **e** royalty
 c topsoil   **f** convoy
3a toil   **e** exploit
 b coy   **f** joyful
 c void   **g** alloy
 d adjoin   **h** boycott

1 The Read and Spell words all have the /oi/ sound. Write any word that you cannot read or any word for which you do not know the meaning.

2 Write the Read and Spell word suggested by each of these pictures.

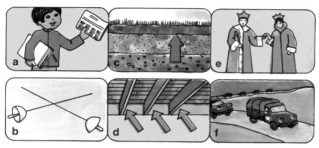

3 Write the Read and Spell words that mean
a to work hard
b shy and modest
c an empty space
d to be next to
e a great deed
f very happy
g a mixture of metals
h to punish by avoiding

1 Roy wrote a report for his science notebook. Proofread his work. Make sure of the facts in the report by reading the entry for *oyster* in the Spelling Dictionary. After you have found the mistakes, write the report correctly.

129

---

11 /tü/ /ᵻʜə/ /wes′tərn/ /īlz/   *They had an enjoyable voyage to the western isles.*
12 /sum/ /un′em ploi′mənt/ /sēmz/ /tü/ /bē/ /un′ə void′ə bəl/   *Some unemployment seems to be unavoidable.*
13 /kou′boiz′/ /hav/ /nō/ /chois/ /but/ /tü/ /join/ /ə/ /round′up′/   *Cowboys have no choice but to join a roundup.*
14 /ūz/ /ə/ /moist/ /tou′əl/ /tü/ /klēn/ /yùr/ /plat′ər/   *Use a moist towel to clean your platter.*

15 /ᵻʜə/ /brīt′nəs/ /uv/ /ᵻʜə/ /kom′ət/ /ə stoun′dəd/ /us/   *The brightness of the comet astounded us.*

Mastery Test 29b
 1 /poi′zən/ *poison*
 2 /rē join′/ *rejoin*
 3 /kôf/ *cough*
 4 /ə noi′/ *annoy*
 5 /rē jois′/ *rejoice*
 6 /em ploi′mənt/ *employment*

1 (See Teaching Suggestions.)

2 (See the entries for *avoidable* and *unavoidable* in the Spelling Dictionary as model answers.)

Another Word from the Mexicans
coyote /kī ō′ tē/ or /kī′ ōt/
(/kō yō′ tā/ may be written in some regions.)

Mastery Test
For complete directions and an explanation of the testing program, see the Introduction to this Teacher's Edition.

Oysters are found along the seacoasts in many parts of the world. Most people consume oysters because they taste good. People no that oysters are rich in vitemins, too.

Pearls are produced inside some oysters the pearl forms on the inside shell around a tiny grain of sand. Drops of liquid from the oysters body trickle around the grain of sand and harden. Little by little, as the drops harden, a smooth and shiny pearl is formed.

The best pearls are found in oysters that live in the cold waters of the northern latitudes.

2 Read the dictionary entry below.

| A lexicographer often shows prefixes, like *un*, as entry words in a dictionary. | • **un-** /un/ *Prefix.* **1.** Not: *Unchanged* means "not changed." **2.** Do the opposite of: *Undress* means "to do the opposite of dress." |

Write complete dictionary entries for *avoidable* and *unavoidable*. Give all necessary information in each entry. Compare your work with the entries in the Spelling Dictionary.

Another Word from the Mexicans

Because we are neighbors of the Spanish-speaking Mexicans, many Spanish words have been added to our language. *Coyote* is one such word. It is the Mexican Spanish word for the prairie wolf of western North America. In English the word is pronounced /kī′ ōt/ or /kī ō′ tē/. The word originally came from the Nahuatl Indian word *coyotl*.

Write the word *coyote* and the pronunciation that you prefer to use for it.

130

---

7 /tin′ foil′/ *tinfoil*
8 /ə point′/ *appoint*
9 /ə void′ ə bəl/ *avoidable*
10 /pou′ ər/ *power*
11 /wē/ /kükt/ /oi′ stərz/ /ôn/ /our/ /broil′ ər/ /fôr/ /tü/ /ourz/ *We cooked oysters on our broiler for two hours.*
12 /püt/ /ə/ /lās/ /doi′ lē/ /un′ dər/ /ᴛʜat/ /bōl/ /uv/ /flou′ ərz/ *Put a lace doily under that bowl of flowers.*

13 /kan/ /ū/ /hir/ /ᴛʜə/ /koinz/ /ᴛʜat/ /jing′ gəl/ /sō/ /noi′ zə lē/ /in/ /mī/ /pok′ ət/ *Can you hear the coins that jingle so noisily in my pocket?*
14 /ī/ /kām/ /hir/ /tü/ /sē/ /ᴛʜə/ /splen′ dər/ /uv/ /ᴛʜis/ /roi′ əl/ /man′ shən/ *I came here to see the splendor of this royal mansion.*
15 /īl/ /māk/ /an/ /ə point′ mənt/ /tü/ /sē/ /ᴛʜə/ /den′ tist/ /nekst/ /wēk/ *I'll make an appointment to see the dentist next week.*

Combinations with /ô/

Study Chart

Word Types	Review Words	Sound-Spellings	How do we spell these?
■	haunt raw halt	/hônt/ /rô/ /hôlt/	/ô/ /ô/ /ô/
◀ y ey	naugh ty	/nô' tē/	/ô/ /ē/
◀ er or ar	daugh ter au thor	/dô' tər/ /ô' thər/	/ô/ /ər/ /ô/ /ər/
■■	foot ball	/fut' bôl'/	/u/ /ô/
■■	fau cet sau sage	/fô' sət/ /sô' sij/	/ô/ /ə/ /ô/ /ij/
■■■	as tro naut di no saur	/as' trə nôt/ /dī' nə sôr/	/a/ /ə/ /ô/ /ī/ /ə/ /ô/
◀■	re call	/rē kôl'/	/rē/ /ô/
■▶	a gree able a gree ment	/ə grē' ə bəl/ /ə grē' mənt/	/ə/ /ē/ /ə bəl/ /ə/ /ē/ /mənt/
◀■▶	dis a gree ment	/dis' ə grē' mənt/	/dis/ /mənt/

New Words

gaunt	sau cer	wal let	cau tion
squawk	law yer	tom a hawk	cau tious
malt	bas ket ball	au to graph	pre cau tion
laun dry	wal rus	ex haust	

131

Teaching Suggestions

This is the last of the four units in which the digraphic-vowel spellings are recycled through the various word-type patterns. In this unit the *au*, *aw*, and *a(l)* spellings of /ô/ are featured. /ô/ is sometimes spelled *o* in the initial or medial position of a syllable and sometimes spelled *ou*, as in *brought*, *ought*, and *thought*. These latter two spellings are not illustrated in this unit. It should be noted, also, that the *a(l)* spelling does not invariably represent /ô/. It does produce a few snurks, such as *half*, *shall*, and *talk*.

Use the Study Chart as usual to establish the spelling generalizations of /ô/ in each of the review words. Help the pupils to apply the generalizations to the new words. Note the three review words *agreeable*, *agreement*, and *disagreement*. These words are presented here because there are no suitable words with /ô/ to illustrate these word-type patterns.

Answers

1 haunt, gaunt, raw, squawk, halt, malt
2 naughty, laundry
3 daughter, saucer, lawyer, author
4 football, basketball
5 fau cet, sau sage, wal rus, wal let
6 as tro naut, di no saur, tom a hawk, au to graph
7 re call, a gree able, a gree ment, dis a gree ment, ex haust, cau tion, cau tious, pre cau tion

●● **Answers**

1a haunt
 b squawk
 c halt
2 gaunt, raw
3 recall, exhaust

Handwriting Models

gaunt   saucer   wallet   caution
squawk   lawyer   tomahawk cautious
malt   basketball autograph precaution
laundry walrus   exhaust

1 We can spell /ô/ with *au, aw,* or *a* when the *a* is followed by *l.* Write the two one-syllable words in which *au* spells /ô/, the two one-syllable words in which *aw* spells /ô/, and the two one-syllable words in which *a(l)* spells /ô/.

2 Write the two words in which *y* spells the soft /ē/ ending

3 Write the three words in which the soft /ər/ ending is spelled *er* and the word in which it is spelled *or.*

4 Write the two compounds in which /ô/ is spelled *a(l).*

5 Write the eye-syllables of the two-syllable words /fô′ sət/, /sô′ sij/, /wôl′ rəs/, and /wôl′ ət/.

6 Write the eye-syllables of the three-syllable words /as′ trə nôt/, /dī′ nə sôr/, /tom′ ə hôk/, and /ô′ tə graf/.

7 Write the eye-syllables of the eight prefix-root, root-suffix, and prefix-root-suffix words.

1 Write the verbs to fit these clues.
a Ghosts do it.
b Parrots and complainers do it.
c Marching soldiers are told to do it.

2 Write the adjectives that mean "very thin and bony" and "uncooked."

3 Write the prefix-root words that mean "to call back" and "to tire out."

132

● Through a combination of writing whole words and eye-syllables, the exercises in this section cause pupils to pay attention again to the various word-type patterns. Pupils should be able to do the exercises independently.

●● The exercises in this section concentrate on the meanings of the words. If the word meanings have been reviewed, the exercises should be done independently by the pupils.

●● The Read and Spell list offers practice in decoding words with the *au, aw,* and *a(l)* spellings of /ô/.

●● The correct proofreading exercise, with corrected errors underscored, is as follows:

"Hot dog" is the nickname for a thin round sausage that is eaten on a long roll. Some hot dogs are almost a block long when they are first made in a sausage factory. The

4 Write new and review words for these pictures.

5 Write the nouns to fit these clues.

a It is used in drugstores and in breweries.

b You need one in court.

c It is a signature.

Read and Spell

launch	scrawny	saunter	applaud	auction
clause	gaudy	drawbridge	falcon	lawful
pawn	faulty	jigsaw	defraud	audible
sprawl	slaughter	outlaw	install	unlawful
scald	pauper	drawback	faultless	exhaustion
waltz	falter	withdraw	audience	installment

1 Write any Read and Spell word that you cannot read or any word for which you do not know the meaning.

2 Write Read and Spell verbs for the sentences below.

a It will ____ the wolf.

b They will ____ her.

133

4a laundry **d** football
  b astronaut **e** dinosaur
  c walrus **f** faucet
5a malt
  b lawyer
  c autograph

●● **Answers**
2a scald
  b applaud

---

ground sausage _meat_ is _poured_ by machines into a folded sausage skin. The skin slowly un-folds as it is stuffed _until_ it stretches out for nearly a block. At a signal, another machine snips the long sausage into parts, pinches the ends of each little section together, and pro-duces many hot dogs.

Some other words from the French, in addition to _plateau_, in which _eau_ spells /ō/ are _beau, bureau, chateau,_ and _trousseau._

Mastery Test 30a
 1 /skwôk/ _squawk_
 2 /môlt/ _malt_
 3 /lôn′ drē/ _laundry_
 4 /hôlt/ _halt_
 5 /ô′ thər/ _author_
 6 /ə grē′ ə bəl/ _agreeable_
 7 /lô′ yər/ _lawyer_
 8 /dī′ nə sôr/ _dinosaur_
 9 /rē jois′′/ _rejoice_
10 /broil′ ər/ _broiler_

133

3a scrawny   c gaudy
 b audible   d faulty
4a waltz   c drawbridge
 b jigsaw   d auction
5a pawn   d gaudy
 b defraud   e pauper
 c sprawl   f launch

3 Write Read and Spell adjectives for these sentences.

a This dog is _____.   **c** He looks _____.

b She is _____.   **d** The brakes were _____.

4 Write Read and Spell nouns for the sentences below.

a They're dancing a _____.   **c** The _____ is up.

b It's a _____ puzzle.   **d** They're at an _____.

5 Write Read and Spell words for these sound-spellings.
a /pôn/   **c** /sprôl/   **e** /pô′ pər/
b /dē frôd′/   **d** /gô′ dē/   **f** /lônch/

1 Marla wrote a report about one of her favorite foods. Proof-read her report. After you have found her mistakes, write the report correctly.

134

---

11 /ī/ /askt/ /ᵺə/ /fā′ məs/ /fut′ bôl′/ /plā′ ər/
/fôr/ /hiz/ /ô′ tə graf/   *I asked the famous football player for his autograph.*
12 /är/ /hôks/ /and/ /ē′ gəlz/ /bōth/ /bėrdz/
/uv/ /prā/   *Are hawks and eagles both birds of prey?*
13 /hėr/ /nô′ tē/ /dô′ tər/ /brōk/ /ᵺə/
/lā′ dēz/ /sô′ sər/   *Her naughty daughter broke the lady's saucer.*
14 /ᵺə/ /fô′ sət/ /ôn/ /our/ /hī′ drənt/
/lēks/   *The faucet on our hydrant leaks.*

15 /dis′ ə grē′ mənts/ /ə mung′/ /frendz/
/är/ /not/ /ôl′ wāz/ /ə void′ ə bəl/
Disagreements among friends are not always avoidable.

Mastery Test 30b
  1 /hônt/ *haunt*
  2 /oi′ stər/ *oyster*
  3 /sô′ sij/ *sausage*
  4 /trou′ zərz/ *trousers*
  5 /rē kôl′/ *recall*

"Hot dog" is the nickname for a thin, round sausage that is eaten on a long role. Some hot dogs are almost a block long when they are first made in a sausage factory. The ground sausage meet is pored by machines into a folded sausage skin. The skin slowly unfolds as it is stuffed. Until it stretches out for nearly a block. At a signal, another machine snips the long sausage into parts, pinches the ends of each little section together, and produces many hot dogs.

2 Read the dictionary entries below.

> A lexicographer may show prefixes, like *dis* and *re*, as entry words in a dictionary.

- **dis-** /dis/ *Prefix.* **1.** The opposite of: *Discontented* is the opposite of *contented.* **2.** Do the opposite.
- **re-** /rē/ or /rə/ *Prefix.* **1.** Again: *Reopen* means "to open again." **2.** Back: *Repay* means "to pay back."

Write a dictionary entry for the word *recall.* Compare your work with the entry in the Spelling Dictionary.

Another Word from the French

Plateau /pla tō'/ comes from a French word for "flat." A plateau is a flat land in the mountains. The *eau* spelling for the /ō/ vowel sound is a typical French spelling. When we borrowed the word *plateau,* we also took the French spelling. There are many French words in the English language that have this spelling pattern.

Write only the sentence that is true from the three below.

a /ə/ /pla tō'/ /iz/ /moun' tə nəs/ /land/.
b /ə/ /pla tō'/ /iz/ /land/ /in/ /ə/ /val' ē/.
c /ə/ /pla tō'/ /iz/ /ə/ /flat/ /land/ /in/ /ᵵнə/ /moun' tənz/.

135

1 (See Teaching Suggestions.)
2 (See the entry for *recall* in the Spelling Dictionary as a model answer.)

Another Word from the French
c A plateau is a flat land in the mountains.

Mastery Test
For complete directions and an explanation of the testing program, see the Introduction to this Teacher's Edition.

---

6 /bas' kət bôl'/ *basketball*
7 /tom' ə hôk/ *tomahawk*
8 /eg zôst'/ *exhaust*
9 /rô/ *raw*
10 /wôl' rəs/ *walrus*
11 /ᵵнə/ /trē' tē/ /wuz/ /ə/ /kô' shəs/ /ə grē' mənt/ /bə twēn'/ /tü/ /kun' trēz/ *The treaty was a cautious agreement between two countries.*
12 /as' trə nôts/ /tāk/ /men' ē/ /prə kô' shəns/ /bə fôr'/ /ēch/ /flīt/ *Astronauts take many*

precautions before each flight.
13 /our/ /gīd/ /kô' shənd/ /us/ /tü/ /woch/ /our/ /wôl' əts/ *Our guide cautioned us to watch our wallets.*
14 /ᵵнə/ /pùr/ /beg' ər/ /had/ /ə/ /wird/ /and/ /gônt/ /lùk/ *The poor beggar had a weird and gaunt look.*
15 /klōz/ /wèr/ /dis plād'/ /ôn/ /ᵵнə/ /koun' tər/ /uv/ /ᵵнə/ /stôr/ *Clothes were displayed on the counter of the store.*

Study Chart

Word Types	Review Words	Sound-Spellings	How do we spell these?
■	carve sharp	/kärv/ /shärp/	/är/ /är/
y ey	part‚y‚ arm‚y‚	/pär′ tē/ /är′ mē/	/är/ /ē/ /är/ /ē/
er or ar	bar‚ber‚ har‚bor‚	/bär′ bər/ /här′ bər/	/är/ /ər/ /är/ /ər/
le el al	mar‚ble‚ mar‚vel‚ car‚niv‚al‚	/mär′ bəl/ /mär′ vəl/ /kär′ nə vəl/	/är/ /əl/ /är/ /əl/ /är/ /ə/ /əl/
■ ■	barn‚yard‚	/bärn′ yärd′/	/är/ /är/
■ ■	car‚ton‚ arc‚tic‚	/kärt′ ən/ /ärk′ tik/	/är/ /ə/ /är/ /i/
■ ■ ■	car‚pen‚ter‚	/kär′ pən tər/	/är/ /ə/ /ər/
◄ ■	re‚mark‚	/rē märk′/	/rē/ /är/
■ ►	harm‚ful‚	/härm′ fəl/	/är/ /fəl/

New Words

harsh	tar‚dy‚	gar‚gle‚	farm‚land‚	bar‚be‚cue‚
chart	par‚lor‚	par‚cel‚	art‚ist‚	re‚gard‚
bar‚ley‚	arm‚or‚	card‚in‚al‚	car‚toon‚	mar‚vel‚ous‚

136

Teaching Suggestions

The previous fourteen units have dealt with short-vowel spellings, long-vowel spellings, and digraphic-vowel spellings in all of the various word-type patterns. This unit begins a series of four units in which the fourth basic vowel-spelling group, the vowel-r spellings, is recycled through the word-type patterns. In this unit the *ar* spelling of /är/ is featured in each review and new word.

Use the Study Chart to introduce the unit as usual. Since there is only one spelling generalization involved in the spelling of /är/, you may want to spend an extra amount of time discussing the spelling options used for the soft-syllable endings /ē/, /ər/, and /əl/ and the other affixes of the review words. As usual, help the pupils to apply the generalizations to the new words.

136

Handwriting Models

harsh   *parlor*   *cardinal*   *barbecue*
chart   *armor*   *farmland*   *regard*
barley   *gargle*   *artist*   *marvelous*
tardy   *parcel*   *cartoon*

1 Write the four one-syllable words in which *ar* spells /är/.

2 We can spell the soft /ē/ ending with *y* or with *ey*. Write the three two-syllable words in which *y* spells /ē/ and the two-syllable word in which *ey* spells /ē/.

3 We can spell the soft /ər/ ending with *er* or with *or*. Write the two-syllable word in which *er* spells /ər/ and the three two-syllable words in which *or* spells /ər/.

4 We can spell the soft /əl/ ending with *le, el,* or *al*. Write the two two-syllable words in which *le* spells /əl/, the two two-syllable words in which *el* spells /əl/, and the two words in which *al* spells /əl/.

5 Write the four eye-syllables of the two compound words.

6 Write the eye-syllables of the two-syllable words /kärt′ ən/, /ärk′ tik/, /är′ tist/, and /kär tün′/.

7 Write the eye-syllables of the two three-syllable words /kär′ pən tər/ and /bär′ bə kū/.

8 Write the eye-syllables of the two prefix-root words.

9 We spell the /fəl/ suffix with _____ and the /əs/ suffix with _____. Write the two words with these suffixes.

1 Write synonyms from the new and review lists for *slice, container, late, drawing, wonder,* and *wonderful*.

2 Write review-word antonyms for *dull, tropic,* and *helpful*.

137

● **Answers**
1 carve, sharp, harsh, chart
2 party, army, tardy, barley
3 barber, harbor, parlor, armor
4 marble, gargle, marvel, parcel, carnival, cardinal
5 barn yard, farm land
6 car ton, arc tic, art ist, car toon
7 car pen ter, bar be cue
8 re mark, re gard
9 ful, ous, harmful, marvelous

●● **Answers**
1 carve, carton, tardy, cartoon, marvel, marvelous
2 sharp, arctic, harmful

●   The exercises in this section occur in a familiar pattern. They deal with the words according to their word-type contexts.

●●   These exercises are routine, but they do require a knowledge of the word meanings. Exercise 1 deals with synonyms and Exercise 2 with antonyms. Exercises 4 and 5 involve the application of structural generalizations.

●●   The Read and Spell list can be used as a decoding test of words with /är/. As usual, the words illustrate each of the various word-type patterns. Be sure to clarify the word meanings for the pupils before the writing exercises are assigned. Exercise 2 requires pupils to write synonyms, Exercise 3 requires them to write *ing* verb forms, and Exercise 4 involves word meanings.

3a barber   **d** carpenter
 b armor   **e** barnyard
 c harbor   **f** artist
4a carving
 b gargling
 c barbecuing
5 armies, parties

●
●● **Answers**
2 startle, depart, discharge,
    pardon
3 snarling, enlarging,
    sparkling, departing

3 Write the new and review words for these pictures.

4 Write the *ing* verb forms suggested by these pictures.

5 Write the plural forms of the nouns /är′ mē/ and /pär′ tē/.

Read and Spell

snarl	arbor	crowbar	market	impart
charm	partner	cartwheel	architect	argument
parch	sparkle	margin	discharge	harmless
quarry	article	target	enlarge	garment
parsley	startle	pardon	depart	harness
garter	warble	cargo	unharmed	compartment

1 Write any Read and Spell word that you cannot read or any word for which you do not know the meaning.

2 Write synonyms from the Read and Spell list for *frighten, leave, fire,* and *forgive.*

3 Write the *ing* forms of the Read and Spell verbs /snärl/, /en lärj′/, /spär′ kəl/, and /dē pärt′/.

138

●●
  The correct proofreading exercise, with corrected spelling errors underscored and corrected noun errors starred, is as follows:

Persons	Places	Things
daughter	*parlor*	parcel
author	barnyard	*barbecue*
*youth	isle	armor
carpenter	aisle	*carnival*
artist	*mountain	*barley*

 1 /pär′ tē/ *party*
 2 /härsh/ *harsh*
 3 /tär′ dē/ *tardy*
 4 /är′ mē/ *army*
 5 /pär′ lər/ *parlor*
 6 /här′ bər/ *harbor*
 7 /gär′ gəl/ *gargle*
 8 /ô′ tə graf/ *autograph*
 9 /kär′ nə vəl/ *carnival*
10 /prə kô′ shən/ *precaution*
11 /ŧHōz/ /bär′ bərz/ /hav/ /lôst/ /ŧHār/

4 Write words from the Read and Spell list to complete these sentences.

4a arbor   **f** target
  b cargo   **g** architect
  c harness   **h** crowbar
  d quarry   **i** argument
  e charm   **j** cartwheel

a This is a grape _____.

f She's shooting at a _____.

b This ship is loading _____.

g This man is an _____.

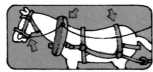

c This is a _____.

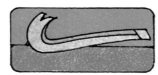

h This is a _____.

d This is a _____.

i They're having an _____.

e He will _____ the snake with his skill.

j She's doing a _____ on the grass.

139

/shärp/ /siz′ ərz/   *Those barbers have lost their sharp scissors.*

12 /men′ ē/ /fā′ məs/ /skulp′ tərz/ /kärvd/ /ŦHār/ /wėrks/ /in/ /mär′ bəl/   *Many famous sculptors carved their works in marble.*

13 /ŦHə/ /är′ tist/ /drü/ /fôr/ /hū′ mər əs/ /kär tünz′/ /fôr/ /ŦHə/ /bùk/ /uv/ /fā′ bəlz/ *The artist drew four humorous cartoons for the book of fables.*

14 /wôl′ rə səz/ /liv/ /in/ /ärk′ tik/ /sēz/ *Walruses live in arctic seas.*

15 /tü/ /māl/ /renz/ /pėrcht/ /hī/ /ôn/ /ŦHə/ /weŦH′ ər/ /vān/   *Two male wrens perched high on the weather vane.*

Mastery Test 31b
1 /mär′ vəl/ *marvel*
2 /rē gärd′/ *regard*
3 /sô′ sər/ *saucer*
4 /bärn′ yärd′/ *barnyard*
5 /wôl′ ət/ *wallet*
6 /oi′ stər/ *oyster*

Answers

1 (See Teaching Suggestions.)
2 (See the entry for *trousers* in the Spelling Dictionary as a model answer.)

A Word from the Portuguese
a Marmalade is made with pieces of fruit.

Mastery Test
For complete directions and an explanation of the testing program, see the Introduction to this Teacher's Edition.

1 Martha wrote these lists of nouns. Proofread her work and write the lists correctly. Change the words that are not nouns into their noun forms.

Persons	*Places*	*Things*
daughter	parlor	parcel
author	barnyard	barbecue
youthful	isle	armor
carpenter	aisle	carnival
artist	mountainous	barly

2 Read the dictionary entry below for the word *pajamas*.

A lexicographer shows both pronunciations for words with two pronunciations.

A lexicographer uses the abbreviations *n.* and *pl.* to show that a noun entry is plural.

• **pajamas** /pə jä′ məz/ *or* /pə jam′ əz/ *n. pl.* Garments to sleep in, consisting of a coat and loose trousers: *The red pajamas are torn.*

Write a dictionary entry for the plural noun *trousers.* Compare your work with the entry in the Spelling Dictionary.

A Word from the Portuguese

The Portuguese word *marmelada* became our word *marmalade,* the jelly with pieces of fruit and fruit rind. The Portuguese got their word from a Latin word that means "sweet apple." The Romans, in turn, got their word from a Greek word, *melimelon,* that means "honey apple."
Write only the sentence that is true from the two below.
a /mär′ mə lād/ /iz/ /mād/ /with/ /pē′ səz/ /uv/ /früt/.
b /mär′ mə lād/ /iz/ /mād/ /uv/ /hun′ ē/.

140

---

7 /kär′ də nəl/ *cardinal*
8 /chärt/ *chart*
9 /bär′ bə kū/ *barbecue*
10 /kärt′ ən/ *carton*
11 /mush′ rümz′/ /frum/ /ŦHat/ /fēld/ /är/ /not/ /härm′ fəl/ /rē märkt′/ /ŦHə/ /fär′ mər/ *"Mushrooms from that field are not harmful,"* remarked the farmer.
12 /ŦHis/ /färm′ land′/ /wùd/ /bē/ /ek′ sə lənt/ /fôr/ /rāz′ ing/ /bär′ lē/ *This farmland would be excellent for raising barley.*

13 /klev′ ər/ /kär′ pən tərz/ /kan/ /bild/ /mär′ və ləs/ /tā′ bəlz/ /frum/ /pē′ səz/ /uv/ /sē′ dər/ /wùd/ *Clever carpenters can build marvelous tables from pieces of cedar wood.*
14 /ū/ /must/ /sē/ /ŦHə/ /dis plā′/ /uv/ /met′ əl/ /är′ mər/ /in/ /ŦHə/ /mū zē′ əm/ *You must see the display of metal armor in the museum.*
15 /tī/ /tü/ /nots/ /in/ /ŦHə/ /kôrd/ /bə fôr′/ /ū/ /māl/ /ŦHə/ /pär′ səl/ *Tie two knots in the cord before you mail the parcel.*

Study Chart

Word Types	Review Words	Sound-Spellings	How do we spell these?
■	dare stair	/dãr/ /stãr/	/ãr/ /ãr/
◀ y ey	dair,y, li,brar,y,	/dãr' ē/ /lī' brãr' ē/	/ãr/ /ē/ /ī/ /ãr/ /ē/
■■	scare,crow, bare,back, hair,cut, arm,chair,	/skãr' krō'/ /bãr' bak'/ /hãr' kut'/ /ärm' chãr'/	/ãr/ /ō/ /ãr/ /a/ /ãr/ /u/ /ãr/ /ãr/
■■	be,ware,	/bē wãr'/	/ē/ /ãr/
◀■	re,pair,	/rē pãr'/	/rē/ /ãr/
■▶	care,less,	/kãr' ləs/	/ãr/ /ləs/
◀■▶	pre,par,a,tion,	/prep'ə rā' shən/	/shən/
⊕	fare-fair	/fãr/	/ãr/
▽	their	/ŦHãr/	/ãr/

New Words

flare	car,fare,	prair,ie,	hair
pair	hard,ware,	un,fair,	hare
fair,y,	up,stairs,	care,ful,	▽ heir
con,trar,y,	air,craft,	de,clar,a,tion,	

141

Teaching Suggestions

In this unit the *are* and *air* spellings of /ār/ are featured. The /ār/ sounds are alternately shown as /er/ or /ar/ in some dictionaries. Many words in this unit are one of a set of homonyms. That means, of course, that more than the usual number of thirty words might be dealt with while the pupils are studying.

Use the Study Chart to introduce the unit and to establish the spelling generalizations for each of the review words. Help the pupils to apply the generalizations to the new words. Note that the homonyms *fare* and *fair* are presented as review words in the Study Chart. You may also want to discuss the homonyms of the review words *stair* and *their,* which are *stare* and *there-they're* respectively. In the list of new words, *hair* and *hare* are presented as a pair of homonyms. Other new words that have homonyms are *flare, pair,* and *heir.* Their homonyms are *flair, pear-pare,* and *air* respectively. The new word *fairy* and the word *ferry* are not generally considered homonyms.

Answers

1 dare, fare, flare, hare, stair, fair, pair, hair
2 their, there, they're, heir, air
3 library, contrary
4 dairy, fairy
5 scare, bare, hair, chair, fare, ware, stairs, air
6 pair, fair, care, care
7 pre par a tion, de clar a tion

●● Answers

1a fair
 b fair
 c fare
 d hair
 e hare
 f pair
 g pare

Handwriting Models

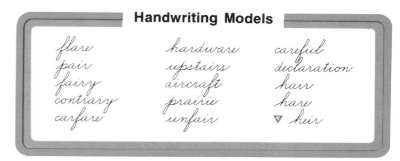

flare   hardware   careful
pair   upstairs   declaration
fairy   aircraft   hair
contrary   prairie   hare
carfare   unfair   ▽ heir

1 We can spell the /âr/ sounds with *are* or with *air*. Write the four one-syllable words in which *are* spells /âr/ and the four one-syllable words in which *air* spells /âr/.

2 Write the two snurks in which *eir* spells /âr/. Also, write the homonyms of the two snurks. (The homonyms are not in the new and review lists.)

3 We can also spell the /âr/ sounds with *ar*. Write the two soft-/ē/-ending words in which *ar* spells /âr/.

4 Write the two /ē/-ending words in which *air* spells /âr/.

5 Write the /âr/ eye-syllables of the eight compound words.

6 Write the two /âr/ eye-syllables of the prefix-root words and the /âr/ eye-syllable of the root-suffix words.

7 Write the four eye-syllables of each prefix-root-suffix word.

1 Write the correct homonyms to complete the sentences below and on the next page.
a She paid a _____ /fâr/ price for old coins.
b The weather will be _____ /fâr/ today.
c Do you have your _____ /fâr/ for the bus?
d He has blond _____ /hâr/.
e The _____ /hâr/ lost the race to the tortoise.
f I bought a _____ /pâr/ of gloves.
g Father, please _____ /pâr/ the apple. (Not a unit word.)

142

● The exercises in this section are routine and should be done independently by the pupils. Note, however, that Exercise 2 requires pupils to write several words that are not in the new or review lists. Pupils who have not participated in a previous discussion about these words may need special help.

●● Exercise 1 of this section requires pupils to write several words that are not in the lists. Exercise 2 involves word meanings.

●● The Read and Spell list is composed of more words with /âr/. The various word-type patterns illustrated in the Study Chart are again shown here. The list should be used as a decoding test in the usual manner. Discuss the meanings. The writing exercises require a knowledge of the word meanings.

●● The correct proofreading exercise, with corrected spelling errors underscored and corrected list errors starred, is as follows:

h The prince is _____ /ãr/ to the king's throne.

i The _____ /ãr/ is fresh by the seashore. (Not a unit word.)

j Please do not _____ /stãr/ at us. (Not a unit word.)

k Go up the _____ /stãrz/ to the attic.

2 Write new and review words for the sentences below.

a She's going to _____ that _____.

b He's riding _____ over the _____.

c He'd better be _____ of that dog _____.

d Thomas Jefferson has finished _____ of the _____ of Independence.

e That's a _____ next door to the _____ store.

f They lit _____ so the _____ could land.

143

h heir
i air
j stare
k stairs
2a repair, armchair
   b bareback, prairie
   c careful, upstairs
   d preparation, Declaration
   e dairy, hardware
   f flares, aircraft

Synonyms
flare-blaze
mend-repair
*against-contrary
daring-bold

Homonyms
fair-fare
pear-pair
there-their
stare-stair

Antonyms
fair-unjust
*careless-careful
foul-fair
warfare-peace

1 /ärm′ chãr′/ *armchair*
2 /bãr′ bak′/ *bareback*
3 /fãr′ ē/ *fairy*
4 /kär′ fãr′/ *carfare*
5 /dãr/ *dare*
6 /ãr′ kraft′/ *aircraft*
7 /prep′ ə rā′ shən/ *preparation*
8 /un fãr′/ *unfair*
9 /koin/ *coin*
10 /kô′ shəs/ *cautious*
11 /kãr′ fəl/ /bãr′ bərz/ /giv/ /gùd/ /hãr′ kuts′/

Answers

2 comparable, lair, fairness,
   spare, despair, blare
3a rare, ordinary
  b comparing, dictionaries
  c preparing, spareribs
  d barefoot, carefree

bare	chair	fairground	carefree	despair
mare	lair	nightmare	barefoot	impair
spare	hairy	welfare	prepare	fairness
rare	dictionary	chairman	declare	various
blare	necessary	sparerib	compare	comparable
stare	ordinary	downstairs	unaware	contrariness

1 Write any Read and Spell word that you cannot read o
any word for which you do not know the meaning.

2 Write synonyms from the Read and Spell list for *similar*
den, justice, save, hopelessness, and *blast.*

3 Write Read and Spell words, their *ing* forms, or their plurals

a This is a _____, not an _____, beast.

b She's _____ the _____.

c She's _____ the _____ for the barbecue.

d He's a _____ boy, but he's _____ as can be.

144

Careful barbers give good haircuts.
12 /ᵷНǝ/ /ãrz/ /kãm/ /swift′ lē/ /tü/ /hir/
/ᵷНãr/ /ants/ /wil/ /red/   *The heirs came*
swiftly to hear their aunt's will read.
13 /ᵷНǝ/ /fãr/ /tü/ /rīd/ /tü/ /ᵷНǝ/ /lī′ brãr′ ē/
/iz/ /nīn′ tē/ /sents/   *The fare to ride to the*
library is ninety cents.
14 /ī/ /nō/ /ᵷНat/ /ǝ/ /māl/ /kãr′ dǝ nǝl/ /iz/
/red/   *I know that a male cardinal is red.*
15 /ᵷНǝ/ /wir′ ē/ /man/ /went/ /up′ stãrz′/ /tü/

/rē tīr′/ /fôr/ /ᵷНǝ/ /nīt/   *The weary man went*
upstairs to retire for the night.

Mastery Test 32b
  1 /bē wãr′/ *beware*
  2 /dãr′ ē/ *dairy*
  3 /ãr′ tist/ *artist*
  4 /kãr tün′/ *cartoon*
  5 /kãr′ lǝs/ *careless*
  6 /dek′ lǝ rā′ shǝn/ *declaration*

144

1 Lou wrote pairs of synonyms, antonyms, and homonyms. Proofread his work for spelling and for words that are written in the wrong list. After you have found his mistakes, write the lists correctly.

Synonyms	*Antonyms*	*Homonyms*
flare – blaze	*fair – unjust*	*fair – fare*
mend – repare	*against – contrary*	*pear – pair*
careless – carefull	*foul – fair*	*there – thier*
daring – bold	*warfare – peace*	*stare – stair*

2 Read the dictionary entry below.

A lexicographer may show a suffix like *ful* as an entry word in the dictionary.	► **-ful** /fəl/ *Suffix.* **1.** Full of: *Cheerful* means "full of cheer." **2.** Showing: *Careful* means "showing care." **3.** Enough to fill: *Cupful* means "enough to fill a cup."

Write a dictionary entry for each of the words *hopeful* and *spoonful*. Compare your work with the entries in the Spelling Dictionary.

Another Word from the Italians

The Italian word *spago* means "a string or cord." The Italian word *spaghetto* means "little string." The English word *spaghetti* came from this word. Spaghetti is long, thin sticks made of flour and water.

Write only the sentences that are true from the four below. Spell all the words correctly.

a The word *spaghetti* means /ə/ /lit′ əl/ /stik/.
b The Italian word *spaghetto* means /ə/ /lit′ əl/ /string/.
c Spaghetti /iz/ /mād/ /uv/ /flour/ /and/ /milk/.
d Spaghetti /iz/ /mād/ /uv/ /wôt′ ər/ /and/ /flour/.

145

Answers
1 (See Teaching Suggestions.)
2 (See the entries for *hopeful* and *spoonful* in the Spelling Dictionary as model answers.)

Another Word from the Italians
b The Italian word *spaghetto* means "a little string."
d Spaghetti is made of water and flour.

Mastery Test
For complete directions and an explanation of the testing program, see the Introduction to this Teacher's Edition.

---

7 /skãr′ krō′/ *scarecrow*
8 /mär′ və ləs/ *marvelous*
9 /flãr/ *flare*
10 /rē pãr′/ *repair*
11 /ə/ /pãr/ /uv/ /hãrz/ /ran/ /bī/ /ŦHə/ /bärn/   *A pair of hares ran by the barn.*
12 /īl/ /bī/ /plī′ wùd′/ /fôr/ /ŦHə/ /stãrz/ /at/ /ə nuŦH′ ər/ /härd′ wãr′/ /stôr/ /snärld/ /ŦHə/ /kus′ təm ər/   *"I'll buy plywood for the stairs at another hardware store," snarled the customer.*
13 /its/ /lōn′ lē/ /hir/ /ôn/ /ŦHə/ /prãr′ ē/ /rē märkt′/ /ŦHə/ /pī′ ə nir′/   *"It's lonely here on the prairie," remarked the pioneer.*
14 /ŦHats/ /kon′ trer ē/ /tü/ /our/ /ə grē′ mənt/ /hē/ /sed/   *"That's contrary to our agreement," he said.*
15 /shē/ /prē fėrz′/ /tü/ /wosh/ /hėr/ /hãr/ /ôn/ /ə/ /fãr/ /dā/   *She prefers to wash her hair on a fair day.*

33 Combinations with /ôr/

Study Chart

Word Types	Review Words	Sound-Spellings	How do we spell these?
■	sport score hoarse	/spôrt/ /skôr/ /hôrs/	/ôr/ /ôr/ /ôr/
■ y ey	glor‚y‚ fac‚tor‚y ter‚ri‚tor‚y	/glôr′ ē/ /fak′ tər ē/ /ter′ ə tôr′ ē/	/ôr/ /ē/ /a/ /ər/ /ē/ /er/ /ē/
■ er or ar	or‚der	/ôr′ dər/	/ôr/ /ər/
■ le el al	nor‚mal	/nôr′ məl/	/ôr/ /əl/
■■	fore‚man score‚card	/fôr′ mən/ /skôr′ kärd′/	/ôr/ /ə/ /ôr/ /är/
■■	or‚chard or‚phan	/ôr′ chərd/ /ôr′ fən/	/ôr/ /ər/ /ôr/ /ə/
■■■■	or‚ig‚in‚al	/ə rij′ ə nəl/	/ij/ /əl/
◄■	ex‚plore	/eks plôr′/	/eks/ /ôr/
◄■►	im‚port‚ant	/im pôrt′ ənt/	/im/ /ôr/ /ənt/

New Words

fort	di‚rect‚or‚y	mor‚tar	for‚bid	cor‚ri‚dor
ore	for‚mer	or‚al	ig‚nore	ex‚port
hoard	hor‚ror	fore‚cast	ab‚sorb	de‚port‚ment

146

Teaching Suggestions

This unit features the *or, ore,* and *oar* spellings of /ôr/ in conjunction with the various word-type patterns. As indicated in an earlier unit of this text, the /ôr/ sounds are pronounced /ōr/ in some regions of our country. You are urged to exercise whatever preference may locally prevail between the /ôr/ and /ōr/ pronunciations of words spelled *or, ore,* and *oar.* In so doing, you might help pupils understand that dictionary makers cannot cover all of the speech variations used throughout the country. Pupils should also understand that lexicographers are reporters, not arbiters — their work is not divinely inspired.

Use the Study Chart as a vehicle of discussion regarding the spelling generalizations of /ôr/. Pupils should observe that /ôr/ is not heard in the review words *factory* and *original,* even though the *or* spelling is used. In both cases the *or* spelling occurs in unstressed syl-

Handwriting Models

fort former forecast corridor
ore horror forbid export
hoard mortar ignore deportment
directory oral absorb

1 We can spell /ôr/ with *or, ore,* or *oar.* Write the two one-syllable words in which *or* spells /ôr/, the two one-syllable words in which *ore* spells /ôr/, and the two one-syllable words in which *oar* spells /ôr/.

2 Write the four words in which the /ē/ ending is spelled *y.*

3 We can spell the /ər/ ending with *er, ar,* or *or.* Write the two words in which the /ər/ ending is spelled *er,* the word in which it is spelled *ar,* and the two words in which it is spelled *or.*

4 Write the three words in which the soft /əl/ ending is spelled *al.*

5 Write the three /ôr/ eye-syllables used in the four compound words.

6 Write the eye-syllables of the words /ôr′ chərd/, /ôr′ fən/, /ig nôr′/, and /ab sôrb′/.

7 Write the /ôr/ eye-syllables of the two words with the /eks/ prefix.

8 We can spell the /ənt/ suffix with *ant* or with *ent.* We spell the /mənt/ suffix with *ment.* Write the eye-syllables of the words with these suffixes.

1 Write antonyms from the lists for the words *silent, unimportant,* and *latter.*

147

● Answers
1 sport, fort, score, ore, hoarse, hoard
2 glory, factory, territory, directory
3 order, former, mortar, horror, corridor
4 normal, original, oral
5 fore, score, for
6 or chard, or phan, ig nore, ab sorb
7 plore, port
8 im port ant, de port ment

●● Answers
1 oral, important, former

lables. Separating the words into eye-syllables will help the pupils think stress on all the syllables and establish spelling clues. It will be worthwhile to have some discussion of the meanings of the words.

● The exercises in this section are routine. They require the pupils to write a combination of whole words and eye-syllables. The format should be quite familiar.

●● These exercises require the pupils to deal with antonyms, *ing* verb forms, noun plurals, synonyms, and word meanings.

●● The Read and Spell list continues to be offered as a decoding test or for decoding practice. Pupils should discuss the word meanings before they do the writing exercises, which are unusually large in number but should be quite familiar in format.

2a scoring **d** absorbing
  b ordering **e** exploring
  c ignoring **f** hoarding
3 factories, territories,
  glories, directories
4 normal, corridor, horror,
  deportment, foreman,
  original
5a scorecard **d** fort
  b directory **e** orchard
  c factory **f** mortar
6a orphan **c** hoarse
  b ore **d** sport

2 Write the *ing* verb forms suggested by these pictures.

3 Write the plural forms of the words /fak′ tər ē/, /ter′ ə tôr′ē/, /glôr′ ē/, and /də rek′ tər ē/.

4 Write synonyms from the lists for the words *usual, hallway, terror, behavior, boss,* and *earliest.*

5 Write a new or review word to complete each sentence.

a This is a ____.   **c** This is a ____.   **e** This is an ____.

b This is a ____.   **d** This is a ____.   **f** This is ____.

6 Write a new or review word to complete each sentence.
a A child whose parents are dead is an ____.
b Rock containing metal is called ____.
c A deep, rough voice is a ____ voice.
d Baseball is a popular ____.

148

●● The correct proofreading exercise is:
  1. Does a pupil with good deportment behave well? yes
  2. Is a corridor a long hall? yes
  3. Do men mine ore in an orchard? no
  4. Does cotton cloth absorb moisture? yes
  5. Did early explorers ride horses through their territories? yes
  6. Do most farmers ignore weather forecasts? no

Mastery Test 33a
  1 /ab sôrb′/ *absorb*
  2 /ig nôr′/ *ignore*
  3 /fôr′ kast′/ *forecast*
  4 /eks′ pôrt/ *export*
  5 /ôr′ fən/ *orphan*
  6 /eks plôr′/ *explore*
  7 /kãr′ fəl/ *careful*
  8 /nôr′ məl/ *normal*
  9 /kôf/ *cough*
  10 /pär′ səl/ *parcel*
  11 /ŦHə/ /fôr′ mən/ /tōld/ /ŦHə/ /bil′ dərz/ /tü/ /ūz/ /ŦHis/ /môr′ tər/ *The foreman told the*

Read and Spell

snort	soar	moral	uproar	deport
thorn	boar	morsel	borrow	transform
port	porter	foremost	hornet	torment
pore	border	forearm	origin	gorgeous
core	formal	corkscrew	report	portable
coarse	mortal	shortstop	import	porous

Write words from the Read and Spell list for all the exercises in this section.

1 Write any Read and Spell word that you cannot read or any word for which you do not know the meaning.

2 Write three one-syllable words in which *or* spells /ôr/.

3 Write two one-syllable words in which *ore* spells /ôr/.

4 Write three one-syllable words in which *oar* spells /ôr/.

5 Write two words in which *er* spells the soft /ər/ ending.

6 Write three words in which *al* spells the soft /əl/ ending.

7 Write one word in which *el* spells the soft /əl/ ending.

8 Write five compound words.

9 Write four prefix-root words.

10 Write four root-suffix words.

11 Write the two- and three-syllable words /hôr′ nət/, /bôr′ ō/, and /ôr′ ə jin/.

1 Mort wrote yes-no questions as a game for a class party. Proofread his work. After you have found his mistakes, write the questions correctly and answer each question by writing *yes* or *no* after it.

149

builders to use this mortar.

12 /pùt/ /ŦHēz/ /bas′ kət bôl′/ /skôrz/ /ôn/ /yùr/ /skôr′ kärd′/ *Put these basketball scores on your scorecard.*

13 /in/ /fôr′ mər/ /yirz/ /ŦHə/ /ōld/ /fôrt/ /wuz/ /ŦHə/ /sēn/ /uv/ /much/ /biz′ ə nəs/ *In former years the old fort was the scene of much business.*

14 /dü/ /ū/ /think/ /ŦHat/ /wē/ /hôrd/ /tü/ /much/ /sil′ vər/ /ôr/ *Do you think that we hoard too much silver ore?*

15 /ŦHat/ /pōl/ /iz/ /az/ /hī/ /az/ /ŦHə/ /ches′ nut′/ /trē/ *That pole is as high as the chestnut tree.*

Mastery Test 33b

1 /kôr′ ə dər/ *corridor*

2 /hôr′ ər/ *horror*

3 /ôr′ əl/ *oral*

4 /glôr′ ē/ *glory*

5 /prãr′ ē/ *prairie*

6 /ter′ ə tôr′ ē/ *territory*

7 /fak′ tər ē/ *factory*

8 /fôr′ bid′/ *forbid*

1 (See Teaching Suggestions.)

2 (See the entry for *order* in the Spelling Dictionary as model answers for *in order to* and *out of order*.)

Another Word from the Chinese
board, or, short, oars

Mastery Test
For complete directions and an explanation of the testing program, see the Introduction to this Teacher's Edition.

---

1. Does a pupil with good deportment behave well?
2. Is a corridor a long haul?
3. Do men mine oar in an orchard?
4. Does cotton cloth absorb moisture?
5. Did early explorers ride hoarses through their territorys?
6. Do most farmers ignore weather forcasts?

2 Sometimes an entry word may be used in expressions that have a special meaning.

| A lexicographer lists special expressions in alphabetical order according to the first word in the expression. | • **order** /ôr′ dər/ *n.* **1.** The way one thing follows another. **2.** Command: *The order must be obeyed.* **3.** Request for goods. —*v.* **1.** Command. **2.** Request goods. **by order of,** According to an order given by a proper person: *The bank was closed by order of the governor.* **in order,** Working right: *The TV set is in order.* |

Write an explanation of the expressions *in order to* and *out of order*. Use each expression in one or more sentences to help make the meaning clear. When you have finished, compare your work with the entry in the Spelling Dictionary.

Another Word from the Chinese

The word *sampan* comes from the two words *san,* meaning "three," and *pan,* meaning "board" or "plank." A *san-pan* was a little three-plank boat. Today a Chinese *sampan* is a flat-bottomed skiff that is rowed by two short oars.
Write the four words from the paragraph above that have the /ôr/ sounds.

150

---

9 /kən trãr′ ē/ *contrary*
10 /spôrt/ *sport*
11 /in′ sekts/ /swüpt/ /doun/ /ôn/ /fä′ ₮Hərz/ /pēch/ /ôr′ chərd/ *Insects swooped down on Father's peach orchard.*
12 /₮His/ /də rek′ tər ē/ /in klüdz′/ /₮Hə/ /ə dres′ əz/ /uv/ /im pôrt′ ənt/ /pē′ pəl/ *This directory includes the addresses of important people.*
13 /yür/ /də pôrt′ mənt/ /wuz/ /mär′ və ləs/

/dē klãrd′/ /₮Hə/ /tē′ chər/ /in/ /ə/ /hôrs/ /vois/ *"Your deportment was marvelous,"* declared the teacher in a hoarse voice.*
14 /₮Hā/ /wėr/ /pōld/ /in/ /ôr′ dər/ /tü/ /ē lekt′/ /ə/ /prez′ ə dənt/ *They were polled in order to elect a president.*
15 /hav/ /ū/ /sēn/ /₮Hə/ /ə rij′ ə nəl/ /ôr′ dər/ /fôr/ /tü/ /poundz/ /uv/ /kůk′ ēz/ *Have you seen the original order for two pounds of cookies?*

Combinations with /èr/
Study Chart

Word Types	Review Words	Sound-Spellings	How do we spell these?
■	stern twirl blurt	/stèrn/ /twèrl/ /blèrt/	/èr/ /èr/ /èr/
◄ y ey	dirty	/dèr' tē/	/èr/ /ē/
◄ er or ar	mirror burglar	/mir' ər/ /bèr' glər/	/ir/ /ər/ /èr/ /ər/
◄ le el al	purple	/pèr' pəl/	/èr/ /əl/
■■	murmur purpose	/mèr' mər/ /pèr' pəs/	/èr/ /ər/ /èr/ /əs/
◄■	deserve	/dē zèrv'/	/dē/ /èr/
■►	nervous terrible	/nèr' vəs/ /ter' ə bəl/	/èr/ /əs/ /er/ /ə bəl/
◄■►	conference	/kon' fər əns/	/kon/ /ər/ /əns/
Ⓗ	fur-fir	/fèr/	/èr/

New Words

nerve	stur dy	hur dle	pre serve	dis turb ance
thirst	mur der	fer tile	cur rent	▽ ber ry
burst	cir cu lar	cur tain	ser vant	▽ bur y

151

Teaching Suggestions

This is the last of the four units that deal with the vowel-r spellings in combination with the various word-type patterns. This unit features the *er, ir,* and *ur* spellings of /èr/. The /èr/ sounds occur only in stressed syllables. The similar /ər/ sounds occur in unstressed syllables and are usually spelled, as the pupils have observed throughout this text, with *er, or,* or *ar.* You may want to again call attention to the similarity of these sounds.

Use the Study Chart to introduce the unit and to establish the /èr/ spelling generalizations of the review words. Pupils should observe that, although they have not been so marked, both *mirror* and *terrible* are snurks. *Mirror* is a snurk because the *ir* spells /ir/ instead of the expected /èr/. *Terrible* is a snurk because the *er* spells /er/ instead of the expected /èr/. In the list of new words, *berry* and *bury* are shown as snurks. Pupils should determine why they are

Handwriting Models

nerve   circular   current
thirst   hurdle   servant
burst   fertile   disturbance
sturdy   curtain   ▽ berry
murder   preserve   ▽ bury

1 We can spell /èr/ with *er, ir,* or *ur.* Write the two one
syllable words in which *er* spells /èr/, the three one-syllable
words in which *ir* spells /èr/, and the three one-syllable words
in which *ur* spells /èr/.

2 Write the four words in which *y* spells the soft /ē/ ending

3 Write the word in which the soft /ər/ ending is spelled *er*
the word in which it is spelled *or,* and the two words in which
it is spelled *ar.*

4 In a few words we spell the soft /ər/ ending with *ur.* Write
the review word in which *ur* spells /ər/.

5 Write the three two-syllable words in which *le* spells the
soft /əl/ ending.

6 Write the eye-syllables of the words /pèr' pəs/, /kèr' tən/
/dē zèrv'/, /prē zèrv'/, and /ter' ə bəl/.

7 Write the words with the /əs/ and /ənt/ suffixes.

8 Write the eye-syllables of the two prefix-root-suffix words.

9 Write the correct homonym to complete each sentence
a Some animals grow thick _____ in winter.
b People often use _____ trees as Christmas trees.
c Pirates used to _____ their gold.
d We make coffee from the _____ of the coffee plant.

152

---

snurks. They are generally considered to be
homonyms.

● These exercises follow the well-estab-
lished format of recent units. Pupils should
work these exercises independently.

●● Exercises 1 and 2 require application of
structural generalizations. Exercise 4 requires
knowledge of word meanings.

●
●● The Read and Spell list contains more /èr/
words for decoding. Knowledge of word meanings is required for the writing exercise, which
follows a familiar format.

●●
●● The correct proofreading exercise, with
corrected errors underscored, is as follows:

Mirrors have interested people throughout
the ages. There are many old <u>tales</u> *of magic*
mirrors. One legend tells about a mirror that

1 Write the *er* and *est* forms of /dėr′ tē/ and /stėr′ dē/.

2 Write the *ing* forms of /dē zėrv′/ and /prē zėrv′/.

3 Write the words /stėrn/, /twėrl/, and /blėrt/.

4 Write new and review words to complete these sentences.

a She is holding a ____ with a ____ shape.

b He likes to hear the ____ of the ____.

c This ____ seems to be very ____.

d These ____ grapes grow in ____ soil.

e Her ____ is to create a ____.

f He will leap over the last ____ and ____ across the finish line.

153

●● **Answers**
1 dirtier, dirtiest, sturdier, sturdiest
2 deserving, preserving
3 stern, twirl, blurt
4a mirror, circular
  b murmur, current
  c servant, nervous
  d purple, fertile
  e purpose, disturbance
  f hurdle, burst

howed thoughts instead of images. Another story is about a huge <u>circular</u> mirror that warned the king of traitors and false friends. An old Greek legend is my favorite. <u>It's about a mirror that showed scenes of the past, present, and future.

I wonder if some people still <u>believe</u> mirrors have magic powers. Perhaps that is why they say that breaking a mirror means seven years of bad luck.*

Mastery Test 34a
1 /blėrt/ *blurt*   **6** /pėr′ pəl/ *purple*
2 /kėr′ tən/ *curtain* **7** /up′ stärz′/ *upstairs*
3 /dėr′ tē/ *dirty*   **8** /nėrv/ *nerve*
4 /bėrst/ *burst*   **9** /hėr′ dəl/ *hurdle*
5 /kär′ fəl/ *careful* **10** /thėrst/ *thirst*
11 /ī/ /līk/ /tü/ /woch/ /ŦHə/ /sėr′ kū lər/ /mō′ shən/ /uv/ /ŦHə/ /hwėrl′ pül′/ *I like to watch the circular motion of the whirlpool.*
12 /blud/ /flōz/ /thrü/ /yùr/ /vānz/ /tü/ /yùr/ /härt/ *Blood flows through your veins to*

Answers

2a surfboard
 b percolator
 c verse
 d turtle
 e serpent
 f carburetor
 g hurl
 h vertical
 i murderous (surly)

Read and Spell

verse	surly	hurtle	person	exert
churn	thirsty	turtle	service	convert
hurl	thirty	vertical	serpent	invert
lurch	carburetor	surfboard	furnish	commerce
scurry	percolator	curbstone	reserve	murderous
curtsy	emperor	observe	disturb	permanent

1 Write any Read and Spell word that you cannot read ⊂
any word for which you do not know the meaning.

2 Write Read and Spell words to complete these sentence⊆

a She's on a
———.

d This is a
friendly ———.

g He's going to
——— the ball.

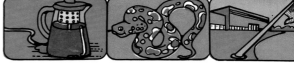

b This is a ———.

e This is some
———!

h It's not ———.

c The poet is
writing ———.

f He's fixing
the ———.

i He looks ———

154

---

your heart.
13 /ī/ /fôr′ bid′/ /ū/ /tü/ /māk/ /ə/ /pub′ lik/
/dis tėr′ bəns/ /hir/   *I forbid you to make a*
public disturbance here.
14 /ᵵHə/ /vān/ /chīld/ /twėrld/ /ə round′/ /in/
/frunt/ /uv/ /ᵵHə/ /mir′ ər/   *The vain child*
twirled around in front of the mirror.
15 /ᵵHis/ /fėr′ təl/ /färm′ land′/ /iz/
/kėr′ ənt lē/ /ūzd/ /fôr/ /rāz′ ing/ /ber′ ēz/
This fertile farmland is currently used for
raising berries.

Mastery Test 34b
 1 /pėr′ pəs/ *purpose*
 2 /stėr′ dē/ *sturdy*
 3 /härd′ wār′/ *hardware*
 4 /skwėrt/ *squirt*
 5 /nėr′ vəs/ *nervous*
 6 /lôn′ drē/ *laundry*
 7 /ter′ ə bəl/ *terrible*
 8 /mėr′ dər/ *murder*
 9 /kon′ fər əns/ *conference*
 10 /sėr′ vənt/ *servant*
 11 /ᵵHis/ /hev′ ē/ /fėr/ /kōt/ /iz/ /tü/ /wärm/

1 Bernice read a book about legends and wrote these paragraphs. Proofread her work and write the paragraphs correctly.

> Mirrors have interested people throughout the ages. There are many old tails of magic mirrors. One legend tells about a mirror that showed thoughts instead of images. Another story is about a huge circuler mirror that warned the king of traitors and false friends. An old greek legend is my favorite its about a mirror that showed scenes of the past, present, and future.
>
> I wonder if some people still beleive mirrors have magic powers. Perhaps that is why they say that breaking a mirror means seven years of bad luck.

2 Read the dictionary entry below for the word *build.*

A lexicographer shows the irregular form of verbs when *ed* cannot be added to the entry.

- **build** /bild/ *v.* **1.** Make by putting materials together: *People build houses. Birds build nests.* **2.** Develop: *They built fine reputations.* **built, building.**

Write a complete dictionary entry for the word *burst.* Compare your work with the entry in the Spelling Dictionary.

Another Word from the Romans

The English word *versus* came from a Latin word meaning "against." The Latin word came from an older Latin word meaning "to turn." To turn and face another person was to oppose that person. If we say today "the Giants versus the Cardinals," we mean that the Giant team will play against the Cardinal team.

Write a synonym from the paragraph above for *versus.*

155

Answers
1 (See Teaching Suggestions.)
2 (See the entry for *burst* in the Spelling Dictionary as a model answer.)

Another Word from the Romans
against

Mastery Test
For complete directions and an explanation of the testing program, see the Introduction to this Teacher's Edition.

tü/ /wâr/ *This heavy fur coat is too warm to wear.*
12 /kamp′ ərz/ /shùd/ /bē/ /kār′ fəl/ /tü/ /prē zèrv′/ /ŦHēz/ /jī′ ənt/ /fèr/ /trēz/ *Campers should be careful to preserve these giant fir trees.*
13 /mī/ /loi′ əl/ /frend/ /iz/ /ded/ /and/ /ber′ ēd/ /mèr′ mərd/ /ŦHə/ /king/ *"My loyal friend is dead and buried," murmured the king.*
14 /shē/ /red/ /loud′ lē/ /sō/ /ŦHat/ /ŦHə/ /ô′ dē əns/ /kùd/ /hir/ /hèr/ *She read loudly so that the audience could hear her.*
15 /ŦHis/ /bèr′ glər/ /dē zèrvz′/ /stèrn/ /trēt′ mənt/ /sed/ /ŦHə/ /juj/ *"This burglar deserves stern treatment," said the judge.*

Study Chart

Word Type	Review Words	How do we spell these ear-syllables?
◀■▶	en joy able	/en joi′ ə bəl/
◀■▶	in vis ible	/in viz′ ə bəl/
◀■▶	pre dic tion	/prə dik′ shən/
◀■▶	pro tec tion	/prə tek′ shən/
◀■▶	con fid ent	/kon′ fə dənt/
◀■▶	com pan ion	/kəm pan′ yən/
◀■▶	re place ment	/rə plās′ mənt/
◀■▶	de scend ant	/də sen′ dənt/
◀■▶	dis grace ful	/dis grās′ fəl/
◀■▶	ex pres sion	/eks presh′ ən/

New Words

con trac tion	dis a gree able	re spons ible
ex cell ence	im peach ment	re gard less
pro ces sion	de light ful	con tin ent
re sist ance	com mo tion	▽ un pleas ant
re luc tant	en large ment	con ver sa tion
in struc tion	pre scrip tion	con ve ni ent
un ea si ness	pre vi ous	

1 Prefixes are usually soft syllables. Write the correct spellings for these prefixes: /en/, /em/, /in/, /prə/, /kən/, /kəm/, /rə/, /də/, /dis/, /eks/, /un/, /im/.

2 Suffixes, too, are usually soft syllables. Write the correct spellings for these suffixes: /ə bəl/, /shən/, /ənt/, /əns/, /mənt/, /fəl/, /ləs/, /əs/.

156

Teaching Suggestions

This unit brings together all of the common prefixes and suffixes that have been presented throughout this text. When the pupils become familiar with the standard affix spellings and habitually separate the long words into their component eye-syllables, these prefix-root-suffix words become relatively easy to spell.

Use the Study Chart to review the familiar prefix and suffix spellings. Pupils should note that the spelling errors that may occur by confusing some suffixes, such as *able* and *ible,* may be circumvented by careful observation.

● The exercises in this section cause pupils to write the prefixes, the suffixes, and the root eye-syllables.

●● The exercises in this section focus on the function of suffixes and on the flexibility of the affixes in conjunction with the roots.

●
●● The Read and Spell words repeat the prefix-root-suffix pattern. Pupils who have learned to see long words as a series of eye-syllables should be able to decode these words.

Handwriting Models

contraction	*disagreeable*	*responsible*
excellence	*impeachment*	*regardless*
procession	*delightful*	*continent*
resistance	*commotion*	▽ *unpleasant*
reluctant	*enlargement*	*conversation*
instruction	*prescription*	*convenient*
uneasiness	*previous*	

3 Write the root eye-syllables of the words with these prefixes: *re, com, dis, im, pre, in, ex, un, con, de, en, pro.*

Some of the words you will write in this section are not in the new or review lists.

1 Write nouns by adding noun suffixes to the verbs *resist, protect, impeach, descend, enlarge,* and *disagree.*

2 Write nouns by changing the adjective suffixes of *reluctant, confident, excellent,* and *convenient* to noun suffixes.

3 Write adjectives by adding adjective suffixes to *delight, response,* and *regard.*

4 Write three prefix-root-suffix words using the /kən/, /rə/, and /eks/ prefixes, the root *trac,* and the /shən/ suffix.

5 Write two prefix-root-suffix words using the /rə/ and /dis/ prefixes, the root *place,* and the /mənt/ suffix.

6 Write three prefix-root-suffix words using the /in/, /də/, and /kən/ prefixes, the root *scrip,* and the /shən/ suffix.

7 Write three prefix-root-suffix words using the /kəm/, /də/, and /eks/ prefixes, the root *pres,* and the /shən/ suffix.

8 Write three prefix-root-suffix words using the /kəm/, /də/, and /prə/ prefixes, the root *mo,* and the /shən/ suffix.

157

3 re: place, sist, luc, spons, gard;
com: pan, mo;
dis: grace, a gree;
im: peach;
pre: dic, scrip, vi;
in: vis, struc;
ex: pres, cell;
un: ea si, pleas;
con: fid, trac, tin, ver sa, ve ni;
de: scend, light;
en: joy, large;
pro: tec, ces

●● **Answers**
1 resistance, protection, impeachment, descendant, enlargement, disagreement
2 reluctance, confidence, excellence, convenience
3 delightful, responsible, regardless
4 contraction, retraction, extraction
5 replacement, displacement
6 inscription, description, conscription
7 compression, depression, expression
8 commotion, demotion, promotion

Mastery Test 35a
1 /nėrv/ *nerve*
2 /hėr′ dəl/ *hurdle*
3 /kėr′ tən/ *curtain*
4 /kon′ fə dənt/ *confident*
5 /prē′ vē əs/ *previous*
6 /in viz′ ə bəl/ *invisible*
7 /də sen′ dənt/ *descendant*
8 /rə gärd′ ləs/ *regardless*
9 /kən trak′ shən/ *contraction*
10 /rə zis′ təns/ *resistance*
11 /ə/ /trip/ /ə krôs′/ /ғнə/ /kon′ tə nənt/ /iz/ /sėr′ tən/ /tü/ /bē/ /en joi′ ə bəl/

Read and Spell

extension	enrollment	enrichment	explosion
deportment	promotion	comparable	renewable
projection	contraption	disgraceful	excitement
respectable	description	unselfishness	contestant
unpardonable	unevenness	disturbance	dependence
exception	execution	unskillful	indifferent
reduction	compartment	discussion	conclusion
invasion			disappointment

1 Write any Read and Spell word that you cannot read or any word for which you do not know the meaning.

2 Write Read and Spell nouns by adding suffixes to these verbs. In some cases you will have to change the root when you add the suffix.

a	excite	**f**	disturb	**k**	promote
b	disappoint	**g**	conclude	**l**	execute
c	enroll	**h**	explode	**m**	invade
d	project	**i**	discuss	**n**	describe
e	reduce	**j**	enrich	**o**	extend

3 Write Read and Spell adjectives by adding adjective suffixes to *renew*, *disgrace*, and *respect*.

4 Write an antonym from the Read and Spell list for each of these words.

a	skillful	**c**	evenness	**e**	independence
b	selfishness	**d**	pardonable	**f**	demotion

1 Tom's assignment was to write synonyms for ten adjectives from the new and review lists. Proofread his work. After you have found his mistakes, write the words and their synonyms correctly. (You will have to substitute correct synonyms for two incorrect ones.)

158

A trip across the continent is certain to be enjoyable.
12 /hü/ /iz/ /rə spon′ sə bəl/ /fôr/ /ᵮHis/ /dis grās′ fəl/ /kə mō′ shən/ /ᵮHə/ /bôs/ /də man′ dəd/ *"Who is responsible for this disgraceful commotion?" the boss demanded.*
13 /ᵮHis/ /flou′ ər/ /haz/ /ə/ /dis′ ə grē′ ə bəl/ /sent/ *This flower has a disagreeable scent.*
14 /ᵮHə/ /dôg/ /gāv/ /its/ /ō′ nər/ /luv/ /and/ /prə tek′ shən/ *The dog gave its owner love and protection.*

15 /in struk′ shənz/ /fôr/ /dü′ ing/ /ᵮHə/ /proj′ ekt/ /är/ /in klü′ dəd/ *Instructions for doing the project are included.*

Mastery Test 35b
  1 /kôr′ ə dər/ *corridor*
  2 /də pôrt′ mənt/ *deportment*
  3 /un ē′ zē nəs/ *uneasiness*
  4 /rə luk′ tənt/ *reluctant*
  5 /ek′ sə ləns/ *excellence*
  6 /rə plās′ mənt/ *replacement*

1. *convenient* – *suitable*
2. *previous* – *earlier*
3. *disagreeable* – *unpleasant*
4. *delightful* – *pleasing*
5. *confident* – *certain*
6. *sturdy* – *harsh*
7. *dirty* – *soiled*
8. *terrible* – *awfull*
9. *stern* – *strong*
10. *reluctant* – *unwilling*

2 Read the dictionary entry below for the word *inconvenient*.

> A lexicographer shows many prefix words as entries in a dictionary. → • **inconvenient** /in′ kən vēn′ yənt/ *adv.* Not convenient; troublesome; causing bother, difficulty, or discomfort: *It is inconvenient for you to leave at this time.*

Write a dictionary entry for the word *invisible*. Compare your work with the entry in the Spelling Dictionary.

A Word from the Africans

The word *banjo* comes from the African word *mbanza*. A banjo is a stringed musical instrument something like a guitar. It has a long neck and a round body that looks like a drum. The plural form of *banjo* is *banjos* or *banjoes*.

Write only the sentence that is true from the three below. Spell the words correctly.

a /ə/ /ban′ jō/ /haz/ /ə/ /lông/ /bod′ ē/.
b /ə/ /ban′ jō/ /iz/ /ə/ /smôl/ /drum/.
c /ə/ /ban′ jō/ /iz/ /ə/ /stringd/ /in′ strə mənt/.

159

Answers
1 (See Teaching Suggestions.)
2 (See the entry for *invisible* in the Spelling Dictionary as a model answer.)

A Word from the Africans
c A banjo is a stringed instrument.

Mastery Test
For complete directions and an explanation of the testing program, see the Introduction to this Teacher's Edition.

---

7 /prē skrip′ shən/ *prescription*
8 /eks presh′ ən/ *expression*
9 /im pēch′ mənt/ *impeachment*
0 /prə dik′ shən/ *prediction*
1 /mī/ /frend/ /iz/ /ə/ /də līt′ fəl/ /kəm pan′ yən/ *My friend is a delightful companion.*
2 /ī/ /sent/ /ū/ /an/ /en lärj′ mənt/ /uv/ /mī/ /fāv′ ə rət/ /fō′ tō/ *I sent you an enlargement of my favorite photo.*
3 /ə/ /prə sesh′ ən/ /müvd/ /slō′ lē/ /doun/ /ŦHə/ /īl/ *A procession moved slowly down the aisle.*
14 /ŦHōz/ /tü/ /men/ /är/ /hav′ ing/ /an/ /un plez′ ənt/ /kon′ vər sā′ shən/ *Those two men are having an unpleasant conversation.*
15 /īl/ /gō/ /tü/ /ŦHə/ /lī′ brär′ ē/ /hwen/ /its/ /kən vēn′ yənt/ *I'll go to the library when it's convenient.*

Answers

1 or din ar y
nec es sar y
e vap or ate
ge o graph y
man u fac ture
in de pend ence
ther mom e ter
al li ga tor
par tic u lar
a rith me tic

2 a bil it y
ma ter i al
col o ni al
ac tiv it y
me chan ic al
ma jor it y
op er a tor
ac com pan y
au to mat ic
cir cum fer ence
ap pre ci ate
al to geth er

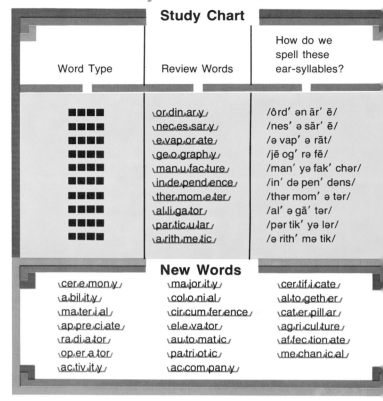

36 Four-Syllable **Words**

Study Chart

Word Type	Review Words	How do we spell these ear-syllables?
■■■■	or din ar y	/ôrd′ ən ãr′ ē/
■■■■	nec es sar y	/nes′ ə sãr′ ē/
■■■■	e vap or ate	/ə vap′ ə rāt/
■■■■	ge o graph y	/jē og′ rə fē/
■■■■	man u fac ture	/man′ yə fak′ chər/
■■■■	in de pend ence	/in′ də pen′ dəns/
■■■■	ther mom e ter	/thər mom′ ə tər/
■■■■	al li ga tor	/al′ ə gā′ tər/
■■■■	par tic u lar	/pər tik′ yə lər/
■■■	a rith me tic	/ə rith′ mə tik/

New Words

cer e mon y	ma jor it y	cer tif i cate
a bil it y	col o ni al	al to geth er
ma ter i al	cir cum fer ence	cat er pill ar
ap pre ci ate	el e va tor	ag ri cul ture
ra di a tor	au to mat ic	af fec tion ate
op er a tor	pa tri ot ic	me chan ic al
ac tiv it y	ac com pan y	

1 Write the eye-syllables of each of the review words.

2 Write the eye-syllables of these new words: /ə bil′ ə tē
/mə tir′ ē əl/, /kə lō′ nē əl/, /ak tiv′ ə tē/, /mə kan′ ə kəl
/mə jôr′ ə tē/, /op′ ər ā′ tər/, /ə kum′ pə nē/, /ô′ tə mat′ ik
/sər kum′ fər əns/, /ə prē′ shē āt′/, /ôl′ tə geth′ ər/.

160

Teaching Suggestions

This last unit features four-syllable words. In our elementary vocabulary, two out of every three words are multisyllabic. Of these multisyllabic words, about 62 percent are two-syllable words, 26 percent have three syllables, 10 percent have four syllables, and only 2 percent have more than four syllables.

Use the Study Chart and the list of new words to review the spelling generalizations and to provide practice in separating words into four eye-syllables. With this many syllables, the markings are rather arbitrary. Pupils may

separate long words into eye-syllables to su their individual convenience.

● These exercises are designed to focus o eye-syllables and meanings.

●● These exercises are routine and can b done independently by the pupils.

●●
●● The Read and Spell words all have fou syllables.

The writing exercises are routine.

Handwriting Models

ceremony   majority   certificate
ability   colonial   altogether
material   circumference   caterpillar
appreciate   elevator   agriculture
radiator   automatic   affectionate
operator   patriotic   mechanical
activity   accompany

3 Write a new word to complete each sentence below.

a He's getting a ___.

c The ___ is crowded.

e That ___ is sick.

b She's very ___.

d The boy is ___.

f That's a hot ___.

1 Write the *ing* forms of the verbs *evaporate, accompany, manufacture,* and *appreciate.*

2 Write the plural forms of the nouns *activity, ceremony, ability,* and *majority.*

3 Write new and review adjectives that mean "normal," "like a machine," "apart from others," and "moving by itself."

4 Write new and review nouns that mean "the science of numbers," "having to do with farming," and "special acts."

161

3a certificate   **d** affectionate
b patriotic   **e** caterpillar
c elevator   **f** radiator

●● **Answers**
1 evaporating, accompanying, manufacturing, appreciating
2 activities, ceremonies, abilities, majorities
3 ordinary, mechanical, particular, automatic
4 arithmetic, agriculture, ceremony

The correct proofreading exercise is:

A woolly bear is not a bear. It's an ordinary caterpillar with stripes around its body. People once thought that the woolly bear's stripes could forecast weather.

"Wide stripes mean a mild winter," declared my uncle. "Narrow stripes mean a long, frozen season."

We learned in science that there are always some woolly-bear caterpillars with wide stripes and some with narrow stripes. Woolly bears are not weather forecasters!

Mastery Test 36a
1 /prē′ vē əs/ *previous*
2 /kon′ tə nənt/ *continent*
3 /mə jôr′ ə tē/ *majority*
4 /ak tiv′ ə tē/ *activity*
5 /ser′ ə mō′ nē/ *ceremony*
6 /ôrd′ ən ār′ ē/ *ordinary*
7 /ag′ rə kul′ chər/ *agriculture*
8 /man′ yə fak′ chər/ *manufacture*
9 /mə kan′ ə kəl/ *mechanical*
10 /ə vap′ ə rāt/ *evaporate*
11 /ᵮHā/ /bōs′ təd/ /ə bout′/ /hav′ ing/
/ô′ tə mat′ ik/ /el′ ə vā′ tərz/ /at/ /ᵮHār/ /skül/

161

Answers

2a cemetery
  b photographer
  c astronomer
  d dictionary
  e literature
  f escalator
3a immediate   **d** rectangular
  b electrical   **e** sympathetic
  c political   **f** scientific

Read and Spell

territory	photographer	emergency	favorable
immediate	scientific	electrical	ambassador
impractical	dictionary	architecture	rectangular
perishable	investigate	escalator	elaborate
epidemic	temperature	sympathetic	additional
cemetery	astronomer	customary	fashionable
congratulate	democratic	political	irregular
literature			energetic

1 Write any Read and Spell word that you cannot read ⌐ any word for which you do not know the meaning.

2 Write Read and Spell nouns to complete these sentences

a This is a ____.   **c** He is an ____.   **e** He's writing ____

b She is a ____.   **d** This is a ____.   **f** This is an ____.

3 Write Read and Spell adjectives for these sound-spellings
  a /ə mē′ dē ət/   **d** /rek tang′ gyə lər/
  b /ə lek′ trə kəl/   **e** /sim′ pə thet′ ik/
  c /pə lit′ ə kəl/   **f** /sī′ ən tif′ ik/

1 Shirley wrote a report for her science class. Proofread he work and write the report correctly.

162

They boasted about having automatic
elevators at their school.
12 /ə/ /fuz′ ē/ /kat′ ər pil′ ər/ /āt/ /ôl/ /ŦHə/
/lēvz/ /ôn/ /ŦHə/ /bou/   *A fuzzy caterpillar
ate all the leaves on the bough.*
13 /its/ /nes′ ə sãr′ ē/ /tü/ /pùt/ /ŦHə/ /rīt/
/ə dres′/ /ôn/ /ŦHə/ /pär′ səl/   *It's necessary
to put the right address on the parcel.*
14 /ŦHãr/ /är/ /ôl′ tə geŦH′ ər/ /tü/ /men′ ē/
/vej′ ə tə bəlz/ /in/ /ŦHis/ /süp/   *There are
altogether too many vegetables in this soup.*
15 /al′ ə gā′ tərz/ /är/ /not/ /nōn/ /az/

/ə fek′ shə nət/ /pets/   *Alligators are not
known as affectionate pets.*

Mastery Test 36b
  1 /pər tik′ yə lər/ *particular*
  2 /jē og′ rə fē/ *geography*
  3 /pā′ trē ot′ ik/ *patriotic*
  4 /op′ ər ā′ tər/ *operator*
  5 /ə kum′ pə nē/ *accompany*
  6 /in′ də pen′ dəns/ *independence*
  7 /sər kum′ fər əns/ *circumference*
  8 /ə prē′ shē āt′/ *appreciate*

A woolly bear is not a bear. Its an ordinary cater-pillar with stripes around it's body. People once thought that the woolly bears stripes could forecast weather.

"Wide stripes mean a mild winter, declared my uncle. Narrow stripes mean a long, frozen season."

We learned in science that their are always some woolly-bear caterpillars with wide stripes and some with narrow stripes. Woolly bears are not weather forecasters!

2 Read the dictionary entry below for the word *alligator*.

A lexicographer may show a labeled illustration of the entry word.

about 12 feet

• **alligator** /al′ ə gā′ tər/ *n.* Large rep-tile with a rather thick skin, similar to the crocodile but having a shorter and flatter head. Alligators live in the warm parts of America.

Write a dictionary entry for the word *caterpillar*. Make a drawing of a caterpillar to accompany the entry. Label the drawing to show that a caterpillar is about 2¹/₂ inches long. Compare your work with the entry in the Spelling Dictionary.

Another Word from the Hawaiians

A *ukulele* /ū′ kə lā′ lē/ is a small four-stringed guitar of Portuguese ori-gin that became popular in Hawaii during the 1880's. The word is made from two Hawaiian words, *uku*, which means "small person," and *lele*, which means "jumping." The word *ukulele*, like the word *kimono*, is often misspelled.

Write the plural form or forms of *ukulele*, *banjo*, *pajamas*, *barbecue*, *hoof*, and *alligator*.

163

9 /sər tif′ ə kət/ *certificate*
0 /kon′ vər sā′ shən/ *conversation*
1 /ᵺat/ /yung/ /skol′ ər/ /haz/ /mär′ və ləs/ /ə bil′ ə tē/ /in/ /ə rith′ mə tik/ *That young scholar has marvelous ability in arithmetic.*
2 /ᵺə/ /thər mom′ ə tər/ /nir/ /ᵺə/ /rā′ dē ā′ tər/ /went/ /up/ /āt/ /də grēz′/ *The thermometer near the radiator went up eight degrees.*
3 /hü/ /iz/ /rə spon′ sə bəl/ /fôr/ /get′ ing/ /us/ /ə nuf′/ /mə tir′ ē əlz/ /tü/ /fin′ ish/ /our/ /proj′ ekt/ *Who is responsible for*

getting us enough materials to finish our project?
14 /men/ /wôr/ /lärj/ /shü/ /buk′ əlz/ /in/ /kə lō′ nē əl/ /dāz/ *Men wore large shoe buckles in colonial days.*
15 /wē/ /spent/ /tü/ /nīts/ /in/ /an/ /in/ /ᵺat/ /iz/ /kən vēn′ yənt/ /tü/ /ᵺə/ /lāk/ *We spent two nights in an inn that is convenient to the lake.*

GUIDE TO THE DICTIONARY

The Spelling Dictionary has the new words from the unit lists, words from other languages that are presented in the units, and many additional words that are needed for the exercises. Guide words are given at the top of each page. A pronunciation key is shown at the bottom of every right-hand page.

The pronunciation of an entry word is shown between slant marks.

- **cautious** /kô′ shəs/ *adj.* Very careful; not taking chances.

Spaces are used to show the ear-syllables of an entry word.

- **prescription** /prē skrip′ shən/ *n.* Written order for preparing and using a medicine.

The primary accent is shown by the darker accent mark.
The secondary accent is shown by the lighter accent mark.

- **patriotic** /pā′ trē ot′ ik/ *adj.* Having or showing love for one's country.

The part or parts of speech for an entry word are shown by abbreviations.

- **feast** /fēst/ *n.* Rich meal for a special occasion; banquet. —*v.* Eat a rich meal.

The plural of a noun is shown if it is formed any way other than by adding *s* or *es* to the singular, or if there might be some doubt about the plural.

- **directory** /də rek′ tər ē/ *n.* List of names and addresses. *pl.* **directories.**

The *er* and *est* forms of adjectives are shown when the spelling of the entry word changes before the endings are added.

- **crafty** /kraf′ tē/ *adj.* Skillful in deceiving others. **craftier, craftiest.**

The past tense and *ing* forms of verbs are shown when the spelling of the entry word changes before the endings are added.

- **vibrate** /vī′ brāt/ *v.* Move rapidly to and fro; quiver. **vibrated, vibrating.**

The past tense and *ing* forms of irregular verbs are shown.

- **wring** /ring/ *v.* Twist with force. **wrung, wringing.**

Words with the same spelling and very different meanings are shown as separate entry words.

- **squall**[1] /skwôl/ *n.* Sudden, violent gust of wind, often with rain, snow, or sleet.

- **squall**[2] /skwôl/ *v.* Cry or scream loudly. —*n.* Loud, harsh cry.

The authors are indebted to Scott, Foresman and Company for permission to use and to adapt definitions from the Thorndike-Barnhart Intermediate Dictionary by E. L. Thorndike and Clarence L. Barnhart. Copyright © 1974 by Scott, Foresman and Company.

SPELLING DICTIONARY

- **ability** /ə bil′ ə tē/ *n.* **1.** Power: *the ability to work.* **2.** Skill: *She has great ability as an actress.* **3.** Talent: *musical ability.* *pl.* **abilities.**
- **absolute** /ab′ sə lüt/ *adj.* **1.** Complete; entire: *Try to tell the absolute truth.* **2.** Not limited in any way: *The emperor was an absolute ruler.*
- **absorb** /ab sôrb′/ *v.* **1.** Take in; suck up: *The sponge absorbed all the water.* **2.** Interest very much: *The boy was so absorbed by the baseball game that he did not notice the rain.*
- **accompany** /ə kum′ pə nē/ *v.* **1.** Go along with: *May I accompany you on your walk?* **2.** Be or happen along with: *rain accompanied by strong wind.* **accompanied, accompanying.**
- **achieve** /ə chēv′/ *v.* **1.** Do: *Did you achieve what you had planned to do?* **2.** Reach by one's own effort: *She achieved fame as a swimmer.* **achieved, achieving.**
- **activity** /ak tiv′ ə tē/ *n.* **1.** Being active: *Children engage in more physical activity than old people.* **2.** Action: *the activities of the enemy.* **3.** Thing to do: *My favorite activity is playing football.* *pl.* **activities.**
- **actor** /ak′ tər/ *n.* Person who acts on the stage, in movies, on television, or over radio.
- **affectionate** /ə fek′ shə nət/ *adj.* Loving; fond: *an affectionate puppy.*
- **agent** /ā′ jənt/ *n.* **1.** Person or company that acts for another. **2.** Any power or cause that produces an effect: *Yeast is an important agent in causing bread to rise.*
- **agreeable** /ə grē′ ə bəl/ *adj.* **1.** Pleasant; pleasing: *The child had an agreeable manner.* **2.** Willing: *We'll go if Mother is agreeable.* *syn.* **pleasant.**
- **agriculture** /ag′ rə kul′ chər/ *n.* Farming; the raising of crops and farm animals.
- **ailment** /āl′ mənt/ *n.* Illness; sickness: *His ailment was only a headache.*
- **aimless** /ām′ ləs/ *adj.* Without direction; without purpose: *They spend too much time in aimless daydreaming.*
- **aircraft** /ãr′ kraft′/ *n.* Any airplane, airship, helicopter, or balloon. *pl.* **aircraft.**

- **aisle** /īl/ *n.* **1.** Passage between rows of seats. **2.** Any long, narrow passage.
- **alcohol** /al′ kə hôl/ *n.* Colorless liquid that makes certain other liquids intoxicating, and that is used in medicines, in manufacturing, and for fuel.
- **alias** /ā′ lē əs/ *n.* A name used instead of one's real name; a false name.
- **allow** /ə lou′/ *v.* Let; permit.
- **allowance** /ə lou′ əns/ *n.* Limited share set apart: *Her weekly allowance is five dollars.*
- **aloha** /ä lō′ ə/ *or* /ä lō′ hä/ *n., interj.* **1.** Greetings; hello. **2.** Farewell; good-bye.
- **altogether** /ôl′ tə geŦĦ′ ər/ *adv.* Completely; entirely: *The house was altogether destroyed.*
- **ancestor** /an′ ses′ tər/ *n.* Person from whom one is directly descended.
- **annoy** /ə noi′/ *v.* Make somewhat angry; disturb: *The baby annoys his sister.*
- **annoyance** /ə noi′ əns/ *n.* **1.** Feeling of dislike or trouble: *She showed annoyance at the delay.* **2.** Something that causes a feeling of dislike or trouble; disturbance: *Heavy traffic on our street is an annoyance.*
- **antonym** /an′ tə nim/ *n.* Word that means the opposite of another word: *"Hot" is the antonym of "cold."*
- **appoint** /ə point′/ *v.* **1.** Name a person for a position or job; choose. **2.** Decide on; set.
- **appointment** /ə point′ mənt/ *n.* **1.** Act of naming for an office or position. **2.** Office; position. **3.** Engagement to be somewhere or to meet someone.
- **appreciate** /ə prē′ shē āt′/ *v.* **1.** Value; recognize the worth of: *He appreciates music.* **2.** Be thankful for: *I appreciate your help.* **appreciated, appreciating.**
- **approve** /ə prüv′/ *v.* **1.** Think or speak well of; be pleased with. **2.** Consent to: *Congress approved the bill.* **3.** Give a favorable opinion: *approve of an action.* **approved, approving.**
- **armor** /är′ mər/ *n.* A covering, usually of metal or leather, worn to protect the body in fighting.

/a/ ran /ā/ rain /ã/ care /ä/ car /e/ hen /ē/ he /ėr/ her /i/ in /ī/ ice /o/ not /ō/ no /ô/ off
/u/ us /ū/ use /ü/ tool /ù/ took /ou/ cow /oi/ boy /ch/ church /hw/ when /ng/ sing /sh/ ship
/ŦĦ/ this /th/ thin /zh/ vision /ə/ about, taken, pencil, lemon, circus

- **artist** /är' tist/ *n.* **1.** Person who paints, draws, or otherwise creates pictures. **2.** Person who is skilled in any of the fine arts, such as music, sculpture, or literature.
- **astound** /ə stound'/ *v.* Surprise greatly.
- **athlete** /ath' lēt/ *n.* Person trained in the exercise of physical strength, speed, and skill: *Baseball players are athletes.*
- **atlas** /at' ləs/ *n.* Book of maps.
- **atmosphere** /at' mə sfir/ *n.* **1.** Air that surrounds the earth. **2.** Mass of gases that surrounds any heavenly body: *The atmosphere of Venus is cloudy.* **3.** Air in any given place: *The atmosphere in the cellar is damp.*
- **attendant** /ə ten' dənt/ *n.* Person who waits on another. —*adj.* Accompanying: *Sneezing is an attendant discomfort of a cold.*
- **autograph** /ô' tə graf/ *n.* Person's name written by himself: *Many people collect autographs of celebrities.* —*v.* Write one's name in or on: *The author autographed her book for us.*
- **automatic** /ô' tə mat' ik/ *adj.* **1.** Moving or acting by itself: *an automatic elevator.* **2.** Done without thought or attention: *Breathing and swallowing are automatic.*
- **avenue** /av' ə nū/ *n.* Broad street, often bordered by trees.
- **avoidable** /ə void' ə bəl/ *adj.* Able to be avoided, or kept away from.

b

- **backbone** /bak' bōn'/ *n.* **1.** The main bone down the middle of the back. **2.** The most important part.
- **baker** /bāk' ər/ *n.* Person who makes or sells bread, pies, cakes, etc.
- **balance** /bal' əns/ *n.* **1.** Instrument for weighing. **2.** Equality in weight, amount, force, etc. **3.** Steadiness. **4.** Difference between the debit and credit sides of (an account): *a balance of $20 in the bank.* —*v.* **1.** Weigh in a balance. **2.** Make or be equal in weight, amount, force, etc. **3.** Make or keep steady: *balance a coin on its edge.* **balanced, balancing.**
- **bamboo** /bam bü'/ *n.* Woody, treelike grass with a tall, stiff, hollow stem, used in making canes, fishing poles, furniture, etc. *pl.* **bamboos.**
- **banjo** /ban' jō/ *n.* Musical instrument having four or five strings, played by plucking the strings. *pl.* **banjos** or **banjoes.**
- **barbecue** /bär' bə kū/ *n.* **1.** Outdoor meal in which meat is roasted over an open fire. **2.** Grill; open fireplace for cooking meat, usually over charcoal. **3.** Meat roasted over an open fire. —*v.* **1.** Cook meat over an open fire. **2.** Cook meat or fish in a highly flavored sauce. **barbecued, barbecuing.**
- **barley** /bär' lē/ *n.* A grasslike plant grown in cool climates and used for its grain.
- **base**¹ /bās/ *n.* **1.** The part of a thing on which it rests; the lowest part, or bottom: *The base of the lamp was broken.* **2.** Foundation. **3.** A station in games like baseball. **4.** Starting place; headquarters.
- **base**² /bās/ *adj.* **1.** Low; mean: *To betray a friend is a base action.* **2.** Inferior: *Lead is a base metal.*
- **basin** /bā' sən/ *n.* **1.** Wide, shallow dish; bowl. **2.** Amount a basin can hold: *a basin of water.* **3.** Shallow area containing water: *Part of the harbor is a basin for yachts.*
- **basketball** /bas' kət bôl'/ *n.* **1.** Game played with a large, round ball between two teams of five players each. The players try to toss the ball through a ring to which a net is attached that is open at the bottom. **2.** Ball used in the game of basketball.
- **bass**¹ /bās/ *n.* **1.** Lowest male voice in music. **2.** Singer with the lowest male voice in music. **3.** Part in music for such a singer. —*adj.* Having a deep, low sound.
- **bass**² /bas/ *n.* Fish used for food. *pl.* **bass** or **basses.**
- **bathe** /bā℻/ *v.* **1.** Take a bath; give a bath to. **2.** Go swimming. **bathed, bathing.**
- **beehive** /bē' hīv'/ *n.* **1.** Hive, or house, for bees. **2.** Busy, swarming place.
- **belief** /bə lēf'/ *n.* **1.** What is held to be true or real: *It was once a common belief that the earth is flat.* **2.** Faith; trust.
- **bench** /bench/ *n.* **1.** A long seat, usually of wood or stone. **2.** A strong, heavy table used by a carpenter or by any worker with tools.
- **berry** /ber' ē/ *n.* **1.** Any small, juicy fruit with many seeds. **2.** Dried seed or kernel of grain or other plants. *pl.* **berries.**
- **berth** /bèrth/ *n.* Place to sleep on a ship, train, or airplane.
- **billboard** /bil' bôrd'/ *n.* Outdoors signboard.
- **birdhouse** /bèrd' hous'/ *n.* House for the nests of wild birds.
- **birth** /bèrth/ *n.* **1.** Being born: *The baby weighed 8 pounds at birth.* **2.** A beginning: *the birth of a nation.*
- **blight** /blīt/ *n.* **1.** Any disease that causes plants to wither. **2.** Anything that causes destruction or ruin. —*v.* Cause ruin; destroy.

- **blister** /blis′ tər/ *n.* **1.** Baglike place in the skin filled with watery matter: *My wet shoes made blisters on my heel.* **2.** Swelling on the surface of metal, paint, or wood.
- **blond** /blond/ *adj.* **1.** Light in color: *blond hair.* **2.** Having yellow or light-brown hair: *Have you seen that blond girl with my sister?* — *n.* Person with blond hair. (Spelled **blonde** when referring to a girl or a woman.)
- **blowout** /blō′ out′/ *n.* The bursting of an automobile tire.
- **boast** /bōst/ *v.* **1.** Speak too well of oneself or what one owns. **2.** Be proud of. **3.** Have something to be proud of: *Our school boasts a new library.* — *n.* Statement in praise of oneself.
- **bomb** /bom/ *n.* Container filled with an explosive. — *v.* Hurl bombs at; drop bombs on.
- **booster** /bü′ stər/ *n.* One who helps or encourages another; one who helps a cause.
- **booth** /büth/ *n.* **1.** Place where goods are shown or sold at a fair, market, or convention. **2.** Small, closed place for a telephone or motion-picture projector. *pl.* **booths** /büꟘHz/ or /büths/.
- **bough** /bou/ *n.* **1.** One of the main branches of a tree. **2.** Branch cut from a tree.
- **bouquet** /bō kā′/ or /bü kā′/ *n.* **1.** Bunch of flowers. **2.** Fragrance: *These spices and herbs have a wonderful bouquet.*
- **bow**[1] /bou/ *n.* A bending of the head or body in greeting, respect, etc. — *v.* Bend the head or the body in greeting, respect, etc.
- **bow**[2] /bou/ *n.* Forward part of a ship, boat, or airplane.
- **bow**[3] /bō/ *n.* **1.** Weapon for shooting arrows. **2.** Slender rod with horsehairs stretched on it, for playing the violin. **3.** Curve: *the bow of the lips.* **4.** Loop; knot.
- **brand** /brand/ *v.* **1.** Mark by burning the skin with a hot iron. **2.** Put a mark of disgrace on. — *n.* **1.** Certain kind or make: *a brand of flour.* **2.** An iron stamp for burning a mark.
- **bray** /brā/ *v.* Make a loud, harsh cry like that of a donkey. — *n.* Loud, harsh cry of a donkey; any loud, harsh cry.
- **brew** /brü/ *v.* **1.** Make a drink by soaking, boiling, or mixing. **2.** Plot; plan; bring about: *The boys are brewing some mischief.* **3.** Begin to form: *The storm is brewing.* — *n.* Drink that is brewed.

- **brief** /brēf/ *adj.* **1.** Lasting only a short time: *a brief meeting.* **2.** Using few words: *a brief statement.*
- **brightness** /brīt′ nəs/ *n.* Much light; brilliance: *the brightness of the sun.*
- **broil** /broil/ *v.* **1.** Cook by putting or holding directly over or under heat or fire. **2.** Be very hot: *You will broil in this hot sun.*
- **broiler** /broil′ ər/ *n.* **1.** Pan or rack used over or under a flame for cooking food. **2.** Young chicken suitable for broiling.
- **bronco** /brong′ kō/ *n.* Wild or partly wild horse that has been tamed. *pl.* **broncos.**
- **broth** /brôth/ *n.* Thin soup: *This broth is made of meat and vegetables.*
- **browse** /brouz/ *v.* **1.** Skim through a book reading passages here and there. **2.** Look through a group of things in search of something of interest: *browse through a library.* **browsed, browsing.**
- **bruise** /brüz/ *n.* **1.** Injury to the body that does not break the skin. **2.** Injury to the outside of a fruit, vegetable, or plant. — *v.* **1.** Hurt; injure: *bruise her feelings by harsh words.* **2.** Injure the outside of. **3.** Become bruised: *His flesh bruises easily.* **bruised, bruising.**
- **buckle** /buk′ əl/ *n.* **1.** Fastening for two loose ends of a belt, strap, etc. **2.** Metal ornament for a shoe. **3.** A distortion; bulge. — *v.* **1.** Fasten together with a buckle. **2.** Bulge; bend; kink; wrinkle. **buckled, buckling.**
- **buffalo** /buf′ ə lō/ *n.* The bison of North America, a wild ox with a great, shaggy head and short front legs. *pl.* **buffaloes, buffalos,** or **buffalo.**
- **build** /bild/ *v.* **1.** Make by putting materials together. **2.** Develop: *A lawyer builds his case on facts.* **built, building.**
- **bulky** /bul′ kē/ *adj.* Taking up too much space; large; hard to handle. **bulkier, bulkiest.**
- **bullet** /bùl′ ət/ *n.* Piece of metal shaped to be fired from a pistol, rifle, or other small gun.
- **bulletin** /bùl′ ə tən/ *n.* **1.** Short statement of news. **2.** Publication appearing at regular intervals.
- **burst** /bèrst/ *v.* **1.** Break open or apart suddenly: *The flowers burst into bloom.* **2.** Explode: *The bomb will burst.* **3.** Go, come, or do suddenly: *The children burst into the room without knocking.* **4.** Be very full: *The barns are bursting with grain.* **burst, bursting.** — *n.*

/a/ ran /ā/ rain /ã/ care /ä/ car /e/ hen /ē/ he /èr/ her /i/ in /ī/ ice /o/ not /ō/ no /ô/ off
/u/ us /ū/ use /ü/ tool /ù/ took /ou/ cow /oi/ boy /ch/ church /hw/ when /ng/ sing /sh/ ship
/ꟘH/ this /th/ thin /zh/ vision /ə/ about, taken, pencil, lemon, circus

1. Outbreak: *a burst of laughter.* **2.** Sudden display: *a burst of speed.*

- **bury** /ber′ ē/ *v.* **1.** Put a dead body in the earth, in a tomb, or in the sea. **2.** Cover up; hide: *The squirrels buried nuts in the garden.* **buried, burying.**
- **butcher** /buch′ ər/ *n.* One who kills or sells animals for food. —*v.* **1.** Kill animals for food. **2.** Kill people or animals needlessly, cruelly, or in large numbers.

C

- **calendar** /kal′ ən dər/ *n.* Table showing the months, weeks, and days of the year.
- **camel** /kam′ əl/ *n.* Large, four-footed animal with one or two humps on its back.
- **candidate** /kan′ də dāt/ *n.* Person who is proposed for or seeks some office or honor.
- **caravan** /kar′ ə van/ *n.* Group of persons traveling together.
- **cardinal**[1] /kär′ də nəl/ *adj.* Chief; principal: *The cardinal value of his plan is that it is simple.*
- **cardinal**[2] /kär′ də nəl/ *n.* **1.** An American songbird. **2.** One of the high officials of the Roman Catholic Church.
- **carefree** /kãr′ frē′/ *adj.* Without worry; happy; gay: *The children spent a carefree summer.*
- **careful** /kãr′ fəl/ *adj.* **1.** Watchful; cautious: *Be careful with my bicycle.* **2.** Done with thought or effort: *careful work.*
- **carfare** /kãr′ fãr′/ *n.* Money paid for riding on a passenger vehicle.
- **carol** /kar′ əl/ *n.* Song or hymn of joy: *Christmas carol.* —*v.* Sing joyously: *Birds carol in the early morning.*
- **carrot** /kar′ ət/ *n.* **1.** Plant that has a long, tapering, orange-red root. **2.** Root of this plant, which is eaten as a vegetable.
- **cartoon** /kär tün′/ *n.* **1.** Sketch or drawing that shows persons, things, or events in an exaggerated way: *Political cartoons often represent the United States as a tall man called Uncle Sam.* **2.** Comic strip.
- **caterpillar** /kat′ ər pil′ ər/ *n.* Larva, or worm-like form in which insects such as the butterfly and the moth hatch from the egg.

- **caution** /kô′ shən/ *n.* **1.** Unwillingness to take a chance: *Use caution in crossing a busy*

street. **2.** Warning: *That sign is a caution to drivers.* —*v.* Warn; urge to be careful.

- **cautious** /kô′ shəs/ *adj.* Very careful; not taking chances: *a cautious driver.*
- **cedar** /sē′ dər/ *n.* Evergreen tree with branches that spread widely and with fragrant, reddish, durable wood.
- **celery** /sel′ ə rē/ *n.* Vegetable whose long, crisp stalks are whitened by keeping them covered as they grow.
- **cell** /sel/ *n.* **1.** Small room in a prison or monastery. **2.** Any small, hollow space: *the cells of a honeycomb.* **3.** A very small unit of living matter.
- **cent** /sent/ *n.* A coin, usually an alloy of copper, of the United States and Canada. 100 cents make a dollar.
- **ceremony** /ser′ ə mō′ nē/ *n.* A special form or set of acts to be done on special occasions: *a wedding ceremony.*
- **certificate** /sər tif′ ə kət/ *n.* Written or printed statement that may be used as proof of a fact: *a birth certificate; a graduation certificate.*
- **chairman** /chãr′ man′/ *n.* **1.** Person in charge of a meeting. **2.** Person at the head of a committee. *pl.* **chairmen.**
- **chart** /chärt/ *n.* **1.** Map. **2.** Sheet of information arranged in pictures, tables, or diagrams. —*v.* Make a map or chart of: *The captain charted the course of the ship.*
- **cheat** /chēt/ *v.* Deceive; trick; play, work, or do business in a dishonest way. —*n.* Person who deceives others; fraud.
- **chestnut** /ches′ nut′/ *n.* **1.** Sweet nut in a prickly burr. **2.** Tree on which this nut grows. **3.** Wood of the chestnut tree. —*adj.* Reddish brown.
- **chime** /chīm/ *n.* Set of musical bells. —*v.* Ring out musically: *The bells chimed at midnight.* **chimed, chiming.**
- **chord** /kôrd/ *n.* Combination of three or more notes of music sounded at the same time in harmony.
- **cinder** /sin′ dər/ *n.* Piece of partly burned wood or coal.
- **circular** /sėr′ kū lər/ *adj.* **1.** Round like a circle: *The full moon has a circular shape.* **2.** Moving in a circle: *A merry-go-round makes a circular motion.* —*n.* Letter, notice, or advertisement sent to each of a number of people.
- **circumference** /sər kum′ fər əns/ *n.* **1.** The boundary line of a circle. **2.** The distance around: *The circumference of the plate is 12 inches.*

- **civil** /siv′ əl/ *adj.* **1.** Having to do with citizens: *civil laws.* **2.** Not naval, military, or connected with the church: *a civil court.* **3.** Polite: *He gave the angry man a civil answer.*
- **clamp** /klamp/ *n.* Brace, band, or wedge used to hold things tightly together. —*v.* Fasten, strengthen, or steady by means of a clamp.
- **clan** /klan/ *n.* Group of related families; group.
- **clause** /klôz/ *n.* **1.** Part of a sentence having a subject and a verb. **2.** Single provision of a law, treaty, or written agreement: *a clause in our lease.*
- **clerk** /klėrk/ *n.* **1.** Woman or man employed to sell goods in a store or a shop. **2.** Man or woman employed in an office to file, type, or keep records. —*v.* Work as a clerk.
- **clever** /klev′ ər/ *adj.* **1.** Bright; intelligent: *a clever girl.* **2.** Skillful in doing a particular thing: *a clever carpenter.*
- **clinic** /klin′ ik/ *n.* A place for the medical treatment of certain people or diseases: *a children's clinic.*
- **clockwise** /klok′ wīz′/ *adj., adv.* In the direction in which the hands of a clock turn; from left to right.
- **cloth** /klôth/ *n.* Material made from wool, cotton, silk, linen, hair, etc., by weaving, knitting, or rolling and pressing.
- **clothe** /klōⓉH/ *v.* **1.** Put clothes on; provide with clothing: *She was clothed in fine garments for the ceremony.* **2.** Cover: *The trees were clothed in colored leaves.* **clothed** or **clad, clothing.**
- **clothes** /klōz/ *n. pl.* Coverings for the body: *The shop has pretty clothes.*
- **coarse** /kôrs/ *or* /kōrs/ *adj.* **1.** Not fine: *coarse sand.* **2.** Rough: *coarse cloth.* **3.** Common; poor; vulgar. **coarser, coarsest.**
- **cocoa** /kō′ kō/ *n.* **1.** Powder made from seeds of the cacao tree. **2.** Drink made from this powder with milk and sugar.
- **coin** /koin/ *n.* Piece of metal stamped by the government for use as money. —*v.* **1.** Make money by stamping metal: *The mint coins millions of dimes each year.* **2.** Make up; invent: *Space travel has led us to coin many new words.*
- **colonial** /kə lō′ nē əl/ *adj.* Having to do with a colony or colonies; having something to do

with the thirteen colonies that became the United States of America.
- **comet** /kom′ ət/ *n.* A bright heavenly body with a starlike center and often with a cloudy tail of light. Comets move around the sun in a long oval course.
- **commerce** /kom′ ėrs/ *n.* Trade; buying and selling in large amounts.
- **commotion** /kə mō′ shən/ *n.* Confusion; disturbance: *The accident caused quite a commotion on the playground.*
- **compact**[1] /kom′ pakt/ *n.* Small case containing face powder and a mirror.
- **compact**[2] /kəm pakt′/ *adj.* **1.** Closely packed together. **2.** Having parts tightly arranged in a small space: *a compact TV set.*
- **compact**[3] /kom′ pakt/ *n.* Agreement: *The Pilgrims made a solemn compact.*
- **compose** /kəm pōz′/ *v.* **1.** Make up: *compose a song.* **2.** Make calm: *You must stop crying and compose yourself.* **composed, composing.**
- **conclusion** /kən klü′ zhən/ *n.* **1.** End: *The conclusion of the story was sad.* **2.** Decision reached by reasoning: *He came to the conclusion that he must work harder.*
- **condense** /kən dens′/ *v.* **1.** Make denser; become more compact or more strong: *Light is condensed by means of lenses.* **2.** Change from a gas to a liquid. **3.** Put into fewer words: *Condense your report into four lines.* **condensed, condensing.**
- **consume** /kən süm′/ *v.* **1.** Use up: *Students consume much of their time studying.* **2.** Eat or drink up: *We consumed all the sandwiches at lunchtime.* **3.** Burn up: *Fire consumed the house.* **consumed, consuming.**
- **continent** /kon′ tə nənt/ *n.* One of the seven great masses of land on the earth: *North America, South America, Australia, Europe, Africa, Asia, and Antarctica are continents.*
- **contract** /kon′ trakt/ *n.* Written agreement enforceable by law. /kən trakt′/ *v.* **1.** Draw together; make or become smaller. **2.** Shorten by omitting some letters or sounds.
- **contraction** /kən trak′ shən/ *n.* **1.** Process of contracting. **2.** State of being contracted. **3.** A shortened form: *"Don't" is a contraction of "do not."*
- **contrary** /kon′ trer ē/ *adj.* Completely different: *Her taste in movies is contrary to mine.*

/a/ ran   /ā/ rain   /ā/ care   /ä/ car   /e/ hen   /ē/ he   /ėr/ her   /i/ in   /ī/ ice   /o/ not   /ō/ no   /ô/ off
/u/ us   /ū/ use   /ü/ tool   /u̇/ took   /ou/ cow   /oi/ boy   /ch/ <u>ch</u>urch   /hw/ <u>wh</u>en   /ng/ si<u>ng</u>   /sh/ <u>sh</u>ip
/ⓉH/ <u>th</u>is   /th/ <u>th</u>in   /zh/ vi<u>s</u>ion   /ə/ <u>a</u>bout, tak<u>e</u>n, penc<u>i</u>l, lem<u>o</u>n, circ<u>u</u>s

—n. The opposite: *You like hot weather; I like the contrary.* /kən trer' ē/ *or* /kən trär' ē/ *adj.* Stubborn: *That child is contrary today.*

● **convenient** /kən vēn' yənt/ *adj.* **1.** Saving trouble; easy to use: *a convenient tool.* **2.** Not troublesome: *Will it be convenient for you to come early?* **3.** Handy: *a convenient place to meet.*

● **conversation** /kon' vər sā' shən/ *n.* Friendly talk; exchange of ideas by talking informally together.

● **cookbook** /kùk' bùk'/ *n.* Book of recipes.

● **cookie** /kùk' ē/ *n.* Cooky.

● **cooky** /kùk' ē/ *n.* Small, flat, sweet cake. *pl.* **cookies.**

● **cord** /kôrd/ *n.* **1.** Thick string; thin rope: *He tied the parcel with cord.* **2.** Something resembling a cord: *the cord of an electric iron.* **3.** Measure of cut wood: *We bought a cord of fireplace wood.* **4.** Nerve or tendon in the body: *vocal cords; spinal cord.*

● **corridor** /kôr' ə dər/ *n.* Long hallway: *Our classroom is at the end of a corridor.*

● **costume** /kos' tüm/ *or* /kos' tūm/ *n.* **1.** Dress belonging to another time or place, worn by actors and actresses. **2.** A complete set of outer garments.

● **cotton** /kot' ən/ *n.* **1.** Soft white fibers of a plant, used in making cloth. **2.** Plant producing these fibers. **3.** Thread or cloth made of cotton. *—adj.* Made of cotton: *a cotton dress.*

● **cough** /kôf/ *v.* Force air from the lungs with sudden effort and noise. *—n.* Act or sound of coughing.

● **council** /koun' səl/ *n.* Group of people called together to discuss questions and give advice.

● **countdown** /kount' doun'/ *n.* The calling out of the passing seconds before the launching of a missile or rocket.

● **coward** /kou' ərd/ *n.* A person who lacks courage or is afraid; one who runs from danger; one who is not brave.

● **cowbell** /kou' bel'/ *n.* Bell hung around a cow's neck to indicate the animal's whereabouts.

● **coyote** /kī ō' tē/ *or* /kī' ōt/ *n.* Small wolf living on the prairies of western North America. *pl.* **coyotes** *or* **coyote.**

● **crafty** /kraf' tē/ *adj.* Skillful in deceiving others: *The crafty fox lured the rabbit from its hole.* **craftier, craftiest.**

● **crawfish** /krô' fish'/ *n.* Fresh-water animal looking much like a small lobster; crayfish. *pl.* **crawfish** *or* **crawfishes.**

● **crime** /krīm/ *n.* Very wrong deed that is against the law: *Murder is a crime.*

● **crude** /krüd/ *adj.* **1.** In a raw or natural state: *crude oil.* **2.** Coarse: *a crude log cabin.* **3.** Lack of refinement: *crude manners.* **cruder, crudest.**

● **cruise** /krüz/ *n.* Pleasure voyage. *—v.* Sail about from place to place. **cruised, cruising.**

● **cucumber** /kū' kum bər/ *n.* **1.** Long green vegetable with firm flesh and seeds, often eaten in thin slices as a salad or used to make pickles. **2.** The vine a cucumber grows on.

● **cupcake** /kup' kāk'/ *n.* Small cake baked in a pan shaped like a cup.

● **curb** /kèrb/ *v.* Restrain; hold back: *Curb your laughter.* *—n.* **1.** Check; restraint: *a curb on expenses.* **2.** A raised concrete or stone border along the edge of a pavement or sidewalk.

● **cure** /kūr/ *v.* **1.** Make well. **2.** Get rid of: *cure a cold.* **3.** Preserve by drying or salting: *The bacon was cured by the farmer.* **cured, curing.** *—n.* Remedy: *a cure for a headache.*

● **current** /kèr' ənt/ *n.* **1.** Flow; stream: *a current of water.* **2.** Flow of electricity through a wire. **3.** Movement of events: *the current of public opinion.* *—adj.* Of the present time: *current events.*

● **curtain** /kèr' tən/ *n.* **1.** Cloth hung at windows or doors for protection or ornament. **2.** A hanging screen that separates a stage from the part of a theater where the audience sits.

● **custom** /kus' təm/ *n.* **1.** A usual action; habit. **2.** A long-established habit that has almost the force of law. **customs,** *n. pl.* **1.** Taxes paid to the government on things brought in from a foreign country. **2.** The office where such imported things are checked.

d

● **daily** /dā' lē/ *adj.* Done, happening, or appearing every day. *—adv.* Day by day. *—n.* Newspaper printed every day. *pl.* **dailies.**

● **damp** /damp/ *adj.* Slightly wet; moist. *—n.* Moisture: *We could feel the damp in the air.*

● **darkness** /därk' nəs/ *n.* Lack of light: *Do not be afraid of the darkness.*

● **dauntless** /dônt' les'/ *adj.* Brave; not able to be frightened or discouraged.

● **decay** /dē kā'/ *v.* **1.** Rot. **2.** Grow less in power, wealth, strength, or beauty: *Many nations that were strong once have now decayed.* *—n.* **1.** Rotting: *The decay in the tree trunk caused the tree to fall.* **2.** The lessening of beauty, wealth, or power.

- **declaration** /dek′ lə rā′ shən/ *n.* Public statement: *The royal declaration was announced in every city.*
- **decoy** /dē koi′/ *v.* Lead into danger by means of trickery. /dē′ koi/ *n.* Artificial bird used to lure birds into a trap or near a hunter.
- **delicatessen** /del′ ə kə tes′ ən/ *n.* Store selling prepared foods, pastries, cooked meats, cheese, and the like.
- **delightful** /də līt′ fəl/ *adj.* Giving pleasure; very pleasing: *a delightful party.*
- **dent** /dent/ *n.* Hollow made by a blow or by pressure. —*v.* **1.** Make a dent in. **2.** Become dented: *Soft wood dents easily.*
- **dentist** /den′ tist/ *n.* Doctor whose work is the care of the teeth.
- **deportment** /də pôrt′ mənt/ *n.* Behavior; conduct; way a person acts.
- **descendant** /də sen′ dənt/ *n.* **1.** Person born of a certain family or group. **2.** Offspring; child, grandchild, great-grandchild, etc.
- **destroy** /dē stroi′/ *v.* **1.** Break to pieces; ruin; spoil. **2.** Put an end to; do away with.
- **difference** /dif′ ər əns/ *n.* **1.** Being different. **2.** The result of subtracting: *The difference between 6 and 10 is 4.* **3.** A dispute.
- **digit** /dij′ it/ *n.* **1.** Any of the figures 0, 1, 2, 3, 4, 5, 6, 7, 8, 9. (Sometimes 0 is not included as a digit.) **2.** Finger; toe.
- **diminish** /də min′ ish/ *v.* Make or become smaller in amount, size, or importance: *The heat diminished as the sun went down.*
- **directory** /də rek′ tər ē/ *n.* List of names and addresses. *pl.* **directories.**
- **disagreeable** /dis′ ə grē′ ə bəl/ *adj.* **1.** Not pleasant: *Rainy weather is disagreeable.* **2.** Unfriendly; unkind: *a disagreeable person.*
- **discount** /dis′ kount/ *v.* Take off a certain amount from a price. —*n.* The amount taken off from a price.
- **disgust** /dis gust′/ *n.* Strong dislike: *We feel disgust for a bad taste.* —*v.* Arouse disgust in: *The smell of a pigpen disgusts many people.*
- **dismiss** /dis mis′/ *v.* **1.** Send away; allow to go: *The class was dismissed at noon.* **2.** Remove from office or service: *They were dismissed from their jobs for laziness.*
- **display** /dis plā′/ *v.* **1.** Show; expose to view. **2.** Let appear; reveal: *Don't display your temper.* —*n.* **1.** Exhibition. **2.** A showing off.

- **disturbance** /dis tèr′ bəns/ *n.* **1.** A destroying of peace, quiet, or rest. **2.** A thing that destroys peace, quiet, or rest.
- **divisible** /də viz′ ə bəl/ *adj.* **1.** Capable of being divided. **2.** Capable of being divided without leaving a remainder: *The number 8 is divisible by 4.*
- **dizzy** /diz′ ē/ *adj.* **1.** Not steady: *He became dizzy from the blow on the head.* **2.** Having the sensation that things are whirling: *A merry-go-round makes me dizzy.* **3.** Confused. **dizzier, dizziest.**
- **dodge** /doj/ *v.* **1.** Move quickly to one side. **2.** Move quickly to get away from. **3.** Get away from by some trick: *He dodged all the questions.* **dodged, dodging.**
- **doily** /doi′ lē/ *n.* Small piece of lace, linen, plastic, or paper used under plates, other dishes, or vases. *pl.* **doilies.**
- **donate** /dō′ nāt/ *v.* Give; contribute. **donated, donating.**
- **dough** /dō/ *n.* Mixture of flour, milk, and other materials from which cake, pie crust, bread, etc., are made.
- **dove** /duv/ *n.* Bird with a thick body, short legs, and a beak enlarged at the tip; pigeon.
- **downfall** /doun′ fôl′/ *n.* **1.** Sudden overthrow or ruin. **2.** Heavy fall of rain or snow.
- **downstream** /doun′ strēm′/ *adv., adj.* With the current of a stream; down a stream.
- **dragon** /drag′ ən/ *n.* An imaginary huge, fierce animal that looks like a winged snake and breathes out fire and smoke.
- **drawl** /drôl/ *v.* Talk in a slow, lazy way. —*n.* Slow, lazy way of talking.
- **dread** /dred/ *v.* Fear greatly: *Cats dread water.* —*n.* Fear, especially fear of what may happen. —*adj.* Dreadful.
- **drift** /drift/ *v.* **1.** Be carried along by currents of air or water. **2.** Carry along. **3.** Go along without knowing where one is. **4.** Heap or be heaped up by the wind. —*n.* **1.** Anything carried along by the wind, water, or ice. **2.** Snow or sand heaped up by the wind.
- **driveway** /drīv′ wā′/ *n.* Road to drive on, often leading from a house or garage to the public road.
- **drought** /drout/ *n.* **1.** Long period of dry weather. **2.** Lack of water; dryness.
- **drug** /drug/ *n.* Substance other than food, that produces a change in the body's func-

/a/ ran   /ā/ rain   /ä/ care   /ä/ car   /e/ hen   /ē/ he   /ėr/ her   /i/ in   /ī/ ice   /o/ not   /ō/ no   /ô/ off
/u/ us   /ū/ use   /ü/ tool   /ù/ took   /ou/ cow   /oi/ boy   /ch/ church   /hw/ when   /ng/ sing   /sh/ ship
/ᴛʜ/ this   /th/ thin   /zh/ vision   /ə/ about, taken, pencil, lemon, circus

tion: *Some drugs are medicines that help the body; some drugs are poisons that harm the body.* —*v.* **1.** Give harmful drugs to: *The witch drugged Snow White.* **2.** Affect the senses in an unnatural way: *The wine drugged the man.* **drugged, drugging.**

- **drumstick** /drum′ stik′/ *n.* **1.** Stick for beating a drum. **2.** Lower half of the leg of a cooked chicken or turkey.
- **dune** /dūn/ *or* /dün/ *n.* Mound or ridge of loose sand heaped up by the wind.
- **dynamite** /dī′ nə mīt/ *n.* Powerful explosive commonly used to blast rocks. —*v.* Blow up with dynamite. **dynamited, dynamiting.**

e

- **eager** /ē′ gər/ *adj.* Wanting very much.
- **earphone** /ir′ fōn′/ *n.* Receiver for a telephone, telegraph, radio, or TV set that is placed over the ear.
- **earring** /ir′ ring′/ *n.* Ornament for the ear.

- **element** /el′ ə mənt/ *n.* **1.** One of about 100 simple substances from which all other things are made up. **2.** Simple or necessary part: *We learn the elements of arithmetic in the elementary school.*
- **elevator** /el′ ə vā′ tər/ *n.* **1.** Moving platform or cage to carry persons or things up and down in a building or mine. **2.** Building for storing grain. **3.** Movable, flat piece on the tail of an airplane to cause it to go up or down.
- **energy** /en′ ər jē/ *n.* **1.** Vigor; will to work: *The child is too full of energy to sit still.* **2.** Force: *We used much energy to clean the yard.* *pl.* **energies.**
- **engage** /en gāj′/ *v.* **1.** Take part: *engage in an activity.* **2.** Occupy: *Work engages their attention all day.* **3.** Promise to marry: *He is engaged to my sister.* **engaged, engaging.**
- **enjoy** /en joi′/ *v.* **1.** Have or use with joy: *We enjoyed our visit to the park.* **2.** Have the benefit of: *She enjoys good health.*
- **enlargement** /en lärj′ mənt/ *n.* Anything that is a larger form of something else. An enlargement is often made from a small photograph.
- **equator** /ē kwā′ tər/ *n.* An imaginary circle around the middle of the earth, halfway between the North Pole and the South Pole.

- **estimate** /es′ tə māt/ *v.* Form an opinion: *We estimated the cost at twelve dollars.* **estimated, estimating.** /es′ tə mət/ *n.* Opinion about how much, how many, or how good: *His estimate of the cost was twelve dollars.*
- **exceed** /ek sēd′/ *v.* **1.** Be more or greater than: *The sum of 5 and 7 exceeds 10.* **2.** Go beyond: *Do not exceed the speed limit.*
- **excellence** /ek′ sə ləns/ *n.* Very high quality: *She was praised for the excellence of her work.*
- **exert** /eg zèrt′/ *v.* Use fully: *A clever fighter exerts both strength and skill.*
- **exhaust** /eg zôst′/ *v.* **1.** Empty completely: *exhaust the oil well.* **2.** Use up: *exhaust the supply of water.* **3.** Tire out: *The long walk exhausted me.* —*n.* Used steam or gasoline that escapes from an engine.
- **export** /eks′ pôrt/ *or* /eks pôrt′/ *v.* Send goods out of one's country for sale and use in another: *The United States exports automobiles.* /eks′ pôrt/ *n.* Article exported: *Cotton is an export of the United States.*
- **extend** /eks tend′/ *v.* **1.** Stretch out: *extend your hand.* **2.** Give; grant: *extend help to the poor.*
- **extreme** /eks trēm′/ *adj.* **1.** Very great; very strong: *They took extreme measures to stop the riot.* **2.** At the very end: *The extreme north stops at the North Pole.* **extremer, extremest.**

f

- **fable** /fā′ bəl/ *n.* **1.** Story that is made up to teach a lesson: *"The Hare and the Tortoise" is a fable.* **2.** Story that is not true: *Her story about a summer trip is just a fable.*
- **fairground** /fār′ ground′/ *n.* Place outdoors where fairs are held.
- **fairy** /fār′ ē/ *n.* A tiny imaginary being, very lovely and delicate, who has power to help or harm human beings. *pl.* **fairies.** —*adj.* Having to do with fairies: *a fairy tale; a fairy godmother.*
- **falsehood** /fôls′ hùd′/ *n.* Lie; untruth; false statement.
- **farmhouse** /färm′ hous′/ *n.* House to live in on a farm.
- **farmland** /färm′ land′/ *n.* Land used for farming.
- **fashion** /fash′ ən/ *n.* **1.** The way a thing is shaped or done. **2.** Style. —*v.* Make; shape; form.
- **fatal** /fā′ təl/ *adj.* **1.** Causing death: *a fatal accident.* **2.** Causing ruin: *The rain was fatal*

to our picnic. **3.** Important; fateful: *At last the fatal day of the test arrived.*

● **feast** /fēst/ *n.* Rich meal for a special occasion; banquet. —*v.* Eat a rich meal; provide a rich meal for.

● **fertile** /fèr′ təl/ *adj.* **1.** Able to bear fruit, seeds, or young: *a fertile plant or animal.* **2.** Able to develop into a new individual: *Chicks hatch from fertile eggs.* **3.** Able to produce much: *fertile soil.*

● **fifty** /fif′ tē/ *n., adj.* Five times ten; 50. *pl.* **fifties.**

● **film** /film/ *n.* **1.** Very thin coating: *a film of oil on the water.* **2.** Roll of material used to take photographs: *film for a camera.* **3.** Motion picture: *a film about animals.* —*v.* **1.** Cover with a film. **2.** Make a motion picture of.

● **fireplace** /fīr′ plās′/ *n.* Place built to hold a fire.

● **fishhook** /fish′ hük′/ *n.* Hook for catching fish.

● **flair** /flâr/ *n.* Natural talent: *a flair for writing rhymes.*

● **flare** /flâr/ *v.* **1.** Flame up briefly: *The wind made the torches flare.* **2.** Spread out in the shape of a bell: *Her skirt flares at the bottom.* **flared, flaring.** —*n.* **1.** A blaze; unsteady light: *the flare of a match.* **2.** A burst of sudden feeling: *a flare of anger.* **3.** A bell-shaped spreading out: *the flare of a skirt.*

● **flesh** /flesh/ *n.* **1.** The soft substance of the body that covers the bones and is covered by skin. **2.** Meat. **3.** The soft part of fruits or vegetables: *The flesh of a peach is pale yellow.*

● **flood** /flud/ *v.* **1.** Fill to overflowing. **2.** Flow over. —*n.* Flow of water over usually dry land.

● **foil**[1] /foil/ *v.* Outwit; prevent from carrying out.

● **foil**[2] /foil/ *n.* Metal hammered or rolled into a thin sheet.

● **foil**[3] /foil/ *n.* Long, narrow sword used in fencing.

● **fond** /fond/ *adj.* Loving: *a fond look.*

● **fondness** /fond′ nəs/ *n.* A liking: *I have a fondness for candy.*

● **footstep** /füt′ step′/ *n.* **1.** A person's step. **2.** Distance covered in one step. **3.** Sound of steps coming or going.

● **footstool** /füt′ stül′/ *n.* Low stool on which to place the feet when seated.

● **forbid** /fôr′ bid′/ *v.* Not allow; make a rule against: *The teacher forbade us to leave our seats.* **forebad** or **forebade, forbidden** or **forbid, forbidding.**

● **fore** /fôr/ *adj.* At the front. —*interj.* In golf, a warning shout to keep someone from being hit by the ball.

● **forearm** /fôr′ ärm′/ *n.* The part of the arm between the wrist and the elbow.

● **forecast** /fôr′ kast′/ *v.* Predict; tell what is coming: *Cooler weather is forecast for tomorrow.* **forecast** or **forecasted, forecasting.** —*n.* Prediction: *What is the forecast for tomorrow?*

● **foreman** /fôr′ mən/ *n.* Person in charge of workers. (*Supervisor* now preferred.) *pl.* **foremen.**

● **former** /fôr′ mər/ *adj.* **1.** The first of two: *Canada and the United States are in North America; Montreal is in the former country.* **2.** Earlier; past.

● **fort** /fôrt/ *n.* Strong building or place that can be defended against an enemy.

● **foundry** /foun′ drē/ *n.* Place where metal is melted and molded. *pl.* **foundries.**

● **fraction** /frak′ shən/ *n.* **1.** One or more of the equal parts of a whole: $1/3$ and $1/4$ are fractions. **2.** Not all of a thing; very small part.

● **freckle** /frek′ əl/ *n.* Small, light-brown spot that some people have on the skin.

● **freight** /frāt/ *n.* Goods that a train, truck, ship, or aircraft carries.

● **friction** /frik′ shən/ *n.* **1.** A rubbing of one thing against another, such as skates on ice or a brush on shoes. **2.** Resistance to motion of surfaces that touch: *Oil reduces friction.* **3.** Disagreement: *Friction between the two nations brought them close to war.*

● **frightful** /frīt′ fəl/ *adj.* **1.** Dreadful: *a frightful explosion.* **2.** Ugly; shocking: *frightful clothes; a frightful condition.*

● **funnel** /fun′ əl/ *n.* **1.** Open vessel ending at the bottom in a tube. **2.** Anything shaped like a funnel. **3.** Smokestack or chimney on a steamship or steam engine.

● **fuzzy** /fuz′ ē/ *adj.* Covered with fine, loose down; covered with fuzz. **fuzzier, fuzziest.**

g

● **gargle** /gär′ gəl/ *v.* Wash the throat or mouth with a liquid kept in motion by the outgoing

---

/a/ ran   /ā/ rain   /ã/ care   /ä/ car   /e/ hen   /ē/ he   /èr/ her   /i/ in   /ī/ ice   /o/ not   /ō/ no   /ô/ off
/u/ us   /ū/ use   /ü/ tool   /ù/ took   /ou/ cow   /oi/ boy   /ch/ church   /hw/ when   /ng/ sing   /sh/ ship
/ᴛʜ/ this   /th/ thin   /zh/ vision   /ə/ about, taken, pencil, lemon, circus

breath: *He gargled with hot salt water to relieve his sore throat.* **gargled, gargling.** —*n.* Liquid used for gargling.

● **gasoline** /gas′ ə lēn/ *n.* Colorless liquid made from petroleum, that burns easily and is used to run automobiles, aircraft, and the like. (Also spelled **gasolene.**)

● **gaunt** /gônt/ *adj.* Very thin and bony, with hollow eyes and a starved look: *Hunger had made him gaunt.*

● **geyser** /gī′ zər/ *n.* Spring that sends up fountains or jets of hot water or steam.

● **glare** /glãr/ *n.* **1.** Strong, unpleasant light. **2.** Fierce, angry stare. —*v.* **1.** Shine strongly or unpleasantly. **2.** Stare with anger. **glared, glaring.**

● **gloomy** /glü′ mē/ *adj.* **1.** Dark; dim: *a gloomy winter day.* **2.** Sad: *She is in a gloomy mood.* **3.** Discouraging: *a gloomy predicament.* **gloomier, gloomiest.**

● **grace** /grās/ *n.* **1.** Beauty of form or movement. **2.** Short prayer of thanks given before or after meals.

● **grapevine** /grāp′ vīn′/ *n.* Vine that grapes grow on.

● **grassland** /gras′ land′/ *n.* Land with grass on it, used for pasture.

● **grease** /grēs/ *n.* Soft, melted animal fat. —*v.* Rub grease on. **greased, greasing.**

● **greasy** /grē′ sē/ *adj.* **1.** Having grease on it: *greasy hands.* **2.** Oily; having much grease in it: *Greasy food is hard to digest.* **greasier, greasiest.**

● **grief** /grēf/ *n.* Heavy sorrow; deep sadness. *syn.* **sorrow. come to grief,** Have trouble.

● **groove** /grüv/ *n.* **1.** Long, narrow cut or furrow. **2.** Fixed way of doing things. —*v.* Make a cut, rut, or narrow channel with a tool: *The counter of the sink is grooved.* **grooved, grooving.**

● **grouchy** /grouch′ ē/ *adj.* Ill-tempered; surly. **grouchier, grouchiest.**

● **group** /grüp/ *n.* Persons or things together; clan. —*v.* Form into a group.

● **grownup** /grōn′ up′/ *n.* Adult: *Many grownups attended the school play.* —*adj.* Arrived at full growth; adult.

● **growth** /grōth/ *n.* **1.** Development. **2.** Amount grown: *one year's growth.*

h

● **hair** /hãr/ *n.* **1.** Fine, threadlike growth from the skin of people and animals. **2.** Mass of such growths: *The child's hair is brown.*

● **handcuff** /hand′ kuf′/ *n.* Device to keep persons from using their hands, usually one of two steel bracelets joined by a short chain and fastened around the wrists. —*v.* Put handcuffs on.

● **hangar** /hang′ ər/ *n.* Shed for airplanes or airships.

● **hardware** /härd′ wãr′/ *n.* Articles made from metal: *Locks, hinges, nails, screws, or knives are hardware.*

● **hare** /hãr/ *n.* Animal with long ears, a divided upper lip, a short tail, and long hind legs. A hare is much like a rabbit, but larger. *pl.* **hare** or **hares.**

● **harsh** /härsh/ *adj.* **1.** Rough to the touch, taste, eye, or ear: *a harsh voice.* **2.** Cruel; unfeeling; severe: *a harsh leader.*

● **hawk** /hôk/ *n.* Bird of prey with a strong, hooked beak. —*v.* Hunt with trained hawks.

● **height** /hīt/ *n.* **1.** Measurement from top to bottom; how high anything is. **2.** A fairly great distance up.

● **heir** /ãr/ *n.* Person who has the right to somebody's property or title after the death of its owner.

● **helpful** /help′ fəl/ *adj.* Giving help; useful.

● **hew** /hū/ *v.* Cut; chop with an ax. **hewed, hewn** or **hewed, hewing.**

● **hibernate** /hī′ bər nāt/ *v.* Spend the winter in an inactive state. **hibernated, hibernating.**

● **hoard** /hôrd/ *v.* Save and store away: *Squirrels hoard nuts for the winter.* —*n.* What is saved and stored away: *The squirrel's hoard was kept in a tree.*

● **hoarse** /hôrs/ *adj.* **1.** Sounding rough and deep: *a hoarse voice.* **2.** Having a rough voice. **hoarser, hoarsest.**

● **hobble** /hob′ əl/ *v.* **1.** Limp. **2.** Tie the legs of a horse together: *The horse was hobbled so that it would not run away.* **hobbled, hobbling.** —*n.* Rope or strap used to tie a horse's legs together.

● **hobby** /hob′ ē/ *n.* Something a person especially likes to do or study that is not his main business. *pl.* **hobbies.**

● **hockey** /hok′ ē/ *n.* Game played by two teams on ice or on a field. Ice hockey is played on an ice rink by two teams of six players on skates. The object of the game is to put a round rubber disk, called the puck, into the opponent's goal with a hockey stick.

● **hoist** /hoist/ *v.* Lift up; raise, often with ropes and pulleys: *hoist a flag; hoist the sails.* —*n.* **1.** A hoisting; a lift: *She gave me a hoist up the wall.* **2.** Elevator.

- **holy** /hō' lē/ *adj.* **1.** Belonging to a deity; sacred. **2.** Like a saint. **3.** Worthy of reverence. holier, holiest.
- **honey** /hun' ē/ *n.* Thick, sweet yellow liquid made by bees out of drops collected from flowers.
- **hoof** /hùf/ *or* /hüf/ *n.* **1.** Hard foot covering of certain animals. **2.** The whole foot of certain animals. *pl.* **hoofs** or **hooves.**
- **hopeful** /hōp' fəl/ *adj.* Full of or showing hope: *They are hopeful of more success in the future.*
- **hopscotch** /hop' skoch'/ *n.* Game played by jumping into or across numbered squares.
- **horror** /hôr' ər/ *n.* Terror; very strong dislike: *The child has a horror of snakes.*
- **horseback** /hôrs' bak'/ *n.* The back of a horse. —*adv.* On the back of a horse: *They like to ride horseback.*
- **host**[1] /hōst/ *n.* **1.** Person who receives another person as his guest. **2.** Keeper of an inn or hotel.
- **host**[2] /hōst/ *n.* A large number: *a host of stars in the sky.*
- **hostess** /hō' stəs/ *n.* Woman who receives another person as her guest.
- **household** /hous' hōld'/ *n.* All the people living in a house.
- **hue** /hū/ *n.* Color; shade; tint: *Her coat showed most of the hues of the rainbow.*
- **humid** /hū' mid/ *adj.* Moist; damp: *Air by the sea is often humid.*
- **humorous** /hū' mər əs/ *adj.* Funny; amusing: *a humorous story.*
- **hurdle** /hèr' dəl/ *n.* **1.** Barrier for people or horses to jump over in a race. **2.** Obstacle; difficulty. —*v.* Jump over: *The horse hurdled the fence easily.* **hurdled, hurdling.**
- **husky** /hus' kē/ *adj.* **1.** Dry in the throat; hoarse. **2.** Big and strong. **huskier, huskiest.**

i

- **idle** /ī' dəl/ *adj.* **1.** Doing nothing; not busy; not working. **2.** Lazy; not willing to do things. **3.** Worthless; useless: *idle pleasures.* **idler, idlest.** *ant.* **busy.** —*v.* Be idle; do nothing. **idled, idling.**
- **idol** /ī' dəl/ *n.* **1.** Image that is worshiped as a god. **2.** Person or thing that is loved very much: *The baby was the idol of the family.*

- **igloo** /ig' lü/ *n.* An Eskimo hut that is shaped like a dome and is often made of blocks of hard snow. *pl.* **igloos.**
- **ignore** /ig nôr'/ *v.* Pay no attention to; disregard: *The driver ignored the policeman's whistle.* **ignored, ignoring.**
- **I'll** /īl/ **1.** I shall. **2.** I will.
- **impeachment** /im pēch' mənt/ *n.* Act of accusing a public official of wrong conduct before a court of justice.
- **import** /im' pôrt/ *n.* **1.** Article brought into a country from another. **2.** Importance: *matters of great import.* /im pôrt'/ *v.* Bring article or articles into a country for sale or use.
- **improve** /im prüv'/ *v.* **1.** Make better: *He improved his ability to bowl.* **2.** Become better: *Her health is improving.* **improved, improving.**
- **inconvenient** /in' kən vēn' yənt/ *adj.* Not convenient; not easy to use: *The shelves are so high that they are inconvenient to reach.*
- **infect** /in fekt'/ *v.* **1.** Cause disease by introducing germs: *Dirt infects an open cut.* **2.** Influence in a bad way.
- **instruction** /in struk' shən/ *n.* Teaching; education; knowledge.
- **invisible** /in viz' ə bəl/ *adj.* Not visible; not able to be seen.
- **involve** /in volv'/ *v.* **1.** Have as a necessary part; take in; include: *Housework involves cooking.* **2.** Bring (into difficulty, danger, etc.): *One foolish mistake can involve you in trouble.* **3.** Entangle; complicate. **4.** Take up the attention of; occupy: *She was involved in working on a puzzle.* **involved, involving.**
- **isle** /īl/ *n.* Small island.

j

- **jewel** /jü' əl/ *n.* **1.** Precious stone; stone of great value. **2.** A valuable ornament to be worn, set with precious stones. **3.** Person or thing that is very precious. —*v.* Set with jewels.
- **join** /join/ *v.* **1.** Bring together; unite. **2.** Become a part of: *join a club.*
- **journey** /jèr' nē/ *n.* Trip: *Our journey lasted two weeks. pl.* **journeys** —*v.* Take a trip: *We journeyed across the sea.*
- **joyride** /joi' rīd'/ *n.* A ride in an automobile for pleasure.

/a/ ran /ā/ rain /ã/ care /ä/ car /e/ hen /ē/ he /èr/ her /i/ in /ī/ ice /o/ not /ō/ no /ô/ off
/u/ us /ū/ use /ü/ tool /ù/ took /ou/ cow /oi/ boy /ch/ church /hw/ when /ng/ sing /sh/ ship
/ŦH/ this /th/ thin /zh/ vision /ə/ about, taken, pencil, lemon, circus

- **jubilee** /jü′ bə lē/ *n.* **1.** An anniversary thought of as a time of rejoicing. **2.** Time of great joy.
- **judgment** /juj′ mənt/ *n.* **1.** Opinion: *In my judgment she is prettier than her sister.* **2.** Good sense. **3.** Decision made by a judge or others in a court of law.
- **junk**[1] /jungk/ *n.* Old metal, paper, rags, etc. —*v.* Throw away or discard as junk.
- **junk**[2] /jungk/ *n.* A Chinese sailing ship.

k

- **kangaroo** /kang′ gə rü′/ *n.* Mammal of Australia having small forelegs and very strong hind legs. The female has a pouch in front in which she carries her young. *pl.* **kangaroos.**
- **karate** /kə rä′ tē/ *n.* A Japanese method of fighting without weapons by striking at the opponent with the hands or feet.
- **kimono** /kə mō′ nə/ *n.* **1.** A loose outer garment held in place by a sash, worn by Japanese men and women. **2.** A woman's loose dressing gown. *pl.* **kimonos.**
- **kindergarten** /kin′ dər gärt′ ən/ *n.* School or class for children who are not yet old enough to enter the first grade.
- **knew** /nü/ *or* /nü/ *v.* See **know.** *He knew the answer.*
- **know** /nō/ *v.* **1.** Have the facts of; be skilled in. **2.** Be acquainted with. **knew, known, knowing.**
- **known** /nōn/ *v.* See **know.** *He was known for his artistic ability.*
- **kosher** /kō′ shər/ *adj.* Right or clean according to Jewish law: *kosher food.*
- **kowtow** /kou′ tou′/ *v.* Show exaggerated respect for: *There is no need to kowtow to your boss.*

l

- **latitude** /lat′ ə tüd/ *or* /lat′ ə tūd/ *n.* **1.** Distance north or south of the equator measured in degrees. **2.** Freedom from narrow rules.
- **laundry** /lôn′ drē/ *n.* **1.** Room or building where clothes are washed and ironed. **2.** Clothes washed or to be washed. *pl.* **laundries.**
- **lawless** /lô′ ləs/ *adj.* **1.** Paying no attention to the law: *A thief leads a lawless life.* **2.** Having no laws.
- **lawyer** /lô′ yər/ *n.* Person who knows the laws and gives advice about matters of law or acts for another person in court.

- **legal** /lē′ gəl/ *adj.* **1.** Of law: *legal advice.* **2.** Lawful: *Hunting is legal during the official hunting season.*
- **likewise** /līk′ wīz′/ *adv.* **1.** The same: *See what I do; I hope you'll do likewise.* **2.** Also: *I must go home, and she likewise.*
- **liquid** /lik′ wid/ *n.* Substance that is not a solid or a gas; substance that flows freely, like water. —*adj.* In liquid form; melted.
- **loan** /lōn/ *n.* **1.** A lending. **2.** Anything lent, such as money. —*v.* Make a loan.
- **local** /lō′ kəl/ *adj.* **1.** Of a place; having to do with a certain place or places: *local news.* **2.** Of just one part of the body: *a local pain.*
- **location** /lō kā′ shən/ *n.* **1.** A locating: *the location of the camp.* **2.** A being located. **3.** Position; place: *a bad location.*
- **lone** /lōn/ *adj.* **1.** Alone; solitary: *The lone cub was playing.* **2.** Standing apart; isolated: *a lone house.*
- **lonely** /lōn′ lē/ *adj.* **1.** Feeling oneself alone and longing for friends. **2.** Alone: *a lonely tree.* **lonelier, loneliest.**
- **loop** /lüp/ *n.* **1.** Part of a curved string, wire, or cord that crosses itself. **2.** Thing, bend, course, or motion shaped like such a curved object: *In writing, "b" and "l" have loops.* —*v.* **1.** Make a loop of; make a loop in. **2.** Fasten with a loop: *He looped the sail to the mast.*
- **lowland** /lō′ land′/ *n.* Land that is lower and flatter than the neighboring country.
- **loyal** /loi′ əl/ *adj.* **1.** True and faithful to love, promise, or duty. **2.** Faithful to one's kind, government, or country: *a loyal citizen.*

m

- **mainland** /mān′ land′/ *n.* The main part of a continent apart from the outlying islands.
- **major** /mā′ jər/ *adj.* Larger; greater: *The major part of a baby's life is spent sleeping.* —*n.* An officer in the army, ranking next above a captain.
- **majority** /mə jôr′ ə tē/ *n.* The larger number; more than half: *A majority of the children have read that book.* *pl.* **majorities.**
- **malt** /môlt/ *n.* Grain, usually barley, soaked in water until it sprouts and tastes sweet.
- **mammal** /mam′ əl/ *n.* Warm-blooded animal with a backbone and young that are nursed by the mother.
- **marmalade** /mär′ mə lād/ *n.* Sweet preserve, similar to jam, made of fruit such as oranges.
- **marvelous** /mär′ və ləs/ *adj.* Excellent;

176

splendid; extraordinary: *a marvelous time; marvelous weather.*

- **master** /mas' tər/ *n.* Person who rules or commands people or things. —*adj.* Expert; skilled: *master builder.* —*v.* Become skillful at: *She mastered ice-skating quickly.*
- **matchless** /mach' ləs/ *adj.* So great or wonderful that it cannot be equaled: *The rescuers showed matchless courage.*
- **material** /mə tir' ē əl/ *n.* What a thing is made from or done with: *dress material; writing materials.* —*adj.* Of the body: *Food and shelter are material needs.*
- **mattress** /mat' rəs/ *n.* Covering of strong cloth stuffed with cotton, straw, etc., used on a bed or as a bed. A spring mattress contains wire springs.
- **mayor** /mā' ər/ *n.* Person at the head of a city or town government.
- **meadow** /med' ō/ *n.* Piece of grassy land; field of grass.
- **mechanical** /mə kan' ə kəl/ *adj.* **1.** Having to do with machinery. **2.** Worked by machinery: *a mechanical toy.* **3.** Without expression: *Their singing was very mechanical.*
- **medal** /med' əl/ *n.* Piece of metal, like a coin, given as an honor to somebody or to celebrate some event.
- **melon** /mel' ən/ *n.* Large, juicy fruit of the vine.
- **menu** /men' ū/ *n.* List of foods to be served.
- **method** /meth' əd/ *n.* **1.** Way of doing something. **2.** System in doing things.
- **microbe** /mī' krōb/ *n.* Living organism of a very small size; germ.
- **microphone** /mī' krə fōn/ *n.* Instrument for magnifying small sounds or for transmitting sounds: *Radio and television stations use microphones for broadcasting.*
- **miser** /mī' zər/ *n.* Person who loves money for its own sake and lives poorly in order to save money.
- **moccasin** /mok' ə sən/ *n.* **1.** Soft shoe, often made from the skin of a deer. **2.** Poisonous snake found in the southern part of the United States.
- **molar** /mō' lər/ *n.* Tooth with a broad surface for grinding.
- **mortar** /môr' tər/ *n.* Mixture of lime, cement, sand, and water for holding bricks or stones together.

- **moth** /môth/ *n.* A winged insect very much like a butterfly, but flying mostly at night. *pl.* **moths** /môᴛʜz/ *or* /môths/.
- **mountainous** /moun' tən əs/ *adj.* **1.** Covered with mountain ranges. **2.** Huge: *a mountainous wave.*
- **movie** /mü' vē/ *n.* Motion picture.
- **murder** /mėr' dər/ *n.* Unlawful, intentional killing of a human being. —*v.* Killing a human being intentionally.
- **muscle** /mus' əl/ *n.* **1.** The tissue in the bodies of people and animals that can be tightened or loosened to make the body move. **2.** Special bundle of such tissue that moves a particular bone or part of the body: *your arm muscles.*
- **museum** /mū zē' əm/ *n.* Building or rooms in which a collection of objects illustrating science, ancient life, art, or other subjects is kept and displayed.
- **mushroom** /mush' rüm'/ *n.* Small fungus shaped like an umbrella and growing very rapidly. —*v.* Grow rapidly.
- **mustang** /mus' tang/ *n.* Small wild or half-wild horse of the North American plains.

n

- **napkin** /nap' kin/ *n.* Piece of cloth used at meals to protect the clothing or to wipe the lips or fingers.
- **narrow** /nar' ō/ *adj.* **1.** Not wide; having little width. **2.** Limited; small: *a narrow circle of friends.* **3.** With little margin: *a narrow escape.* —*v.* Make or become narrower.
- **nectar** /nek' tər/ *n.* **1.** Sweet liquid found in many flowers. **2.** In mythology, the drink of the Greek gods.
- **neglect** /nə glekt'/ *v.* **1.** Leave uncared for: *Don't neglect the plants.* **2.** Omit: *Don't neglect to feed the cat.* —*n.* **1.** Want of attention to what should be done. **2.** Being neglected.
- **nephew** /nef' ū/ *n.* Son of one's brother, sister, brother-in-law, or sister-in-law.
- **nerve** /nėrv/ *n.* **1.** Fiber or bundle of fibers connecting the spinal cord or brain with the eyes, ears, muscles, and glands. **2.** Courage.
- **newsstand** /nüz' stand'/ *or* /nūz' stand'/ *n.* Place where newspapers and magazines are sold.
- **nickname** /nik' nām'/ *n.* Name added to or used instead of a person's real name.

/a/ ran /ā/ rain /ä/ care /ä/ car /e/ hen /ē/ he /ėr/ her /i/ in /ī/ ice /o/ not /ō/ no /ô/ off
/u/ us /ū/ use /ü/ tool /u̇/ took /ou/ cow /oi/ boy /ch/ church /hw/ when /ng/ sing /sh/ ship
/ᴛʜ/ this /th/ thin /zh/ vision /ə/ about, taken, pencil, lemon, circus

- **niece** /nēs/ *n.* Daughter of one's brother, sister, brother-in-law, or sister-in-law.
- **ninety** /nīn' tē/ *n., adj.* 90. *pl.* **nineties.**
- **ninth** /nīnth/ *adj.* Next after the eighth: *the ninth girl in line.* —*n.* **1.** The one next after the eighth one: *the ninth in line.* **2.** One of nine equal parts: *I ate a ninth of the pie.*
- **noble** /nō' bəl/ *adj.* **1.** Fine and good in character. **2.** High and great by birth, rank, or title. **3.** Excellent; splendid; magnificent: *a noble scene.* **nobler, noblest.** —*n.* Person high and great by birth, rank, or title.
- **noisily** /noi' zə lē/ *adv.* In a noisy way: *The children played noisily in the back yard.*
- **noodle** /nü' dəl/ *n.* Mixture of flour and water, or flour and eggs, like macaroni, but made in flat strips.
- **nook** /nùk/ *n.* Cozy little corner; hidden spot; sheltered place.
- **novel** /nov' əl/ *adj.* Strange; new: *Flying gives some people a novel sensation. His invention was a novel idea.* —*n.* Long story with characters and a plot.
- **numb** /num/ *adj.* Having lost the power of feeling or moving: *My fingers are numb with cold.* —*v.* **1.** Make numb. **2.** Dull the feelings of: *numbed with grief.*
- **numeral** /nü' mər əl/ *or* /nū' mər əl/ *n.* Figure or group of figures standing for a number: *7, 25, 463, and X are numerals.*
- **nylon** /nī' lon/ *n.* Strong, elastic, and durable substance used to make clothing, stockings, bristles, etc. —*adj.* Made of nylon.

o

- **obstinate** /ob' stə nət/ *adj.* Stubborn.
- **occupy** /ok' yə pī/ *v.* **1.** Live in: *occupy a house.* **2.** Fill; take up: *occupy all the space.* **3.** Keep busy. **4.** Hold: *occupy an important position.* **5.** Take possession of. **occupied, occupying.**
- **odor** /ō' dər/ *n.* Smell: *the odor of roses.*
- **offspring** /ôf' spring'/ *or* /of' spring'/ *n.* The young of a person, animal, or plant; descendant. *pl.* **offsprings** or **offspring.**
- **oilcan** /oil' kan'/ *n.* **1.** Can for holding oil. **2.** Can with a spout for dispensing oil.
- **omit** /ō mit'/ *v.* **1.** Leave out: *He made spelling mistakes because he omitted letters in words.* **2.** Fail to do; neglect: *She omitted making her bed.* **omitted, omitting.**
- **operator** /op' ər ā' tər/ *n.* Person who causes something to run or work: *a telephone operator; the operators of a railroad.*

- **opponent** /ə pō' nənt/ *n.* Person who is on the other side in a game, fight, or discussion: *She defeated her opponents in the election.*
- **oral** /ôr' əl/ *adj.* **1.** Spoken; using speech: *An oral agreement is not enough; we must have a written agreement.* **2.** Of the mouth: *The oral opening in an earthworm is small.*
- **order** /ôr' dər/ *n.* **1.** The way one thing follows another: *alphabetical order.* **2.** Condition in which everything is in its right place: *to put a room in order.* **3.** Condition; state: *The room was in bad order.* **4.** State or condition in which laws are obeyed: *Order was established by the police.* **5.** Principles and rules by which a meeting is run. **6.** Command; a telling of what to do. **7.** Paper saying that money is to be paid or something handed over: *a postal money order.* **8.** Statement to a store or tradesman telling what you wish. **9.** Brotherhood of monks, friars, or knights: *the Franciscan order.* —*v.* **1.** Command; tell what to do. **2.** Give an order for. **by order of,** According to an order given by a proper person. **in order, 1.** In the right arrangement. **2.** Working right. **in order to,** As a means to. **out of order, 1.** In the wrong order or arrangement. **2.** Not working right.
- **ore** /ôr/ *n.* Mineral or rock containing enough of a metal or metals to make mining it profitable.
- **ounce** /ouns/ *n.* **1.** Unit of weight; 1/16 of a pound in avoirdupois and 1/12 of a pound in troy weight. In the metric system, one avoirdupois ounce equals 28.3495 grams. **2.** Measure for liquids; sixteen ounces equals one pint. In the metric system, one liquid ounce equals 29.5737 cubic centimeters. **3.** A little bit; a small amount. *abbr.* **oz.**
- **oval** /ō' vəl/ *adj.* Shaped like an egg or like an elipse. —*n.* Something having an oval shape.
- **owner** /ō' nər/ *n.* One who owns: *She is the owner of the prize dog.*
- **oyster** /oi' stər/ *n.* A kind of shellfish much used as food. Oysters are found in shallow waters along seacoasts. Some oysters that live in tropical waters produce pearls. Pearls are produced when a grain of sand gets inside the oyster's shell and is covered with thin layers of liquid from the oyster's body.

p

- **pair** /pār/ *n.* **1.** Set of two: *pair of shoes.* **2.** Two mated animals. **3.** Single thing consisting of two parts that cannot be used separately: *a pair of scissors; a pair of pants.* *pl.* **pair** or **pairs.** —*v.* Arrange or be arranged in pairs.

● **pajamas** /pə jä′ məz/ *or* /pə jam′ əz/ *n. pl.* Garments to sleep in, consisting of a coat and trousers. (Also spelled **pyjamas.**)

● **panel** /pan′ əl/ *n.* **1.** Strip or surface that is different in some way from what is around it: *The front panel in her skirt was made of lace.* **2.** Group formed for discussion: *A panel of teachers discussed the subject of homework.* **3.** Board containing instruments, controls, or indicators used in operating an automobile, aircraft, or the like. —*v.* Arrange in panels; furnish with panels: *We will panel the walls with wood.*

● **panic** /pan′ ik/ *n.* Unreasoning fear; fear causing a person or group of persons to lose control of themselves: *There was a panic when fire broke out in the store.* —*v.* Be affected with panic: *The audience panicked when fire broke out.* **panicked, panicking.**

● **pantry** /pan′ trē/ *n.* Small room or closet for keeping food and cooking materials. *pl.* **pantries.**

● **parcel** /pär′ səl/ *n.* **1.** Bundle; package: *Her arms were filled with parcels.* **2.** Piece: *a parcel of land.*

● **pardon** /pärd′ ən/ *n.* **1.** Forgiveness. **2.** Legal document setting a person free. —*v.* **1.** Forgive. **2.** Set free from punishment. **3.** Excuse.

● **pare** /pãr/ *v.* Cut, trim, or shave off the outer part of; peel: *pare an apple.* **pared, paring.**

● **parlor** /pär′ lər/ *n.* **1.** Room for receiving guests; sitting room. **2.** A shop.

● **parrot** /par′ ət/ *n.* Bird with a stout, hooked bill and often bright-colored feathers: *Some parrots repeat words and sentences.*

● **patience** /pā′ shəns/ *n.* Calm bearing of pain, of waiting, or of anything that annoys, troubles, or hurts.

● **patio** /pä′ tē ō/ *or* /pat′ ē ō/ *n.* Terrace; flat, open porch for outdoor eating and lounging. *pl.* **patios.**

● **patriotic** /pā′ trē ot′ ik/ *adj.* Having or showing love for one's country.

● **peace** /pēs/ *n.* **1.** Freedom from war. **2.** Agreement between contending parties to end war: *the Peace of Paris.* **3.** Quiet; calm: *peace of mind.*

● **peanut** /pē′ nut′/ *n.* Seed like a nut, used for food and for cooking oil.

● **pear** /pãr/ *n.* **1.** A sweet, juicy, edible fruit rounded at one end and smaller toward the stem end. **2.** Tree that it grows on.

● **pension** /pen′ shən/ *n.* A regular payment to a person that is not wages. —*v.* Give a pension to: *The army pensioned the soldier after years of loyal service.*

● **photo** /fō′ tō/ *n.* Photograph; picture made with a camera. *pl.* **photos.**

● **phrase** /frāz/ *n.* **1.** Combination of words. **2.** Expression often used: *"Call up" is a phrase used for "make a telephone call to."* —*v.* Express in a particular way: *She phrased her answer very carefully.* **phrased, phrasing.**

● **piano** /pē an′ ō/ *n.* Large musical instrument whose tones come from many wires. The wires are sounded by hammers that are worked by striking keys on a keyboard. *pl.* **pianos.**

● **piece** /pēs/ *n.* **1.** One of the parts into which a thing is divided or broken. **2.** Portion: *a piece of bread.* **3.** One composition in an art: *a piece of music.* **4.** Disk, block, figure, or the like, used in playing games. —*v.* Make or repair by joining pieces. **pieced, piecing.**

● **pint** /pīnt/ *n.* Unit of measure equal to half a quart. In the metric system, one liquid pint equals 0.473 liter.

● **pistol** /pis′ təl/ *n.* Small, short gun held and fired with one hand.

● **plaid** /plad/ *n.* **1.** Piece of woolen cloth having a pattern of checks and stripes. **2.** Pattern of checks and stripes. —*adj.* Having a pattern of checks and stripes: *a plaid coat.*

● **plaster** /plas′ tər/ *n.* Soft mixture of lime, sand, and water that hardens as it dries. —*v.* Cover walls or ceiling with plaster.

● **plastic** /plas′ tik/ *n.* Any of various substances that can be molded or shaped when hot and become hard when cooled. —*adj.* **1.** Made of plastic: *a plastic bottle.* **2.** Easily molded or shaped: *Clay, wax, and plaster are plastic substances.*

● **plateau** /pla tō′/ *n.* Plain in the mountains; large, high plain. *pl.* **plateaus** /pla tōz′/.

● **playmate** /plā′ māt′/ *n.* Person who plays with another.

● **pledge** /plej/ *v.* Promise solemnly. **pledged, pledging.** —*n.* **1.** Solemn promise. **2.** Thing

/a/ ran /ā/ rain /ã/ care /ä/ car /e/ hen /ē/ he /ėr/ her /i/ in /ī/ ice /o/ not /ō/ no /ô/ off
/u/ us /ū/ use /ü/ tool /u̇/ took /ou/ cow /oi/ boy /ch/ church /hw/ when /ng/ sing /sh/ ship
/ᵀH/ this /th/ thin /zh/ vision /ə/ about, taken, pencil, lemon, circus

given to show favor or love: *The ring was a pledge of his love for the queen.*

- **plenty** /plen' tē/ *n.* All one needs; a large number or amount: *We need plenty of wood for the fire.* —*adj.* Enough; plentiful: *Six potatoes will be plenty.*
- **plume** /plüm/ *n.* Large, long feather.
- **plywood** /plī' wud'/ *n.* Board or boards made of thin layers of wood glued together.
- **pointblank** /point' blangk'/ *adj.* **1.** Aimed directly at a target. **2.** Direct; blunt. —*adv.* In a direct way.
- **poise** /poiz/ *n.* Balance: *The young girl has poise of mind and body and never seems embarrassed.* —*v.* Balance: *He was poised on the edge of the diving board.* **poised, poising.**
- **pole**[1] /pōl/ *n.* Long, slender piece of wood. —*v.* Make a boat go with a pole. **poled, poling.**
- **pole**[2] /pōl/ *n.* **1.** The North Pole and the South Pole, which are the ends of the earth's axis. **2.** Either end of a magnet.
- **politics** /pol' ə tiks/ *n.* Science and art of government: *Roosevelt was engaged in politics for many years.* *pl.* or *sing.*
- **poll** /pōl/ *n.* **1.** Collection of votes: *We had a poll to decide where to have the picnic.* **2.** Number of votes cast: *There was a light poll because of the rain.* **3.** List of voters. **4.** Survey of public opinion. —*v.* Take the votes of: *The people were polled for president.*
- **popcorn** /pop' kôrn'/ *n.* Kind of corn, the kernels of which burst open and puff out when heated.
- **port**[1] /pôrt/ *n.* **1.** Harbor; place where ships can be sheltered. **2.** Place where ships can load and unload; city or town by a harbor.
- **port**[2] /pôrt/ *n.* Left side of a ship or aircraft when one faces the front, or bow. —*adj.* On the left side of a ship or aircraft.
- **pose** /pōz/ *n.* **1.** Position of the body. **2.** Pretense. —*v.* **1.** Put in a certain position. **2.** Hold a position: *pose for a photographer.* **3.** Take a false position for effect: *pose as a rich woman.* **posed, posing.**
- **poster** /pō' stər/ *n.* Large printed sheet, or notice, put up in a public place.
- **postpone** /pōst' pōn'/ *v.* Put off until later: *The baseball game was postponed for a day.* **postponed, postponing.**
- **potato** /pə tā' tō/ *n.* Vegetable that grows underground, most widely used in Europe

and America. *pl.* **potatoes.**

- **pound**[1] /pound/ *n.* **1.** Unit of weight. One pound avoirdupois is 16 ounces. One pound troy is 12 ounces. In the metric system, one pound equals 0.4536 kilogram. **2.** Unit of money used in Great Britain. *abbr.* **lb.**
- **pound**[2] /pound/ *v.* **1.** Strike or beat heavily many times. **2.** Crush into powder by beating.
- **pound**[3] /pound/ *n.* An enclosed place in which to keep stray animals: *a dog pound.*
- **powder** /pou' dər/ *n.* **1.** Solid reduced to dust by crushing or grinding. **2.** Some special kind of powder: *face powder.* **3.** Gunpowder. —*v.* Sprinkle with powder.
- **power** /pou' ər/ *n.* **1.** Strength; force. **2.** Ability to do or act. **3.** Authority; right; control; influence. **4.** Person, nation, or anything that has authority or influence: *The five powers had a peace conference.* **5.** The product obtained by multiplying a number by itself one or more times: *16 is the fourth power of 2.*
- **prairie** /prâr' ē/ *n.* Large area of level or rolling land with grass but few or no trees.
- **praise** /prāz/ *v.* **1.** Speak well of. **2.** Worship in words or song: *praise God.* **praised, praising.** —*n.* Act of saying that a thing or person is good; words that tell the value of a person.
- **pray** /prā/ *v.* **1.** Ask from God; speak to God. **2.** Ask earnestly.
- **precaution** /prə kô' shən/ *n.* Care taken beforehand.
- **prefer** /prē fėr'/ *v.* Like better: *She prefers reading to sewing.* **preferred, preferring.**
- **prescription** /prē skrip' shən/ *n.* Written order for preparing and using a medicine.
- **preserve** /prē zėrv'/ *v.* **1.** Save; keep safe. **2.** Keep up; maintain. **3.** Prepare food to keep it from spoiling. **preserved, preserving.** —*n.* Place where wild animals or fish are protected. **preserves** /prə zėrvz'/ *n. pl.* Fruit cooked with sugar and sealed from the air.
- **preview** /prē' vū'/ *n.* Previous view or inspection; advance showing. —*v.* View beforehand: *We previewed the movie before it was shown for the public.*
- **previous** /prē' vē əs/ *adj.* Coming before; earlier: *He made a better grade on a previous test.*
- **prey** /prā/ *n.* **1.** Animal hunted or seized for food: *Mice are the prey of cats.* **2.** Habit of hunting and killing other animals for food: *Hawks are birds of prey.* **3.** Victim: *He is a prey to fear.* —*v.* **1.** Hunt and kill for food:

Cats prey upon mice. **2.** Do harm: *Worry preys on her mind.*

- **proceed** /prō sēd'/ *v.* **1.** Move forward. **2.** Carry on any activity: *proceed to open the door.*
- **procession** /prə sesh' ən/ *n.* Something that moves forward; persons marching: *A funeral procession filled the street.*
- **proclaim** /prō klām'/ *v.* Make known publicly and officially.
- **project** /proj' ekt/ *n.* **1.** Plan; scheme. **2.** Undertaking; enterprise. /prō jekt'/ *v.* **1.** Plan; scheme. **2.** Stick out: *The rocky point projects far into the water.* **3.** Throw forward.
- **proof** /prüf/ *n.* **1.** Way or means of showing the truth of something: *I have proof of my story.* **2.** Act of testing.
- **propose** /prō pōz'/ *v.* **1.** Put forward for consideration. **2.** Present the name of someone for office or membership. **3.** Intend; plan. **4.** Make an offer of marriage. **proposed, proposing.**
- **pry**[1] /prī/ *v.* Look with curiosity; peep: *He sometimes pries into other people's affairs.* **pried, prying.**
- **pry**[2] /prī/ *v.* **1.** Raise or move by force: *Pry up the stone with your pickax.* **2.** Get with much effort: *We finally pried the secret out of her.* **pried, prying.**
- **public** /pub' lik/ *n.* People in general; all the people. —*adj.* **1.** Concerning or belonging to the people as a whole. **2.** Not private.
- **punch**[1] /punch/ *v.* **1.** Hit with the fists. **2.** Pierce a hole in. —*n.* **1.** Quick blow or thrust. **2.** Tool for making holes.
- **punch**[2] /punch/ *n.* Drink made of different liquids, often fruit juices.
- **puppet** /pup' ət/ *n.* **1.** A small doll, often moved by wires. **2.** Anybody who is not independent, but does what somebody else says.

q

- **quail**[1] /kwāl/ *n.* Any of various plump game birds, especially the bobwhite. *pl.* **quails** or **quail.**
- **quail**[2] /kwāl/ *v.* Lose courage; shrink back with fear: *The dog quailed at the loud noise.*
- **queer** /kwir/ *adj.* Strange; odd; peculiar.
- **quite** /kwīt/ *adv.* **1.** Completely; entirely: *I am quite alone.* **2.** Really; truly: *quite a change in the weather.* **3.** Very: *quite hot.*

r

- **raccoon** /ra kün'/ *n.* **1.** Small, bushy animal with grey fur and a ringed tail, that lives in wooded areas and is active at night. **2.** Fur of this animal. (Also spelled **racoon.**)
- **racket**[1] /rak' ət/ *n.* **1.** Loud noise; din: *Don't make a racket when others are studying.* **2.** Dishonest scheme for getting money from people.
- **racket**[2] /rak' ət/ *n.* Oval frame with a network of strings and a long handle. It is used to hit the ball in games like tennis.
- **racoon** /ra kün'/ *n.* Raccoon.
- **radiator** /rā' dē ā' tər/ *n.* **1.** Device for heating a room, consisting of pipes through which hot water or steam passes. **2.** Device for cooling water: *the radiator of a car.*
- **rainbow** /rān' bō'/ *n.* Bow, or arch, of seven colors seen sometimes in the sky when the sun shines through mist or spray.
- **reason** /rē' zən/ *n.* **1.** Cause: *Tell me your reason for not coming.* **2.** Power to think things out. **3.** Common sense. —*v.* **1.** Think things out: *A baby cannot reason.* **2.** Consider; argue: *It is hard to reason with an angry person.*
- **reasonable** /rē' zən ə bəl/ *adj.* **1.** Sensible; not foolish: *You can depend on my mother to act in a reasonable way.* **2.** Fair: *a reasonable request.* **3.** Inexpensive: *a reasonable price.*
- **rebel** /reb' əl/ *n.* Person who resists or fights against authority: *The rebels fought against the government forces.* —*adj.* Defying the law: *a rebel army.* /rē bel'/ *v.* **1.** Resist or fight against: *The oppressed people rebelled against the wicked ruler.* **2.** Feel dislike for: *They rebelled at having to stay indoors on such a fine day.* **rebelled, rebelling.**
- **recall** /rē kôl'/ *v.* **1.** Call back to mind; remember: *Mother recalls stories she heard years ago.* **2.** Order back: *recalled to duty.* **3.** Withdraw: *recall the orders.* —*n.* Act of calling back.
- **reduce** /rē düs'/ *or* /rē dūs'/ *v.* **1.** Make less; make smaller. **2.** Become less in weight. **3.** Bring down: *Misfortune reduced them to begging.* **4.** Change to another form: *If you reduce 3 ft., 6 in. to inches, you have 42 inches.* **reduced, reducing.**

/a/ ran /ā/ rain /ã/ care /ä/ car /e/ hen /ē/ he /ėr/ her /i/ in /ī/ ice /o/ not /ō/ no /ô/ off
/u/ us /ū/ use /ü/ tool /ů/ took /ou/ cow /oi/ boy /ch/ church /hw/ when /ng/ sing /sh/ ship
/ŦH/ this /th/ thin /zh/ vision /ə/ about, taken, pencil, lemon, circus

- **refuse**[1] /rē fūz'/ v. **1.** Say "no" to: *refuse the offer.* **2.** Say "no": *be free to refuse.* **3.** Say one will not do it: *refuse to obey.* **refused, refusing.**
- **refuse**[2] /ref' ūs/ n. Useless stuff; waste; rubbish.
- **regard** /rē gärd'/ v. **1.** Look at closely. **2.** Consider; think of. —n. **1.** Respect. **2.** Consideration; thoughtfulness.
- **regardless** /rə gärd' ləs/ adj. Careless; without heed: *We will go to the meeting, regardless of the weather.*
- **rejoice** /rē jois'/ v. **1.** Be glad: *He rejoiced at our success.* **2.** Make glad: *The people were rejoiced by their victory.* **rejoiced, rejoicing.**
- **relief** /rē lēf'/ n. **1.** Help in time of pain or trouble. **2.** The lessening or freeing from a pain, burden, or difficulty. **3.** Change of persons on duty. **4.** Person or persons who relieve others from duty. **5.** Freedom from a post of duty: *The nurse had two hours' relief from her post.* **on relief,** Being given help from public funds.
- **relieve** /rē lēv'/ v. **1.** Make easier; reduce the pain or trouble of. **2.** Set free (a person on duty) by taking that place. **3.** Bring aid to; help. **relieved, relieving.**
- **reluctant** /rə luk' tənt/ adj. Unwilling; slow to act because of unwillingness: *I am reluctant to go out in cold weather.*
- **reptile** /rep' tīl/ or /rep' təl/ n. Cold-blooded animal that creeps or crawls: *Snakes, turtles, crocodiles, alligators, and lizards are reptiles.*
- **resist** /rē zist'/ v. **1.** Act against; oppose: *The team resisted all efforts to discourage them.* **2.** Keep from; withstand: *He couldn't resist laughing.*
- **resistance** /rə zis' təns/ n. **1.** Act of striving against: *The bank clerk resisted the robbers.* **2.** Power to strive against: *She has no resistance to germs and is often ill.*
- **responsible** /rə spon' sə bəl/ adj. **1.** Expected to be accountable for: *The pupils are responsible for their own books.* **2.** Deserving credit or blame: *The rain was responsible for a poor corn crop.* **3.** Trustworthy; dependable; reliable: *A responsible person should be chosen.*
- **retire** /rē tīr'/ v. **1.** Give up an office, occupation, etc.: *Baseball players retire young.* **2.** Go away to be quiet. **3.** Withdraw. **retired, retiring.**
- **rhinoceros** /rī nos' ər əs/ n. Large, thick-skinned animal of Africa and Asia with one or two upright horns on the snout. pl. **rhinoceroses** or **rhinoceros.**
- **ring**[1] /ring/ n. **1.** Circle. **2.** Thin band of metal or other material worn on the finger.
- **ring**[2] /ring/ v. **1.** Give forth a clear sound, as a bell does. **2.** Cause a bell to sound. **rang, rung, ringing.**
- **rival** /rī' vəl/ n. Person who wants and tries to get the same thing as another: *The boys were rivals for the same class office.* —adj. Wanting the same thing as another: *rival teams; rival stores.* —v. Equal; match: *The sunset rivaled the sunrise in beauty.*
- **roast** /rōst/ v. **1.** Cook by dry heat; bake. **2.** Make or become very hot. —n. Piece of baked meat. —adj. Prepared by roasting: *roast beef.*
- **roundhouse** /round' hous'/ n. Building for storing or repairing locomotives.
- **roundup** /round' up'/ n. Act of bringing cattle together from long distances.
- **rowdy** /rou' dē/ adj. Rough; disorderly: *a rowdy person.* **rowdier, rowdiest.** —n. A rough, disorderly person: *The rowdies ran across the lawn noisily.* pl. **rowdies.**
- **rumor** /rü' mər/ n. News without any proof that it is true; vague, general talk: *I heard the rumor about her trip, but I did not believe it.* —v. Tell or spread a rumor.
- **rung** /rung/ v. See **ring**[2]. *The bell was rung at noon.*

s

- **sacred** /sā' krəd/ adj. **1.** Holy: *A mosque is a sacred building.* **2.** Connected with religion: *sacred music.* **3.** Worthy of reverence: *the sacred memory of a dead hero.* **4.** Not to be violated or disregarded: *She made a sacred promise.*
- **sacrifice** /sak' rə fīs/ n. **1.** Offering to a god. **2.** Loss: *She will sell her house at a sacrifice.* —v. **1.** Give or offer to a god: *Some ancient people sacrificed animals at their religious ceremonies.* **2.** Give up: *He sacrificed many pleasures in order to care for his old grandfather.* **sacrificed, sacrificing.**
- **salesman** /sālz' mən/ n. Man whose work is selling. pl. **salesmen.**
- **salesmen** /sālz' mən/ n. pl. See **salesman.**
- **samovar** /sam' ə vär/ n. Metal urn with a faucet, used mostly in Russia for boiling water for tea.
- **sampan** /sam' pan/ n. Small, flat-bottomed boat used in the Orient, propelled by oars and sometimes having a sail.

- **sandal** /san' dəl/ *n.* Kind of shoe made of a sole fastened to the foot by straps.

- **sandwich** /sand' wich/ *n.* Two or more slices of bread with filling between them. —*v.* Put in between: *They were sandwiched in the seat between two fat people.*
- **sardine** /sär dēn'/ *n.* Kind of small fish preserved in oil for food. *pl.* **sardines** or **sardine.**
- **saucer** /sô' sər/ *n.* Shallow dish to set a cup on.
- **scent** /sent/ *n.* **1.** Smell: *The scent of flowers filled the garden.* **2.** Sense of smell: *Many dogs have a keen scent.* **3.** Smell left in passing: *Dogs track other animals by their scent.*
- **scheme** /skēm/ *n.* **1.** A plan; a program of action. **2.** A plot: *a scheme to cheat the government.* **3.** System of connected things, parts, etc.: *a color scheme.* —*v.* Plan; plot: *They schemed to bring jewels into the country without paying duty.* **schemed, scheming.**
- **scholar** /skol' ər/ *n.* **1.** A learned person: *The professor was a famous Latin scholar.* **2.** Pupil; learner: *Each scholar spends three hours a night doing homework.*
- **scissors** /siz' ərz/ *n.* Tool or instrument for cutting that has two blades so fastened that they will work toward each other. *pl.* or *sing.*
- **scooter** /sküt' ər/ *n.* Child's vehicle consisting of a board for the feet between two wheels, one in front of the other, steered by a handlebar and pushed by one foot.
- **screwdriver** /skrü' drī' vər/ *n.* Tool for putting in or taking out screws by turning them.
- **sculptor** /skulp' tər/ *n.* Person who carves or models figures.
- **seaport** /sē' pôrt'/ *n.* Port or harbor on the seacoast; city or town with a harbor that ships can reach from the sea.
- **sell** /sel/ *v.* **1.** Exchange for money or other payment. **2.** Keep for sale: *A butcher sells meat.* **3.** Be on sale: *Strawberries sell well in the spring.* **sold, selling.**
- **send** /send/ *v.* **1.** Cause to go or to be carried: *send a letter.* **2.** Cause to come or occur: *God sends rain.* **sent, sending.**

- **sent** /sent/ *v.* Past tense of *send: They sent two spaceships toward the sun.*
- **servant** /sėr' vənt/ *n.* **1.** Person employed in a household. **2.** Person devoted to any service: *Police officers are public servants.*
- **shamrock** /sham' rok'/ *n.* Bright green, three-leaved plant like clover.
- **shield** /shēld/ *v.* Protect; defend: *His friends shielded him from danger.* —*n.* **1.** Piece of armor carried on the arm. **2.** Anything used to protect.
- **shorthand** /shôrt' hand'/ *n.* Method of writing rapidly with symbols.
- **shortstop** /shôrt' stop'/ *n.* Baseball player stationed between second and third base.
- **shove** /shuv/ *v.* Push; jostle: *He shoved the chair under the table. She was shoved by the crowds in the store.* **shoved, shoving.** —*n.* Push: *a gentle shove to send the boat out into the water.*
- **shovel** /shuv' əl/ *n.* Tool with a broad scoop, used to lift and throw loose matter: *a snow shovel; a coal shovel.* —*v.* **1.** Lift and throw with a shovel: *They shoveled the sand into a cart.* **2.** Make with a shovel: *They shoveled a path through the snow.*
- **shriek** /shrēk/ *n.* Loud, sharp, shrill sound: *the shriek of the whistle.* —*v.* Make a loud, sharp, shrill sound.
- **shrivel** /shriv' əl/ *v.* Dry up; wither; shrink and wrinkle: *The grass shriveled in the hot sun.*
- **sideburns** /sīd' bėrnz'/ *n. pl.* Growth of hair down the sides of a man's face in front of the ears. (Sideburns were so named because they were worn once by General Ambrose *Burnside.* The syllables of his name were reversed to form the word *sideburns.*)
- **siege** /sēj/ *n.* **1.** The surrounding of a fortified place by an army trying to capture it. **2.** Any long or persistent effort to overcome resistance: *a siege of illness.*
- **sieve** /siv/ *n.* Utensil having holes in the bottom to let liquids and small particles pass through, but not the larger pieces.
- **signal** /sig' nəl/ *n.* Sign giving notice of something. —*v.* **1.** Make a signal. **2.** Make known by a signal.
- **single** /sing' gəl/ *adj.* **1.** Just one. **2.** For only one. **3.** Without others; alone. **4.** Not married. —*v.* **1.** Pick from among others;

/a/ ran /ā/ rain /ã/ care /ä/ car /e/ hen /ē/ he /ėr/ her /i/ in /ī/ ice /o/ not /ō/ no /ô/ off
/u/ us /ū/ use /ü/ tool /ù/ took /ou/ cow /oi/ boy /ch/ church /hw/ when /ng/ sing /sh/ ship
/ᵺ/ this /th/ thin /zh/ vision /ə/ about, taken, pencil, lemon, circus

select: *They singled out one student.* **2.** In baseball, make a one-base hit. **singled, singling.** —*n.* In baseball, a one-base hit.

● **ski** /skē/ *n.* One of a pair of long, slender pieces of wood, plastic, or metal fastened to the shoes to enable a person to glide over snow. *pl.* **skis** or **ski.** —*v.* Glide over the snow on skis. **skied, skiing.**

● **sleet** /slēt/ *n.* Half-frozen rain. —*v.* Come down in sleet.

● **slogan** /slō′ gən/ *n.* Motto: *"Safety first" is our slogan.*

● **smear** /smir/ *v.* **1.** Cover or stain with something sticky, greasy, or dirty. **2.** Rub or spread oil, grease, or paint. **3.** Receive a mark or stain: *Wet paint smears easily.* **4.** Spoil: *smear a reputation.*

● **smell** /smel/ *n.* **1.** Odor; scent. **2.** Sense of smelling: *Smell is keener in dogs than in people.* —*v.* **1.** Recognize by breathing in through the nose. **2.** Give out an odor: *The garden smells of roses.* **3.** Sniff at: *She picked the rose and smelled it.* **smelled** or **smelt, smelling.**

● **smoothness** /smü͡ŦH′ nəs/ *n.* Even surface; quality of being even; without roughness.

● **snarl**¹ /snärl/ *v.* **1.** Growl and show the teeth. **2.** Say or express with a snarl. —*n.* Sharp, angry words; sharp, angry growl.

● **snarl**² /snärl/ *n.* Tangle: *snarls in the hair.*

● **snatch** /snach/ *v.* Seize suddenly; grab. —*n.* Small amount; bit: *We heard snatches of the music.*

● **sneer** /snir/ *v.* **1.** Show scorn by words or looks. **2.** Say with scorn or contempt: *"Bah,"* sneered the man. —*n.* Look or words showing scorn.

● **soccer** /sok′ ər/ *n.* Game played between two teams of eleven players each, using a round ball that may be struck with any part of the body except the hands and arms.

● **soda** /sō′ də/ *n.* **1.** Any of several substances containing sodium. **2.** Baking soda; sodium bicarbonate. **3.** Soda water.

● **softball** /sôft′ bôl′/ *n.* **1.** A game like baseball, but played with a larger and softer ball. Softball rules are the same as those in baseball, except that a softball pitcher throws the ball underhand instead of overhand. **2.** Ball used in this game.

● **solar** /sō′ lər/ *adj.* **1.** Of the sun: *a solar eclipse.* **2.** Determined by the sun: *solar time.*

● **solo** /sō′ lō/ *n.* Piece of music for one voice or instrument. *pl.* **solos.**

● **soot** /sut/ *n.* Black substance in the smoke from burning coal, wood, oil, or other fuel.

● **spaghetti** /spə get′ ē/ *n.* Mixture of flour and water in slender sticks like macaroni, but thinner.

● **spark** /spärk/ *n.* **1.** Small bit of fire. **2.** Flash that occurs when electricity jumps across an open space. **3.** Flash; gleam. **4.** A glittering bit: *The moving sparks we saw were fireflies.* —*v.* Send out bits of fire; produce sparks.

● **splendor** /splen′ dər/ *n.* **1.** Great brightness; brilliance: *The sun set in great splendor.* **2.** Glory; pomp: *The pageant was a scene of splendor.*

● **sponge** /spunj/ *n.* **1.** Water animal with a tough, elastic skeleton. **2.** Framework of this animal, used for cleaning, soaking up water, etc. **3.** Similar article made of plastic or rubber. —*v.* **1.** Wipe away with a sponge: *Sponge the mud spots off the car.* **2.** Live at the expense of another in a mean way: *The lazy cousins sponge on their family.* **sponged, sponging.**

● **sponsor** /spon′ sər/ *n.* Person who is responsible for a person or thing: *the sponsor of a law; the sponsor of a student applying for a scholarship.* —*v.* Act as a sponsor for: *My scout troop will sponsor one person for summer camp.*

● **spoonful** /spün′ ful′/ *n.* As much as a spoon will hold: *a spoonful of medicine.* *pl.* **spoonfuls.**

● **sprawl** /sprôl/ *v.* **1.** Lie or sit with the limbs spread out, especially ungracefully. **2.** Spread out in an awkward or irregular manner.

● **spread** /spred/ *v.* **1.** Stretch out; open out. **2.** Cover with a thin layer. **3.** Scatter. **4.** Move farther apart. **spread, spreading.**

● **sprout** /sprout/ *n.* Shoot of a plant. —*v.* Begin to grow; shoot forth: *Seeds sprout.*

● **spry** /sprī/ *adj.* Lively; nimble. **sprier, spriest** or **spryer, spryest.**

● **spurt** /spert/ *v.* **1.** Gush out; squirt. **2.** Show great activity for a short time. —*n.* **1.** Sudden rushing forth. **2.** Great increase of effort.

● **sputnik** /sput′ nik/ *n.* An earth satellite put into orbit by the Soviet Union.

● **squad** /skwod/ *n.* **1.** Small number of soldiers grouped for a drill. **2.** Small group of persons working together.

● **squall**¹ /skwôl/ *n.* Sudden, violent gust of wind, often with rain, snow, or sleet.

● **squall**² /skwôl/ *v.* Cry or scream loudly. —*n.* Loud, harsh cry.

- **squash**[1] /skwosh/ *v.* Crush: *The girl squashed the bug.* —*n.* Game somewhat like tennis.
- **squash**[2] /skwosh/ *n.* Vegetable that grows on a vine. *pl.* **squashes** or **squash.**
- **squawk** /skwôk/ *v.* **1.** Make a loud, harsh sound: *Hens and ducks squawk when frightened.* **2.** Complain loudly. —*n.* **1.** Loud, harsh sound. **2.** Loud complaint.
- **squirt** /skwėrt/ *v.* **1.** Force liquid out through a narrow opening. **2.** Come out in a jet or stream. —*n.* Squirting: *a squirt of water from the hose.*
- **stagecoach** /stāj′ kōch′/ *n.* Coach carrying passengers and parcels over a regular route.
- **stake**[1] /stāk/ *n.* Stick or post pointed at one end for driving into the ground. —*v.* **1.** Fasten to a stake or with a stake. **2.** Mark the boundaries of. **staked, staking.**
- **stake**[2] /stāk/ *n.* **1.** Money or thing risked on the result of a game or on any chance: *play for high stakes.* **2.** Something to gain or lose; an interest: *Each of us has a stake in the future of our country.* —*v.* Risk something on the result of a game or on any chance: *They staked their money on the black horse.* **staked, staking.**
- **starve** /stärv/ *v.* **1.** Die because of hunger; suffer because of hunger. **2.** Feel very hungry. **3.** Weaken or kill with hunger: *The men in the fort were starved into surrendering.* **starved, starving.**
- **steady** /sted′ ē/ *adj.* **1.** Regular: *He is making steady progress in school.* **2.** Firm: *This post is steady as a rock.* **3.** Reliable: *a steady worker.* **4.** Calm: *steady nerves.* **steadier, steadiest.** —*v.* Make firm: *She steadied the ladder while I climbed to the roof.* **steadied, steadying.**
- **steak** /stāk/ *n.* Slice of meat or fish for cooking.
- **steep**[1] /stēp/ *adj.* **1.** Having a sharp slope; almost straight up and down. **2.** Unreasonable: *a steep price.*
- **steep**[2] /stēp/ *v.* Soak: *She steeped the tea in boiling water.*
- **steeple** /stē′ pəl/ *n.* High, pointed tower on a church; tower with a spire.
- **stick** /stik/ *v.* Be or become fastened; become fixed; be at a standstill. **stuck, sticking.**
- **stoop**[1] /stüp/ *v.* **1.** Bend forward. **2.** Lower oneself: *They stooped to cheating.* **3.** Carry

head and shoulders bent forward: *The old man stoops.* —*n.* A forward bend.
- **stoop**[2] /stüp/ *n.* Porch or platform at the entrance of a house.
- **strawstack** /strô′ stak′/ *n.* A pile of dried grain stalks after the grain is removed, used for bedding for horses and other animals.
- **strict** /strikt/ *adj.* **1.** Carefully following a rule or seeing that others follow it. **2.** Harsh; severe: *a strict teacher.*
- **stripe** /strīp/ *n.* A long, narrow band of different color or material.
- **stroll** /strōl/ *v.* Take a quiet walk for pleasure. —*n.* A slow, quiet walk.
- **stuck** /stuk/ *v. See* **stick.** *We were stuck in the mud.*
- **stupid** /stü′ pid/ *or* /stū′ pid/ *adj.* **1.** Not intelligent; dull: *a stupid remark.* **2.** Not interesting: *a stupid book.*
- **sturdy** /stėr′ dē/ *adj.* Stout; strong; firm: *a sturdy child; a sturdy chair; a sturdy resistance.* **sturdier, sturdiest.**
- **suffix** /suf′ iks/ *n.* Word part added to the end of a word to change its meaning or form.
- **super** /sü′ pər/ *adj. Slang.* Excellent.
- **surfboard** /sėrf′ bôrd′/ *n.* Long, narrow board for riding the surf.
- **surplus** /sėr′ pləs/ *n.* Amount over and above what is needed; excess: *The bank keeps a surplus of money in reserve.* —*adj.* Extra: *We keep our surplus books in the storeroom.*
- **sway** /swā/ *v.* **1.** Swing back and forth or from side to side: *She swayed in time to the music.* **2.** Cause to move; cause to sway: *The wind swayed the branches.*
- **sweat** /swet/ *n.* **1.** Moisture coming out through the skin: *We wiped the sweat from our faces.* **2.** Moisture collected on a surface: *The sweat on the windows kept us from seeing outside.* —*v.* **1.** Give out moisture through the pores of the skin. **2.** Give out or collect moisture: *A pitcher of ice water sweats.*
- **sweater** /swet′ ər/ *n.* Knitted jacket.
- **swift** /swift/ *adj.* **1.** Moving very fast: *swift cars.* **2.** Coming or happening very quickly: *a swift answer.*
- **swoop** /swüp/ *v.* **1.** Come down with a rush: *Pirates swooped down on the towns along the coast.* **2.** Snatch: *She swooped the child up in her arms.* —*n.* Rapid downward sweep: *With one swoop, the hawk seized the chicken.*

/a/ ran /ā/ rain /ã/ care /ä/ car /e/ hen /ē/ he /ėr/ her /i/ in /ī/ ice /o/ not /ō/ no /ô/ off
/u/ us /ū/ use /ü/ tool /ù/ took /ou/ cow /oi/ boy /ch/ church /hw/ when /ng/ sing /sh/ ship
/ᴛн/ this /th/ thin /zh/ vision /ə/ about, taken, pencil, lemon, circus

- **synonym** /sin′ ə nim/ *n.* Word that means the same or nearly the same as another word: *"Large" and "big" are synonyms.*

t

- **tackle** /tak′ əl/ *n.* **1.** Equipment; apparatus; gear: *fishing tackle.* **2.** Ropes and pulleys for lifting, lowering, or moving. —*v.* **1.** Try to deal with: *She had several problems to tackle.* **2.** Seize: *John tackled the boy and pulled him to the ground.* **tackled, tackling.**
- **tardy** /tär′ dē/ *adj.* **1.** Behind time; late: *They were tardy for school.* **2.** Slow: *The bus was tardier than usual.* **tardier, tardiest.**
- **teammate** /tēm′ māt′/ *n.* A fellow member of a team.
- **telegram** /tel′ ə gram/ *n.* Message sent by telegraph.
- **telegraph** /tel′ ə graf/ *n.* An instrument, system, or process for sending written messages over a far distance. [The Greek word part *tele* means "far" and the Greek word part *graph* means "write."]
- **tenant** /ten′ ənt/ *n.* Person paying rent for the use of land or buildings: *The apartment has room for one hundred tenants.*
- **tepee** /tē′ pē′/ *n.* Tent of the North American Indians made of hides sewed together and stretched over poles. (Also spelled **teepee.**)
- **themselves** /ᴛнem′ selvz′/ *pron.* **1.** *Themselves* is used to make a statement stronger: *The teachers themselves said the test was hard.* **2.** *Themselves* can be used in place of *them* in cases like this: *They hurt themselves sliding downhill.* **3.** Their real selves: *The sick children are not themselves today.*
- **thirst** /thėrst/ *n.* **1.** Desire for something to drink. **2.** Dry feeling in the mouth caused by having had nothing to drink. —*v.* Feel thirsty.
- **thorn** /thôrn/ *n.* Sharp point on the stem or branch of a tree or plant.
- **thoughtful** /thôt′ fəl/ *adj.* **1.** Full of thought. **2.** Considerate of others: *She is always thoughtful of her mother.*
- **thrill** /thril/ *n.* Shivering, excited feeling. —*v.* Have a shivering, excited feeling.
- **thumbtack** /thum′ tak′/ *n.* Tack with broad, flat head that can be pressed into a surface with the thumb.
- **thunder** /thun′ dər/ *n.* **1.** Loud noise that sometimes follows a flash of lightning. **2.** Any noise like thunder. —*v.* **1.** Make a noise like thunder. **2.** Give forth thunder. **3.** Utter very loudly; roar.

- **tidbit** /tid′ bit′/ *n.* Very pleasing bit of food or news.
- **tinfoil** /tin′ foil′/ *n.* Very thin sheet of tin, or tin and lead, used as a wrapping for candy, tobacco, or similar articles.
- **title** /tī′ təl/ *n.* **1.** The name of a book, song, picture, etc. **2.** A name showing rank, occupation, or position in life. **3.** Championship; first-place position: *He won the golf title.* **4.** Legal right to property; evidence of such a right.
- **tobacco** /tə bak′ ō/ *n.* **1.** Prepared leaves of certain plants, used for smoking or chewing or as snuff. **2.** One of these plants. *pl.* **tobaccos** or **tobaccoes.**
- **toil** /toil/ *n.* Hard work; labor. —*v.* Work hard.
- **toll**[1] /tōl/ *v.* Sound with single strokes, slowly and regularly repeated: *toll the bells.* —*n.* Sound of a bell being tolled.
- **toll**[2] /tōl/ *n.* Tax or fee paid for a right; charge for a service: *a toll on long-distance telephone calls.*
- **tomahawk** /tom′ ə hôk/ *n.* Light ax used by North American Indians as a weapon and a tool.
- **tongs** /tôngz/ *n. pl.* Tool for seizing, holding, or lifting.
- **toothbrush** /tüth′ brush′/ *n.* Small brush for cleaning the teeth.
- **tornado** /tôr nā′ dō/ *n.* Violent, destructive wind; violent whirlwind. *pl.* **tornados** or **tornadoes.**
- **trace**[1] /trās/ *v.* **1.** Follow the marks left. **2.** Follow the course of. **3.** Mark out. **4.** Copy by following the lines of with a pencil or pen. **traced, tracing.** —*n.* **1.** Mark left: *traces of rabbits in the snow.* **2.** Little bit; very small amount.
- **trace**[2] /trās/ *n.* Either of the two straps, ropes, or chains by which an animal pulls a wagon or carriage.
- **trademark** /trād′ märk′/ *n.* Mark, symbol, word, or letters owned and used by a manufacturer or merchant to identify goods.
- **trash** /trash/ *n.* Worthless stuff; rubbish.
- **treaty** /trē′ tē/ *n.* An agreement between nations. *pl.* **treaties.**
- **tremble** /trem′ bəl/ *v.* **1.** Shake a little; move gently: *The leaves trembled in the breeze.* **2.** Shake because of fear, cold, excitement, etc. **trembled, trembling.** —*n.* A trembling: *a tremble in her voice.*
- **troop** /trüp/ *n.* **1.** A group or band of persons. **2.** Herd; flock; swarm. **3.** A unit in the cavalry. —*v.* **1.** Move together: *The children trooped*

around the room. **2.** Walk; go; go away.

- **trough** /trôf/ *n.* **1.** Long, narrow container for holding food or water: *He led his horse to the watering trough.* **2.** Anything shaped like a trough.
- **trousers** /trou′ zərz/ *n. pl.* Two-legged outer garment reaching from the waist to the ankles or knees: *He wore the same trousers all week.*
- **truly** /trü′ lē/ *adv.* **1.** In a true manner: *Tell me truly what you think.* **2.** Really: *It was a truly beautiful scene.*
- **truthful** /trüth′ fəl/ *adj.* Honest: *a truthful person.*
- **tuna** /tü′ nə/ *n.* Large sea fish used for food: *Tuna have been known to grow to a length of ten feet or more. pl.* **tuna** or **tunas.**
- **turnstile** /tèrn′ stīl′/ *n.* Post with bars that turn, set in an exit or entrance. The bars are turned to let one person through at a time.

u

- **ukulele** /ū′ kə lā′ lē/ *n.* A small guitar having four strings.
- **umbrella** /um brel′ ə/ *n.* Light, folding frame covered with cloth, used as a protection against rain or sun.
- **unable** /un ā′ bəl/ *adj.* Not able.
- **unavoidable** /un′ ə void′ ə bəl/ *adj.* Not able to be avoided, or kept away from.
- **uneasiness** /un ē′ zē nəs/ *n.* Lack of comfort; restlessness; anxiety.
- **unfair** /un fār′/ *adj.* Not just; not fair.
- **unite** /ū nīt′/ *v.* Join together; make one; join. **united, uniting.**
- **unjust** /un just′/ *adj.* Not fair; not just: *an unjust punishment.*
- **unloose** /un lüs′/ *v.* Release; let loose. **unloosed, unloosing.**
- **unpleasant** /un plez′ ənt/ *adj.* Not pleasant; disagreeable: *unpleasant weather; an unpleasant disposition.*
- **uproot** /up′ rüt′/ *v.* **1.** Tear up by the roots. **2.** Remove completely: *We must uproot cheating from our games.*
- **upstairs** /up′ stārz′/ *adv.* **1.** Up the stairs: *The boy ran upstairs.* **2.** On or to an upper floor: *She lives upstairs.* —*adj.* On an upper floor: *She is waiting in an upstairs room.* —*n.* Upper floor: *The small cottage has no upstairs.*

- **usable** /ūz′ ə bəl/ *adj.* Able to be used: *The old car is not usable because of poor tires.*

v

- **vain** /vān/ *adj.* **1.** Too pleased with oneself; having too much pride in one's looks, ability, etc. **2.** Of no use; unsuccessful. **3.** Of no value: *a vain boast.*
- **valley** /val′ ē/ *n.* **1.** Low land between hills and mountains. **2.** Wide region drained by a river system.
- **vane** /vān/ *n.* Flat piece of metal, or some other device, fixed on a spire or other high object in such a way as to move with the wind and indicate wind direction.
- **vapor** /vā′ pər/ *n.* **1.** Moisture in the air that can be seen; steam from boiling water; fog; mist. **2.** Gas formed from a liquid or solid.
- **vehicle** /vē′ ə kəl/ *n.* **1.** Means of conveying or transporting, such as a carriage, cart, wagon, or car. **2.** Means by which something is told or shown: *Language is a vehicle of thought.*
- **vein** /vān/ *n.* **1.** One of the blood vessels that carry blood to the heart. **2.** Rib of a leaf or of an insect's wing.
- **verse** /vèrs/ *n.* **1.** Poetry. **2.** Group of lines of poetry: *the first verse of ''America.''*
- **vessel** /ves′ əl/ *n.* **1.** Container; hollow holder. **2.** Ship. **3.** Tube carrying blood or other fluid: *Veins and arteries are blood vessels.*
- **vibrate** /vī′ brāt/ *v.* **1.** Move rapidly to and fro: *A snake's tongue vibrates.* **2.** Quiver. **vibrated, vibrating.**
- **vinegar** /vin′ ə gər/ *n.* Sour liquid produced by the fermenting of wine, cider, beer, or the like, and used as flavoring or for preserving food.
- **virus** /vī′ rəs/ *n.* Very small substance that causes disease: *Viruses are so small they cannot be seen through a microscope.*
- **visor** /vī′ zər/ *n.* **1.** The movable front part of a helmet, covering the face. **2.** Brim of a cap that sticks out in the front. **3.** Shade that can be lowered from above to the inside of a car windshield.
- **vitamin** /vī′ tə min/ *n.* Any of certain special substances necessary for the normal growth and proper nourishment of the body.

/a/ ran /ā/ rain /ã/ care /ä/ car /e/ hen /ē/ he /èr/ her /i/ in /ī/ ice /o/ not /ō/ no /ô/ off
/u/ us /ū/ use /ü/ tool /u̇/ took /ou/ cow /oi/ boy /ch/ church /hw/ when /ng/ sing /sh/ ship
/ᴛʜ/ this /th/ thin /zh/ vision /ə/ about, taken, pencil, lemon, circus

- **vivid** /viv' id/ *adj.* Brilliant; strong and clear: *Dandelions are a vivid yellow.*
- **volcano** /vol kā' nō/ *n.* Mountain having an opening through which steam, ashes, and lava are forced out. *pl.* **volcanoes** or **volcanos.**
- **volunteer** /vol' ən tir'/ *n.* **1.** Person who enters any service by choice: *She is a volunteer in the army.* **2.** Person who serves without pay: *The fire fighters in our town are volunteers.* —*v.* Offer one's services.
- **vow** /vou/ *n.* Promise. —*v.* Make a solemn promise.
- **vowel** /vou' əl/ *n.* **1.** An open sound produced by the voice. **2.** Letter that stands for such a sound; *a, e, i, o,* and *u* are vowel letters.

w

- **wallet** /wôl' ət/ *n.* Folding pocketbook.
- **walrus** /wôl' rəs/ *n.* Large sea animal of the arctic regions, resembling a seal but having long tusks.
- **wardrobe** /wôrd' rōb'/ *n.* **1.** Stock of clothes: *They were shopping for their spring wardrobes.* **2.** Room, closet, or piece of furniture for holding clothes.
- **warfare** /wär' fār'/ *n.* War; fighting.
- **weakness** /wēk' nəs/ *n.* **1.** Lack of strength, force, power, or vigor: *Weakness kept him in bed.* **2.** Slight fault: *Her weakness is putting things off until later.* **3.** Fondness: *He has a weakness for sweets.*
- **weapon** /wep' ən/ *n.* **1.** Object or instrument used in fighting: *Swords, guns, and knives are weapons.* **2.** Any means of attack or defense: *Drugs are weapons against disease.*
- **weary** /wir' ē/ *adj.* **1.** Tired: *weary feet.* **2.** Tiring: *a weary day.* **wearier, weariest.** —*v.* Make or become tired. **wearied, wearying.**
- **weird** /wird/ *adj.* **1.** Mysterious; wild; strange: *The witches did a weird dance in the moonlight.* **2.** Odd; queer: *weird shadows.*
- **welfare** /wel' fār'/ *n.* Health, happiness, and prosperity: *My aunt asked about the welfare of everyone in the family.*
- **western** /wes' tərn/ *adj.* Toward the west; in the west; from the west. —*n.* Story, motion picture, or book about life in the western part of the United States.
- **whirl** /hwėrl/ *v.* **1.** Turn or swing round and round. **2.** Move or carry quickly: *whirl away in an airplane.* —*n.* **1.** Whirling movement. **2.** Confused condition.

- **whirlpool** /hwėrl' pül'/ *n.* Current of water whirling violently round and round; whirling storm of wind.
- **whisk** /hwisk/ *v.* **1.** Sweep or brush from a surface. **2.** Move quickly: *The mouse whisked into its hole.* **3.** Whip to a froth.
- **windmill** /wind' mil'/ *n.* Mill or machine worked by the action of the wind upon a wheel of vanes or sails mounted on a tower.
- **wonder** /wun' dər/ *n.* Cause for surprise: *It is a wonder that he is not sick.* —*v.* Be curious about; wish to know.
- **wreckage** /rek' ij/ *n.* What is left by a wreck or wrecks: *The shore was covered with the wreckage of ships.*
- **wrench** /rench/ *n.* **1.** Hard twist. **2.** Tool for turning nuts and bolts. —*v.* Twist or pull suddenly.
- **wring** /ring/ *v.* **1.** Twist with force. **2.** Cause pain or pity in: *The sad story wrung my heart.* **wrung, wringing.**
- **wrung** /rung/ *v. See* **wring.** *The cloth was wrung dry.*

y

- **yacht** /yot/ *n.* Boat for pleasure trips or racing. —*v.* Sail or race on a yacht: *They spent the summer days yachting.*
- **yield** /yēld/ *v.* **1.** Produce: *This farm yields good crops.* **2.** Give up; surrender: *The army yielded to the enemy soldiers.* —*n.* Product; amount yielded: *the farmer's yield of corn.*
- **yoke** /yōk/ *n.* **1.** Wooden frame to fasten two work animals together. **2.** Pair fastened together with a yoke: *He owned a yoke of oxen.* **3.** Part of a garment fitting neck and shoulders closely: *the yoke of her dress.*
- **yolk** /yōk/ *n.* The yellow part of an egg.
- **youth** /ūth/ *n.* **1.** Fact of being young. **2.** Time between childhood and manhood or womanhood. **3.** Young man. **4.** Young people. **5.** First or early part of anything. *pl.* **youths** /ūths/ *or* /ū#Hz/ *or* **youth.**
- **youthful** /ūth' fəl/ *adj.* **1.** Young. **2.** Having the looks or quality of youth: *The old horse ran with a youthful vigor.*
- **yuletide** or **Yuletide** /ūl' tīd'/ *n.* Christmas time; Christmas season.

z

- **zero** /zir' ō/ *n.* The figure or digit 0; nothing. *pl.* **zeros** or **zeroes.**

188